German Aircraft in the Soviet Union and Russia

Yefim Gordon and Sergey Komissarov
with Dmitriy Komissarov

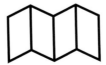

German Aircraft in the Soviet Union and Russia
© 2008 Yefim Gordon and Sergey Komissarov,
with Dmitriy Komissarov

ISBN (13) 978 185780 292 4

Published by Midland Publishing
4 Watling Drive, Hinckley, LE10 3EY, England
Tel: 01455 254 490 Fax: 01455 254 495
E-mail: midlandbooks@compuserve.com
www.midlandcountiessuperstore.com

Midland Publishing is an imprint of
Ian Allan Publishing Ltd

Worldwide distribution (except North America):
Midland Counties Publications
4 Watling Drive, Hinckley, LE10 3EY, England
Telephone: 01455 254 450 Fax: 01455 233 737
E-mail: midlandbooks@compuserve.com
www.midlandcountiessuperstore.com

North American trade distribution:
Specialty Press Publishers & Wholesalers Inc.
39966 Grand Avenue, North Branch, MN 55056, USA
Tel: 651 277 1400 Fax: 651 277 1203
Toll free telephone: 800 895 4585
www.specialtypress.com

© 2008 Midland Publishing
Design concept and layout by
Polygon Press Ltd. (Moscow, Russia)
Line drawings by Vladimir Klimov, Andrey
Yurgenson, and from TsAGI, LII and NII VVS
documents on German aircraft.
Colour artwork by Andrey Yurgenson,
Mikhail Bykov and Sergey Yershov.

The book is illustrated with photos from the
Russian Central State Archive of the National
Economy (TsGANKh), the archive of the M. M.
Gromov Flight Research Institute (LII), the Russian
State Archive of Cine and Photo Documents
(RGAKFD), the Central State Archive of the Soviet
Army (TsGASA), the archive of the Central Aero-
& Hydrodynamics Institute (TsAGI), the personal
archives of Yefim Gordon, Sergey and Dmitriy
Komissarov, Konstantin Udalov, Helmut Walther
and RART, as well as photos by Yefim Gordon,
Sergey Sergeyev, Sergey Komissarov, Victor
Drushlyakov and Ingo Raupach.

Printed in England by Ian Allan Printing Ltd
Riverdene Business Park, Molesey Road,
Hersham, Surrey, KT12 4RG

Contents

Acknowledgements

The authors wish to express their gratitude
to the persons who assisted in and
contributed to the making of this book:

Vyacheslav P. Kondrat'yev, Yuriy V.
Zasypkin, Thomas Müller and Helmut
Walther.

Below: This Soviet-operated Junkers F 13 passenger aircraft is named *Aghitsamolyot Soyuza Osoaviakhima SSSR - 'Zemlya i Fabrika'* (Propaganda aircraft of the USSR's Osoaviakhim Union 'Land and Factory').
Page 4: The tide of the war has turned. This picture shows a selection of captured German aircraft and armour in Moscow's Central Culture & Recreation Park (Gor'kiy Park) in 1943. The aircraft here include Messerschmitt Bf 109Es, Bf 109Fs and a Bf 110, a Junkers Ju 52/3m, a Focke-Wulf Fw 58B and a Heinkel He 111.

INTRODUCTION

The history of flying and aircraft construction in Russia and the Soviet Union is inseparably connected with the progress of aviation in other countries. Imports of aircraft and engines and the influx of new ideas in aircraft design from abroad have played an important role in the development of the Russian aircraft industry, Russian military aviation and air transport. Along with France and Great Britain, Germany occupied an important place among the countries from which aircraft and aero engines found their way to Russia/the Soviet Union; the German influence on Russian/Soviet Aviation can hardly be underestimated.

In this book the authors have tried to mention and describe, in greater or lesser detail, all types of German aircraft that came to be used in Russia – whether it be machines purchased abroad or examples captured in the course of armed conflicts. The period covered in the book spans from 1910 to the present day. The authors have focused their attention on the historical circumstances under which this or that aircraft was acquired, and on its 'operational career' in Russia/the Soviet Union. The technical description of this or that type was often reduced to the minimum required to give a general idea of the aircraft in question. The major landmarks within the period stated above are: early German aircraft in Russia before 1914; German aircraft captured during the First World War and in the course of the subsequent Civil War in Russia; civil and military aircraft of German origin acquired by the Soviet Union in the 1920s and 1930s; captured German aircraft from the Spanish Civil War and the Second World War; the study of German jet aircraft in the USSR in the first post-war years and the work of German design bureaux in the Soviet Union; contacts in the aeronautical sphere in the period from the mid-1950s to the early 1990s; the present-day situation with regard to imports of German aviation technology and hardware into Russia.

When preparing this book the authors have drawn information from various sources, including numerous books published both in Russia and abroad. They wish to single out some of the publications which have proved to be particularly valuable in this respect. Special mention must be made of the book *German Imprint in the History of Russian Aviation* by Dmitriy A. Sobolev and Dmitriy B. Khazanov, which covers in great detail the period from the early 19th century (an attempt of creating a steerable balloon for combat use against Napoleon's army) to the early 1950s when German engineers and scientists built jet aircraft and jet engines for the Soviet aviation industry. Much useful information is to be found in Vadim B. Shavrov's fundamental *History of Aircraft Design in the USSR*, the two volumes of which cover the period from early 1900s to 1950. The use of German aircraft in the USSR up to 1941 is dealt with in detail in the book *Soviet Aircraft and Aviation 1917-1941* by Lennart Andersson; this Swedish author is to be congratulated on the results of his painstaking research which provide insight into the story of the Soviet-German co-operation in the aeronautical sphere between the two world wars. Two more books deserve mention here. It is the book *Under the Red Star* by Carl-Fredrik Geust dealing with captured German aircraft of 1941-1945, and the two-volume work by Andrey O. Aleksandrov and Gennadiy F. Petrov on German aircraft in Russian and Soviet service between 1914 and 1951. The reader will find in the present book fairly frequent references to these authors (as well as to some other researchers), especially in cases of discrepancies appearing in the different sources.

The use of German aircraft in the USSR has become an object of attention of many Russian aviation historians in the last two decades. Their findings, reflected in books and magazine articles, have also proved very useful in the preparation of this book. The authors wish to mention the names of such researchers as Andrey Aleksandrov, Yevgeniy Arsen'yev, Viktor Bakurskiy, Yuriy Borisov, Andrey Firsov, Vladimir Il'yin, Dmitriy Khazanov, Sergey Kolov, Vyacheslav Kondrat'yev, Konstantin Kosminkov, Vladimir Kotel'nikov, Mikhail Maslov, Gennadiy Petrov, Ivnamin Sultanov, Nikolay Yakubovich (the list is not exhaustive), whose articles and books dealing with various types of German aircraft contained interesting facts about their 'careers' in the Russian/Soviet service.

Finally, in dealing with the story of the testing of captured German aircraft in the USSR during the Second World War and the immediate post-war years, the authors have made use of technical descriptions and test reports prepared by TsAGI and NII VVS.

With all the above stated in mind, the authors would like to make the following point. Some readers may find that many materials and photos presented in this book are not new and have appeared previously in numerous books and articles (as testified by the above references and bibliography list at the end of the book). This is true, we frankly admit it. Yet, as a rule, the books published earlier (especially those outside Russia) did not contain detailed information on the testing of German aircraft in the USSR and their evaluation by Soviet aviation specialists; nor did they contain the numerous illustrations prepared by Soviet engineers in the middle of the past century in the process of studying German aircraft or by German designers and engineers who worked for the Soviet Union after the end of the war. These materials may prove both interesting and useful to those who take interest in the history of Soviet aircraft construction. As for the materials published by the authors in some of their earlier books in the Red Star series, we have decided to include them in this book for the sake of a complete and integrated presentation of the subject matter, which otherwise might appear fragmentary. Besides, not all the readers of the present book may be in possession of our previous publications.

The authors do not purport to cover in this book an exhaustive list of German aircraft which at various times were used or evaluated in the Soviet Union and Russia. Nevertheless, they hope that their effort in presenting a large amount of illustrations and expanded comment within the covers of this book was justified.

Note on transcription

Some Russian abbreviations and acronyms are deciphered in the text. The Russian words are rendered phonetically to facilitate their correct pronunciation, the stressed syllables being highlighted in bold type.

4

Chapter 1

GERMAN AIRCRAFT IN RUSSIA

1909-1917

The period described in this chapter starts with the first known cases of German aircraft being imported into Russia and includes the First World War, during which a number of aircraft of German origin (including Austrian-designed aircraft of German manufacture) were captured by the Russian troops and pressed into service with the air units of the Russian army. The revolutionary events of November 1917, which led to the collapse of the Russian Empire and the emergence of Soviet Russia, provide a natural limit to the time frame dealt with here. However, the history of the captured German aircraft extends beyond that time limit, since they were inherited by the nascent air elements of the Red Army and were used in the ensuing Civil War. In the course of that war further examples of German aircraft of World War I vintage were captured or otherwise obtained by Soviet Russia. For the sake of continuity it was deemed expedient to present the whole story of the captured aircraft, including their use in Soviet Russia, within this chapter.

First aircraft of German origin in Russia

Hans Grade's aircraft

The first practical aeroplane of German origin imported into Russia was designed by Hans Grade, a German aircraft construction pioneer who had built the first German aircraft to take to the air in 1908. The machine brought to Russia was a very small mono-plane which was powered by an engine of a very modest output. This aeroplane was built in small numbers, and several examples were sold to owners outside Germany. Two examples of Grade's aircraft found their way to Russia. One of them was put on show at the First International Aeronautical Exhibition in Moscow in 1911; the other one was acquired by an owner in the Caucasian area of the Russian Empire.

Hans Grade had built several aircraft, featuring a monoplane layout and differing in some details; the different versions were designated A, B, 'new B', and C. It is not known which of these found their way to Russia. Typically, Grade's aircraft had wings of an elegant planform slightly reminiscent

of a bird's wings. Their common feature was the fuselage consisting of a metal tube frame carrying the engine with a two-blade tractor propeller. Attached to the rear end of the fuselage frame was the tubular tail boom carrying the empennage. The main undercarriage legs were attached to the fuselage frame and formed a cabane above it which served as a meeting point of the numerous bracing wires above the wings. Bracing wires coming from the lower surface of the wings converged at the axles of the undercarriage wheels.

Yuriy Kremp's aircraft

This aircraft was built in Moscow in 1909 and was, in fact, a scaled-down copy of Hans Grade's aircraft. This was not really surprising, because its designer, Yuriy Kremp, had worked in Germany as Hans Grade's assistant, prior to coming to Russia. Before his association with Grade, Kremp had built a monoplane aircraft in Germany.

The aircraft built by Yuriy Kremp in Moscow was extremely simple in its layout (as was Hans Grade's aircraft). The fuselage was a triangular-section truss built up from water pipes joined together by pins and bolts (unlike Grade's aircraft whose fuselage was a simple beam with a tubular wire-braced tail boom). Mounted at the front end was a two-cylinder engine with a two-blade tractor propeller. The wings were flat (without a curved airfoil) and were formed by the tubular leading-edge and trailing-edge spars joined by ribs and covered with fabric. They were supported by bracing wires extending from the wings' lower surface to the lower part of the fuselage truss and from the wings' upper surface to a cabane above the fuselage. Judging by an available picture of this aircraft, it had ailerons mounted on the extended leading edge spar outboard of the angular wingtips. In this it differed from Grade's aircraft which had no ailerons and had rounded wingtips. The propeller was made of wood and had a shape that became standard for the following two decades.

A peculiar feature of Kremp's aircraft was its undercarriage consisting of four skis. Three of them were mounted under the fuselage and the wings, while the fourth one

was attached beneath the rear fuselage. These wooden skis had upturned front ends.

According to a contemporary Russian publication, in the course of the testing in late 1909 or early 1910 Kremp managed to lift the machine into the air and perform a short flight at a height of 6 m (20 ft), but the flight was interrupted by an engine failure. If this information is accepted as true, Kremp's aircraft may well be considered as the first aircraft of Russian origin that managed to take to the air.

In the spring of 1910 Kremp's aircraft was demonstrated at the Moscow Aeronautical Exhibition, whereupon it was preserved for a long time as an exhibit of the Polytechnic Museum in Moscow (unfortunately, the aircraft has not survived).

Several aircraft of German origin were imported into Russia in 1911-1914. Information on them is rather scant; some of these types are listed below.

Harlan

An aircraft built by the Harlan company in Germany attracted the attention of Russian aviation enthusiasts; it was demonstrated to the Russian engineer Antonov (no relative of Oleg K. Antonov) and was brought to Russia, where it was put on show at an exhibition in St. Petersburg in 1911. By that time the aircraft was already obsolete; despite persistent advertising, it failed to evoke much interest and found no Russian buyers.

Etrich Taube

Two examples of the Taube aeroplane designed and built by the Austrian designer Igo Etrich in 1910, were imported into Russia. They were an Etrich XIII Series A and an Etrich XXIII Series C, probably built by the Lohner Werke in Austria. One of these performed six flights in Moscow in 1911, accompanied by two accidents. The Taube (Dove) owed its name to the peculiar planform of its wings and horizontal tail which, indeed, were very similar to those of a bird. In the same year a Taube piloted by M. G. Lerche took part in a long-distance flight from St. Petersburg to Moscow. This machine was powered by a 65-hp Daimler engine. The type was also flown by G. V. Yankovskiy. The Taube monoplane was later

An Etrich Taube monoplane with Imperial Russian Air Fleet roundels on the wings. This is believed to be the aircraft flown by M. G. Lerche from St. Petersburg to Moscow in 1911.

built under licence by several German companies, which makes it eligible for being mentioned here.

Mars aircraft

Two aircraft of different models called Mars built by DFW (Deutsche Flugzeug-Werke) in Germany took part (unofficially) in the contest of military aircraft which was held in St. Petersburg in 1912. One of them was a biplane powered by a 100-hp Argus engine (a scaled-up copy of the Farman IV, which differed from the original in having a fuselage nacelle). The other was a monoplane powered by a 120-hp Daimler engine with a frontal radiator. The two aircraft coped with the contest's programme but failed to show any special advantages and were not purchased by the Russian military customers.

Albatros (Farman)

A single example of a German-built Farman was purchased in 1912. (The Albatros Werke company had started licence production of a Farman type in 1910). This aircraft, powered by a Gnome engine, was manufactured by Albatros Werke. This was the first Russian purchase of an aircraft in Germany.

Fokker Spin

Anthony Fokker, a pilot and aircraft designer of Dutch origin, later to become a figure of world renown, was working in Germany at that time. At the invitation of Abramovich he also took part in the mentioned contest of 1912 in St. Petersburg with his aeroplane, named Spin (Dutch for 'spider'; some sources use the German spelling Spinne). This was a two-seat, wire-braced, mid-wing monoplane powered by a 100-hp Argus engine. This model, identified in some sources as the B-1912, was a development of an earlier single-seat model designated A-1912 and powered by a 50-hp Argus engine. The aircraft featured an extremely simple construction of the wings which were flat, lacking an airfoil section. The wings had a marked dihedral of 9°.

Being an excellent pilot, Fokker personally flew the Spin during the contest. Climbing to 460 m (1,500 ft), he made spectacular turns in a spiral glide. This machine was the only one among the participants of the contest to meet all the requirements; yet it was adjudged only the fourth place, and Fokker failed to obtain any orders for it.

Schneider (?) aircraft

In 1913 one more German aircraft made its appearance in Russia. The aircraft, identified as a Schneider in Russian sources, was imported into the country by the Russian pilot V. Ya. Mikhaïlov who had obtained his pilot's licence at the Johannisthal flying school in Berlin. In late 1913 this aircraft took part in a long-range flight in which the participating aircraft were to cover the St. Petersburg – Moscow – St. Petersburg route within 48 hours. Mikhaïlov was the only one among the participants to have a passenger on board (V. P. Nevdachin, the future aircraft designer). On 4th December their aeroplane covered a distance of 455 versts (485.394 km/301.486 miles; 1 verst = 3,500 ft) in the course of 4 hours and 58 minutes, which was a national endurance record, and had to discontinue the flight in the area of Tver' due to an engine malfunction.

Shavrov identifies this aircraft as the Schneider (Albatros) and describes it as a biplane powered by a 100-hp Mercedes engine. The aeroplane had a tricycle undercarriage, the nosewheel being mounted at the end of a long skid protruding forward nearly to the propeller's rotation plane. Shavrov states that Mikhaïlov flew this aircraft several times in Moscow in the spring of 1914. When the Russian government declared a mobilisation, the military authorities purchased the aircraft from Mikhaïlov.

This was the last German aircraft to be brought to Russia before the First World War.

Fitingoff biplane

In 1912 an aircraft built by the German designer Fitingoff in Russia made its appearance in Petersburg. This is a rather

obscure aircraft which left no traces in archives (its existence is known from the recollections of two persons who took part in the assembly and servicing of the machine, and A. V. Shiukov, a Russian designer, who had heard about it). Fitingoff arrived from Germany in 1912 at the invitation of Wilhelm Lommatzsch (the spelling of the names may be imprecise), the owner of a St. Petersburg company trading in aeroplanes. Fitingoff suggested to Lommatzsch the idea of building an aircraft and got his consent. The aircraft featured a primary structure made of bamboo; this material was even used for the wheels and the propeller. A peculiar feature of this aircraft was its undercarriage: the huge wheels were as tall as a man. This earned the machine the nickname 'Eliah the Prophet's Chariot'. The aircraft was built in Gatchina near St. Petersburg. According to Shavrov, the aircraft proved unsuitable for flights due to insufficient strength (another source cites insufficient stability).

German aircraft acquired by Russia during the First World War

During the First World War a considerable number of German aircraft was captured by Russian troops after forced landings; many of them were almost intact or in reparable condition. They were restored and pressed into service with the Air Units of the Russian Army. The Russian Imperial Air Fleet suffered an acute shortage of serviceable aircraft, and the addition of captured (German and Austrian) machines to its inventory was a welcome means of alleviating this shortage. Sometimes the repairs were made by the frontline aircraft repair workshops, but usually the damaged enemy aircraft were sent to aircraft factories in the rear. Some of these aircraft were modified in the process of repair by Russian aircraft factories. In some cases German aircraft (notably Albatrosses of various models) were copied and put into production; this was especially the case with the Lebedev aircraft factory, which produced several types based on German aircraft.

The number of captured German aircraft used by Russian air units during the First World War is difficult to assess. Some researchers (Vadim B. Shavrov) put it at 120-150 machines, Austrian aircraft included; others speak of 150-170 aircraft.

Captured German aircraft and their Russian copies are listed below in alphabetical order by manufacturer, with some details of their service record.

Albatros aircraft (general remarks)

Most of the German two-seat reconnaissance aircraft used on the Russian front and captured by Russian troops were the machines designed by Albatros Werke.

Russian records of the captured aircraft do not always exactly specify the type, often described in imprecise terms. Shavrov notes, for example, that *'the first Albatros captured by our troops was an aircraft identified as a "three-bay Albatros", after its wing structure. There were, in all, some ten machines powered by Mercedes, Benz, Argus and Austro-Daimler engines delivering 80-100 hp. They attained a speed of some 105 km (65 mph). Already in the early stage of the war they were relatively obsolescent; soon they were supplanted by Albatrosses with a two-bay biplane cell that became standard'*. (The reference to the three-bay machines is presumably applicable to early examples of the Albatros B.I.)

The following captured Albatrosses can be identified by type.

Above: An Albatros B.I captured by Russian forces during the First World War and pressed into Russian service (note the Russian roundels on the upper wings).

Albatros B.I unarmed reconnaissance and training aircraft

The Albatros B.I was a three-bay biplane (subsequent models, starting with the B.II, were two-bay biplanes). It featured a 'reversed' seating arrangement with the pilot seated aft of the observer. The machine was powered by either a 100-hp Mercedes or a 110-hp Benz engine. It was widely used by the German air force for observation during the first year of the war.

According to Sobolev, in 1915-1916 Lebedev's factory restored more than ten Albatros B.I and B.II aircraft powered by 100-hp and 150-hp Mercedes and 120-hp and 140-hp Benz inline water-cooled engines. These machines were officially known as the 'Type A1 biplane – Lebed'-XI' or simply Lebed'-XI. In other sources (Shavrov and others) the Lebed'-XIs are described as

Above: Another Russian Albatros B.I, probably photographed during the winter of 1914-15.

A captured Albatros B.II reconnaissance aircraft. Note that the Russian roundels are applied on a white background – the white squares on which the German crosses had been applied.

Above: Apparently the same B.II as shown on the previous page. Note that the roundels are also applied to the upper surfaces of the lower wings. Note also the long exhaust stubs on the starboard side.

Above: Russian officers pose for a photo with an Albatros B.II while a mechanic turns over the engine.

Albatros copies built by the Lebedev factory. As such they are described below in a special section dealing with Lebed' aircraft.

The Albatros B.I was used by Lebedev as a basis for the LM-1 floatplane (see in the Lebedev section below)

Albatros B.II unarmed reconnaissance and training aircraft
The B.II model, a two-bay two-seat biplane, differed from the B.I in having smaller dimensions but retaining the basic features of the predecessor, such as the seating arrangement and the absence of armament.

It is probable that some captured Albatros B.IIs were used by the Russian army under their own name (apart from those copied or restored by the Lebedev factory as Lebed'-XIs).

The Albatross B.II also served as a basis for the Lebed'-XII (see below)

Albatros C.I reconnaissance and general purpose aircraft
Brought out in the spring of 1915, the C.I model of the Albatros was basically an adaptation of the unarmed B.I to the newly-conceived C class of armed two-seaters. It featured a reversal of the crew positions

from those in the unarmed version – the observer now sat in the rear cockpit furnished with a ring-mounted Parabellum machine-gun. The type was widely used on both the Western and the Eastern fronts for reconnaissance, bombing, photographic and artillery observation duties. The C.Ia version was fitted with a box radiator on the upper wing leading edge instead of the fuselage-mounted Hazet radiators of the C.I.

Andrey Aleksandrov and Gennadiy Petrov have published a picture of an 'Albatros C.I of a Russian aviation battalion'. The aircraft carried Russian army roundels on the fuselage sides; the photo shows a two-seat two-bay biplane with upper and lower wings of equal span having no stagger.

Albatros C.III reconnaissance and artillery co-operation aircraft
The Albatros C.III was developed on the basis of the Albatros C.Ia. This sturdier and more compact model entered service towards the end of 1916 and was used chiefly for armed reconnaissance or, with up to 200 lb of small bombs, on artillery co-operation duties. This model introduced the 'fishtail' contours of the horizontal tail that became characteristic also of the later Albatros designs.

At least one Albatros C.III that had been shot down by Russian troops was restored to airworthy condition from wreckage which looked like a complete write-off, judging by the available photo of the wreckage delivered to the 6th *aviapark* (aircraft repair workshop) in L'vov. The resulting aircraft operated by a Russian air unit was referred to as an 'Albatros fighter'.

Albatros C.X and C.XII reconnaissance aircraft
Lennart Andersson mentions the Albatros C.X and C.XII among the types 'captured or taken over' by the Red Air Fleet after the revolution of November 1917 (see below). It is thus possible that some examples of these aircraft were captured by the Russian army during the First World War, but no record of their service with Russian air force units is available to the authors of this book.

The C.X entered service in early 1917; before October of that year 300 machines were delivered to operational air units where they were used primarily for long-range reconnaissance. This two-seat biplane powered by a 260-hp Mercedes engine was generally similar to the preceding C.VII production model but was somewhat larger and heavier. It had a plywood-skinned slab-sided fuselage and a wing structure of two-bay wire-braced layout. Eventually, the C.X was built by four subcontractors: Ostdeutsche Albatros Werke (OAW), Linke

This Albatros C.III had been shot down and destroyed in 1917 but was rebuilt from the wreckage in this guise and operated by a Russian air unit as the 'Albatros fighter'. Note the non-standard water radiator.

Hoffmann, Bayerische Flugzeug Werke and LFG (Roland). The aircraft had a maximum speed of 175 km/h (109.4 mph) and armament comprising one forward-firing MG and one flexible MG on the rear gun ring.

The C.X was further developed into the production C.XII type (the C.XI remained on the drawing board). The C.XII introduced various refinements, the most noticeable of which were the new elliptical-section fuselage and a tailplane reduced considerably in area. It looked like scaled-up version of the Albatros D.III and D.V fighters with their streamlined monocoque fuselage and characteristic tail surfaces. The type was introduced into service in the autumn of 1917. Powered by the 260-hp Mercedes D.IVa engine, it was the last of the 'big' single-engined Albatros biplanes, featuring a wing span of 14.16 m (46 ft 6½ in).

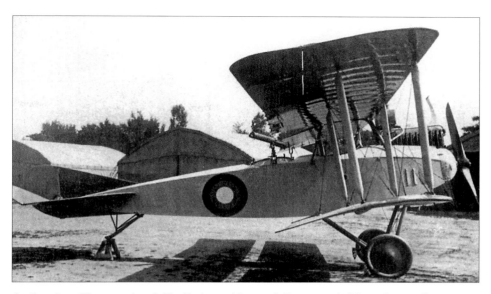

Another view of the same aircraft. The Maxim machine-gun in the rear cockpit is another new item.

Albatros D.V fighter

Again, the Albatros D.V is to be found among the types 'captured or taken over' by the Red Air Fleet after the revolution of November 1917. It is thus possible that some examples of this fighter were captured and used by the Russian army during the First World War.

The Albatros D.V was a further development of the D.III biplane fighter. It was designed in April 1917 and put into production in May 1917, reaching operational units in June of that year. Like its predecessor, the D.V had a monocoque fuselage of a very clean shape, but differed in having a fuselage of oval cross-section and more rounded contours of the rudder. Like the D.III, it was powered by a 175-hp Mercedes D.IIIa engine and armed with two synchronised LMG machine-guns located above the engine. See also the Civil War section below.

Albatros (?) floatplanes

Two (allegedly) 'Albatros' floatplanes were captured by the Russian forces on the Black Sea, according to some sources. The Albatros Werke *did* produce a floatplane; it was the Albatros W.4 single-seat naval fighter which was evolved during the summer of 1916. Based largely on the Albatros D.I landplane fighter design, it was a single-bay biplane with a wooden-framed semi-monocoque fuselage powered by a 160-hp Mercedes D.III engine. It was built in series and used mostly over the North Sea. Lennart Andersson doubts the two floatplanes in question were really Albatrosses; in his opinion, they were more probably other types (Friedrichshafen FF 38s, FF 49s, Gotha WD 14s or Lübeck-Travemündes).

Aviatik (unidentified types)

Automobil und Aviatik AG was one of the German aircraft-manufacturing companies engaged in the series production of military aircraft during the First World War. Originally located at Mühlhausen in Alsace-Lorraine, it was moved to Freiburg. During the war the Austrian branch of the company, bearing the same name (Aviatik GmbH, or the Oester-reichische-Ungarische Flugzeugfabrik Aviatik) was set up in Vienna. This branch produced some designs of its own, among them the Aviatik D.I fighter.

Thus, aircraft bearing the Aviatik brand were manufactured both by Austro-Hungary and by Germany. According to Kenneth Munson, the types built in Germany included the B.I, B.II, C.I, C.II and C.III, while those built in Austro-Hungary comprised the B.II, B.III, C.I, D.I. Thus, sometimes it may be difficult to establish definitely the origin of the captured examples.

Shavrov, in his review of captured German aircraft, states: 'There were a few Aviatik aircraft powered by Daimler engines delivering 120, 165 and 180 hp; their distinctive feature was the thin bracing struts extending to the ends of the upper wing'. This description does not permit to identify precisely the types involved, but could well suit the Austrian-built Aviatik B.II (see below); mention of the Daimler engines also points to their Austrian origin.

Sobolev quotes a report from the Russian press of 1915 relating an episode in which an Austrian Aviatik was forced to land, its two crewmembers surrendering to the Russian troops. 'The Austrian aeroplane captured by our forces was a brand new machine powered by a 120-hp engine, which was quite intact.'

Here are basic facts about some of German-produced Aviatik types:

The Aviatik B.I was a two-seat reconnaissance biplane, built in a two-bay and three-bay configuration. It was powered by a 100-hp Mercedes D.I engine driving a tractor propeller. The pilot occupied the rear cockpit, with the observer seated in the front cockpit. Several machines were put into operation in 1914. The B.II model had a lighter airframe and was fitted with a more powerful engine (the 120-hp Mercedes D.II).

The Aviatik C.I was a reconnaissance aircraft, first flown in 1915 in Freiburg. Initially it retained the same crew seating as the B.I, with the pilot in the rear seat, but later the seating was changed to permit the installation of a turret in the rear cockpit (this version was known as the C.Ia). The next model manufactured in series was the C.III with improved aerodynamics. The C.Is and C.IIIs were used by the German Air Force on all fronts until the end of 1916 for short-range reconnaissance, artillery observation and bombing sorties. Both models were powered by the 160-hp Mercedes D.III engines.

Aviatik B.II reconnaissance and light bomber aircraft (Austrian-built)

In parallel with the German production of Aviatik B types, the Oesterreichische-Ungarische Flugzeugfabrik Aviatik manufactured its own Aviatik B.II and B.III aircraft in three series (Series 32, or B.II; Series 33, or B.III; and Series 34, or a developed version of the B.II). The B.II was a two-seat biplane powered by a 120-hp Austro-Daimler engine (in contrast, the German-built Aviatik B.II was normally powered by the Mercedes D.II).

In early 1916 the XVII Air Corps of the Russian Imperial Air Force obtained one Aviatik B II powered by a 150-hp Daimler engine. Aleksandrov and Petrov, who cite this fact, have also published a picture showing an Aviatik B.II after a crash-landing. The caption states: 'Aviatik B.II of the 5th Austrian Air Division. While on a reconnaissance flight on 5th January 1916*

Above: An Austrian-built Aviatik B.II with Russian markings operated by the 18th Corps Aviation Division. This may be 34.18 of Flik 5 which force-landed in Russian-held territory on 5th January 1916.

Three-quarters rear view of an Imperial Russian Air Fleet Aviatik B.II, showing the placement of the insignia and the shape of the horizontal tail.

the aircraft suffered engine failure and made a forced landing. The aircraft was subsequently employed by the Russian 18th Corps' Aviation division until January-February 1917'. (Note the Austrian origin of the aircraft coded 34.18.)

Aviatik B.III reconnaissance and light bomber aircraft (Austrian-built)

An example of the Aviatik B.III was captured by Russian troops, as witnessed by a picture published in the book by Aleksandrov and Petrov. This must have been an Austrian-built aircraft. The B.III was a further development of the Austrian-built B.II, differing from its predecessor in having a greater span, a more powerful 160-hp engine and a communal cockpit. It was armed with a Schwarzlose machine-gun. The B.III served extensively on the Russian front.

Brandenburg

Shavrov, in his review of the captured types, states: *'Among the lesser-known types mention can be encountered of a Brandenburg powered by a 220-hp Hiero engine'.* It is unclear what type of aircraft he refers to in this case. 'Brandenburg' is a shortened version of the Hansa Brandenburg company name. Among the aircraft designed by this company and series-built in Germany and in Austria there are at least two types which, in some production batches, were fitted with Hiero

engines. These are the Hansa Brandenburg C.I reconnaissance aircraft and the Hansa Brandenburg D.I fighter. Both of them, although of German origin, were built entirely in Austro-Hungary and for the Austrian Air Force. See also Hansa-Brandenburg below.

DFW B.I reconnaissance and training aircraft

Designed and built just before the outbreak of the war, the DFW B.I was a three-bay two-seat biplane powered by a 100-hp Mercedes D.I inline engine, with seven-section Hazet radiators on the fuselage sides. Its peculiar wing planform with the leading edge curving backward gently at the tips soon earned it the nickname 'Flying Banana'. There was no armament.

The DFW was used in modest numbers in World War I. At least one example was captured by the Russian forces in mid-1915 and put into service with the 4th *aviapark* at Lida, Belorussia. Interestingly, it wore the Russian roundels on the undersurfaces of both upper and lower wings. At that time the machine was referred to as a 'Mars'.

Etrich Taube reconnaissance and training aircraft

The Taube monoplane designed by the Austrian engineer Igo Etrich was developed in 1910; from 1911 onwards it was built under licence by the German company E. Rumpler Luftfahrzeugbau GmbH. By 1914

they had been appreciably improved as compared to the original model. The two-seat military version of 1912 was to become the most widely built version of all.

The Austrian machines were of two types, designated A.I when fitted with an 85 Austro-Daimler engine and A.II with the 120-hp Austrian engine.

The Taube multi-purpose aircraft of several externally similar types were series-built under licence and further developed during World War I by several German companies – Rumpler, Albatros, D.F.W., Gotha, Halberstadt, Jeannin, Kondor, Krieger, L.F.G. and others. When the war started, Tauben were used for reconnaissance, training and liaison. They remained in service with the German Air Force until 1916. Of the 500 or so Tauben built for the German air force, the greater part were probably built by Rumpler. Most of the German-built Tauben retained the original wood-and-fabric construction, but those built by D.F.W. and Jeannin featured steel-tube frames and were known as Stahltauben (Steel doves). German-built machines were usually powered by Mercedes or Argus engines delivering 100 hp.

An Albatros-built Taube (alias Albatros FT) of the German Air Force was captured by the XX Air Corps of the Russian Imperial Air Fleet near Riga in the winter of 1914-15. It was powered by a 100-hp Mercedes engine and had an abbreviated tail and a revised landing gear. Sobolev quotes a news item from a contemporary Russian newspaper which reported the capture of two German Tauben that had made forced landings in the Lublin area after being damaged by ground fire.

Fokker (unidentified) (Fokker B?)

Shavrov, Aleksandrov and Petrov all mention a Fokker powered by an Oberursel rotary engine (rated at 100 hp, according to Aleksandrov and Petrov) among the captured fighters. Oberursel engines of different power output were installed in several Fokker fighter types, but the 100-hp engine appears to have been used only on Fokker Bs with different model numbers which were used by the air force of Austro-Hungary as unarmed reconnaissance aircraft. In particular, the 80-hp or 100-hp Oberursel was fitted to the Fokker B.I.

Fokker E

Aleksandrov and Petrov mention the Fokker E among captured aircraft. E stands for *Eindecker* – monoplane. Fokker had four low-wing designs (E.I to E.IV) and a parasol fighter (E.V). It is not clear which of these types is alluded to in this case, but the Fokker E.V is mentioned in the Civil War section (see below).

Friedrichshafen FF 33
reconnaissance floatplane

An example of this aircraft fell into Russian hands on 20th September 1916, when it made a forced landing in the Gulf of Riga after a reconnaissance mission. For its subsequent story see AB-1 in the Lebedev seaplanes section below.

The Friedrichshafen FF 33 was the most numerous among the marine aircraft used by the German Navy during the First World War This twin-float two-seat biplane was built in a great number of versions which can be classified into two categories: the unarmed three-bay reconnaissance versions and the smaller, lighter fighter models with two-bay wings. The captured example must have been of the former category.

Friedrichshafen FF 49c
reconnaissance floatplane

Shavrov states that two 'Friedrichshafen 49c' reconnaissance floatplanes powered by 220-hp Benz engines were captured on the Black Sea (the designation is misspelled and should be Friedrichshafen FF 49c). The FF 49c two-seat reconnaissance floatplane was a development of the FF 39 which, in turn, was derived from the FF 33. The FF 39 differed from the latter in having slightly bigger dimensions and being powered by the 220-hp Benz Bz IV engine. The FF 49c, developed in mid-1917, differed in having a reinforced airframe. The control surfaces featured horn balances. The aircraft was fitted with armament and a radio.

Some 270 examples of the FF 49c were built, some of them by the Sablatnig and LFG companies. The type was fitted with the 200-hp Benx Bz IV engine. Having a wing span of 17.15 m (56 ft 3¼ in) and an AUW of 2,135 kg (4,708 lb), it attained a maximum speed of 140 km/h (87 mph).

Halberstadt fighter (unknown type)

Shavrov states that the captured fighters included Halberstadt machines powered by the 120-hp and 160-hp Argus engines. The 120-hp Argus engine was fitted to Halberstadt D.III (see below)

Halberstadt C.V long-range photo reconnaissance aircraft

This aircraft, a two-bay biplane powered by the 220-hp Benz Bz. IV, saw action only during the final six months of the war. Yet it was built in substantial numbers by the parent companies and by several other companies under licence and used with considerable success by the German air force.

The Halberstadt C.V is mentioned by Aleksandrov and Petrov among the German types captured by the Russian Army.

Above: A Russian Navy Friedrichshafen FF 33 floatplane. The Russian Emperor Nicholas II (third from left) is pictured beside it with top-ranking Russian and foreign military officials.

The same FF 33 abandoned by the White forces evacuating from Sevastopol' as it was overrun by the Red Army, and consequently captured intact.

Halberstadt D.Ia, D.II, D.III, D.IV fighters

It is assumed by some researchers that Halberstadt fighters of these types were captured by the Russian troops, albeit this assumption may appear dubious, particularly with regard to the D.Ia.

These single-seat fighters were developed and built by Halberstadt Flugzeugwerk from late 1915 onwards. The initial D.I model powered by the 100-hp Mercedes D.I was built in two copies; the D.Ia was fitted with a 120-hp Argus As II engine. The next version was powered by the 120-hp Mercedes D.II and designated Halberstadt D.II; it achieved production status. Manufactured concurrently was the D.III which reverted to the Argus As II engine.

The D.III was followed by the Halberstadt D.IV fitted with the 150-hp Benz Bz III engine; sometimes it was armed with two synchronised machine-guns, the normal armament for all types being one machine-gun. Only a few machines of the D.IV type were built. While the preceding types featured a two-bay biplane wing structure, the D.IV was a single-bay biplane. The last model was the D.V with improved aerodynamics. These fighters were built in relatively small numbers (96 D.IIs, 54 D.IIIs, 90 D.Vs, according to one source). The Halberstadt fighters were used on the Western front, and some D.IVs were supplied to Turkey. Available sources do not mention the Eastern front.

Hansa Brandenburg (general remarks)

Aircraft of various models bearing this name were designed in Germany by the Hansa und Brandenburgische Flugzeugwerke GmbH, and were built both in Germany and in Austro-Hungary. Some types were series-built only in Austro-Hungary for that country's air force. The types built in Austro-Hungary included the Hansa Brandenburg C.I, D.I, while all the other types were built in Germany. The company name is sometimes reduced to Brandenburg when referring to the same models. (See also Brandenburg

A Halberstadt C.V photo reconnaissance aircraft. The machine retains the German lozenge camouflage on the wings and tail surfaces but is devoid of any insignia.

above.) Listed below are some Hansa-Brandenburg types captured by Russian troops.

'Hansa Brandenburg type W floatplane'

Sobolev mentions a 'Hansa-Brandenburg type W floatplane' among the aircraft captured by the Russian army (Sobolev uses the Cyrillic B which corresponds to the English V and German W). According to Sobolev, the circumstances of the aircraft's acquisition were as follows: *'In October 1915 the V. A. Lebedev Joint Stock Society succeeded in obtaining an example of the German Hansa Brandenburg type V floatplane. For reasons unknown, on 28th September this machine (c/n 1122/15B), coded 269, performing a flight from Libawa with two crew on board, made a landing on the forest near the lake of Babite in Kurlandia (a part of present-day Latvia – Auth.). On 17th October another seaplane of the same type was downed by fire from the destroyer RNS (Russian Navy ship) Moskvityanin (Muscovite) near Cerel in the vicinity of the island of Esel. Fragments of this seaplane powered by a 120-hp Mercedes engine must have gone to the Lebedev factory, too'.*

Hansa Brandenburg W 12, W 25, W 32, GW and NW seaplanes

A Russian source states that the Russian naval aviation employed several captured German floatplanes; the types listed are the Hansa-Brandenburg W 12, W 25, W 32, GW and NW seaplanes.

The W 12 was a two-seat naval fighter equipped with floats. This biplane machine made its appearance in 1917 and was built in quantity with the Mercedes D.III or Benz Bz.III engines delivering 150 hp. The W 12 featured a unique empennage layout with the vertical tail not protruding above the rear fuselage, so as to provide unobstructed field of fire for the rear gunner/observer. The armament comprised one or two LMG 08/15 forward-firing machine guns and one flexibly mounted Parabellum machine-gun in the rear cockpit. The production run of this successful fighter totalled 146 machines.

The W 12 underwent some further development which resulted in the W 27 experimental machine and the W 32 series-built version. The W 27 built in single example featured I-type interplane struts and was powered by the 195-hp Benz Bz III engine.

The W 32 basically resembled the W 27, but was powered by the 160-hp Mercedes D.III engine.

The W 25 was a further development of the experimental W 11 single-seat reconnaissance floatplane powered by the 200-hp Benz Bz.IV engine.

The GW torpedo attack seaplane completed its acceptance trials in January 1916; 20 examples were built between April 1916 and November 1917. This twin-float biplane powered by two 160-hp Mercedes D.III engines could carry a 723-kg (1,595-lb) torpedo.

The NW reconnaissance and patrol floatplane was an improved version of the Hansa Brandenburg W two-seat biplane; it made its appearance in 1915 and closely resembled the Albatros B.I, except for its twin-float landing gear. The NW was built in small numbers together with the generally similar GNW aircraft. None of them carried defensive armament.

No details are available on the operation of the captured types by Russian forces. Some of the types listed here were later used by the Red Air Fleet (see Civil War section below).

L.F.G. (Roland) D.II fighter

The German company Luftfahrzeug Gesellschaft m.b.H. (L.F.G.) designed and built aircraft which were marketed under the trade name of Roland. (It was added to the company name: LFG Roland – to distinguish it from the similar acronym of the well-known LVG company.) The progeny of this company included the Roland D.I, D.II. and D.III fighters, the first of which was test flown in 1916 and was manufactured in series, 60 machines being built before the LFG factory was destroyed by a fire. After the restoration of the factory an improved model, the Roland D.II, was placed in production; it was built also by the Pfalz company. The Roland D.II and D.IIa were manufactured in series until February 1917, production totalling 70 and 300 respectively. The final fighter model in this line, the Roland D.III, was built in late 1916 – early 1917 with a total production run of 100 machines (50 of them built by Pfalz).

All three types were equal-span biplanes with no stagger; they had an aerodynamically clean fuselage of wooden monocoque construction. The engine was initially the Mercedes D.III of 160 hp, replaced by the Argus As.III on the Roland D.IIa and D.III. The armament comprised one forward-firing synchronised LMG 08/15 machine-gun.

The Roland fighters saw limited use on the Western front, but were committed to action in some numbers on the Eastern front where some of them were shot down by Russian pilots in aerial combat. Two machines were captured and subsequently operated by a Russian Air force unit. The exact type is not stated, but these machines must be the two L.F.G. Roland D.II fighters that, according to other sources, saw service with the Red Air fleet after the revolution (see below the Civil War section).

L.F.G. (Sablatnig SF-5 floatplane) see Sablatnig SF-5

L.V.G. ('Elfauge') B.I, C.I, C.V, C.VI, D.II

LVG aircraft of different models developed by the Luft-Verkehrs Gesellschaft m.b.H. Johannisthal (LVG) must have been captured by Russian troops, but information on that score is scant. The LVG B.I, C.I, C.V, C.VI, D.II are mentioned by Aleksandrov and Petrov among the German types captured by the Russian Army (see below). They also mention 'LVG with Benz and Mercedes engines (200-220 hp)'.

A captured aircraft described (erroneously?) as Aviatik L.V.G. was delivered to the Lebedev factory in 1915 (see Lebed'-IX below).

More information on LVG types in the Red Air fleet is given in the Civil War section below.

L.V.G. ('Elfauge') B.I reconnaissance and training aircraft

The LVG B.I was an unarmed reconnaissance biplane powered by either the 100-hp Mercedes D.I or the 110-hp Benz engine. In this aircraft the pilot occupied the rear cockpit and the observer sat in the front cockpit for a better view. The type was in German service at the outbreak of the war.

Evidence that the LVG B.I was captured and operated in Russia is provided by a picture showing an aircraft with Russian roundels and captioned: 'Winter photograph of an LVG B.I...' etc. However, this may be a case of misidentification.

In Russia this aircraft, as well as other L.V.G. types, was often referred to as 'Elfauge' (after the German pronunciation of the abbreviation).

L.V.G. ('Elfauge') C.I reconnaissance aircraft

The LVG C.I two-bay biplane of 1915 was an improved and armed version of the LVG B.I/II aircraft. In the C.I the pilot and the gunner/observer exchanged their positions, the gunner being seated behind the pilot. This permitted the installation of a flexible machine-gun on a ring mount in the rear cockpit. The aircraft was fitted with a more powerful 150-hp Benz Bz III engine. It entered limited production, but proved to be an interim type, soon superseded by the next model. The C.II version featured several improvements of the airframe and was fitted with the more powerful Mercedes D.III engine.

Aleksandrov and Petrov have published a picture captioned *'An LVG C.I still in the colours of the Russian air forces'*, apparently a captured machine taken over by the Red Air Fleet after November 1917.

L.V.G. ('Elfauge') C.V and C.VI reconnaissance aircraft

The LVG C.V developed in 1917 reached operational units by the autumn of that year. It was one of the most successful German aircraft used for reconnaissance and artillery observation. This machine with an AUW of 1,533 kg (3,380 lb) was powered by the 200-hp Benz Bz IV engine and attained a maximum speed of 164 km/h (102 mph). The armament comprised one forward-firing LMG 08/15 Spandau and one flexibly mounted Parabellum machine-gun in the

Above: This Roland D.IIa (c/n 539) was shot down by 2nd Lt. A. N. Sveshnikov (centre) and force-landed in Russian-held territory on 9th September 1917. It is prepared for evacuation on a horse-drawn cart.

Another Roland D.IIa (c/n 167/12) captured in the spring of 1917 is being inspected by Russian pilots.

rear cockpit, supplemented by up to 40 kg (88 lb) of light bombs.

The C.VI model, delivered to front-line units in 1918, was a modernised version of the C.V, retaining the predecessor's powerplant but featuring a number of modifications to improve its flying qualities. It could deliver up to 80 kg (176 lb) of bombs.

While the C.V model could theoretically reach the Russian front before November 1917 and thus fall into the hands of the Russian army, this cannot be said about the C.VI (see more about these types in the Civil War section below).

Mars reconnaissance aircraft

According to Shavrov, *'there were a few Bristol (Austrian-built) and Mars reconnaissance aircraft powered by Mercedes and Benz engines delivering up to 220 hp'* among the captured aircraft.

As mentioned earlier, Mars was the name used for some DFW aircraft before the war (see DFW heading). Thus, if there were

any Mars aircraft captured during the hostilities they must have been single examples of pre-war manufacture. No further details are available.

Roland – see L.F.G. (Roland) above

Rumpler B.I, C.I, C.IV, C.V reconnaissance aircraft and light bombers

Shavrov mentions the use by the Russian Air Force of captured Rumpler aircraft, 'powered by Mercedes and Opel engines with an output of 100, 110, 160 hp and more'. Other sources specify the Rumpler B.I, C.I, C.IV and C.V. In particular, a B.I bearing the number 213 on the fin (sometimes misidentified as a Mars) belonged to the 6th *aviapark*.

The mentioned types were developed by Rumpler Flugzeug-Werke GmbH. The Rumpler B.I, designed before the outbreak of the war, was an unarmed two-seat, two-bay biplane powered by a 100-hp Mercedes D.I engine. During 1914-15 it saw service

Above: A captured LVG C.I in Russian markings. The upper engine cowling and tyres have been removed. The aircraft was subsequently captured by the Red Army during the Russian civil war.

Above: A Rumpler B.I serialled 213 seen at the 6th Aviapark in L'vov. The aircraft is fitted with a 100-hp Mercedes engine.

on both Eastern and Western Fronts. Its armed counterpart was the Rumpler C.I, which made its appearance in early 1915. The initial production version of the C.I carried only a single Parabellum gun on a ring mounting for self-defence; later machines also had a synchronised Spandau machine-gun installed on the port side of the engine.

The Rumpler C.III (the C.II was projected but not built) was a development of the C.I. Design changes included the installation of the 220-hp Benz Bz. IV engine, a rudder with no fixed fin, a propeller spinner, shorter undercarriage legs, pronounced forward wing stagger and balanced ailerons and elevators. It was built in limited numbers and was soon superseded by the improved C.IV.

The Rumpler C.IV two-seat reconnaissance aircraft developed in 1916 was fitted with a more powerful engine (the 260-hp Mercedes), featuring a propeller spinner and other minor changes. This two-bay biplane had a maximum speed of 171 km/h (106 mph) at 1,000 m (3,380 ft) and a service ceiling of 6,405 m (21,000 ft). It was armed with one forward-firing synchronised Spandau machine-gun and one flexible MG in the rear cockpit. The aircraft performed well, particularly in regard to its rate of climb and speed at high altitude. It was used for long-range reconnaissance. Available sources state that the C.IV was operated on the Western front, making no

Wearing typical World War I period flying helmets, the pilot and observer pose with their Rumpler C.IV reconnaissance aircraft at Komendantskiy airfield, Petrograd, in 1922. Note the excellent condition of the aircraft. The insignia appear to have been overpainted.

mention of the Eastern front; yet it may have found its way to the Russian front, too.

See also the Civil War section below.

Sablatnig SF5 floatplane

Several (two?) examples of the Sablatnig SF5 reconnaissance floatplane (designed by Sablatnig Flugzeufbau GmbH and built under licence by LFG) were captured at the Black Sea. They were erroneously called LVG in Russia. Shavrov spells the designation as Sablatnig-5, probably reflecting the spelling used in Russian documents. No information is available about their service record in the Russian army before the revolution. See also the Civil War section below.

The SF5 was a higher-performance reconnaissance derivative of the earlier SF2 trainer floatplane which, in turn, was the production version of the initial SF1 model. The SF5 was a two-seat twin-float biplane powered by the 150-hp Benz Bz.III engine. In all, 91 machines were manufactured by Sablatnig, L.F.G. and L.V.G. in 1917 and early 1918. They were unarmed and were probably used mainly for training.

'Schneider'

Shavrov states that captured 'Schneider reconnaissance aircraft' were used in small numbers by the Russian army. They were powered by Mercedes engines of 100, 110, 120 and 130 hp and by 150-hp Benz engines. However, no aircraft were produced under this name in Germany or Austro-Hungary (as far as the authors of this book know). Available sources do not mention a company bearing the name Schneider, but do note that the designer of the L.V.G. company was Franz Schneider, of Swiss origin. This prompts one to suppose that the aircraft in question could in actual fact have been L.V.G. aircraft (see also the Civil War section).

Lebedev's work on the restoration and copying of captured German aircraft

V. A. Lebedev, one of the first Russian sports pilots, started his activities in aircraft construction in 1912, initially engaging in the manufacture of propellers and aircraft repair. In 1914 he built his aircraft manufacturing factory in St. Petersburg and started turning out aeroplanes of French types. In the summer of 1915 a captured Albatros aircraft of a 1914 model, powered by a 100-hp engine, was delivered to the factory. It was used by the factory designers as a pattern for the manufacture of Albatros copies incorporating various changes to suit the different engines subsequently installed. These aircraft, as well as copies of aircraft of other foreign types, were aptly designated Lebed' with a new number for

Above: An Albatros B.II converted to a Lebed'-XI. Note the non-standard engine cowling.

Above: This Albatros B.III has been converted to a Lebed'-XI after capture by Russian forces, featuring non-standard vertical boxy water radiators instead of Hazet radiators.

The LM-1 (Lebed'-Morskoy) fighter seaplane afloat on the Neva River in St. Petersburg. Note the strong forward inclination of the float struts.

each succeeding design (Lebed', derived from the factory owner's surname, means 'swan'). When captured German aircraft arrived at the factory, they were repaired and sent to operational units; some of them were copied and put into production. Described below are Lebed' aircraft that were either direct copies or derivatives of various German aircraft. In literature they are normally numbered by Roman figures, but alternative spelling with Arabic figures is used sometimes.

Lebed'-IX

A single example of the Lebed'-IX was built in 1916. It was reportedly a repaired captured L. V. G. aircraft of an unknown model. The aircraft remained a one-off, albeit the Lebedev company claimed in its advertising material that series production of the machine was to be started. The uncertainty about the original type is compounded by the following account (Sobolev): *'According to official declarations*

of the Lebedev factory about its production, in 1915 there were two types related to captured aircraft: "Aviatik" L.V.G. and Albatros of an unspecified model. The Aviatik was received [by the factory] in 1916 and was delivered to an operational unit in early 1916 under the designation Lebed'-IX'. (The combination of the Aviatik and L.V.G. names appears to be an error – which of the two types was actually involved? – Auth.)

Above: The first prototype of the Lebed'-XII reconnaissance aircraft (c/n 442) powered by a Salmson water-cooled radial engine at Komendantskiy airfield in 1916. The pennant-type fuselage insignia usually carried by Russian Imperial Air Fleet aircraft in those days are missing.

Right: The nose of the same aircraft giving details of the engine, propeller hub and water radiators.
Left: A Lebed'-XII fitted with skis for winter operations.

Lebed'-XI (A1 type biplane) two-seat reconnaissance aircraft

About ten examples of this aircraft were built in 1915-1916. It cannot be established with certainty which German aircraft served as a prototype for copying because the examples built differed both in the biplane cellule construction and the engine types. There were six versions of two-bay and three-bay wing boxes, the span varying from 13 to 14.5 m (from 42 ft 7¾ in to 46 ft). The engines used were the 100-hp and 150-hp Mercedes, the 120-hp, 140-hp and 150-hp Benz and 160-hp Maybach inline engines. Presumably several types of captured Albatros aircraft lent their features to different examples of the Lebed'-XI. Several examples of the Lebed'-XI were fitted with 150-hp Salmson water-cooled radial engines (they differed from the similarly powered Lebed'-XII in having a large propeller spinner).

Sobolev, speaking of the same ten machines, describes them as rebuilt captured aircraft of the Albatros B.I and B.II types, not new-build machines, and cites the official designation 'A1-Lebed'-XI' in which the A letter indicated that it was an Albatros type, the Arab figure (1) denoting the version (or example rebuilt?).

Lebed'-XII (Lebed'-12) reconnaissance aircraft

This was also a modified Albatros (no definite model can be cited as its pattern). The aircraft was powered by Salmson radials of different types. These engines were available in bigger numbers than engines of other types; this explains the fact that the Lebed'-XII was built in relatively large numbers despite its unremarkable performance. The prototype of this aircraft (c/n 422) powered by a 130-hp Salmson was flown in December 1915; later it was tested with a 140-hp Salmson engine. As early as June 1915 an order for 225 examples was placed; in the course of the subsequent two years it was fulfilled almost completely. Production machines began to leave the factory in August 1916; 216 aircraft had been completed and tested before 1st March 1919 (the production went on after the revolution and the advent of Soviet power and was halted in 1918). Most of the production machines were powered by 150-hp engines. The aircraft was used for reconnaissance missions, but was not popular with pilots because of difficult handling and several cases of uncontrollable dive. The aircraft was also used as a trainer in several Russian flying schools. It remained in service after November 1917 and was used at the fronts of the Civil War by the various opposing parties; the last examples of this aircraft were operated in the Soviet Union until 1924.

Lebed'-XII *bis*

This designation is used in some sources for the Lebed'-XIIs fitted experimentally with different engines. Notably, an example was equipped with a 140-hp Hispano-Suiza engine, and another with a 120-hp Green engine.

Lebed'-XIII, Lebed XV

In the spring of 1916 the Lebed'-XIII made its appearance. Powered by a 150-hp Salmson radial, it was in all probability an improved version of the Lebed'-XII. The same goes for the Lebed'-XV powered by a 225-hp Renault which appeared at about the same time.

Lebed'-XVI

This aircraft represented a fairly radical modification of the Lebed'-XII, being converted into a twin-engined machine powered by two 80-hp Le Rhône rotary engines. These were placed between the biplane wings on a mounting formed by inverted V-struts. Further changes included an increase in the wing span; the fuselage was redesigned to provide accommodation for three crew members. In addition to the normal crew complement of pilot and rear gunner, one more defensive machine gun station was added in the nose, now free from the powerplant. In this configuration the aircraft departed rather far from the original Albatros concept and thus can be regarded only as a 'distant relative' of the latter.

The aircraft was tested in early 1917, but failed to arouse any interest in the Military Department.

Lebed'-XVII (Lebed'-17) reconnaissance aircraft

This two-seat single-bay biplane was a derivative of the Lebed'-XII reconnaissance aircraft. It incorporated various structural and aerodynamic improvements as compared to the basic model; one of these was the very neat cowling enclosing its Salmson engine of 140 or 150 hp. The aircraft differed from its predecessors in being provided with a small centre section to the upper wing increasing its robustness.

The Lebed'-XVII was built and tested in August 1917. Several machines were built by the end of the year. At least one of these was taken over by the Red Air Fleet and sported red stars on its fuselage and rudder.

Lebed'-XVIII (Lebed'-18) reconnaissance aircraft

Three more Lebed' models defined as 'German type' aeroplanes were developed by the Lebedev factory in 1917. These were the Lebed'-XVIII, Lebed'-XXI and Lebed'-XXIV. They had different engines (230-hp Fiat, 150-hp Salmson and 200-hp Hispano-

Suiza respectively). In comparison with the Lebed'-XII they incorporated certain modifications similar to those effected on the later, improved models of the German Albatros. In January 1917 Lebedev proposed to the Military department the manufacture of 300 machines of the Lebed'-XVIII, but no production order was granted.

Lebed'-XXI (Lebed'-21) reconnaissance aircraft

The first example of this Salmson-powered aircraft passed acceptance on 30th August 1917; later a further 6 examples were accepted by the customer. Shavrov describes it as a 'two-seat monoplane reconnaissance aircraft with modest performance characteristics' which remained in service until 1921.

Lebed'-XXIV (Lebed'-24)

According to Shavrov, this biplane 'of a German type' was to be fitted with either the 230-hp Fiat or the 200-hp Hispano-Suiza engine. It was the subject of negotiations in 1917; they resulted in an order for 200 machines, but the order was not fulfilled because Russia's allies stopped the deliveries of the mentioned engines to Russia in the second half of 1917.

Albatros with a 150-hp Sunbeam engine

Several examples of this three-bay biplane were delivered by the Lebedev factory in late 1916, when this type was already obsolescent.

Lebed' (Albatros-based design) with the Russian M-101 engine

In 1916 the Lebedev factory built a Lebed' aircraft (modelled on an Albatros) powered by the Russian-built M-101 (M-100) engine. This was the 101-hp engine developed by the Duflon and Konstantinovich aero engine company on the basis of captured 100-hp Mercedes inline engines. The plans for starting series production of this engine came to nothing. As for the aircraft, no information on its testing has been discovered.

Lebedev-built Albatros with a 100-hp Fiat engine

This aircraft was under test in late 1916/early 1917. This was an early model of the Albatros dating back to 1914. Three examples were manufactured and accepted for operational service, despite their rather inferior performance, which included a top speed of 95 km/h (59 mph).

Several types of captured German aircraft were repaired or built anew at Lebedev's factory in 1915-16. These included a three-bay Albatros powered by a

Above: A red-starred Albatros C.XII assembled at the 4th aircraft repair depot in Nizhniy Novgorod and taken over by the Red Air Fleet. The aircraft is fitted with skis.

100/120-hp Austro-Daimler engine, other Albatros machines with different engines (150-170-hp Isotta-Fraschini, 160-hp Mercedes, 150-hp Benz), Rumpler and Aviatik aircraft of unspecified types with different engines, and other types.

Lebedev's seaplanes based on German designs

Lebed' Morskoy-1 (LM-1) floatplane

At an early stage of the war the Russian Naval Department formulated a requirement for a hydroplane with a long range, intended for reconnaissance missions on the Black Sea. V. A. Lebedev responded with a proposal to build two aeroplanes based on an Albatros type ('Albatros 4a' is cited in Russian sources). They were to be fitted with interchangeable landing gear (wheels, skis or floats); the endurance was expected to be up to six hours. An agreement between the company and the authorities was reached in February-March 1915. The finished aero-

planes, equipped with floats, were to be delivered for testing in Sevastopol' in May 1915.

The type received the designation Lebed' Morskoy-1 (*morskoy* means maritime or naval) or LM-1; it was based on a three-bay Albatros B.I, with some modifications to the airframe. For example, the area of the vertical tail was increased by the installation of a dorsal fin. The aircraft was fitted with two main floats and one tail float. The British 150-hp Sunbeam was selected as the powerplant. The engines arrived in the autumn of 1915, causing a delay in the delivery of the two LM-1s.

The aircraft was tested in Petrograd in the autumn of 1915; four-blade and two-blade propellers were used alternatively during the tests. In the meantime, a decision had been taken in favour of equipping Russian naval aviation with flying boats, rather than float aeroplanes. In consequence, the LM-1 was not put into production. One of the two prototypes was placed in storage, while the other one was

refitted with a wheel undercarriage and saw limited use.

AB-1 reconnaissance floatplane (Friedrichshafen FF 33)

In 1916 the Lebedev factory received one more piece of war booty – this was a captured floatplane identified as an 'Albatros with Benz-1 engine' (hence the designation AB-1 conferred on it then). In actual fact, it was a Friedrichshafen FF 33 reconnaissance biplane. This particular machine was captured by Russian troops on 20th September 1916 near the island of Runo in the Gulf of Riga. The aircraft made a forced landing when returning to base from a reconnaissance mission. After some repairs the machine was ferried to Reval (Tallinn) where it was assigned to a naval air unit under the designation AB-1. However, its operational use did not last long. In April 1917 it was transferred to the Lebedev factory for the purpose of copying. On the basis of this sample two copies were built at Lebedev's factory in Taganrog at the end of 1917; they were powered by 200-hp Hispano-Suiza engines. There were plans for series production of this aircraft, but they failed to materialise.

German aircraft taken over or captured by the Red Air Fleet after the revolution and during the Civil War

A.E.G. C IV reconnaissance and artillery observation aircraft

According to some reports, at least one A.E.G. C IV served with the Red Air Fleet. This two-seat two-bay biplane was the most important among the C-models manufactured by A.E.G. (Allgemeine Elektrizitäts Gesellschaft). It was brought out in 1916 and remained in operational use throughout the rest of the war, some 400 examples having

Snowbound and looking rather sorry for itself, this Red Air Fleet Albatros C.XII carries the star insignia differently. The stars are obviously hand-painted.

been built by A.E.G. and by Fokker's Schwerin factory. The A.E.G. C.IV was armed with a forward-firing synchronised Spandau machine-gun and a ring-mounted Parabellum gun in the rear cockpit. It was powered by a 160-hp Mercedes D.III engine.

Albatros B.II, D.V, C.X, C.XII, C.XV

Albatros aircraft of different models were used by the Red Air Fleet during the first years after the revolution. Some were original German machines, and others were aircraft built, repaired or re-engined by the Lebedev firm during the First World War, including the Lebed'-series machines. According to Lennart Andersson, the original Albatros aircraft taken over or captured by the Red Air Fleet included B.IIs, D.V fighters, C.Xs and C.XIIs (with the 260-hp Mercedes), aircraft with the 220-hp Benz (used by the 17th Air Detachment in 1922) and with the 110-hp Mercedes. In 1921 the Albatros were used on all fronts and two were employed by the Il'ya Muromets Division. A few Albatros were also used by military flying schools.

Mention has been made earlier in this chapter of two 'Albatros' floatplanes captured by the Russian army at the Black Sea. These machines (c/ns 663 and 674) with 220-hp Benz engines were taken over by the Red Army. They were operated by the 4th **Ghidrootryad** (Seaplane detachment) at Sevastopol' until written off in 1924. As noted above, the 'Albatros' is a misidentification. Lennart Andersson remarks that the engine type would make them Friedrichshafen FF 38s, FF 49s, Gotha WD 14s or Lübeck-Travemündes.

Aleksandrov and Petrov have published a photo of an Albatros C.XII of a Red Army aviation battalion carrying a red star on the fin, on the undersurface of the lower wings and, curiously, under the nose. The aircraft was fitted with paired simple skis replacing each of the wheels. Another picture shows a different Albatros C.XII in service with a Red Army aviation battalion, this time fitted with single skis of a streamlined shape.

The Albatros C.XV was brought out in 1918 as a slightly larger version of the C.XII with overhung ailerons. Only a handful was built. One such aircraft was captured by the Russian Air Fleet and subsequently used by the Western Volunteer Army against the Red Army in 1919 during the Civil War.

'Albatros 16' and 'Albatros-17'

The two types, with designations spelled as above, were mentioned by Shavrov among the German aircraft captured during the Civil War. He describes the former as a two-seat biplane with internally wire-braced fuselage, powered by a 165-hp Mercedes engine. The

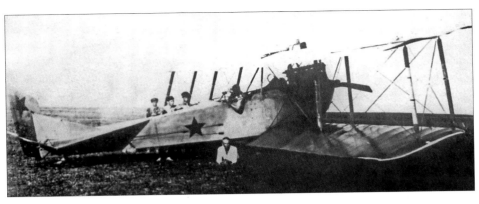

Above: A Brandenburg C.I in Red Air Fleet markings.

latter aircraft of the same layout featured a monocoque fuselage and was powered by a 220-hp Benz engine. No further details were given except that the 'Albatros-17' 'was used on the Eastern front' (whatever this may mean). Since these designations are not to be found among the aircraft produced by Albatros-Werke, it remains unclear what type of aircraft was actually involved.

See also Albatros XVII in the next chapter.

Above: A DFW C.V in Red Air Fleet markings undergoes field maintenance. This view shows the distinctive shape of the wings and horizontal tail.

Two views of a DFW C.V apparently operated by the White forces (and retaining the pre-1917 Russian roundels) after nosing over on landing. The observer is in a hurry to exit the aircraft... who wouldn't be?

Above: A Red Army Air Force Friedrichshafen G.IIIa undergoes repairs in Lithuania after nosing over on landing; a new forward fuselage structure is grafted on, replacing the crushed nose.

One of at least two Friedrichshafen G.IIIa bombers operated by the Red Army Air Force is shown at rest. Curiously, the red star on the starboard lower wing is painted on upside down.

Aviatik

According to Lennart Andersson, one Aviatik of unknown type was present in the Red Air Fleet in August 1922. This must have been one of the Aviatik types captured by the Russian army during the First World War (see above).

Brandenburg C.I (Austrian) reconnaissance aircraft

As related by Lennart Aandersson, four Austrian-built Brandenburg aircraft were in service with the Red Air Fleet at the end of 1920, probably captured in the Ukraine. At the end of 1921 only one remained. A Brandenburg with 160-hp Austro-Daimler engine, almost certainly the same machine, was with the Ukrainian Aviakhim (voluntary society in support of aviation and chemical defence) in October 1926. The Swedish author further remarks that *'two Schneiders (c/n 6926, possibly Brandenburg C.I 69.26, and c/n 363) were converted into photographic aircraft; one was used by the **Vys**shaya **a**erofotogram**mich**eskaya **shko**la*

(Higher School for Aerial Survey – Auth.) and both were offered to Dobrolet (one of the Soviet airlines of the period, see Chapter 2 – Auth.) in February 1924 but not accepted'.

Vyacheslav Kondrat'yev and Dmitriy Khairulin relate that in March-April 1919 five German and Austrian-built aircraft *'two Brandenburgs and three El'fauges (that is, LVGs – Auth.) captured during the recent retreat of the German and Austrian troops from the Ukraine'* were selected for flights to Hungary after the (short-lived) Communist revolution there. They go on to state, *'All the aircraft were new machines of recent models'.* The exact models of the Brandenburgs are not specified.

The Hansa Brandenburg C.I reconnaissance aircraft, first flown in the first half of 1916, was a two-seat, two-bay biplane of wooden construction. It had an open common cabin for the crew of two. Although of German origin, the Hansa Brandenburg C.I was built entirely in Austro-Hungary and was operated principally by the Austrian air force. It was powered by different engines

ranging from 160 to 230 hp; one of the versions was fitted with the 220-hp Benz Bz IVa engine. Initial version was armed with one engine on a flexible mount in the rear cabin; later machines were also fitted with a forward firing fixed machine-gun. Up to 100 kg (220 lb) of light bombs could be carried under the lower wings.

DFW C.V front-line reconnaissance aircraft

Several types of front-line reconnaissance aircraft were developed by DFW (Deutsche Flugzeug-Werke), among them the C.IV, C.V and C.VI models. The C.IV, a two-seat two-bay biplane powered by a 150-hp Benz Bz.III engine, first appeared in the early 1916. This efficient machine was overshadowed by the even better C.V which was developed from it. While retaining basically the same airframe, the C.V was powered by the much more powerful Bz.IV engine of 200 hp. The C.V was in fact a general-purpose aircraft, being used for reconnaissance and photographic work, artillery co-operation and infantry contact patrols. The favourable response from pilots led to large-scale production of the type by several companies – DFW, Halberstadt, Aviatik and Schütte-Lanz. Its armament comprised one forward-firing LMG 08/15 Spandau machine-gun and one flexibly mounted Parabellum machine gun in the rear cockpit. The DFW C.V was manufactured in slightly modified form by the LVG company as the LVG C.V; the two companies' aircraft were very similar externally, which led to some cases of misidentification.

Aleksandrov and Petrov have published a picture of a biplane carrying Red Army Air Force markings (red stars) on the upper wings and the rudder which they identify as the DFW C.V. It is a two-seat, two-bay biplane with a characteristic sweptback tailplane.

An example of the DFW C.V was flown by pilot Tarasov, according to Kondrat'yev and Khairulin. They have also published a picture of a DFV C.V, a machine operated by the 24th Reconnaissance Air Detachment at the Ukrainian Front, after a crash landing in March 1919. Another DFW of an unspecified type is mentioned by these authors as captured by Polish troops on the territory of the Ukraine after their invasion in April 1920.

Fokker D.VIII/E.V fighter

Two Fokker D.VIII/E.V fighters were captured in 1920 (apparently during the Soviet-Polish war of 1920 – Auth.). One of them, flown by the Polish pilot Julian Jasiński, became the booty of the Red Army after being shot down. It was repaired and assigned to the 2nd Independent Fighter Detachment at Kharkov, where it was used as a fighter-trainer until 1925. This story (as related above by Lennart

Andersson) can be supplemented by the following account belonging to Kondrat'yev and Khairulin: In June 1920, during the Soviet-Polish war, an example of the Fokker E.V was captured by Soviet troops at the Lithuanian-Belorussian section of the front. *'At the beginning of the month the Red troops captured a fairly rare Fokker E.V parasol fighter. A young Polish pilot, Jasiński by name, who was fresh out of flying school, flew this fighter to the frontlines but lost his bearings and landed in Soviet territory. The interesting war booty became the property of the Slavnoye Air Group (Slavnenskaya aviagruppa), but, as far as is known, this fighter was not committed to combat.'*

The Fokker E.V monoplane made its appearance in 1918 and entered production in June of that year. It had great agility, and excellent take-off, climbing and diving qualities. The type featured cantilever wings of fairly thick airfoil section mounted above the fuselage on a framework of diagonal struts supporting the wing centre section to which the outer wing panels were attached. The powerplant, fuselage and tailplane were similar to those of the Fokker D.VI, while the vertical tail was identical to that of the D.VII. The armament comprised two synchronised LMG 08/15 machine-guns.

After a series of crashes which occurred shortly after the service introduction of the E.V, these machines were returned to the factory where they received reinforced wings in September 1918. In October 1918 production resumed under the new designation Fokker D.VIII (by that time the Germans started allotting the D index to all their fighters), but the Armistice put an end to the career of this successful fighter.

Friedrichshafen G.IIIa (G.IVa?)

Albeit not exactly a captured aircraft, it merits inclusion here due to the circumstances of its acquisition. According to Lennart Andersson, in January-February 1920 four examples of this twin-engined bomber were used for what one would call today a humanitarian mission. At the request of the Austro-German Prisoner of War Repatriation Commission they were sent by the Deutsche Luft-Reederei from Königsberg (now Kaliningrad, Russia) to Smolensk, carrying medical supplies and members of the commission. One had to discontinue the flight and landed in Poland, but the other three reached their destination.

As Lennart Andersson states further, one of the machines was allowed to return in March (it was carrying a Soviet trade representative to Berlin), but the other two were confiscated by the Soviet authorities and soon went into service with the RKKVF (Red Air Fleet). One of them, equipped to

A dismantled Junkers CL.I attack aircraft (c/n 1803/18) at the Moscow aircraft depot. The aircraft, which belonged to Kampfgeschwader Sachsenberg, was captured in Latvia in the spring of 1919.

carry eight passengers, was assigned to a Special Missions Flight and later to the headquarters of Aviaeskadra No. 1 in Moscow, while the other was used in the Ukrainian and Western Military Districts.

Shavrov, obviously referring to the same episode, albeit in vague terms, identifies the aircraft as a Friedrichshafen G.IVa powered by two 260-hp Mercedes engines. In his account of events, German pilots flew a single aircraft of this type to Moscow carrying medical supplies; he remarks that 'this was not a war booty aircraft'. Another example of the same type was allegedly purchased in 1922.

Aleksandrov and Petrov have published a picture of one of these machines, captioned thus: *'At least one Friedrichshafen G.IIIa fell into Russian hands and was later used as a personal transport by Lev Trotsky. The aircraft later made a crash-landing in Lithuania. This photo shows the aircraft undergoing repairs in a Lithuanian hangar. Following the completion of repairs, the aircraft continued to fly in Lithuania.'*

Halberstadt CL.IV

According to L. Andersson, two Halberstadt CL.IVs (identified as 423 and 1770) and possibly some CL.IIs were captured by the Red Army. One Halberstadt CL.IV (423) was used by the Reconnaissance Air Squadron at Kiev and was retained at the 4th Permanent Air Reserve Unit in Leningrad until some time after April 1924.

The CL (light C) category of warplane was introduced by the German High command at the beginning of 1917. The CL aircraft were to act as escorts to the heavier C type (reconnaissance) aircraft and to undertake ground attack and close support

work. The Halberstadt CL.II was a two-seat biplane armed with single or twin forward-firing synchronised Spandau guns and a rearward-firing flexibly mounted Parabellum gun; it entered service in the summer of 1917. An aerodynamically redesigned and improved version, the CL.IV, was introduced into service in 1918. Both versions were powered by the 160-hp Mercedes D.III engine.

For the Halberstadt C.V, see Chapter 2.

Hansa Brandenburg C.I – see Brandenburg C.I above

Hansa Brandenburg W 12 fighter floatplane

According to some sources, the Red Army operated the Hansa Brandenburg W 12 floatplanes in the Black Sea area. No further details are given. It stands to reason to assume that these were the two W 12s that had been captured by the Russian Imperial Navy from the Germans during the First World War (see above).

Shavrov, speaking of the Hansa Brandenburg floatplanes in Red Army service, states: *'There were single examples on the Black Sea (W 12, W 22, W 32)'*. The W 22 is presumably a misprint for the W 25; in general, these are the types already mentioned in the First World War section (see above).

Junkers D.I fighter and CL.I attack aircraft

The Junkers D.I (J 9 in prototype form) was the first all-metal fighter in the world. Featuring a cantilever low-wing monoplane layout, it was first flown in May 1918. Only 41 production examples were built before the end of the war, a further 31 examples being built after the end of hostilities – between

Above: B. K. Velling, a Red Army Air Force pilot (left), and his LVG C.V in Turkestan (that is, Central Asia).

The pilots and mechanics of the Red Army Air Fleet's 20th Aviation Battalion pose with an LVG C.V on 30th August 1922.

November 1918 and February 1919; 12 of them were built under licence by the Fokker company. The single-seat D.I was powered initially by the 160-hp Mercedes D-III and later by the 185-hp BMW IIIa engine.

The Junkers CL.I (J 10) ground attack aircraft was a two-seat development of the D.I. It differed from the single-seater in having a longer fuselage with a second cockpit for the gunner/observer. The wing span was increased; the undercarriage was slightly altered and reinforced. The CL.I was fitted with the 180-hp Mercedes D.IIIa engine. Only 47 had been delivered before the Armistice.

In 1919 the all-metal Junkers aircraft were actively operated by the German voluntary corps in the course of the civil war in the Baltic area. It was then that the two types fell into the hands of the Red Army. Lennart Andersson presents this as follows: '*Two Junkers D.Is and one Junkers CL.I (s/n 1803/18) were captured on the Polish front in 1920 but they were not assembled. One fuselage was sent to TsAGI in Moscow for examination by the Material Test Section.*'

A slightly different version of the story is presented by Kondrat'yev and Khairulin in their book on aviation activities in the Civil War in Russia. In November 1918 the Red Army launched an offensive against German

troops in Belorussia and the Baltic area, initially gaining some success and occupying Riga in January 1919. However, soon the Latvian troops assisted by the Landeswehr (voluntary formations consisting mainly of local Germans and former German army personnel) repelled this offensive. Among the German-staffed units was an air unit known as Kampfgeschwader Sachsenberg (Sachsenberg Bomber Wing); it was led by Gotthard Sachsenberg, a former German marine aviation pilot. His unit boasted the latest hardware, including some 30 brand-new Junkers D.1 and CL.1 all-metal aircraft. German pilots flew reconnaissance and bombing missions against the Soviet troops. L. Andersson writes: '*As far as is known, they lost at least two Junkers aircraft, one of which made a forced landing behind the front line because of malfunctions, and the other one, in unserviceable and dismantled condition, was simply abandoned during a retreat at the Alt-Autz airfield. Both machines, captured by the Red troops, were taken to Moscow for evaluation* (the machines are not identified by type, but are presumably the CL.Is – Auth.). *Furthermore, there is some evidence indicating that on 18 March 1919 the Red Army troops shot down by ground fire a Junkers D.I in the Mitawa (Jelgava) area. The machine was piloted by*

the German ace Josef Jakobs who managed to make a safe landing and make his way to his own troops. The subsequent fate of the aircraft is not known.'

Among the colour profiles published by Kondrat'yev and Khairulin is a profile of the Junkers CL.I from Kampfgeschwader Sachsenberg bearing German insignia and the inscription *Junk. CL.I Jfa 12604/18* on the fuselage. The caption states that this is a machine captured by the Red Army on the territory of Latvia in the spring of 1919. Accompanying photos show the two Junkers CL.Is captured – s/ns 1803/18 and 12604/18, both in dismantled condition at the Moscow aircraft repair depot.

Interestingly, in 1923 the Soviet aeronautical magazine *Vesnik Vozdushnovo Flota* (Air Fleet Herald) published an article titled 'Some data on the construction of Junkers all-metal aeroplanes'. It was written on the basis of studying the captured machines (see above) and of the information from western publications.

LFG Roland D II fighter

Evidence about the use of this fighter type by the Red Air Fleet comes from Lennart Andersson and two Russian researchers. The Swedish author writes:

'*A single LFG Roland fighter with 180-hp Opel engine (s/n 301, probably D.II 301/17) was used by the 2nd Aviaotryad (Air Detachment) of the Istrebitel'naya Eskadril'ya (Fighter Squadron) at Kiev and then by the 2nd Otdel'nyi istrebitel'nyi aviaotryad (2nd Independent Fighter Detachment) at Khar'kov. In 1924 it was at the 2nd Postoyannaya aviabaza*' (Permanent Air Base).

Kondrat'yev and Khairulin have published a picture captioned: '*A Roland D.II fighter. Only two such aircraft found their way to Russia as World War I war booty. The machine depicted on the photo was operated by the 1st Squadron of the Moscow Revolutionary Air Detachment. Pilot Ya. P. Shuman is in the cockpit. Khar'kov, January 1918.*'

The circumstances of acquisition of the mentioned aircraft are not stated, but it may be presumed that these were the fighters that had been captured and used by the Imperial Russian Air Service (see the First World War section above).

LVG C.II, LVG C.V, LVG C.VI

Externally similar DFW and LVG aircraft of different models remained on the territory of Poland and the Ukraine after the withdrawal of German troops from these countries in early 1919. They got involved in various conflicts that took place in that area during the Civil War in Russia. To quote Lennart Andersson again:

'Several LVG aircraft of different types were captured by the Red Army. In April 1919 V. Khodorovich flew from Vinnitsa to Budapest in a LVG C.V. By December 1920 ten LVGs of different marks were on the RKKVF (Red Air Fleet) inventory. In 1921 they were employed in Turkestan and in the Ukraine. At the beginning of 1922 there were fourteen LVGs, of which three were assigned to the Razvedyvatel'naya Eskadril'ya (Reconnaissance Air Squadron) in Moscow. Known LVG C V (220-hp Benz) c/ns: 38/139, 107, 116, 10400 and 1987'.

Kondrat'yev and Khairulin have published colour profiles of aircraft used during the Civil War (presumably prepared on the basis of pictorial evidence). Among these is profile of the LVG C.II of the 45th Reconnaissance Air Detachment, used on the Western front in the autumn of 1919. Another profile shows the LVG C.V belonging to pilot Tarasov of the 24th Reconnaissance Air Detachment at Vinnitsa, March 1919. Yet another profile depicts the LVG C.V flown by Khodorovich of the Air Detachment for International Communication at Vinnitsa, April 1919 (see below). Curiously, the aircraft retains crosses on the fuselage and rudder, and the inscription: LVG C. v. 9667/17.

The episode with Khodorovich and his flight to Hungary is described by Kondrat'yev and Khairulin as follows:

On 21st March 1919 the Hungarian Soviet Republic was proclaimed in Budapest. Vladimir I. Lenin, the leader of the Russian Soviet Republic, reacted to this by issuing an order calling for the immediate establishment of air communication with Hungary. N. V. Vasil'yev, commander of (Soviet) Ukraine's Air Fleet, was entrusted with fulfilling the task. Five German- and Austrian-built captured aircraft were selected for the flights to Hungary. These were two Brandenburgs and three LVGs captured during the recent retreat

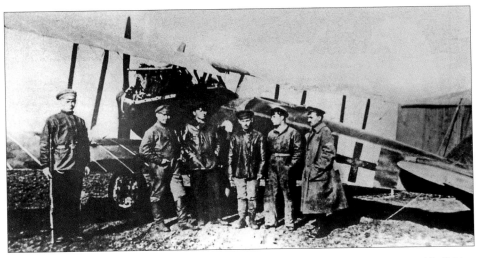

Above: Soviet officials pose with an LVG C.VI wearing what was reported as a red cross on a white field (the aircraft may have been used for delivering medicines to Russia in 1920). Note the armed sentry.

of German and Austrian troops from the Ukraine. A special unit called Air Detachment for International Communication (sometimes called Special Missions Detachment) was formed in Vinnitsa. V. Khodorovich was the only pilot in this detachment to have some experience of long-distance flights. On 12th April 1919 he set off for the first 'international flight' performed by the Soviets. He was flying a two-seat LVG (an LVG C.V, according to some sources), carrying Ferenc György, a Hungarian Communist, as his passenger. After a five-hour flight his aircraft landed safely near Budapest. Shortly thereafter Khodorovich returned to Vinnitsa, flying the same route with a cargo of diplomatic and military mail. This celebrated episode often cited in Soviet historiography had a less glorious sequel. In August 1919 Khodorovich defected to Denikin's White Guard troops, using the same LVG that he had flown to Budapest.

Kondrat'yev and Khairulin have also published a picture of the LVG C.V belonging

to the 1st Fighter Detachment and depicted at Khodynka airfield in Moscow, August 1919. Another picture shows one more LVG C.V on the territory of the Central aviapark (aircraft depot) in Moscow.

They have also published a picture of an LVG C.V of the 4th Air Detachment at Tashkent in the spring of 1922.

Pictures of several examples of the LVG aircraft in Soviet service were published by Andrey Aleksandrov and Gennadiy Petrov. In some cases the type is not identified, in others the C.V or C.VI model is indicated. One of the pictures shows a C.VI in Smolensk in 1923, another depicts a machine belonging to the 20th Aviation Battalion in August 1922, yet another shows an LVG C V of the 14th Aviation Battalion. There is a photo of an LVG C.V in Turkestan and a picture of an LVG C.VI with unusual markings, probably a red cross on a white field (this aircraft may have been used to deliver medicines to Russia in 1920). One of the pictures is captioned: 'LVG C.V bombers

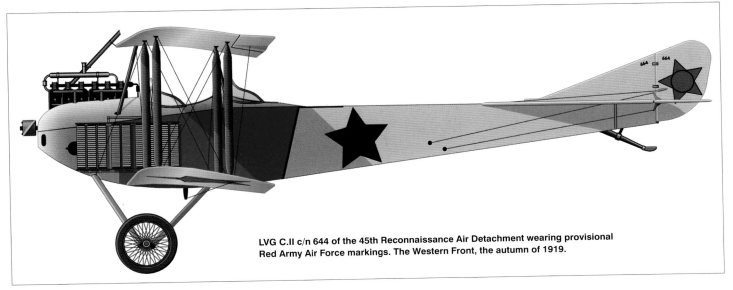

LVG C.II c/n 644 of the 45th Reconnaissance Air Detachment wearing provisional Red Army Air Force markings. The Western Front, the autumn of 1919.

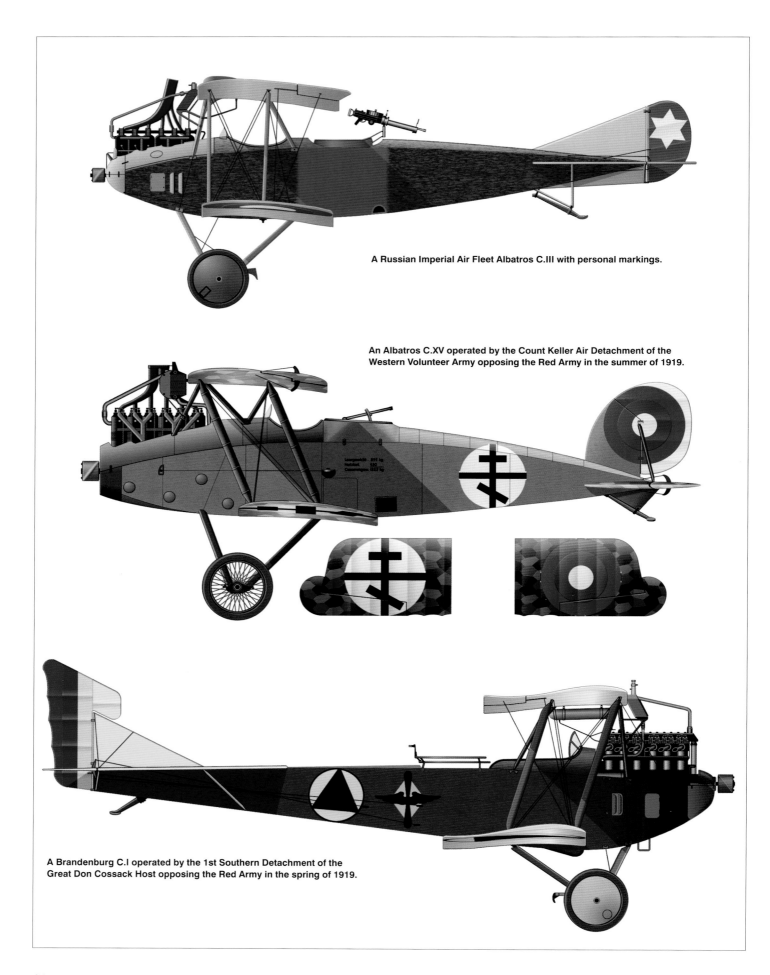

A Russian Imperial Air Fleet Albatros C.III with personal markings.

An Albatros C.XV operated by the Count Keller Air Detachment of the Western Volunteer Army opposing the Red Army in the summer of 1919.

A Brandenburg C.I operated by the 1st Southern Detachment of the Great Don Cossack Host opposing the Red Army in the spring of 1919.

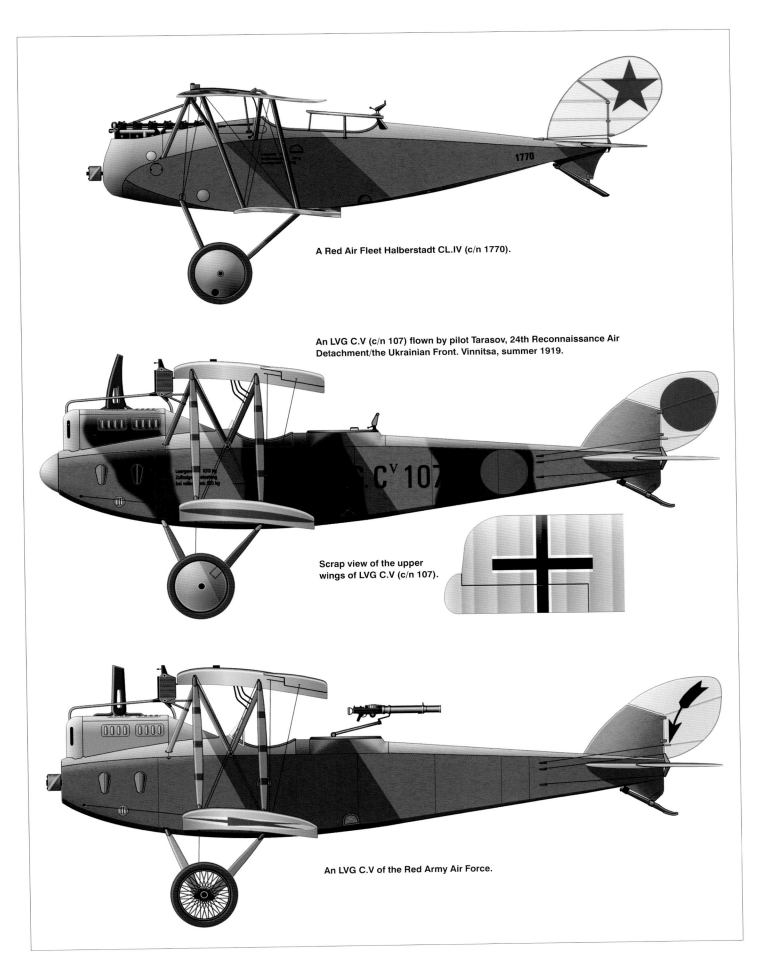

A Red Air Fleet Halberstadt CL.IV (c/n 1770).

An LVG C.V (c/n 107) flown by pilot Tarasov, 24th Reconnaissance Air Detachment/the Ukrainian Front. Vinnitsa, summer 1919.

Scrap view of the upper wings of LVG C.V (c/n 107).

An LVG C.V of the Red Army Air Force.

Red Army Air Force personnel pose for a photo with a Rumpler C.IV in Petrograd in 1922. Note the observer holding the camera over the side of the cockpit.

in service with an aviation unit of the Red Army. These aircraft were supposedly purchased after the October Revolution; however, this cannot be confirmed. A number of these aircraft were stationed on the Turkestan Front in Central Asia, where this photo was taken, most likely in the 1920s'. It must be borne in mind that a certain number of LVG aircraft were purchased by Soviet Russia in 1922 (see next chapter).

Rumpler C.I, C.IV and C.V reconnaissance aircraft

A few captured Rumpler aircraft must have been inherited by the Red Air Fleet from the Imperial Russian Air Fleet.

According to Lennart Andersson, in 1922 the Red Air Fleet operated at least six Rumpler aircraft, some of which were assigned to the DVK (Divizion vozdooshnykh korabley, Division of Air Cruisers – a unit operating the Sikorsky 'Il'ya Muromets' heavy bombers) and to the 1st and 7th Independent Reconnaissance Air Detachments. One was transferred to the Dobrolyot stateowned air transport society for use in the photographic role in 1924; it was registered RR-DLD in April 1925. In the same year a local branch of the ODVF (Obshchestvo droozey Vozdooshnovo flota – the Society of Friends of the Air Fleet) received an aircraft referred to as 'Schneider', which was in fact a German-built Rumpler C.I. Another Rumpler was handed over to Aviakhim (the Society for the Support of Aviation and the Chemical Industry) at Volzhsk.

There is photographic evidence of the use of the Rumpler C.IV and C.V in the Red Air Fleet (several pictures of both types have been published by Aleksandrov and Petrov). Three of the pictures show C.IVs in Petrograd in 1922. The pictures show a twoseat, two-bay biplane with upper and lower

wings of equal span, powered by an inline engine with the exhaust pipe on the port side protruding above the upper wing. The radiator is located in the centre section of the upper wing which is characteristically supported by two slanting struts in an inverted-V arrangement joining the wing trailing edge and the fuselage.

For details of the types mentioned, see the First World War section above.

Rumpler C.VII reconnaissance aircraft

According to Kondrat'yev and Khairulin, an example of this aircraft was captured by Soviet troops during the Polish-Soviet war in September 1919. According to this account, a Rumpler C.VII from the (Polish) 1st Eskadra descended very low during a reconnaissance mission to identify an infantry detachment and was met by concentrated rifle fire. The engine cut after being hit by a bullet, and the pilot had to make a landingin Soviet-held territory. The crew escaped, but the aircraft was captured by the Russians (its fate is not known).

The Rumpler C.VII was a further development of the Rumpler C.IV to which it was almost identical in appearance, except that it had a horizontal exhaust manifold instead of the upward-exhausting one of the C.IV. A specialised high-altitude photo reconnaissance variant was the C.VII Rubild.

Sablatnig SF 5 floatplane

'Two Sablatnig SF 5 floatplanes with 160hp Benz engines, identified as 1358 and 1462 (probably German Marine serials), were captured on the Black Sea. They were called 'LVG' by the Russians because they were licence-built by LFG. Used by the 4th Gidrootryad (Hydroplane Detachment) at Sevastopol until 1923, both were written off

in 1924-25.' This account borrowed from Lennart Andersson almost certainly refers to the Sablatnig SF5 aircraft captured by the Imperial Russian Navy during the First World War and inherited by the Red Air Fleet (see the First World War section above).

'Schneider' (unidentified and misidentified types)

According to Shavrov, the Red Army Air Force had at is disposal two (presumably captured) examples of aircraft referred to as 'Schneider', powered by the 220-hp Benz engine. One of them was converted into a three-seat passenger aircraft which received the name Sinyaya ptitsa (Blue Bird). The conversion was effected at the Aviarabotnik (Aviation Worker) aircraft factory at the initiative of military pilot I. A. Valentey who enlisted the assistance of engineer N. Ye. Shvaryov. The rear cockpit of the gunner was converted into an enclosed twoseat passenger cabin with the seats facing each other. The pilot sat in an open cockpit. The fuselage was painted blue, hence the name. The aircraft was tested in 1923 and showed disappointing results, because with two passengers on board it became tailheavy and unstable.

Lennart Andersson remarks: 'It is possible that some of the captured aircraft referred to as 'Schneider' were in actual fact LVGs – as early models of the LVGs were designed by an engineer named Schneider. 'The LVG C.II with the 160-hp Mercedes engine is the most likely candidate…' (see LVG C.II above).

Also see above Brandenburg C.I (supposedly misidentified as Schneider).

Another 'Schneider', a machine with 160-hp Mercedes engine used by the ODVF (c/n 1091), was in fact a Rumpler (see above).

Chapter 2

GERMAN AIRCRAFT IN SOVIET RUSSIA AND THE USSR

1918-1936

This chapter is devoted to the period spanning from the Bolshevik revolution to the beginning of the Spanish Civil War in 1936. The radical political transformations in Russia that took place in late 1917/early 1918 and the end of the First World War form the natural starting point. The choice of the year of 1936 as the other end of the time bracket is due to the fact that the Spanish Civil War was, in effect, an indirect confrontation between the Soviet Union and Germany, and may well be treated in conjunction with the Second World War period that followed immediately afterwards.

The story of German aircraft captured by the Russian Army during the First World War and inherited by Soviet Russia, as well as those captured during the Russian Civil War, was described for the sake of continuity in the previous chapter. Thus, the present chapter starts with the establishment of ties between Soviet Russia and Germany in the field of aviation and the 'normal' acquisitions of German aircraft by Soviet Russia which took place from 1921 onwards, after the end of the Civil War.

The beginning of Soviet-German co-operation in aviation matters

Germany's defeat in the First World War placed her into the unenviable position of a country deprived of many elements of its sovereignty and subjected to restrictive control measures on the part of the victor powers, as stipulated by the Versailles Treaty. These restrictions affected, above all, the domain of military activities. Germany was forbidden to possess and develop modern types of armament, such as aircraft, tanks and submarines.

Russia, after the Bolshevik revolution of November 1917 and the peace treaty concluded by the Entente states with Germany without Russian participation, found herself in political isolation. The Entente states, hostile to the new regime, severed diplomatic relations with Soviet Russia.

This state of political isolation characteristic for both Russia and Germany motivated the two countries to establish co-operation in the defence industry sphere. Such co-operation would enable Russia to profit by the German scientific, technological and mil-

itary experience for strengthening the Russian economy and her armed forces. As for Germany, co-operation with Russia would make it possible to develop German war industry abroad in contravention of the restrictions imposed by the Allies.

Clearly, this co-operation constituted a blatant breach of the stipulations of the Versailles Treaty. Hence all negotiations between Soviet Russia (or, from 30th December 1922 onwards, the Soviet Union) and Germany on co-operation in the manufacture and development of military hardware were conducted in utmost secrecy.

The first contacts on the above-stated matters took place after the Soviet defeat in the war with Poland in 1920, when the Soviet Government found itself compelled to seek peaceful co-existence with the capitalist world. Mutual visits by special delegations undertaken in the course of 1921 culminated in the signing of an agreement between the Russian Soviet Federative Socialist Republic (actually, the Red Army) and the German Reichswehr on co-operation in military-industrial matters. The problems of aircraft industry occupied a prominent place in this context. The abovementioned agreement with the Reichswehr contained a clause providing for the transfer to Russia of a German enterprise engaged in the manufacture of aircraft and aero engines. Furthermore, the agreement envisaged sending German technical specialists and the most up-to-date examples of aircraft to Russia.

The signing of the Rapallo peace treaty between the RSFSR and Germany on 16th April 1922 provided a legal basis for political and economic co-operation between the two countries. The treaty signified the resumption of diplomatic and economic relations between them and declared the intention of both sides to treat favourably the economic needs of each other. In the wake of the Rapallo Treaty, appropriate steps were undertaken to make use of German assistance in the development of aircraft industry in the Soviet Union (see below). In the meantime, to bridge the gap, the Soviet Government purchased abroad some 150 German aircraft of various types dating back to the period of the First World War.

German aircraft of First World War vintage purchased by Soviet Russia in 1921-1923

Listed and described below are the aircraft of German origin acquired by Soviet Russia in 1921-23. For the most part these were obsolescent aircraft; some of the machines purchased (notably, the Halberstadt aircraft) proved to be so worn out that flying them was simply dangerous. In consequence, their acquisition was not a major contribution to bolstering Soviet Russia's air power. Nevertheless, they merit being mentioned here. The aircraft are arranged in alphabetical order. Note that the Fokker designs included here are those which were developed by the Fokker Flugzeugwerke GmbH in Germany prior to the emigration of Anthony Fokker to the Netherlands where he founded the N.V. Nederlandsche Vliegtuigenfabriek on 21st July 1919. His subsequent designs manufactured in the Netherlands, such as the Fokker D.XI and Fokker D.XIII fighters and Fokker F.III passenger aircraft, are not regarded as aircraft of German origin and thus are outside the scope of this book. However, in view of their parentage it seems right to enumerate here the post-war Fokker types that were imported into the Soviet Union. These were: Fokker D.XI and Fokker D.XIII fighters; Fokker C.IV and C.V reconnaissance aircraft; Fokker S.II trainer; Fokker F.III, F.V and F.VII passenger aircraft. Of these, the D.XI and C.IV were imported in considerable numbers and occupied an important place in the inventory of the Soviet Air Force for some time. The F.III airliner, ten examples of which were bought by the Soviet government for Deruluft, played a significant role in the activities of this joint Soviet-German air transport company. The F.III is a special case dealt with separately (see below)

Fokker C.I and C.III reconnaissance and trainer aircraft

The Fokker C.I reconnaissance aircraft was developed by the Fokker Flugzeugwerke GmbH at Schwerin in 1918 as a two-seat variant of the D.VII fighter, with controls only in the front cockpit. It was a biplane of mixed construction powered by a 185-hp BMW IIIa water-cooled inline engine. Its peculiarity

Above: One of the three two-seat Fokker C.Is bought in 1922 for use as conversiuon trainers for the Fokker D.VII fighter. Note the airfoil-section fuel tank perched on the landing gear axle.

test centre (*Naoochno-opytnyy aerodrom* – lit. Research & Experimental Airfield) in the spring of 1924, where it was used for experimental purposes until 1928. The twelve C.IIIs were assigned to the 1st Higher School of Military Pilots. In 1928 the Military School of Aerial Combat at Orenburg had four and the Combined School of Military Pilots and Mechanics also used a single Fokker C.III. The last aircraft of this type was finally withdrawn from use in 1929. The designation of the C.I was sometimes spelled in documents as 'Tse-odin' after the Russian pronunciation of the Latin C.

Fokker D.VII fighter

Designed in 1917 by Fokker's chief designer Reinhold Platz, the Fokker D.VII biplane came to be recognised as the best German fighter of the First World War. It exhibited outstanding agility and excellent controllability and became the mainstay of the German Luftstreitkräfte. The Fokker V 11 prototype was first flown in January 1918 and a batch of 400 was immediately ordered after a competition for single-seat fighters at Adlershof the same month. The Fokker D.VII entered large-scale production at the Fokker and Albatros factories and began to reach operational units in April; by November 1918 nearly 800 were in service. Many were smuggled from the Fokker works at Schwerin in Germany to Holland in railway wagons in 1919. They were later sold to several countries, including Soviet Russia. Fifty D.VIIs were sold by Fokker to the Soviet Government in 1922. They were handed over in Amsterdam to representatives of the Russian Trade Commission in Berlin. Upon delivery to Leningrad in May 1922 the fighters were assigned to the 1st OIAE at Gatchina, Leningrad, and the 3rd OIAE at Kiev. A sin-

was a fuel tank mounted on the undercarriage axle. The aircraft was built in small numbers, but it appeared too late to become operational with the German air force. Lennart Andersson states that 'a number of C.Is was taken from Germany to Holland in 1919', adding that three C.Is were sold to Soviet Russia with the fifty Fokker D.VIIs in 1922, followed by twelve C.IIIs in 1923. The latter type was an unarmed conversion trainer variant of the C.I, with dual controls and without the fuel tank on the undercarriage axle. Both types were acquired by the

Soviet side for use as trainers. The C.Is had 185-hp BMW engines, while the C.IIIs were fitted with 160/180-hp Mercedes engines. The C.Is, which were armed with Vickers machine-guns, arrived in Leningrad in May 1922 and were distributed to the 1st and 3rd Independent Fighter Squadrons (OIAE – *otdel'naya istrebitel'naya aviaeskadril'ya*) at Leningrad and Kiev and to the Moscow Aviation School.

The last Fokker C.I (c/n 118) had been transferred from the 1st Higher School of Military Pilots in Moscow to the NOA flight

Left: One of the 12 Fokker C.III trainers bought in 1923. It was similar to the C.I, except for the engine type and the configuration of the rear cockpit.
Below and below left: A C.III in service with the 1st Higher School of Military Pilots in Moscow. Note the 'pharaoh's head' artwork.

Above: All 12 Fokker C.IIIs operated by the 1st Higher School of Military Pilots; the nearest aircraft is the one depicted on the oppsite page. The tactical numbers are repeated but the tail insignia are different, indicating different squadrons. Note the two aircraft of other types at the far end of the flight line.

gle aircraft was assigned to the Commander of the Leningrad Military District and three to the lst Higher School of Military Pilots in Moscow.

Early in 1925 the D.VIIs were replaced by Fokker D.XIs in the air squadrons at Leningrad and Kiev and were handed over to the 1st Independent Naval Fighter at Peterhof near Leningrad and to the 1st Independent Fighter Detachment at Yevpatoriya on the Black Sea. From 1928 these fighters were used for advanced training by several schools of military pilots and a few air units. By the end of 1932 only four were in the inventory of the VVS RKKA (*Voyenno-voz-dooshnyye seely Raboche-krest'yanskoy krasnoy armii* – Red Army Air Force, or Red Air Fleet), and one was still left in December 1933. In the Soviet Air Force the Fokker D.VII was often referred to as the FD-VII.

Halberstadt C.V reconnaissance aircraft

The Halberstadt C.V was flown for the first time in 1918 and became operational only during the last six months of the war. The machine was intended for high-altitude long-distance reconnaissance and for gathering photographic intelligence. It was a two-seat, two-bay biplane powered by a 220-hp Benz Bz IV engine. Armament comprised a fixed forward-firing 7.9-mm Spandau machine gun and a flexible Parabellum

Above: A Red Air Fleet Fokker D.VII.

This Halberstadt C.V flown by Red Air Fleet pilot L. Popov flipped over on its back after losing a wheel in May 1924.

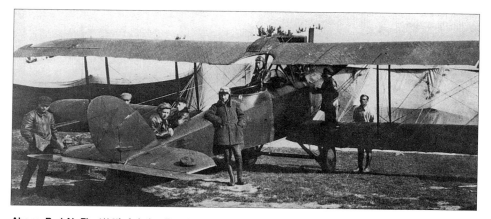

Above: Red Air Fleet/14th Aviation Battalion pilots and mechanics pose with one of the unit's LVG C.Vs. The red star insignia are almost invisible on the green background of the wings and tail.

Twenty LVG C.VIs were operated by the Red Air Fleet in 1922-24. This one is seen after a landing mishap.

stadt C.Vs were purchased by Soviet Russia in 1922. They were delivered to Leningrad in June of that year and were assigned to the 1st Independent Reconnaissance Air Detachment based near Leningrad. As noted above, the machines were very worn out, and their service in the original role did not last long. In 1923 they were relegated to training duties, being distributed to a number of flying schools. All of these aircraft were withdrawn from use after a short time.

Luft-Verkehrs-Gesellschaft LVG C.VI reconnaissance and artillery spotting aircraft

The LVG C.VI two-seat biplane, which was very similar to the preceding C.V model, was among the most successful German reconnaissance and artillery spotting aircraft of the First World War. It entered squadron service in 1918; about 1,100 C.VIs were built before the end of hostilities (according to other sources, some 500 C.Vs and C.VIs were recorded in service three months before the Armistice). The aircraft was powered by the 220-hp Benz Bz VI engine (some sources quote the 200-hp Benz Bz IV). The armament consisted of one fixed forward-firing Spandau machine-gun and one flexibly mounted Parabellum machine-gun for the observer in the rear cockpit. Up to 250 lb of small bombs could be carried.

After the war the LVG C.VI aircraft were acquired by the military air services of several European countries. Soviet Russia also took interest in this aircraft. In 1922 twenty examples of the type were purchased by the Soviet Government (available sources do not specify the circumstances of the deal). The aircraft were delivered in April/May 1922.

The LVG was called the 'El'fauge' in the Soviet Union after the pronunciation of its

machine-gun in the rear cockpit. About 550 were built by the Halberstädter Flugzeugwerke GmbH, BFW, Aviatik and DFW.

The C.V model was among the Halberstadt machines of different models that were captured or interned by Germany's adversaries and by neutral Holland during the last phases of the First World War. In the following period some of these aircraft were sold to a number of countries. Eighteen Halber-

One of the ten Fokker F.III passenger aircraft ordered by the German-Soviet airline Deruluft is seen in manufacturer's colours prior to the application of the registration and the operator's logo on the white diamond on the fuselage side. Note the pilot's windshield, a part which was omitted on some of the aircraft.

designation in German. The imported machines were assigned to several Reconnaissance Air Detachments based at Tashkent and a Reconnaissance Air Detachment at Severnaya, north of Moscow. The LVG C.VIs remained on charge in these units until 1924. Single examples of the type were also used by other air units based at Leningrad and Khar'kov. Two machines were used at the NOA in 1923.

A few examples of the LVG C VI were also used for civil duties in the Soviet Union. Two machines registered RR11 and RR14 were acquired by Deruluft for local flights and communications between their airports; the former of the two saw service from December 1922 until 1926, while the other one, delivered in June 1923, was withdrawn from use in October 1924. In 1923 a single example of the C.VI was purchased in Berlin by a construction organisation called Kashirstroy for personal transport between the organisation's Moscow offices and construction sites outside the city.

Fokker passenger aircraft in the Soviet Union

As noted above, in 1919 Anthony Fokker moved to the Netherlands, and his subsequent activities in the field of aircraft manufacture are associated with that country. However, there was a transition period during which the facilities belonging to Fokker at Schwerin, Germany, continued their work producing the prototypes of two passenger aircraft – the Fokker F.II and Fokker F.III. This allows us to regard the latter type as an aircraft having its origins in Germany and thus eligible for inclusion in this book.

Fokker F.III and Grulich V 1/V 1a passenger aircraft

The Fokker F.III passenger aircraft was an improved version of the Fokker F.II which had started its life on the drawing board in early 1919 and had been flown in prototype form in Germany in October 1919. The more powerful F.III accommodating five passengers in an enclosed cabin was first flown on 20th November 1920. The prototype was built at Schwerin because the facilities in the Amsterdam factory were not yet equipped for this work and Reinhold Platz, Fokker's chief designer, had more experienced personnel at his disposal at Schwerin. This cantilever shoulder-wing monoplane could be powered by a number of different engines ranging from the 230-hp Armstrong-Siddeley Puma to the 360-hp Rolls-Royce Eagle VIII. The first production aircraft delivered to KLM in 1921 were also built at Schwerin. Additionally, F.IIIs were built under licence by Deutsche Aero Lloyd at Staaken airfield, Berlin.

Above: The nose of another F.III showing a differently shaped cowling and windshield, twin wheels instead of single ones and the placement of the wings above the fuselage on short cabane struts.

Above: Deruluft's first F.III, RR1 (c/n 1652), arrived in Moscow on 30th April 1922. This machine was later reregistered RRUAU and later still as CCCP-222. This one lacks the windshield and has twin wheels.

RR1 is recovered from the scene of a crash landing in Lithuania; the wings are towed on a trailer behind the pasenger car. The aircraft was repaired but crashed again near Smolensk, Russia, in 1924.

Above: Two of Deruluft's Fokker F.IIIs, RR6 (c/n 1656) and RR10 (c/n 1660), in front of a hangar. The aircraft were later reregistered D-906 and D-910 respectively.

Above: RR2 (c/n 1653) was one of two Fokker F.IIIs rebuilt to Grulich V 1 configuration. The longer nose, larger vertical tail, wide-chord ailerons and revised undercarriage are well visible here.

RR1 and RR3 (c/n 1654) inaugurated the Moscow-Königsberg service. The latter aircraft, which appears to have a two-bladed propeller, was reregistered D-1389 for a while before reverting to RR3.

Ten F.IIIs powered by Rolls-Royce Eagle VIII engines were bought by the Soviet Government for Deruluft; they carried the registrations RR1 to RR10. These machines ordered in 1922 were partly built in Germany and completed at the Fokker plant at Veere in the Netherlands. The first machine, RR1, arrived in Moscow on 30th April 1922. Two of these aircraft were modified to a new version. Developed by Dipl Ing Karl Grulich, the chief designer of the Deutsche Aero Lloyd workshops at Berlin-Staaken, the new version had a more comfortable six-seat passenger cabin in a reshaped fuselage, a new two-seat cockpit with dual controls, a wide-chord fin, a new rudder and a new undercarriage. Other changes included an increase in the wing area and a more forward position of the engine. The examples registered RR2 and RR5 were rebuilt to this standard, receiving the designation Grulich V 1. In June 1928 RR5 was further modified when it was fitted with a 420-hp Gnome-Rhône Jupiter radial engine. In this configuration it was designated Grulich V 1a.

In 1926 half of Deruluft's fleet was re-registered and received German registrations. Five of the Fokkers received German D-numbers. Acquisition of the new Dornier Merkur aircraft by Deruluft led to the transfer of three Fokker F.IIIs to the Ukrainian air transport society Ukrvozdukhput' (= Ukrainian Air Route) in 1927-1928. They were initially registered RRUAO, RRUAU and RRUAW (sic – the registrations were painted on with no hyphen or space after the country prefix), two of them later being re-registered CCCP-222 and CCCP-223 after the formation of the Soviet Union. Of the remaining Deruluft Fokkers, three had crashed and another three were transferred to the Air Force for use as trainers. RR5 was possibly sold to Osoaviakhim (**Ob**shchestvo sode**y**stviya avi**ah**tsii i khi**mich**eskoy pro**mysh**lennosti – Society for the Support of Aviation and the Chemical Industry), a paramilitary organisation for air-minded youth, in 1929.

Junkers aircraft in the Soviet Union (1922-1936)

The Soviet Government started selecting industrial partners in Germany capable of assisting in the establishment of the Soviet aircraft industry even before the Rapallo treaty was signed. In 1921-1922 negotiations were conducted with several German aircraft and aero engine manufacturing companies. The choice was made in favour of Junkers Flugzeugwerk AG. Guided by the wish to gain access to the most advanced methods of aircraft construction, the Soviet side attached particular importance to the experience of the Junkers company in the field of designing and building all-metal aircraft. Preliminary negotiations with the Junkers company took place in December

Above: The plant at Fili (the former 1st BTAZ) where the Junkers concession was set up in 1922.
Below left: Paul Spalek, the technical director of the Junkers plant at Fili.
Below right: The office of Junkers Flugzeugwerke AG in Nikol'skaya Street in Moscow from where the concession was managed.

1921. Original Soviet plans envisaged erecting aircraft plants in Moscow, Petrograd (later Leningrad; now St. Petersburg) and in the Volga area with German assistance, but these ambitions had to be curtailed for financial reasons. Finally it was decided to reduce the project to the transfer of only one factory to the Junkers company for the purpose of organising production of all-metal aircraft and aero engines. The factory in question was located at Fili, then a western suburb of Moscow (now a part of the city). It had been founded in 1916-17 as the Russo-Balt automobile factory, restyled as the 1st Armour Vehicle and Automobile Factory (BTAZ – *Bronetahnkovyy i avtobil'nyy zavod*) after the revolution. The plant had stood idle for nearly five years and required repairs.

An agreement with Junkers on the terms of the concession was reached not least thanks to the interest the Reichswehr had in the matter. This organisation sponsored the Junkers company financially, expecting to turn the plant at Fili into a testing ground for the development of military aviation hardware for German needs and an eventual source of deliveries of military aircraft to Germany.

By the end of 1922 the terms of co-operation had been finalised, and on 26th November 1922 the Junkers company and the Soviet Government signed Agreement No.1 which granted to Junkers a concession for the manufacture of aircraft and aero engines in the Soviet Union. Simultaneously Agreements No.2 and No. 3 were signed, dealing with air transport and aerial photography respectively. All this was veiled in secrecy, since these agreements constituted a breach of the bans imposed by the Versailles treaty on export of German aviation technology. Under the terms of the concession, the plant at Fili was leased to

A delegation from Junkers examines the still-empty workshops at Fili.

Above: The Junkers F 13 (Ju-13) assembly line at Fili. The fuselage build-up area is shown here. The unpainted aircraft is fitted with temporary iron wheels used for moving the incomplete airframe around.

Junkers for thirty years; the production capacity of the plant was to be no less than 300 aircraft and 450 aero engines per year.

The first order was issued to Junkers by the Red Army Air Force on 26th November 1922, the day of signing the concession agreement (on 4th December, according to another source). It envisaged the manufacture by Junkers of 100 aircraft at Fili. By April 1924 the company was to produce 20 Ju-20 (alias J 20) two-seat floatplanes, 50 Ju-21 (J 21) two-seat reconnaissance aircraft and 30 Ju-22 (J 22) single-seat fighters. (In this case Ju is a German-style transliteration of the Cyrillic letter Ю used in the designations that were adopted in Soviet documents – Ю-21 etc.). This order was amended later.

Above: Ground personnel removes the canvas covers from a Junkers F 13 registered D 257 (c/n 647) and delivered to the Red Army Air Force in May 1923. The combination of a German civil registration with hastily applied Red Army Air Force insignia is noteworthy; the star on the rudder looks definitely lop-sided.

The same machine, '257 Black', after crashing in Moscow on 18th November 1923 (by then the D prefix had been removed). Military pilot B. K. Velling was killed in the crash.

Practical implementation of this production programme proceeded at a slower pace than intended, to the dissatisfaction of the Soviet customer. There were also serious complaints concerning the quality of the aircraft built; yet, the machines were accepted due to the acute need for new aircraft in the Red Army Air Force. In all, by the end of 1924 the Junkers plant at Fili had turned out 20 Ju-20 floatplanes and 61 Ju-21 reconnaissance aircraft, supplemented by a small number of the Junkers F 13 six-seat passenger aircraft (Ju-13 in Russian parlance); they were mostly assembled from imported subassemblies. That was far from the 400-aircraft target figure stipulated by the agreement.

Further functioning of the concession soon ran into problems – mainly due to disagreements on the issue of prices. Negotia-

Above: URSS-144, an F 13 operated by the Dobrolyot airline whose name appears on the engine cowling as Dobrolyot Joint-Stock Co. Note the tie-down ropes.

tions on a new order for 60 modernised Ju-21s held in 1924 stalled because Junkers had put a bigger price tag on its aircraft. In early 1925 the work at the plant came virtually to a halt and the personnel was reduced to a fraction of the original strength. The wisdom of letting the concession go on was called into question. This matter caused disagreements among the Soviet leaders. Finally, on 24th January 1925 the Politbureau of the Communist Party's Central Committee adopted a decision calling for efforts to preserve the concession agreement with Junkers on condition of ensuring more satisfactory production results.

Subsequent negotiations with Junkers centred on the latter's proposal for starting the manufacture of the JuG-1 (K-30) three-engined bomber at Fili. They resulted in an evaluation order for three machines, followed by an order for a further 12 bombers. This led to a temporary re-activation of the plant, albeit the aircraft in question were not actually put into production there and had to be built abroad.

In the meantime, a revised draft concession agreement was submitted by the Soviet authorities for the consideration of the Junkers company. In return for more favourable financial terms the Soviet side expected Junkers to increase the plant's capacity to 400 aircraft per year by 1926, to start using *kol'chugaluminiy* (duralumin of Soviet manufacture) and to design and build one or two new prototype aircraft every year. The Junkers company was unwilling to accept such obligations, while pressing for still more favourable financial terms. The Soviet side came to the conclusion that further negotiations were of no use. Given the

considerable positive results achieved by the Soviet aircraft industry by that time, the co-operation with Junkers no longer appeared a matter of prime importance. On 4th March 1926 the Politbureau issued instructions calling for the termination of the concession agreement with Junkers. In the course of the subsequent negotiations one more attempt was made to save the concession, but to no avail. In the end, the contracting parties reached an agreement on terminating the Junkers concession which was endorsed on 1st March 1927. The Fili plant was taken over by the Soviet Government and incorporated into the Soviet aircraft industry under the name GAZ No. 7 (*Gosoodarstvennyy aviazavod* – state aircraft factory). Renamed Plant No. 22 in 1928, it was tasked with the manufacture of Tupolev's all-metal aircraft (at present it is the site of the Mikhail V. Khrunichev State Research and Production Space Centre).

Summing up the results of the Junkers activities at Fili, Russian researchers note that co-operation with Junkers provided some useful insight into the German methods of all-metal aircraft construction and helped train Soviet specialists well versed in the Western-style production management. On the whole, however, the results obtained

An air-to-air of another Dobrolyot Junkers F 13 registered R-RECI (c/n 651) and delivered in July 1923. This machine was operated on the Moscow-Tiflis service

This F 13 is inscribed *Vse v Osoaviakhim! Aghitsamolyot Osoaviakhima RSFSR* (Everybody join the Osoaviakhim! Propaganda aircraft of the Russian Federative Soviet Socialist Republic's Osoaviakhim).

fell far short of expectations. The functioning of the Junkers factory in the USSR failed to become the mainstay for the development of advanced aircraft manufacture in the USSR and even hampered it to some extent because the Soviet financial resources and the attention of the country's leaders were diverted from the proper encouragement of indigenous projects in the field of aircraft construction.

The scant results of the undertaking were in no small degree due to the unwillingness of Hugo Junkers to invest sufficient sums in the Fili plant and to render effective assistance to the Soviet side in launching indigenous production of duralumin and aero engines. But part of the blame rests with the bureaucratic procrastination and lack of flexibility on the part of the Soviet leaders. Yet, basically the termination of the concession was due to the fact that the Soviet aircraft industry proved capable of sustainable development on its own. True, it did need an influx of advanced design features and experience from the West, but forthwith that was to be ensured through more efficient forms of co-operation, notably licence production of aircraft and engines and the training of Soviet specialists abroad.

Interestingly, in 1928 the Junkers company, using its contacts with the Soviet military attaché in Berlin, unofficially raised the issue of resuming its activities in the USSR; in particular, it was willing to build an aircraft plant in the USSR on the terms of a concession agreement. This fact was mentioned by Jan Berzin, the chief of the Soviet military intelligence, in his secret report on the Soviet-German military co-operation, dated 24th December 1928. However, these soundings found no response.

The Junkers aircraft that were either imported from Germany or produced at the Junkers plant at Fili in the period between the mid-1920s and the mid-1930s are described below.

Junkers F 13 (Ju-13, F-13, PS-2) passenger and transport aircraft

The Junkers type that gained the widest use in the USSR was the F 13, a six-seat passenger aircraft of all-metal construction first flown as J 13 in Dessau in 1919. In the Soviet Union, the official F 13 designation was initially ignored, and the aircraft was known at first as Ju-13. This designation was applied to the initial version powered by the 185-hp BMW IIIa engine. The designation F-13 was adopted in Soviet service for the Junkers L-5-powered version, although, in fairness, all the machines of this type operated in the USSR ought to have borne the F 13 designation.

An F 13 made its first appearance in Moscow in May 1922. In the subsequent years more than sixty Junkers Ju-13s and F-13s gave service in the USSR ('nearly seventy', as Dmitriy Sobolev puts it). By far most of the machines were imported from Germany. According to Lennart Andersson, the 'Soviet' F 13s were not built by the Junkers factory at Fili, but *a few of the F 13s used in the Soviet Union might have been assembled at Fili from Dessau-built sub-assemblies*'. For a short period the F 13s were serviced and repaired by this plant until the workshop of Dobrolyot (the forerunner of Aeroflot) in Moscow could take over this kind of work in 1924-25. Sobolev states that the Germans *did* assemble several examples of the F 13 at Fili, albeit not for the USSR (there they conducted the assembly of the military version of the F 13 for export to Persia; the aircraft was fitted with a machine-gun installation behind the pilot's seat and could be used as a bomber or transport aircraft).

Russian historians relate that five completely new Junkers F 13s were built from Soviet-produced duralumin (Kol'chugaluminiy) in Dobrolyot's Central workshops where the company had organised repairs and restoration work on these aircraft after major accidents.

In the 1920s the Ju-13 was the main aircraft type on Soviet passenger air routes. It entered service in 1922 to ensure communications between Moscow and Nizhniy Novgorod where the famous All-Russian fair was held; later the Ju-13 was operated on the routes of the Soviet air transport organisations: Dobrolyot, Ukrvozdukhput', Siblyot, Zakavia, and the joint Soviet-German company Deruluft. For example, ten machines acquired by Dobrolyot in 1923 flew the Moscow – Kazan', Tashkent – Alma-Ata, Tashkent – Bukhara, Bukhara – Khiva and Bukhara – Dyushambe (later renamed Dushanbe) services. In addition to passenger services, the Ju-13s were used in ambulance aviation and even for agricultural flying; a Dobrolyot machine registered URSS-145 (c/n 649) was tested with aerial dusting gear against forest pests near Lake Baikal. The F 13s were also used for propaganda flights staged by the Osoaviakhim paramilitary organisation, and for training in flying schools. As for Deruluft, this company put L 5-powered F 13s into service in 1928. Five of the seven F 13s operated by Deruluft carried Soviet registrations with RR or URSS prefixes.

The Junkers F 13 saw service with the Red Army Air Force as well and was committed to action in Central Asia in the course of operations against the local insurgents (the so-called *basmachi*). For example, in 1924 several missions of this kind were flown in the Khiva area by an F 13 piloted by a German pilot, Otto Wieprich, who was awarded a gold watch in recognition of his contribution. The F 13s were used mostly for reconnaissance missions, but some of them were converted into auxiliary bombers by fitting bomb racks beneath the wings; they were also provided with a Lewis machine-gun mounted in the rear window on each side. About twenty different F 13s were used by the Red Army Air Force, albeit the number on charge at any given time was appreciably smaller.

Of interest is the use of the F 13 in the Soviet Polar aviation. Here is just one episode. Pilot Mikhail S. Babushkin with his Junkers F 13 registered R-RDAS (c/n 671) took part in the efforts to rescue the team of Italian Polar researchers led by Umberto Nobile after the crash of their airship *Italia* in the Arctic. Babushkin's aircraft was based on the icebreaker S/S *Malygin*, but it operated from the adjoining icefield, using a ski undercarriage. Babushkin made several flights in search of the Italian team (to no avail), supplemented by several trial and reconnaissance flights. In all, he made 15 take-offs and as many landings on the ice, which in itself was a pioneering job – before Babushkin, operating from drifting ice had been considered too risky and had not been practised.

The sturdy and reliable Junkers F 13 took part in a number of long-distance flights. One of these was the flight from Moscow to Peking, performed in 1925 by a group of five aircraft. In addition to two R-1 and R-2 reconnaissance aircraft and one AK-1 passenger aircraft, the group included two Junkers F 13s (R-RDAO *Krasnyy Kamvol'shchik* and R-RDAP *Pravda*). Only R-RDAO reached the Chinese capital, the other machine having suffered damage during a landing on the final stretch of the route.

Several Ju-13s were fitted with floats of the same type as on the Ju-20. In the autumn of 1923 one of these aircraft, R-RDAE, was used for paid pleasure flights on the Moskva River in the area of the agricultural exhibition (at present the Central Culture & Recreation Park, aka Gor'kiy Park). Ju-13s fitted with floats (this version was also called F 13W) were also operated in other parts of the country, including the Far East. In 1926 an F 13W registered R-RDAA and named *Mossovet* was flown by pilots V. L. Galyshev and F. I. Groshev along the Yenisey River from Krasnoyarsk to Turukhansk and back. Another machine, registered R-RECG, was used for propaganda flights.

During the final stage of their operational service in Soviet civil aviation, the L 5-powered F 13s had their designation changed to PS-2 (*passazheerskiy samolyot*, passenger aircraft), the PS-1 possibly having been reserved for F 13s with BMW engines.

Alongside with Soviet air transport organisations, the Junkers F 13 aircraft were operated in the Soviet Union by Junkers-Luftverkehr AG (JLAG) on the basis of a concession agreement which was signed in 1922. Under the terms of this agreement Junkers was to set up an air route from Sweden to Persia over the territory of the USSR. To ensure these operations, the company imported ten Junkers F 13 aircraft from Germany. Eventually, fourteen F 13s were operated by JLAG, carrying Soviet registrations in the R-RExx series (R-RECA, R-RECB etc). On 1st June 1923 scheduled flights began on the Moscow – Tiflis (Tbilisi) route. In 1924 the entire route from Sweden to Persia was to be put into operation. However, Junkers refused to open this route unless the Soviet Government granted further financial privileges allegedly required to compensate for the expected losses from the route's operation. In March 1927 the concession agreement on the Sweden-Persia transit air route was cancelled. Yet, a new deal was concluded enabling Junkers to operate an air service between Baku and Teheran from 1928; it was flown for some time by F 13s retaining their Soviet registrations. Eventually these aircraft were returned to Germany or sold, one machine being purchased by the Soviet Air Force.

It remains to be mentioned that in 1924-26 the Soviet Union exported single examples of the Junkers F 13 to several countries. The recipients included Afghanistan (one machine), Persia (two), Mongolia (one) and China (two float-equipped F 13s for the Canton government).

Junkers J 20 (A 20, Ju-20) reconnaissance floatplane

The Junkers J 20 two-seat reconnaissance floatplane was a derivative of the Junkers J 11 reconnaissance seaplane dating back to the First World War. Some sources quote the manufacturer's designation as A 20. In prototype form the machine was powered by a 160-hp Mercedes D IIIa six-cylinder inline engine, but production aircraft assembled at the Junkers plant in Fili were fitted

Above: This Dobrolyot F 13W floatplane, R-RDAA *Mossovet* (c/n 649), is pictured on the Yenisey River during a flight from Krasnoyarsk to Turukhansk and back in 1926 (pilots V. L. Galyshev and F. I. Groshev).

Left: Doborolyot's F 13s R-RDAO *Krasnyy Kamvol'shchik* (c/n 648) and R-RDAP *Pravda* (c/n 673) took part in a flight from Moscow to Peking in June-July 1925.
Right: F 13 R-RDAM *Sibrevkom* ('Siberian Revolutionary Committee', c/n 590) is seen here in the Altai region, probably in 1924.

Above: This ski-equipped F 13, R-RODB No. 2 (c/n 749), was named *Vse v Aviakhim! Aghitsamolyot Aviakhim RSFSR* and used for propaganda flights; this may be the same aircraft as on page 36. Note the design of the skis with stabilising fins at the rear.

with the 185-hp BMW IIIa engine. The first order for 100 aircraft, which was placed by the Soviet Government with the Junkers company at the end of 1922 (on the day the concession agreement was signed), included twenty J 20 aircraft which were to be delivered before April 1924. This order was fulfilled with some delay. In the Soviet service the aircraft was referred to as the Ju 20 (again, this is a German-style transliteration of the Cyrillic Ю-20 designation).

The Ju 20s delivered by Junkers proved to fall short of the standards stipulated by the order. The weight of the aircraft exceeded the specified figure by 25%; the maximum speed proved to be a mere 164 km/h (102 mph) as against the promised 190 km/h (118 mph). The Ju-20 (as well as the Ju-21, see below) lacked synchronising devices for

the guns firing through the propeller disc; in consequence, the machines delivered by the Germans had to be brought up to the required standard at Plant No. 1 in Moscow. (The Ju-20 was designed to take an armament consisting of one, later two, forward-firing machine-guns and a flexible single or twin gun in the rear cockpit. The Soviet examples carried only a single flexible Lewis gun during the latter part of their career.)

According to Sobolev, in addition to the 20 Ju-20s built at Fili, the USSR purchased in Germany some 20 floatplanes of this type, as well as a few Ju-20s on wheel undercarriage. However, Lennart Andersson states the following: 'A sales report prepared at Dessau in 1929 mentions a second batch of twenty aircraft delivered in 1926, but this information is erroneous'.

The Ju-20 reconnaissance aircraft were operated by the naval air element of the Baltic Fleet and Black Sea Fleet until 1930. Aircraft of this type were delivered during the spring of 1924 to the 1st OMRAO (*otdel'nyy morskoy razvedyvatel'nyy aviaotryad* – Independent Naval Reconnaissance Air Detachment) at Oranienbaum and the 2nd OMRAO in Leningrad, where they replaced the Grigorovich M-24 flying-boat. A few Ju-20s were based on the cruisers SNS *Chervona Ukraina* and SNS *Profintern* which entered service with the Baltic Sea and Black Sea Fleets in 1928 and 1927 respectively.

Attempts were made to enhance the performance of the Ju-20 by installing more powerful engines. Two Ju-20s were re-engined with the 240-320-hp BMW IV; one machine was reportedly tested with the 310-

Dobrolyot Junkers F 13 R-RDAO (c/n 648) named *Krasnyy kamvol'shchik* (Red Woolworker). It took part in the Moscow-Peking flight (10th June/13th July 1925), piloted by N. I. Naidyonov and V. D. Osipov.

hp Junkers L 5. During negotiations with Junkers in 1925 the BMW IV-engined J 20 was mentioned, but no orders followed.

From 1930 onwards the Ju-20s were relegated to civil duties and were operated in small numbers by the Soviet Polar aviation in northern regions of the country (thanks to its metal construction the aircraft was suitable for operation in the harsh conditions of the High North). It was with this type of aircraft that the first Soviet flights in the Arctic were conducted back in 1924 when pilot Boris I. Chukhnovskiy performed 11 flights in the Ju-20 from the continent to the island of Novaya Zemlya. In the early 1930s the Ju-20s must have been used for ice observation in northern regions.

A single example registered CCCP-25 was used in support of the fishing industry, searching for fish shoals in the Caspian Sea in 1930. Three aircraft based in Moscow were used for aerial photography in 1931. By the mid-1930s the type had disappeared from service.

Junkers J 21 (T 21, H 21, Ju-21) reconnaissance aircraft

The Junkers J 21 (referred to in some sources as the T 21) was a two-seat reconnaissance aircraft, a parasol monoplane in which the wings were supported above the fuselage on eight struts. The fuselage centre section housed two cockpits, of which the rear one (the observer's cockpit) was configured as a turret, to which a rotating gun-ring was attached. Armament included two forward-firing Vickers machine-guns, a flexible single gun in the rear cockpit and bombs. In the Soviet Union it was known as Ju-21 (Ю-21 in Cyrillic characters). It was powered by the BMW IIIa engine delivering 185 hp. The first order placed by the Red Army Air Force with the Junkers company after the signing of the concession agreement (see above) included 50 two-seat Ju-21 reconnaissance aircraft (as well as the Ju-20 and Ju-22 types).

As was the case with the J 20, the J 21 manufactured at Fili (the licence-built version was referred to by Junkers as H 21) fell short of the specified performance; for example, the weight of the Ju-21 manufactured by Junkers proved to exceed the design figure by about 25%; in consequence, the maximum speed attained was only 195 km/h as against the 210km/h promised by the company. Other characteristics (rate of climb, range and ceiling) also fell short of the stipulated figures.

According to Dmitriy Sobolev, by the end of 1924 the Junkers factory at Fili had manufactured 61 Ju-21 aircraft. One more batch of this type was manufactured in 1925. Lennart Andersson assesses the total num-

Above: F 13W R-RDAE *Prombank* (c/n 656) on a slipway on the Moskva River in Moscow. Note the downward-extended rudder and forward boarding steps of the floatplane version.

Above: The same aircraft in landplane configuration on skis (F 13S). Like some other Dobrolyot Junkers F 13s, R-RDAE carried the Soviet coat-of-arms near the cockpit.

At some stage of its career R-RDAE had a different name, 'Latvian Rifleman'. The name was carried in Latvian (*Latvju Strelneeks*) to port and in Russian (*Latyshskiy Strelok*) to starboard.

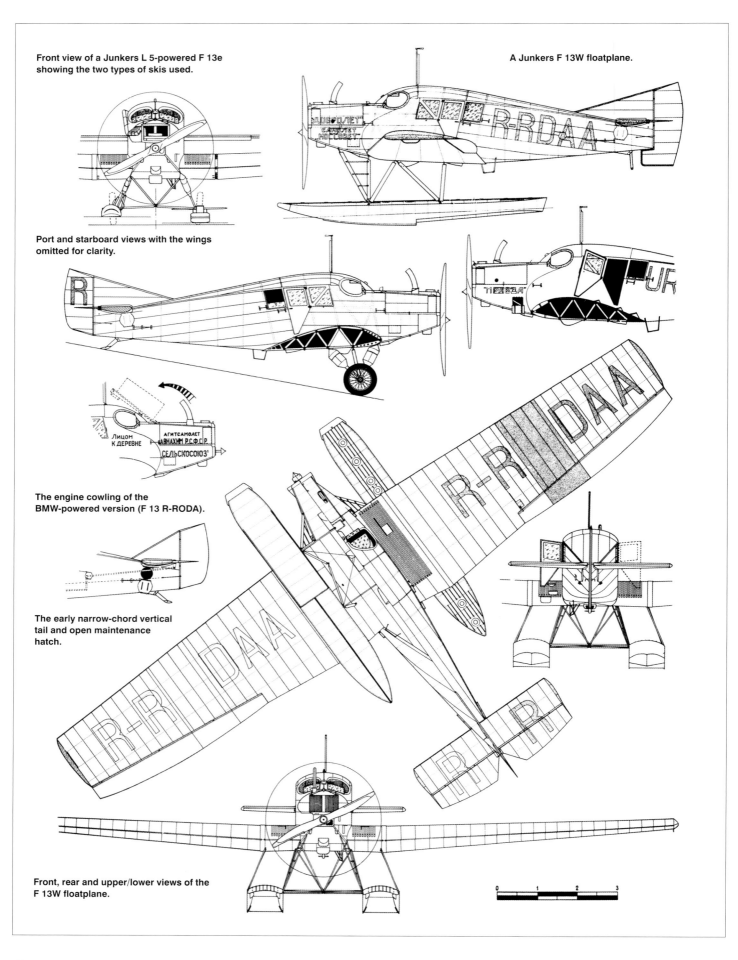

Front view of a Junkers L 5-powered F 13e showing the two types of skis used.

A Junkers F 13W floatplane.

Port and starboard views with the wings omitted for clarity.

The engine cowling of the BMW-powered version (F 13 R-RODA).

The early narrow-chord vertical tail and open maintenance hatch.

Front, rear and upper/lower views of the F 13W floatplane.

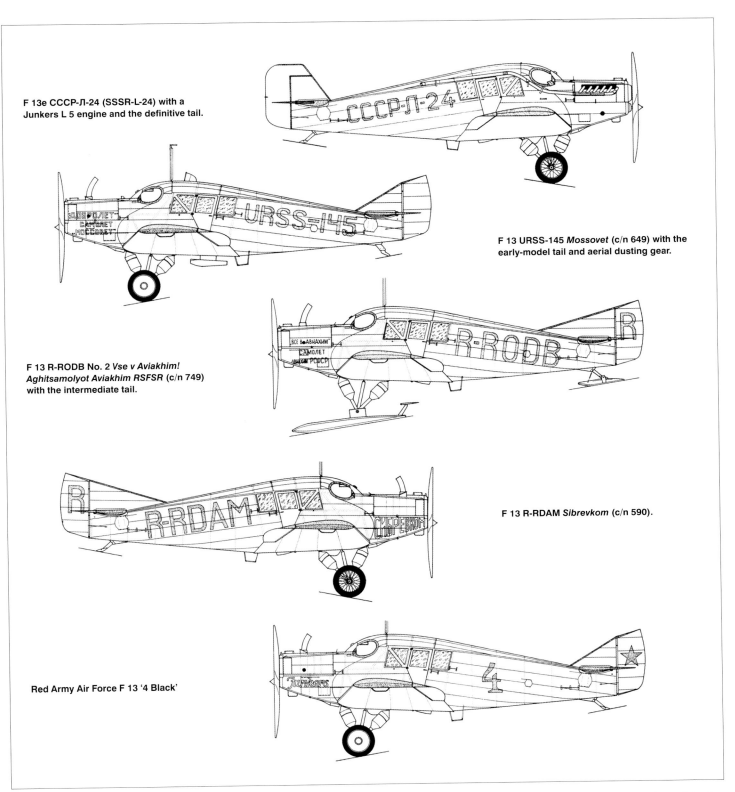

F 13e СССР-Л-24 (SSSR-L-24) with a Junkers L 5 engine and the definitive tail.

F 13 URSS-145 *Mossovet* (c/n 649) with the early-model tail and aerial dusting gear.

F 13 R-RODB No. 2 *Vse v Aviakhim! Aghitsamolyot Aviakhim RSFSR* (c/n 749) with the intermediate tail.

F 13 R-RDAM *Sibrevkom* (c/n 590).

Red Army Air Force F 13 '4 Black'

ber of Ju-21s accepted by the VVS between the end of 1924 and the beginning of 1926 appears to be seventy-nine, in addition to the two prototypes delivered in 1923 (this tallies with the terms of the order, which stipulated the manufacture of 80 Ju-21 aircraft). Interestingly, Lennart Andersson mentions the designation Ju-21a for the last thirty examples under this order, without describing the special features of this version.

The J 21 saw only limited service with the Red Army Air Force in its capacity of a reconnaissance aircraft, due to inadequate performance (rather low speed and insufficient useful load). The maximum speed was 196.4 km/h (122 mph), not 210 km/h (130.5 mph) as promised. Rate of climb and endurance also fell short of expectations and the machine's insufficient payload limited its military value. The Ju-21 equipped various units

of the Red Army Air Force based in the Moscow Military District, the Eastern Military District, the Ukrainian Military District and in the Leningrad Military District. Furthermore, among the units to receive the Ju-21 were reconnaissance air detachments based at Tashkent. These units were employed operationally in the fight against the *basmachi* insurgents in Turkestan during 1925, flying reconnaissance and strafing sorties.

Above: '4 Black', a Red Army Air Force Junkers F 13, after a crash landing.

Above: Another view of '4 Black'; apart from the undercarriage, the damage appears to be superficial. The aircraft was operated by one of the Red Army Air Force units in Turkestan.

Above: In contrast, R-RODB No. 1 (c/n 692) was damaged beyond repair on 16th February 1925. It was named *Krasnyy artel'shchik/Vse v ODVF!* (Red collective worker/Join the Air Fleet Friends Society).

In 1924 the Soviet Government intended to place a repeat order for the J 21 with the Junkers company. It was decided to order 60 machines of the improved Ju-21c version powered by the 240-hp BMW IVa engine. However, the Junkers company agreed to fulfil the order only on condition that the prices be raised, citing increased production costs. The Soviet side insisted on adhering to the previously agreed prices, and the negotiations stalled. (Note: The Ju-21c designation is as spelled by Sobolev. Lennart Andersson spells the designation of this version as 'J 21s' or 'Ju-21s', apparently regarding the 'c' suffix as Cyrillic rather than a Latin character).

Acquisition of some other versions of the J 21 was negotiated by the Soviet authorities. The VVS was interested in obtaining a BMW IV-powered two-seat fighter variant of the J 21. The German company came up with an offer of the J 25 derivative powered by the 240… 320-hp BMW IVa; this offer, received by the VVS in August 1924, was rejected. The J 25 was later re-engined as the J 28 and offered as a two-seat fighter with the BMW IV engine to the Red Army Air Force in 1925, but with the same result.

Starting in 1927, the Ju-21 was gradually supplanted by the Soviet-built R-1 reconnaissance aircraft (a copy of the de Havilland DH.4); the last Ju-21s in the Air Force were replaced by R-1s in the autumn of 1930.

The Ju-21s thus made redundant found new employment in the GVF (Civil Air Fleet). In particular, they proved their worth in the role of aerial photography aircraft. Several machines used for these duties carried registrations in the CCCP-Ф series, Ф (Cyrillic F) being the operator letter for organisations engaged in aerial survey. Several machines used for general duties received registrations in the CCCP-Л series (Л = L, the operator letter for GVF). Examples of both kinds include CCCP-Ф9, CCCP-Ф11, CCCP-Ф14 etc, CCCP-Л53, CCCP-Л72, CCCP-Л78 etc. The last Ju-21 is presumed to have been withdrawn from service with GVF in 1933.

Junkers J 22 (Ju-22) single-seat fighter

This aircraft is usually omitted in Russian accounts of the Junkers types used in the USSR because the plans for its acquisition failed to materialise. Yet, it deserves mention here, since it was included in the first order for 100 assorted aircraft placed by the Soviet government with the Junkers company in late 1922. In addition to the 50 J 21s, it included fifteen J 22 Is and fifteen J 22 IIs, also to be delivered before April 1924.

The J 22 was a single-seat derivative of the J 21 from which it differed in having the

Top: Junkers J 20 (Ju-20) fuselages on the assembly line at Fili. Deliveries of these seaplanes to the Soviet Navy began in 1923.

Second from top: A still-unmarked J 20 afloat beside a slipway. No mounting ring for the machine gun is installed in the rear cockpit.

Above right: A Baltic Fleet Air Arm J 20 with the tactical number '2 White' on the rudder is hoisted aboard the cruiser SNS *Profintern*. The plethora of float mounting struts and the planing bottoms of the floats are well visible.

Right: The cockpit section of the same aircraft, showing the lifting cable attachment points and the machine gun mounting ring.

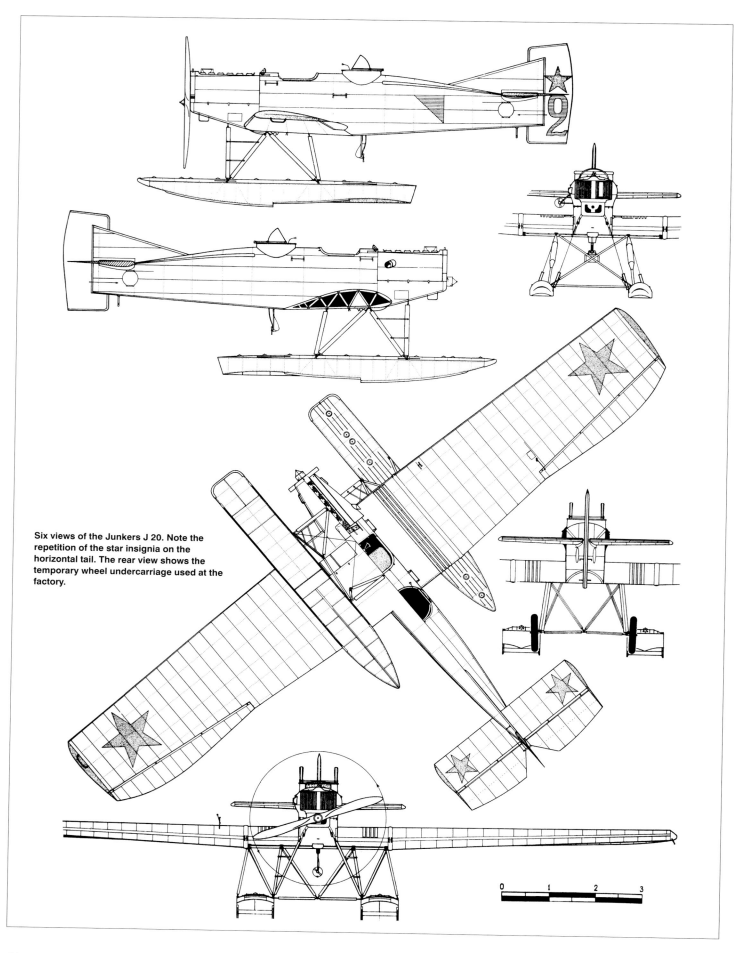

Six views of the Junkers J 20. Note the repetition of the star insignia on the horizontal tail. The rear view shows the temporary wheel undercarriage used at the factory.

0 1 2 3

wings mounted flush against the upper surface of the fuselage in order to improve the pilot's field of view. Its wing span and fuselage length were slightly reduced as compared to the J 21. Two prototypes of the J 22 were built at Dessau and flown in November 1923 and April 1934 respectively; the test results were disappointing, and the type was not accepted by the Red Army Air Force. In consequence, the hundred-aircraft order was changed to call for the delivery of twenty J 20s and eighty J 21s.

Junkers W 33 (V-33, PS-3, PS-4) transport aircraft

In 1926 a modified variant of the F 13 for cargo transport and other utility tasks was developed by the Junkers Flugzeugwerke. There were two versions: the W 33 with the water-cooled 310-hp Junkers L 5 six-cylinder inline engine, and the W 34 with different types of air-cooled radial engines. The W 33 was purchased by the USSR in some numbers in the late 1920s, while the W 34 found its way to the Soviet Union much later, when a few were obtained as war booty during the Second World War.

The Soviet Union purchased some 30 Junkers W 33s in Germany and Sweden. In Soviet service they were initially designated Yunkers V-33 (English rendering of the Cyrillic transliteration of the German designation). In 1933, according to Lennart Andersson, they were redesignated PS-3, the PS denoting *passazheerskiy samolyot* – passenger aircraft (in spite of their cargo role); no confirmation of this from Soviet/Russian sources is available to the authors of the present book). If that was really the case, this was the second use of this designation which had been previously applied to demilitarised R-3 (ANT-3) recon-

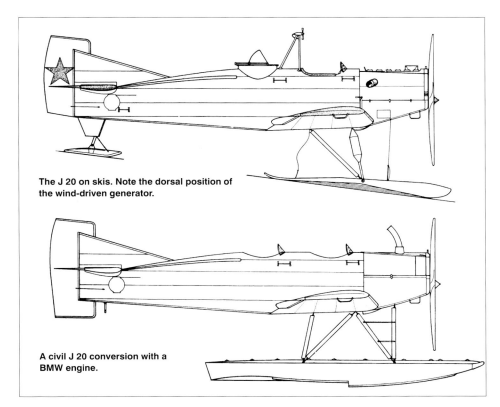

The J 20 on skis. Note the dorsal position of the wind-driven generator.

A civil J 20 conversion with a BMW engine.

naissance aircraft. In that case PS meant *pochtovyy samolyot* – mailplane). Incidentally, the first PS-3 type was operated by the GVF until 1933, so the re-use of the designation in that year seems logical enough (Lennart Andersson styles the mailplane version of the R-3 as P-3).

The first three W-33s were delivered to Dobrolyot in November-December 1928. Initially registered R-RDAH (c/n 2528), R-RDAI (c/n 2529) and R-RDAO (c/n 2533), they were re-registered CCCP-175, CCCP-176 and CCCP-177 respectively in 1929. In 1929-1930 they were supplemented by a further six aircraft, of which the first received the reg-

istration URSS-182 and the other five became CCCP-441 to CCCP-445. All but three of these aircraft were based at Irkutsk, while the three machines registered CCCP-443, CCCP-444 and CCCP-445 were sent to Khabarovsk. The Irkutsk-based machines flew the Irkutsk-Yakutsk and Irkutsk-Bodaibo services, while those based in Krasnoyarsk were used on the route to Sakhalin Island. In most cases the machines were equipped with floats. Further known W 33s used by the East Siberian GVF Directorate at Irkutsk and the Far Eastern Directorate at Khabarovsk include СССР-Л-31, СССР-Л-32, СССР-Л42, СССР-Л-735, СССР-Л-752, СССР-Л20,

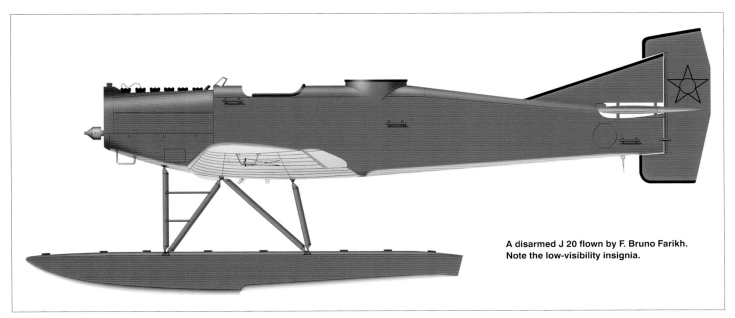

A disarmed J 20 flown by F. Bruno Farikh. Note the low-visibility insignia.

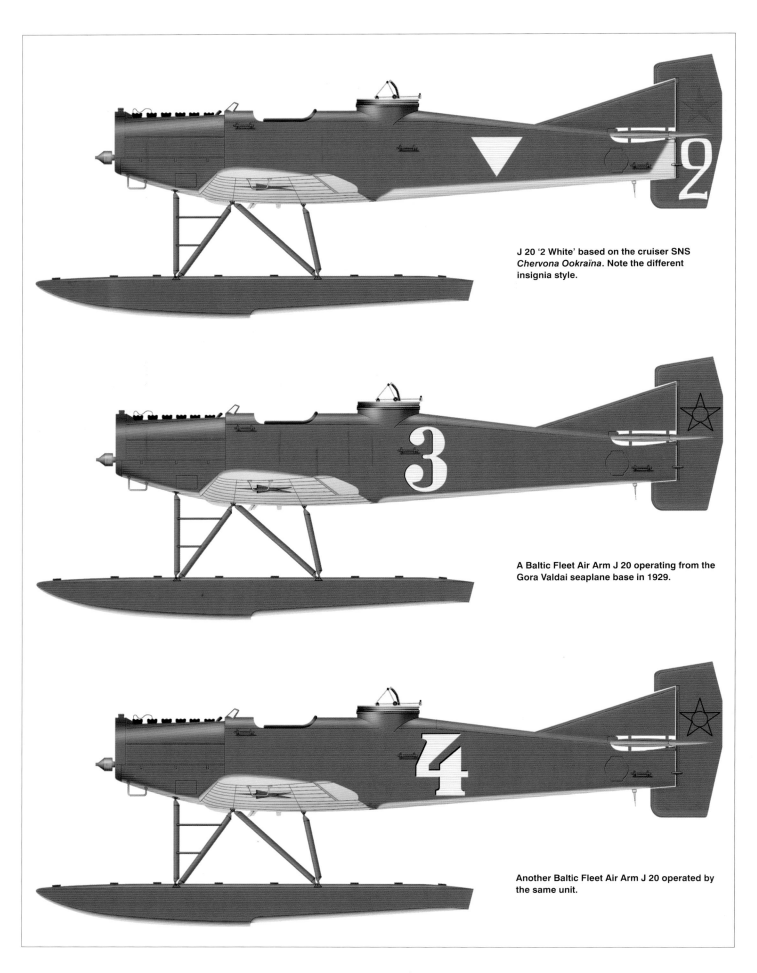

J 20 '2 White' based on the cruiser SNS *Chervona Ookraïna*. Note the different insignia style.

A Baltic Fleet Air Arm J 20 operating from the Gora Valdai seaplane base in 1929.

Another Baltic Fleet Air Arm J 20 operated by the same unit.

CCCP-Л21 and CCCP-Л30 (the three last-mentioned were based at Khabarovsk).

In addition to the imported examples, a small number of W-33s was built in the Soviet Union, making use of the experience gained in the course of servicing and repairing aircraft of this type, as well as the Junkers F 13. Soviet-built W-33s were designated PS-4. According to Russian sources, seven machines were manufactured at Dobrolyot's repair facility in Irkutsk, and a further ten at the Central Aircraft Repair Base in Moscow (restyled as Plant No. 89). Lennart Andersson specifically mentions three such aircraft built at Irkutsk in 1932-34, and six aircraft built in Moscow in 1934. Incidentally, Lennart Andersson uses the PS-4 designation only with regard to the Soviet-built W-33s, while some Soviet publications apply the designation PS-4 indiscriminately to all W 33s operated in the USSR, regardless of their origin.

The Soviet-built PS-4 was slightly modernised as compared to the original W 33, featuring an enclosed cockpit. The first PS-4, completed in August 1932, was delivered to Glavsevmorput' (Administration of the Northern Sea Route). Lennart Andersson identifies it as CCCP-H-4, but this must be an error (this registration belonged to a JuG-1 since February 1932). The actual registration must have been CCCP-H-5, for which photo proof exists. Another known Irkutsk-built PS-4 was CCCP-Л1402. The Moscow-built examples included CCCP-Л1414, CCCP-Л1415, CCCP-Л1416, CCCP-Л1417, CCCP-H62 and CCCP-H63.

The PS-3/PS-4 aircraft were operated both as landplanes on wheels and skis and as floatplanes. They were mostly used in Siberia for cargo transportation, the floatplane version making use of the numerous rivers for their operation. The W 33 in all its guises remained in service in the Soviet Union for more than 10 years, single examples still flying as late as 1945.

A special chapter in the W 33's Soviet career is its use in polar aviation. To quote Lennart Andersson, Glavsevmorput' received CCCP-H4 (CCCP-H-5? – Auth.) in October 1932 and CCCP-H63 and CCCP-H64 in January 1935. From the summer of

Above: A rare photo of the J 20 in flight. The machine is the same example as depicted on page 43. Note the placement of the insignia on the undersurfaces and the green planing bottoms of the floats.

Above: CCCP-Ф15 (SSSR-F15), a Junkers J 21 decommissioned and transferred to Dobrolyot for photo mapping duties. On this machine the fuel tanks have short rear ends.

Above: A J 21 in Red Army Air Force service. The tanks have longer and more pointed rear ends.

2nd Aviation Battalion J 21s lined up for a parade in the 1930s. The first four machines carry the tactical numbers '1 White' through '4 White'. The upper cowling panels and the machine-guns have been removed because of high ambient temperatures creating the risk of overheating.

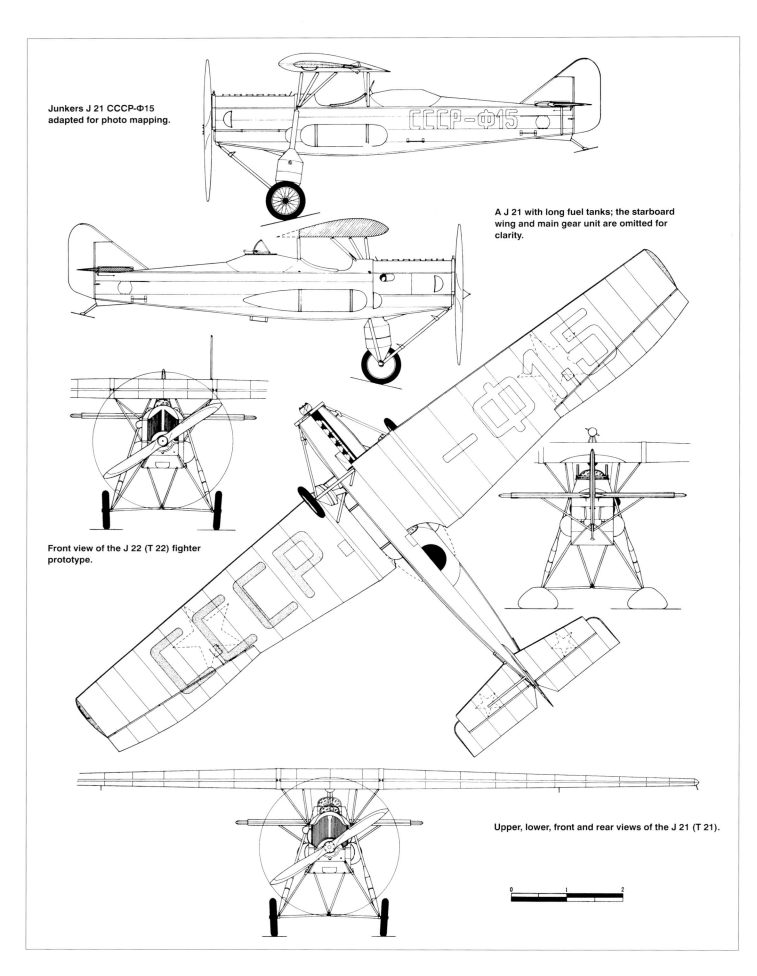

Junkers J 21 CCCP-Ф15 adapted for photo mapping.

A J 21 with long fuel tanks; the starboard wing and main gear unit are omitted for clarity.

Front view of the J 22 (T 22) fighter prototype.

Upper, lower, front and rear views of the J 21 (T 21).

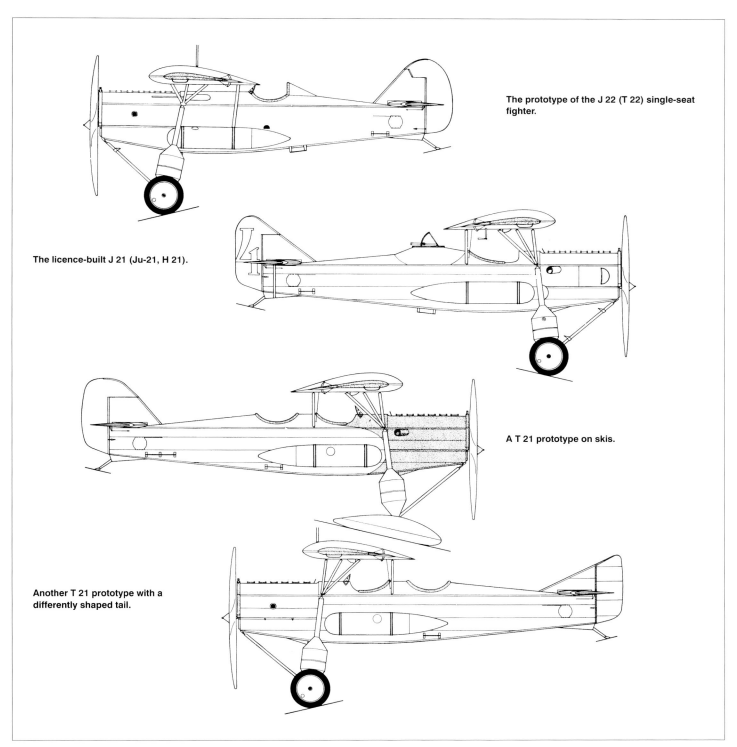

The prototype of the J 22 (T 22) single-seat fighter.

The licence-built J 21 (Ju-21, H 21).

A T 21 prototype on skis.

Another T 21 prototype with a differently shaped tail.

1935 these aircraft were included in the Air Group responsible for operating a freight and passenger service along the northern part of the Lena River from Irkutsk to Tiksi. At least two PS-4s were used by Polar Aviation (*Polyarnaya aviahtsiya*/Aviaarktika) in 1939.

One of the episodes related to it is the participation of a W 33 floatplane in an Arctic expedition in 1929. The expedition's purpose was to study the feasibility of air navigation along the Northern Sea route. A crew captained by pilot Otto A. Kal'vitsa performed flights over the northern coasts of the country within the stretch between the Bering Strait and the mouth of the Lena River. The expedition lasted about a month and had to be discontinued due to an engine failure. During that period the aircraft covered a distance of 5,450 km (3,387 miles).

In 1934 two PS-4s participated in the famous operation to rescue the crew and passengers of the icebound steamship S/S *Chelyuskin* that had been crushed by Polar icefields. These were the machines registered СССР-Л-752 and СССР-Л-735 piloted by V. L. Galyshev and I. V. Doronin.

Junkers G-24 (G-23) passenger aircraft

Vadim B. Shavrov wrote thus about the Junkers G 24: *'This was a passenger aircraft powered by three 220-hp BMW engines; it was intended to carry 10 passengers and two crew. In its design it was essentially a scaled-up Junkers F 13. In 1925 a single example of this aircraft was sent to the Soviet Union by the Junkers company for familiarisation and advertising purposes; it performed some demonstration flights, but no purchases ensued'.*

Above: This J 21 (H 21), c/n 504, became the 100th Junkers aircraft manufactured by the Fili plant; it was built in 1925.

Above: This J 21 coded '2 White' crash-landed near Samsonovo railway station in 1924 and looks like a total loss. Note the original short external tanks.

This demilitarised J 21 bears the unusual civil registration ДЛ-12 (that is, DL-12).

Curiously, Dmitriy A. Sobolev refers to the same aircraft as the G-23, stating: 'The Junkers company came up with a proposal for the setting up of the manufacture of the three-engined JuG-1 bomber which was a military version of the new G 23 passenger aircraft. In the spring of 1925 a G 23 was demonstrated in Moscow for advertising purposes; it performed demonstration flights'.

The apparent confusion with the designations has its explanation. Both of them were applicable! In September 1924 the Junkers company commenced flight testing of the G 24 nine-passenger three-engined

aircraft. However, its progress ran into difficulties because of the restrictions on the performance of civil types, imposed under the terms of the Versailles Treaty. In accordance with the restrictions an aircraft like the G 24 was permitted only if it was fitted with engines which made it severely underpowered and, consequently, useless for commercial purposes. As related by Lennart Andersson, *'the problem was solved by building the aircraft under the paper designation G 23 – a temporary and symbolic step 'backwards' – allegedly a version powered by engines that had been permitted. (One source credits the G 23 with a powerplant*

consisting of one 165-hp engine and two 100-hp engines – *Auth.*). *In reality the aircraft were fitted with the 230hp Junkers L 2s, registered in Sweden and Switzerland and then put into service back in Germany as 'non-German' aircraft! One G 24 (c/n 835) was sent to Copenhagen, and then to Moscow where it arrived on 11th April 1925 and was registered to Junkers-Luftverkehr as R-RECL for demonstrations, before being returned to Germany in June'*. Note the obvious allusion to 'reclame' (French for advertising) in the registration!

L. Andersson further states that one Junkers G 24 was ordered for Dobrolyot, but the order was cancelled on 28th August 1928 and three Junkers W 33s were bought instead.

The G-24 episode is interesting only in connection with the role this aircraft played in the development of the K-30 bomber which, under the JuG-1 designation, was actually ordered by the USSR and served with the Red Army Air Force.

Junkers K 30 (R 42, JuG-1) bomber

In the spring of 1925, during the negotiations on the prospects of the Junkers concession held in Moscow, the Junkers company came up with a proposal envisaging the manufacture at Fili of a three-engined all-metal bomber based on the new Junkers G 24 (G 23) passenger aircraft. Reflecting the dual-role civil/military concept adopted at that time by Junkers, the aircraft featured a spacious fuselage of large cross-section. Outwardly it differed from the airliner version in having two open dorsal turrets in the fuselage roof and a vertically adjustable ventral 'dustbin' type revolving turret located just aft of the wings. The armament comprised a pair of single or twin Lewis machine-guns and a single gun in the ventral turret. A bomb load of 1,000-1,200 kg (2,200-2,650 lb) or a 3.3-m (10 ft 10 in) torpedo could be carried on racks beneath the fuselage. The aircraft was powered by three Junkers L-5 engines rated at 310 hp. Series production of this bomber known as the K 30 had been organised by Junkers in Sweden where AB Flygindustri had been set up at Limhamn to make possible the manufacture of G 24s and K 30s without interference from Allied control authorities. The designation used at that stage was Junkers G.I (*Grossflugzeug* – large aircraft); in its abbreviated form JuG-1 it gained currency in the Soviet Union, and the Soviet Air Force, as well as other Soviet organisations, stuck to it, ignoring the K 30 designation. (Some Soviet documents refer to these aircraft as G-1s, dropping the Ju.)

The proposal looked promising, and in July 1925 the Soviet side, guided by the wish to reinstate production at Fili as quickly as

Above and below: A PS-4 cargo aircraft (a Soviet-built Junkers W 33 with an enclosed cockpit) registered СССР-Л1402 (SSSR-L1402). Note the small cabin glazing area and the optional wheel spats.

possible, decided to make a trial order for three JuG-1 aircraft without waiting for the completion of the new bomber prototype's trials. The price tag of one bomber was 228,000 roubles. A few months later the Air Force Directorate placed an order with the Junkers company for a further 12 JuG-1s at a price of 205,000 roubles per unit. However, subsequent negotiations on the functioning of the concession as a whole ran into difficulties, calling into question the continuation of the concession. In mid-1926 the Air Force Directorate declared the contract for the JuG-1 bombers cancelled, citing the failure of the Junkers company to fulfil a number of obligations under the concession agreement. In the course of further negotiations the parties came to an agreement on the terms under which the concession was terminated; the Soviet side agreed to accept the JuG-1 bombers ordered in 1925.

Since the Junkers factory in Fili was shut down when the concession was terminated, the 15 JuG-1 aircraft ordered in 1925 were manufactured by the Junkers subsidiary in Sweden, which called them R 42s. The first three aircraft were shipped from Limhamn to Leningrad by the end of November 1925. At least one of these machines had the initial shallow broad-chord fin with a curved leading edge which was later replaced by a taller fin with a straight leading edge. To keep the deal secret, the aircraft were shipped to the USSR without armament, in the guise of passenger aircraft. In Moscow they were outfitted at the Fili plant as bombers.

In 1926 the aircraft of the first batch entered service with the Air Force units (official acceptance by the VVS took place in February 1927). The JuG-1s were assigned to the 1st Air Brigade at Gatchina south of Leningrad (renumbered as the 3rd Air Brigade in 1928), equipping the 57th (later also the 55th) Heavy Bomber Squadron. They were operated both in landplane and floatplane versions. The JuG-1s based on the

Above: An original W 33, СССР-176 (ex R-RDAI, c/n 2529), operated by Dobrolyot as a floatplane.

W 33 СССР-Л-31 (ex СССР-177, ex R-RDAO, c/n 2533) nudges onto a slipway at the end of a flight. Note the open cockpit, the larger cabin windows (compare with the PS-4) and the dog-leg exhaust pipe.

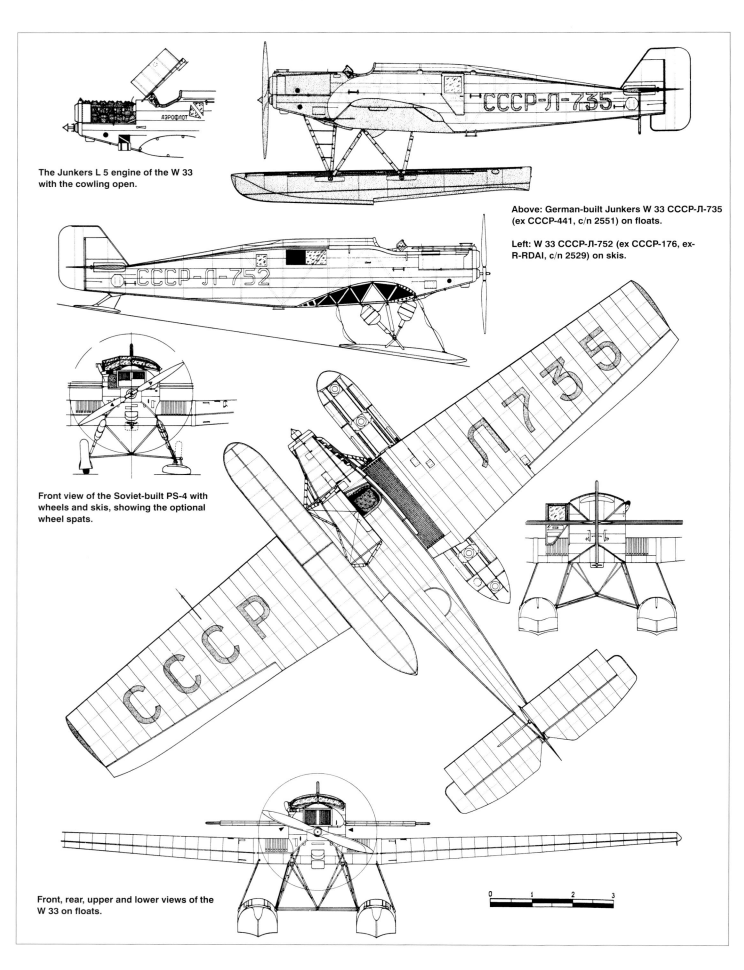

The Junkers L 5 engine of the W 33 with the cowling open.

Above: German-built Junkers W 33 СССР-Л-735 (ex CCCP-441, c/n 2551) on floats.

Left: W 33 СССР-Л-752 (ex CCCP-176, ex-R-RDAI, c/n 2529) on skis.

Front view of the Soviet-built PS-4 with wheels and skis, showing the optional wheel spats.

Front, rear, upper and lower views of the W 33 on floats.

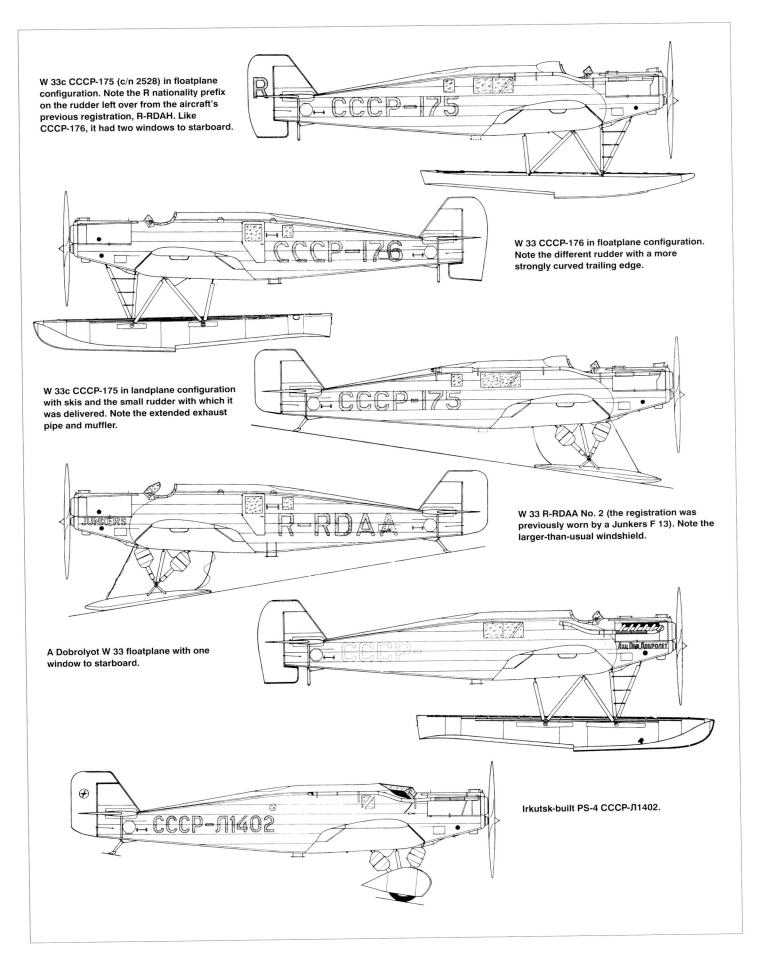

W 33c CCCP-175 (c/n 2528) in floatplane configuration. Note the R nationality prefix on the rudder left over from the aircraft's previous registration, R-RDAH. Like CCCP-176, it had two windows to starboard.

W 33 CCCP-176 in floatplane configuration. Note the different rudder with a more strongly curved trailing edge.

W 33c CCCP-175 in landplane configuration with skis and the small rudder with which it was delivered. Note the extended exhaust pipe and muffler.

W 33 R-RDAA No. 2 (the registration was previously worn by a Junkers F 13). Note the larger-than-usual windshield.

A Dobrolyot W 33 floatplane with one window to starboard.

Irkutsk-built PS-4 CCCP-Л1402.

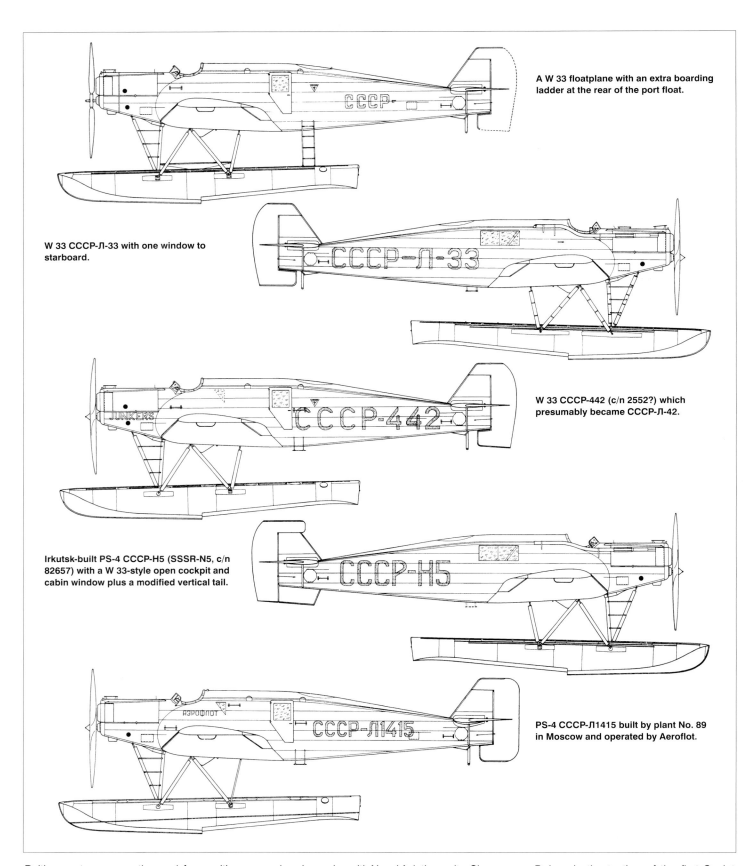

A W 33 floatplane with an extra boarding ladder at the rear of the port float.

W 33 СССР-Л-33 with one window to starboard.

W 33 CCCP-442 (c/n 2552?) which presumably became СССР-Л-42.

Irkutsk-built PS-4 CCCP-H5 (SSSR-N5, c/n 82657) with a W 33-style open cockpit and cabin window plus a modified vertical tail.

PS-4 СССР-Л1415 built by plant No. 89 in Moscow and operated by Aeroflot.

Baltic coast were mostly used for maritime reconnaissance. JuG-1 c/n 906 was tested as a torpedo-bomber (notably, on the Black Sea by the Sevastopol'-based 60th Air Squadron) but the type probably never became operational in that role and only carried bombs and

mines in service with Naval Aviation units. Single examples were used by NII VVS and by the Air Force Academy. The JuG-1 was popular with its crews, but various complaints were voiced about the offensive and defensive armament, which had to be modified.

Delays in the testing of the first Soviet heavy bomber – the TB-1 – prompted the Air Force Administration (UVVS – *Oopravleniye Voyenno-vozdooshnykh seel*) to purchase a further eight JuG-1 bombers in 1927. They were delivered from Limhamn in January

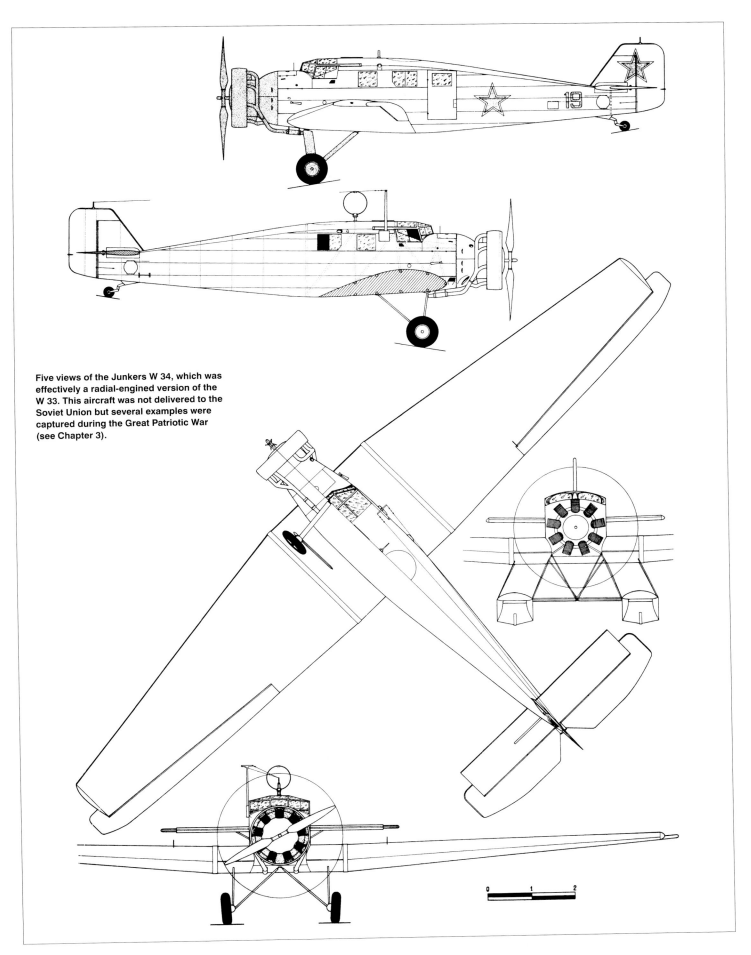

Five views of the Junkers W 34, which was effectively a radial-engined version of the W 33. This aircraft was not delivered to the Soviet Union but several examples were captured during the Great Patriotic War (see Chapter 3).

0   1   2

Above: Maintenance in progress on W 33 CCCP-Л-735 (ex CCCP-441, c/n 2551). Note the built-in step on the side of the cowling facilitating access to the engine.

Above: A ski-equipped W 33. The landing gear design is well visible.

A Junkers JuG-1 in the assembly shop of the Fili factory where it was outfitted as a bomber. This one has the early version of the vertical tail.

1928. Unlike earlier examples, they had Soviet Tur-6*bis* open turrets, Telefunken radios and other changes. In 1928-29 the JuG-1 was the Red Army Air Force's most potent combat aircraft. In 1930-31, after the TB-1 had entered production, the JuG-1s were phased out by the Air Force and transferred to the Civil Aviation. After conversion to nine-seat passenger configuration at the Central Repair Workshop in Moscow, they were used as transport floatplanes on air routes along the Lena River and other Siberian rivers. Naturally, the aircraft were stripped of all military equipment and provided with heating for winter operation. The JuG-1s were also used in other parts of the country. For example, they supplanted for a brief period the Kalinin K-4 on the Moscow-Tiflis (present-day Tbilisi) service; they also served with the Moscow and Ukrainian GVF Departments and were operated in the Soviet republics of Central Asia (Uzbekistan and Turkmenistan). The JuG-1s operated by the Civil Air Fleet (initially by Dobrolyot, later by Aeroflot) carried registrations in the CCCP-Л series (CCCP-Л8, CCCP-Л43, CCCP-Л710, CCCP-Л743 and others – a total of 15 Swedish-built machines). Examples in service with the Sevmorput' (Administration of the Northern Sea route) were registered in

Above: Red Army Air Force personnel pose for a photo with a JuG-1 during an exercise in the Moscow Military District.

the CCCP-H series (for example, CCCP-H4). At least two JuG-1s were built by the GVF repair shops at Irkutsk in 1934; these were CCCP-H17 and CCCP-Л1455.

One of the JuG-1s took part in the search for the Italian expedition led by Umberto Nobile which, as already mentioned, was in distress in the Arctic after the crash of the airship *Italia*. The unmarked aircraft, which was nicknamed **Kras***nyy* **med***ved'* (Red bear),

was loaded on the deck of the icebreaker S/S *Krasin*. On 10th July 1928 a crew captained by Boris G. Chukhnovskiy set off on a reconnaissance flight from an airstrip prepared on the ice near the icebreaker and spotted several of the expedition's participants – the so-called Malmgren group. Rough ice did not permit a landing, but Chukhnovskiy radioed to the icebreaker the location of the group in distress, and two

days later the men were safely on board the ship. Next came the turn of the JuG-1, whose crew also had to be rescued after a forced landing. The aircraft was recovered and subsequently fitted with floats at Spitsbergen on 22nd July.

In line with other Junkers aircraft in Soviet service, the civil JuG-1 was redesignated PS-5 in 1933. Several years later this designation was reused for a civil version of

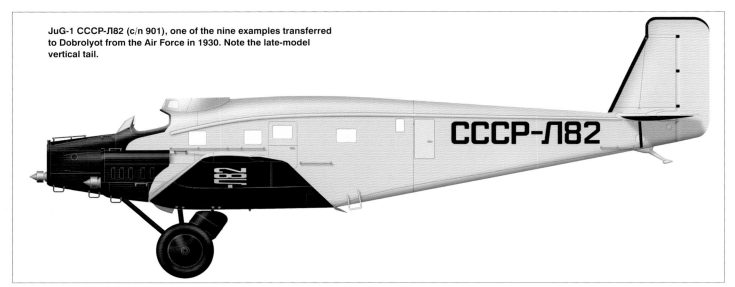

JuG-1 CCCP-Л82 (c/n 901), one of the nine examples transferred to Dobrolyot from the Air Force in 1930. Note the late-model vertical tail.

Above: Red Army personnel poses with a Junkers G 24, the forerunner of the K 30 (JuG-1). This may be the example that was evaluated in the military flying school in Lipetsk.

Above: A demilitarised JuG-1 transferred to the Polar Aviation, outfitted as a floatplane and registered CCCP-H4 (SSSR-N4). A crewman pokes his head out of the dorsal gunner's position.

The rear fuselage of CCCP-H4. A boarding ladder has been placed on the port float while the aircraft is partially beached.

the Tupolev R-10 reconnaissance aircraft, albeit in the latter case PS stood for *pochtovyy samolyot* (mailplane) rather than *passazheerskiy samolyot* (airliner).

Junkers K 47b two-seat fighter

In early 1929 the Soviet authorities signed a contract with the Junkers company providing for the delivery of two K 47b fighters (the aircraft was also known as the A-48 in 'civil' guise). This was a two-seat low-wing all-metal monoplane with twin tails; the wings were braced by ventral V-struts attached to the fixed main landing gear units. It was powered by a 480-hp Siemens Jupiter VI 9Af nine-cylinder radial driving a two-blade propeller. In addition to two fixed forward-firing machine guns, it had one flexible machine-gun in the rear cockpit; the twin tails provided a good field of fire for the gunner.

The two machines (c/ns 3352 and 3353) were manufactured by Junkers' Swedish subsidiary, AB Flygindustri. In December 1929 they were delivered by boat to Leningrad and were assigned to NII VVS (Research Institute of the Soviet Air Force) for evaluation. Prior to testing, they were fitted with armament which comprised two 7.62-mm (.50 calibre) PV-1 machine-guns and one Degtyaryov DA machine-gun of the same calibre. Upon completion of the testing, which produced fairly positive results, one of the aircraft was assigned to the headquarters flight of the 15th Air Brigade at Bryansk in 1931. The other K 47b went to the Air Force Academy in 1933.

The influence of this aircraft is plainly visible in the design of some Soviet two-seat fighters. The types in point are the Grigorovich DI-3 and the Laville DI-4 which, like the German fighter, had twin fins in order to increase the gunner's field of fire. They were, however, quite different in other respects, the DI-3 being a biplane while the DI-4 was a strut-braced high-wing monoplane.

Dornier aircraft in the USSR in the 1920s/early 1930s

The early 1920s saw the establishment of cooperation between the Soviet Union and Dornier Metallbauten GmbH. The founder of this company, Claudius Dornier, started producing all-metal aircraft as early as the First World War period. During the early 1920s he developed the Komet and Merkur passenger aircraft, which were operated by the airlines of several countries; he also produced several successful types of flying boats.

In 1923 the Dornier company offered its Komet II passenger aircraft to the newly established Ukrainian air transport society Ukrvozdukhput'. In addition, it addressed the Soviet government with a proposal envisaging the granting of a concession for the manufacture of Dornier aircraft in the USSR. Ukrvozdukhput' displayed interest for this type of cooperation; it intended to start joint production of Dornier passenger aircraft at the former Anatra aircraft factory in Simferopol'.

This idea failed to gain support from the Soviet leaders, who were primarily interested in military aircraft. The Air Force Directorate turned down the proposal put forward by Dornier and Ukrvozdukhput' and gave some consideration to possible joint production of Dornier-designed military aircraft, but gave up this option on the background of an uncertain situation with the prospects of the Junkers concession. In the end, co-operation with the Dornier company boiled down to purchases of Komet and Merkur passenger aircraft and the acquisition of the Dornier Wal flying boats for the Soviet Navy.

Dornier B Komet I and Komet II passenger aircraft

Based at Friedrichshafen in southern Germany, Dornier Metallbauten GmbH was one of the German industrial enterprises with which the Soviet Union maintained fairly close commercial ties and cooperation during the 1920s and early 1930s. In their efforts aimed at developing air transport in the country the Soviet government turned its attention to the passenger aircraft produced by this company. These were the Dornier Komet aircraft produced in several versions which gained a measure of success. The Komet was a single-engined strut-braced high-wing monoplane of steel and duralumin construction, featuring an enclosed four-seat passenger cabin while the pilot sat

Above: JuG-1 *Krasnyy medved'* (Red bear) aboard the icebreaker S/S *Krasin* passing through the fjords of Norway on 16th June 1928. The aircraft was used in the search for Umberto Nobile's expedition.

Above: The same aircraft on the return trip with floats installed. Interestingly, the *Krasnyy medved'* wore no registration. Note the flag with the 'red bear' above the fuselage.

A Red Army Air Force JuG-1 with the tactical number '1 Red' touches down at Novgorod-Krechevitsy during a Leningrad Military District exercise in June 1930. Note the armed dorsal gunner's position.

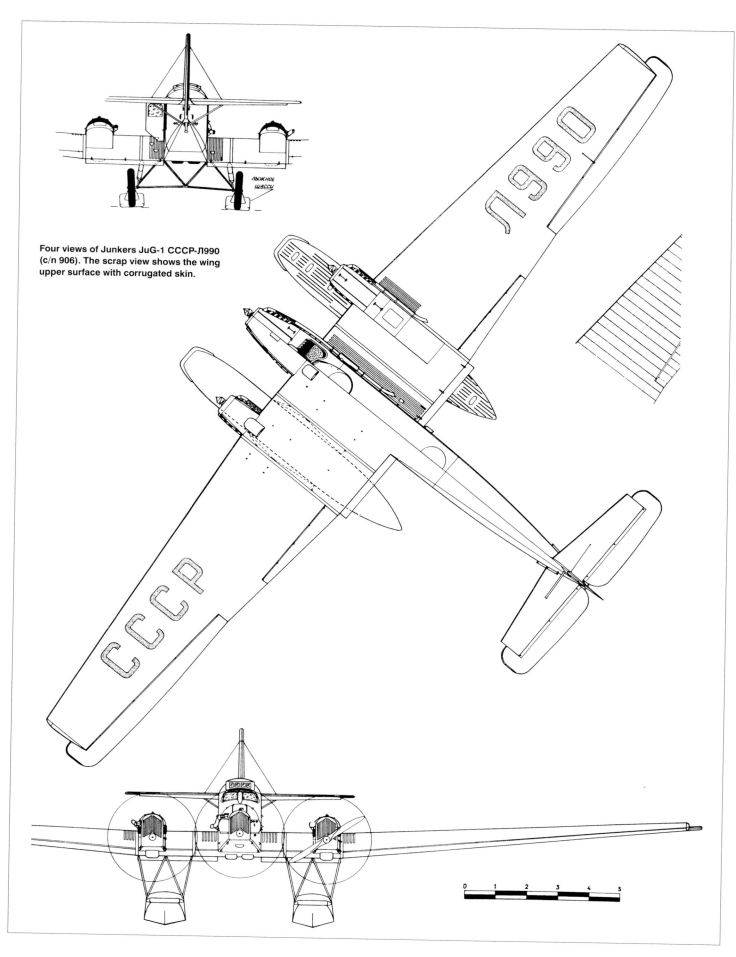

Four views of Junkers JuG-1 СССР-Л990
(c/n 906). The scrap view shows the wing
upper surface with corrugated skin.

ЛЫЖНОЕ
ШАССИ

0 1 2 3 4 5

60

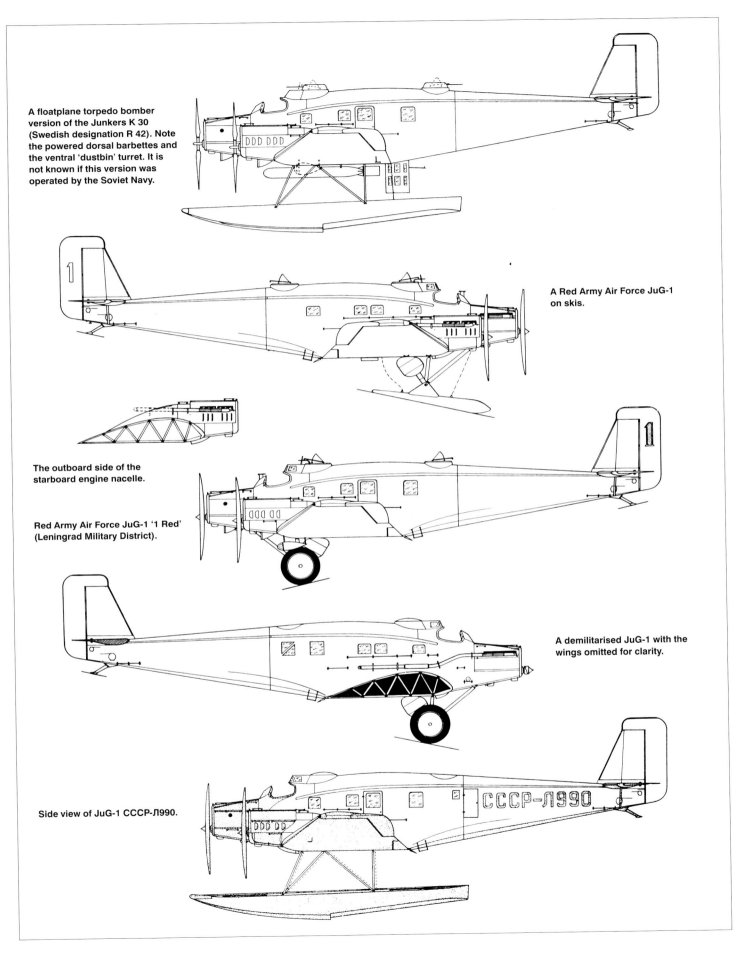

A floatplane torpedo bomber version of the Junkers K 30 (Swedish designation R 42). Note the powered dorsal barbettes and the ventral 'dustbin' turret. It is not known if this version was operated by the Soviet Navy.

A Red Army Air Force JuG-1 on skis.

The outboard side of the starboard engine nacelle.

Red Army Air Force JuG-1 '1 Red' (Leningrad Military District).

A demilitarised JuG-1 with the wings omitted for clarity.

Side view of JuG-1 СССР-Л990.

Junkers JuG-1 '1 Red',
Krechevitsy airfield, Novgorod, Leningrad Military District
June 1930.

Junkers JuG-1 '5 Red', Soviet Navy.
Note that only the rear dorsal turret is armed.

Junkers JuG-1 CCCP-H4.

in an open cockpit. The initial version, first flown on 21st February 1921 and sometimes identified as the Komet I, had a 185-hp BMW IIIa water-cooled six-cylinder engine; it was followed by the improved Dornier B Komet II in October 1922.

Some Russian sources (Shavrov, Sobolev) claim that the introduction of Dornier Komet into Soviet service started with the Komet I, but this is apparently a misunderstanding. According to other sources (notably Lennart Andersson), the first Komets received by the Soviet carrier (Ukrvozdukhput') were of the Komet II version. Six machines of this type were ordered in June 1923 via the Stinnes company, which had the exclusive right to sell Dornier aircraft; of these, two were to be fitted with BMW IIIa engines and four with 260-hp Rolls-Royce Falcon IIIs. Interestingly, Sobolev appears to regard the BMW-powered examples as Komet Is and the Rolls-Royce Falcon-powered machines as Komet IIs (Komet-2). He writes: *'In 1923-1925 the Ukrainian air transport society 'Ukrvozdukhput' purchased in Germany ten (? – Auth.) Komet aircraft for operation on the Khar'kov – Kiev and Khar'kov – Odessa services. Some of them were powered by the BMW IIIa 185-hp engine, while the Komet-2 version had the Rolls-Royce Falcon engine'*. Delivery of these aircraft took place in the period from 30th June 1923 to September. The first two machines (the BMW-powered ones) had frontal radiators and two-blade wooden propellers, while the Rolls-Royce powered aircraft had side-mounted radiators and four-blade propellers. Eventually all six machines were fitted with RR Falcon engines, since the BMW's 185 hp proved insufficient to give the aircraft acceptable field performance.

The six machines were ceremoniously handed over to Ukrvozdukhput' on 30th September 1923 (the first two aircraft) and on 18th November (the remaining four). The aircraft temporarily received alphanumeric registration (RR15 to RR20); later they received new alphabetic registrations ranging from RRUAA to RRUAF. All the machines also had individual names (see below).

For some time the newly acquired aircraft were used for local flights and demonstrations during the winter of 1923-1924. In 1924 they were put on scheduled services on the Khar'kov-Kiev and Khar'kov-Odessa routes, but their use for this purpose did not last long. In 1925, after the arrival of the larger Komet III aircraft, most Komet II machines were relegated to survey work and fitted with aerial cameras. In 1927 one of the aircraft (RRUAB) was destroyed by fire. In the following year the aircraft registered RRUAA crashed. The last four machines

Above: A retouched photo of a Junkers K 47 prototype, D-2012, which was in unarmed configuration with a faired rear seat headrest and an uncowled engine. The Soviet examples looked like this one.

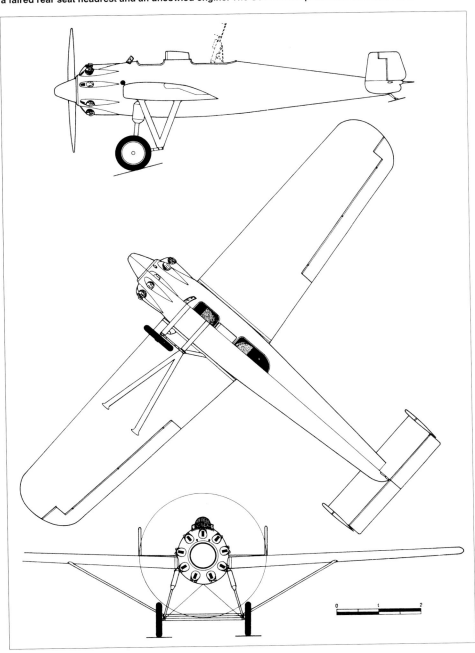

Three views of the armed version of the K 47 with an aft-facing gunner in the rear cockpit (and hence no fairing aft of it), a helmeted cowling and a large propeller spinner.

Above: A brand-new and still unregistered Dornier B Komet II with a BMW IIIa engine.

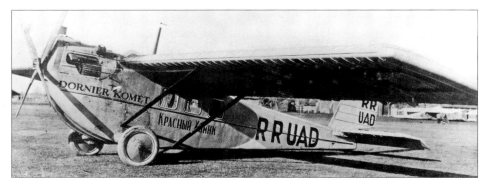

Above: Komet II RR UAD of Ukrvozdukhput' (ex RR18, c/n 9/46) was named *Krasnyy khimik* (Red Chemical Industry Worker) and became CCCP-202. Note how the registration is repeated on the rudder.

The hulk of a Komet II used by Dobrolyot for photo mapping duties, as indicated by the registration C.C.C.P.-Ф27 (SSSR-F27; ex CCCP-118 or CCCP-119, c/n 51 or 53). It was struck off charge in 1933.

Dornier Komet IIs in Soviet service – registrations and names

RRUAA	*Donets-Zheleznodorozhnik* (The Railroader of the Don River Region)
RRUAB	*Ukraina* (The Ukraine)
RRUAC	*Khar'kovskiy metallist* (The Metal Worker of Khar'kov)
RRUAD	*Krasnyy khimik* (The Red Chemical Industry Worker)
RRUAE	*Khar'kovskiy proletariy* (The Proletarian of Khar'kov)
RRUAF	*Ukrvneshtorg* (The Ukrainian Foreign Trade Society)
RRDBA	*Moskovskoye Uchotnoye Obshchestvo Vzaimnovo Kredita*
	(The Moscow Mutual Credit Society)
RRDBB	*Krasnaya Bashkiriya* (Red Bashkiria)

were withdrawn from use in 1929. Two of these had been refitted with 250-hp BMW IV engines.

In addition to the six examples listed above, two more Dornier Komet II aircraft powered by BMW IVs were imported into the Soviet Union in June 1925. Registered R-RDBA and R-RDBB (c/n 53), they were put on local passenger routes in the service of Dobrolyot. The machines were later re-registered CCCP-118 and CCCP-119 and were eventually reassigned for photo mapping work. They were accordingly re-registered CCCP-Ф26 and CCCP-Ф27. It is interesting to compare this information with the following quotation from Sobolev: *'In 1925 the Red Army command purchased from Dornier two Komet-2 aircraft at a price of $34,000 per unit. In accordance with the order specification, the passenger compartment was modified to permit the installation of a Zeiss aerial camera'.*

The GVF designation for the Komet II was DK-II or DK2.

Dornier B Komet III and Merkur passenger aircraft

The Dornier B Komet II in Soviet service were supplemented by the later Komet III model. Despite the common name and a similar strut-braced high-wing layout, it was virtually a completely different aircraft, much bigger and heavier than the Komet II. Its capacity was increased to six passengers in an enclosed cabin plus two crew in an open cockpit. The powerplant was a water-cooled 360-hp Rolls-Royce Eagle with a frontal radiator driving a four-blade propeller. As distinct from the shoulder-wing Komet II, in this case the wing was mounted on short struts above the fuselage.

First flown on 7th December 1924, the Komet III was followed by the Dornier B Merkur on 10th February 1925. This version differed from the Komet III in being powered by the 600-hp BMW VI engine; it also featured a larger fin and a retractable radiator beneath the forward fuselage. Many Komet IIIs were later rebuilt to Merkur configuration.

Eight Komet III and Merkur aircraft were sold to the Soviet Union. Seven of these were Komet IIIs, ordered by Ukrvozdukhput' in 1925 (c/ns 67, 68, 69, 70, 79, 81 and 82). Initially carrying delivery registrations in the RR-number series, they were later registered RRUAG to RRUAN, with the omission of RRUAI. These machines saw service on the Ukrvozdukhput' route between Moscow and Persia with intermediate landings at Khar'kov and Baku. One of the machines, RRUAK (c/n 70), crashed on 19th May 1926, one passenger suffering fatal injuries. As for the aircraft, it was repaired and rebuilt as a Merkur with a BMW engine in 1927.

In 1929 six Komet IIIs belonging to Ukr-vozdukhput' were reregistered CCCP-204 to CCCP-209. In the following year they were transferred to Dobrolyot following a merger between this company and Ukrvozdukhput' that had taken place in January 1930. Their service with Dobrolyot was of short duration, all the machines being transferred to GVF (Civil Air Fleet) flying schools in 1931. They were used by GVF as trainers until 1934, one of the aircraft becoming CCCP-Ш18 (Ш = Sh, a role designator for aircraft operated by GVF's flying schools). The GVF designation for the Komet III was DK-III (DK3).

A single example of the Dornier B Merkur (D-968, c/n 100) was bought by Ukrvoz-dukhput' in 1926; it became RRUAR. Another Merkur (c/n 163) was purchased by Dobrolyot in 1927. Registered RRDAW, it was named *Pravda* (Truth, the Soviet daily newspaper). Thus, in 1929 there were three examples of this type in Soviet service: RRDAW, RRUAK and RRUAR; in that year they were reregistered CCCP-148, CCCP-210 and CCCP-211 respectively. CCCP-211 was cancelled in the same year and CCCP-210 was lost in a crash in January 1931, while the surviving CCCP-148 served with Aeroflot's Central Asian Department until the end of 1932.

Three ex-Deruluft Merkurs were added to the GVF/Aeroflot fleet in 1932, and by the end of that year a total of three were on charge. All had been withdrawn from use by 1934. Noted but unconfirmed 1931-type registrations are CCCP-Л707 and CCCP-Л564. The GVF designation for the Dornier Merkur was DM.

In 1927 Deruluft replaced its Fokker F.IIIs with Dornier Merkurs on the Moscow-Berlin route. From 1926 the Deruluft fleet carried both German and Soviet registration marks, and some of the new Merkurs were given RR-numbers, while the rest had D-numbers. When the Soviet registration system changed in 1929, Deruluft aircraft carried the URSS prefix and numbers in the 300 block. When the system changed again in 1931, a D for Deruluft was added in front of the number.

Dornier J and JII Wal multi-purpose flying boats

The Dornier J Wal (German for 'whale') flying boat was purchased by the Soviet Union in some numbers for both military and civil use in the late 1920s and early 1930s, acquiring considerable importance in both spheres of operation. This aircraft, series-built in Italy and not in Germany because of restrictions imposed on the German aviation after the First World War, attracted the attention of the Soviet military when it came to choosing a naval aircraft capable of performing mar-

Above: CCCP-Ф26, Dobrolyot's other photo mapping Komet II. Note the different registration style.

Above and below: Dobrolyot Komet II C.C.C.P.-118 seen during winter operation on skis on the Arkhangel'sk – Ust'-Sysol'sk service. Note the black panels on the wings disguising exhaust stains.

Dornier Merkur D-1080 (c/n 128?), one of several examples operated by Deruluft. The famous Soviet writer Maksim Gor'kiy is fourth from right.

Above: A Russian-registered Dornier Merkur of Deruluft (RR30, c/n 130) at Königsberg. A further example operated by the same carrier but registered in Germany (D-1079, c/n 127) is visible in the background.

Above: One more Russian-registered Deruluft Merkur, RR35 (c/n 174), seen in 1928. Note the different placement of the airline titles.

Above: Deruluft Dornier Merkur D-1081 (c/n 129) appears to sit in vacuum because the entire (well, almost entire) background has been retouched away by zealous censors!

Mail bags brought by a GAZ-AA 1.5-ton lorry marked *Pochta* (Mail) is loaded into Merkur CCCP-Л74, one of the examples taken over by Aeroflot, circa 1933. Oddly, the registration is not repeated on the wings.

itime patrol duties. Powered by two engines in a tandem installation on the strut-mounted wings, this flying boat was a robust machine with high seaworthiness. In 1925 the Soviet Government ordered two military Wals with 450-hp Lorraine-Dietrich R engines (some sources give the engine type as Lorraine-Dietrich 12Eb). These two machines (c/ns 56 and 57), bearing the temporary Italian registrations I-DOUR and I-DOER, were delivered in September 1926 and entered service with the 60th Air Squadron at Sevastopol'. The evaluation results proved satisfactory; Soviet specialists especially noted the fine workmanship and ease of access to all vital units, in particular to the engines.

A further twenty machines of the type were ordered in the summer of 1927. The engine type specified for this batch was the 500... 730-hp BMW VI which was due to enter licence production in the USSR. These machines incorporated some changes and are referred to in some sources as the DoJ Bis. In 1928 the Soviet customers took delivery of these aircraft (c/ns 90-100 and 127-153). These machines were armed with two Degtyaryov DA machine-guns. The units to which these aircraft were assigned comprised the Sevastopol'-based 60th and 63rd Air Squadrons; in 1932 they were renumbered the 123rd and 124th TBAE (*tyazholaya bombardirovochnaya aviaeskadril'ya* – Heavy Bomber Squadron). The 66th Air Detachment at Leningrad also had a few Wals for a short period.

The military Dornier Wals were modified in service, receiving, in present-day parlance, a mid-life upgrade. The Italian-built machine-gun turrets mounting Lewis guns were replaced by Soviet-manufactured ones mounting twin Degtyaryov DA machine-guns. The fuselage-mounted bomb racks, as well as those mounted on the sponsons, were replaced by bomb racks of improved design.

Several sources, including Shavrov, claim that Plant No. 45 in Sevastopol', which had conducted repairs and upgrading of the Wals, also manufactured six new machines powered by M-17B engines (licence-built copies of the BMW VIE 6,0). Vladimir Kotel'nikov considers these assertions plausible, since this plant had received the machine tools of a repair workshop purchased in Italy together with the second batch of Wals comprising 20 aircraft. Moreover, according to Shavrov, the machines were assembled from imported subassemblies. However, this information cannot be considered as 100% accurate.

By the middle of 1930 the Dornier Wal machines were already becoming obsolescent. From 1930 they underwent various equipment upgrades in the USSR. They began to be supplanted first by the imported Savoia S-62*bis* and its MBR-4 licence-built version (*morskoy blizhniy razvedchik* – short-range maritime reconnaissance aircraft), and then by the Soviet-designed Beriyev MBR-2. In 1937 the Dornier Wal was completely phased out of military service; the remaining machines were turned over to the Polar aviation.

By that time the Soviet Polar aviation had already accumulated some experience of operating the Wal. As early as 1928 the Dobrolyot company purchased in Italy an example of the type which was named *Mossovet* (Moscow City Council) and put on the Irkutsk-Yakutsk route. In the same year one of the Wals from the first batch (c/n 95), named *Sovetskiy Sever* (Soviet North) for the occasion, was placed at the disposal of the Komseverput' Joint-Stock Co. (*Komitet severnovo morskovo putee* – Northern Sea Route Committee) and undertook a 14,000-km (8,280-mile) trans-Arctic proving flight from Vladivostok over Petropavlovsk-na-Kamchatke and Arkhangel'sk to Leningrad, flown by a crew comprising A. A. Volynskiy and E. M. Koshelev. The mission ended in a failure when the aircraft was wrecked by a storm on 22nd August. In 1929 another Wal (c/n 130) was transferred to the Komseverput' organisation and was named *Komseverput' No. 1*. The organisation was engaged in establishing the Arctic shipping route along the north coast of the Soviet Union. The intention was to use the Dornier Wal for ice reconnaissance in the interests of merchant shipping. To this end the machine in question was flown by Boris G. Chukhnovskiy from Sevastopol' to Arkhangel'sk in July 1929 and then was based at the Kara Sea coast. It was intended to assist the icebreaker S/S *Krasin* in guiding the first convoy of merchant ships across the Kara Sea.

In July 1930 Komseverput' No. 1 was transferred to Dobrolyot. Two new Wals were ordered by Komseverput' for Dobrolyot. They were delivered by the Italian pilot De Briganti in July-August 1930 (c/ns 122 and 123); the first of these had the delivery registration I-AAVF. These machines were in most respects identical to the examples previously supplied to the Air Force, but differed in being fitted with a reinforced steel bottom, camera, radio and D/F equipment. Upon delivery they were given the Soviet registrations USSR-471 and USSR-472 and named Komseverput' No. 2 and Komseverput' No. 3 respectively. The machines were immediately put to work on ice reconnaissance. In 1931 the operation of these aircraft became the responsibility of the newly-formed Aviation Service of the Northern Sea Route Committee (*Aviasloozhba Komseverputee*); the three Wal flying boats at its disposal were re-

Above: Dornier Merkur RRDAW (c/n 163) operated by Dobrolyot is named *Ts[entral'nyy] O[rgan] VKP(b) "Pravda"* (The *Pravda* newspaper, the central print organ of the All-Union Communist (Bolshevik) Party).

Above: A trio of Soviet Navy/Black Sea Fleet Air Arm Dornier Wal flying boats in line abreast formation. The white-painted rudders with large tactical numbers are noteworthy.

Another Soviet Navy Wal at rest with both engine cowlings open in the late 1930s, with a sister ship visible behind.

67

Above: A pair of Dornier Wals taxiing at a Soviet Navy base on the Black Sea, with the cruiser SNS *Krasnyy Kavkaz* (Red Caucasus) in the background.

Above: *Sovetskiy Sever* (Soviet North), a Wal flown by A. A. Volynskiy and E. M. Koshelev, is seen during a stopover on a flight along the Northern Sea Route. It wore no markings except a red star on the nose.

CCCP-H1, a Polar Aviation Dornier Wal, partially beached at a seaplane base in the High North.

registered CCCP-H1, CCCP-H2 and CCCP-H3 (Cyrillic H = N, a prefix for the aircraft operated by this organisation and later by Polar Aviation in general). Sadly, CCCP-H3 crashed on 8th September 1932 and had to be written off. CCCP-H2 remained in service until August 1937 when it was lost in a ground accident.

The activities of the Dornier Wal aircraft in service with Komseverput' were not confined to ice reconnaissance. In 1930 CCCP-H1 with a geologist on board made several flights in the area where the famous Tunguska meteorite had fallen in 1907, with the intention of determining precise location of the fall. Yet another task performed by CCCP-H1 was the monitoring of the migration of white whales in the area of the Taimyr Peninsula in the interests of whaling.

According to Sobolev, a special 'Arctic' version of the Dornier Wal was developed in the USSR. At Boris G. Chukhnovskiy's suggestion the boat hull's bottom was reinforced, changes were made in the design of the fuel piping and an emergency fuel jettison system was developed. A thus modified version was built to Soviet order at a factory in Altenrhein, Switzerland.

In December 1932 the Soviet Union ordered two examples of an improved Wal designated Dornier J II. This version differed from its predecessor in having a new vertical tail with rounded rudder top contours and a single radiator of larger type hinged below the rear engine. The examples delivered to the USSR in August 1933 were of the J II Bis version with M-17 engines (a Soviet copy of the BMW VI). Carrying the temporary German registrations D-6 and D-8 (c/ns 238 and 239), they had an open cockpit and an observer's station in the bows and three small circular cabin windows in the hull. One of the Do J II machines received the registration CCCP H10. In 1932-33 many of the Wals delivered previously were re-engined with the M-17s.

Sevmorput' added further examples of Dornier Wal to its fleet in 1933. These included CCCP-H6, CCCP-H7, CCCP-H8, CCCP-H9 and CCCP-H10. An example registered CCCP-H26 was also noted (this was possibly an ex-military machine).

By November 1933 the VVS had eighteen Wals left, while Sevmorput' had six by the end of that year. One of the Sevmorput' machines was written off so that by the end of 1935 five remained.

The Wals were used for expeditions, special flights and the Yenisey River service between Krasnoyarsk and Dudinka. In September 1937 Dornier Wal CCCP-H2 flown by Zadkov participated in the search for Sigizmund A. Levanevskiy's specially modified Bolkhovitinov DB-A bomber (CCCP-H209), which had gone missing when attempting a record-breaking flight to the USA via the North Pole.

The GVF designation for the Dornier Wal was DW. In 1938-39 the Wals serving with Glavsevmorput'/Aviaarktika included CCCP-H235, CCCP-H236, CCCP-H237 and CCCP-H303, and possibly also CCCP-H233, CCCP-H234, CCCP-H238 and CCCP-H239. In 1939 Wals were used on the freight and passenger service between Irkutsk and Tiksi on the Lena River. The Dornier Wal flying boat remained an important component of Soviet Polar aviation up to the German invasion of the USSR in June 1941.

After the outbreak of the war several of these aircraft were transferred to the military aviation and were operated by the North Fleet and by the Pacific Fleet in the course of the second half of 1941. Four Wals operated by the North Fleet until early 1942 performed ice reconnaissance, transported cargoes and flew anti-submarine patrol missions. Four Wals requisitioned from Polar aviation were used by the Pacific Fleet in late 1941 as transport and long-range reconnaissance aircraft.

Successful operation of the Dornier Wal flying boats in the USSR must have influenced the thinking of Soviet aircraft designers to some extent. This influence can be noticed, for example, in the overall layout of the DAR long-range Arctic reconnaissance aircraft built in 1935 under the direction of Robert L. Bartini in the GVF Aircraft

Above: Dornier Wal CCCP-H2 was flown by the famous pilot Vasiliy Molokov from Krasnoyarks to Moscow on 22nd July/19th September 1936. The significance of the wreath on the fuselage is unknown.

Another ex-military Wal operated by Polar Aviation, CCCP-H8, seen here at Tiksi Bay.

Research Institute (NII GVF) at the initiative of Boris G. Chukhnovskiy. This flying boat incorporated such distinctive features of the Dornier machine as the wing set high above the fuselage, flat-bottomed boat-hull fuselage and the engines mounted above the wing in a tandem installation.

Heinkel aircraft in the USSR Late 1920s/early 1930s

The Red Army Air Force began to take an interest in Ernst Heinkel's designs after the delivery of new HD 17 reconnaissance aircraft (HD probably stood for *Heinkel-Doppeldecker* – Helnkel biplane) to the Reichswehr's clandestine flying school in Lipetsk in 1926. The UVVS requested information from Aviatrest (a governing body of the aircraft industry) on aircraft designed by Ernst Heinkel Flugzeugwerke GmbH. A report submitted by Aviatrest in 1927 focused attention on the He 5 maritime reconnaissance aircraft, the HD 23 single-seat biplane fighter and the HD 33 biplane reconnaissance aircraft as promising types, and recommended a purchase of one or two machines of a given type for evaluation, should the Air Force Directorate be interested in licence manufacture of a particular Heinkel aircraft.

Heinkel HE 5c reconnaissance floatplane

In the late 1920s Soviet naval aviation suffered from an acute shortage of modern short-range maritime reconnaissance aircraft. In search of an aircraft capable of replacing the obsolescent Grigorovich flying boats of pre-Revolution vintage and the Italian-built Savoia S.16*ter* flying boats then in service with the Soviet naval air element, the Soviet Navy command turned its attention to the HE.5 three-seat floatplane developed by the Heinkel company in 1926. It was a low-wing monoplane (probably hence the HE for *Heinkel-Eindecker* – Helnkel monoplane) of mixed construction, powered by different engines in different versions. This aircraft was built under licence in Lidingö, Sweden, as the HE.5b maritime reconnaissance aircraft for the Swedish naval aviation.

The aircraft intended for the USSR were powered by BMW VIE 7,3 Vee-12 water-cooled engines which were the most up-to-date engines at that time. With this powerplant the aircraft was redesignated HE.5c. At an AUW of 2,900 kg (6,394 lb) the aircraft had an endurance of 4 hours. Two aircraft of this type (W.Nr. 272 and 289) were acquired by the Soviet government. The first of these was tested in Warnemünde on 17th October 1927. On 31st October it was

Above: One of the two Heinkel He 5c reconnaissance floatplanes purchased from Germany for evaluation.

shipped from Hamburg to Sevastopol' on the Black Sea. The aircraft was devoid of military equipment because the Soviet customers were late in submitting the equipment specification. On 18th January 1928

the aircraft was formally accepted by a commission of the Black Sea Fleet Air Arm. The need to repair some minor damage sustained en route delayed the beginning of the flight test programme until March 1928.

A special commission headed by Commander of the Black Sea Fleet Air Arm V. K. Lavrov was set up to supervise the testing of the HE.5c. The testing of the first machine revealed that the aircraft's performance fell short of the figures claimed by the manufacturer; on the other hand, the pilots liked the machine's handling. However, the take-off and landing qualities were deemed unsatisfactory. Furthermore, when taxiing on water, the aircraft tended to lower its tail and the tail control surfaces were prone to being affected by waves and spray.

On 5th April an official assessment was made of the test results. The aircraft's performance was considered satisfactory, but not the position of the aircraft's CG when operating on water. The aircraft could not be recommended for open-sea operations. It was deemed suitable for operation from

Top left: The first prototype Heinkel HD 37 at plant No. 292 in Saratov. Note the pointed spinner.
Top right, above and right: A silver-doped and unmarked Polikarpov I-7 – the Soviet copy of the HD 37. Note the more bulbous spinner with a Hucks starter dog.

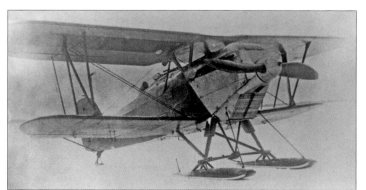

Two views of an I-7 on skis. The aircraft is painted dark green, except for the engine cowling, which is unpainted.

The KR-1 remained in Soviet Navy service until 1938, when it was replaced by the Beriyev KOR-1 floatplane. One of the aircraft was transferred to the Polar Aviation and took part in hydrographic expedition to the Taimyr Peninsula in the Far North in 1932; in 1934 it was based on the icebreaker S/S *Krasin* and used for ice reconnaissance.

Albatros aircraft in the USSR in the 1920s

Three types related to the German Albatros-Werke are described here; this section does not deal with the Albatros aircraft which were imported into the USSR for the needs of the clandestine German flying school at Lipetsk (see a special section on this subject below).

'Albatros XVII' reconnaissance aircraft

A two-seat reconnaissance aircraft bearing this designation was built at the 4th Aviapark at Nizhniy Novgorod; it was completed in April 1921. No Albatros type with a designation including the number XVII existed in Germany. It may be surmised that the aircraft in question was a copy of a captured German Albatros with some modifications. The so-called 'Albatros XVII' was taken to Moscow, finished there and made its first flight on 2nd March 1922 with V. Mel'nikov at the controls. The machine was transferred to the NOA (Flight Test Centre) and remained there until being written off, probably in 1924.

See also 'Albatros-16' and 'Albatros-17' in the previous chapter.

Albatros L 58 passenger aircraft

The L 58 was a high-wing passenger aircraft accommodating four passengers and two crew; it was built in small numbers in 1922-23. This aircraft was to be evaluated by Deruluft which planned to use an L 58 registered RR12 on the Königsberg-Moscow service. Lennart Anderson states that an L 58 took off from Berlin-Staaken on 17th October 1923, bound for Moscow, *'but it is not known if this was the same machine and nothing is known of its ultimate fate'.*

Albatros L 76a fighter/reconnaissance aircraft

The Albatros L 76a was an improved version of the L 65 two-seat fighter/reconnaissance aircraft developed by Albatros-Werke in 1924-1925 for the German Army. Making its appearance in 1927, the L 76a was followed by the slightly different L 77v and L 78 models.

The Soviet Air Force showed some interest for the Albatros two-seater; a production licence for the L 77 was discussed during the spring of 1927 and two examples of the L 76 were acquired by the USSR in late 1927. They were subjected to evaluation at NII VVS and then assigned to operational units in the Moscow and Ukranian Military Districts where they were used as staff aircraft. One of them was still in service in November 1933.

German engines in the Soviet Union

Despite the general backwardness of Russian industry, compounded by the collapse of the nation's economy during the Civil War years, aircraft construction in Soviet Russia/the Soviet Union relatively quickly managed to overcome the initial difficulties and establish itself as a viable branch of the country's economy and defence. Less successful were the efforts aimed at establishing indigenous aero engine production which could not rely on any substantial design experience from the pre-revolutionary period. Before 1917 aero engines were either imported or built at home on the basis of French licences. Thus, in the early 1920s the only aero engine in production was the M-2 (Ron-120), a copy of the Le Rhône Jb delivering 120 hp, which was clearly unsuitable as a powerplant for new military aircraft. Certain hopes were pinned on the Junkers factory at Fili (see above), but Junkers consistently evaded the fulfilment of obligations under the concession agreement related to the establishment of aero engine manufacture in the USSR. According to the agreement, Junkers was to arrange the production of up to 450 engines annually. The types suggested by Junkers were the 310-hp L 4 and the 500-hp L 5. In total, the company was to build 1,125 engines during the term of the agreement, but, in reality, engine production at Fili was never established before liquidation of the concession in 1927.

Under these circumstances the Soviet authorities welcomed the proposal made by Bayerische Motorenwerke AG (BMW) in late 1923 for organising the manufacture of that company's engines in the USSR. However, the bench testing of the BMW IV engine conducted at NAMI (*Naoochnyy avtomotornyy instiltoot* – Automobile & Engine Research Institute) in late 1924 revealed that its real output was a mere 230-240 hp instead of the promised 300 hp, and the interest for the proposal somewhat waned. Nevertheless, in April 1925 negotiations were begun with the BMW company with a view to granting a concession for the production of the BMW IIIa and BMW IV engines at the former Russkiy Reno factory (that is, the Russian branch of Renault) in Rybinsk. In September 1925 a group of Soviet aero-engine specialists headed by V. Ya. Klimov visited Munich to negotiate with BMW. Finally, in December 1925, the idea of concession with the company was abandoned, and discussions on acquiring a manufacturing licence were started (see below).

The BMW IVs were imported in small numbers and were installed in the Kalinin K-1, K-2 and K-3 prototype passenger aircraft. Under a special agreement the BMW company supplied to the USSR the BMW IIIa engines from the beginning of 1925 and, from May of that year, the BMW IVa. By the beginning of July 1925 the Soviets had received eighty-nine BMW IIIas and sixteen BMW IVas. The BMW IVa engines were installed in a small batch of R-II trainers (re-engined R-1 reconnaissance aircraft). The BMW IV also powered the Kalinin K-1 and K-2. The German engines, notably the BMW

The BMW VI engine, complete with BMW logos on the crankcase.

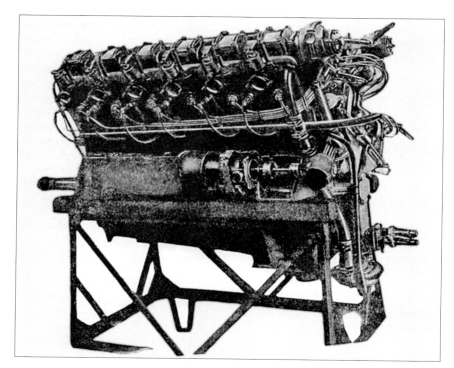

Above and right: The M-17, the Soviet licence-built version of the BMW VI.
Left: An M-17 undergoing bench testing.
Bottom: Transverse and longitudinal cross-sections of the M-17.

III, were mainly delivered to the Junkers concession factory at Fili. There was a Soviet type powered by the BMW IIIa – that was the 2U-B3 transition trainer which was tested in 1926 but not adopted for series production.

The situation became less acute when the Western powers lifted their economic blockade of the USSR in 1924. The Soviet industry started manufacturing under licence the 400-hp Ford Liberty engine as the M-5 and the 300-hp Hispano-Suiza 8Fb as the M-6. However, this could not be a long-term solution and the introduction of more modern and powerful engines was a

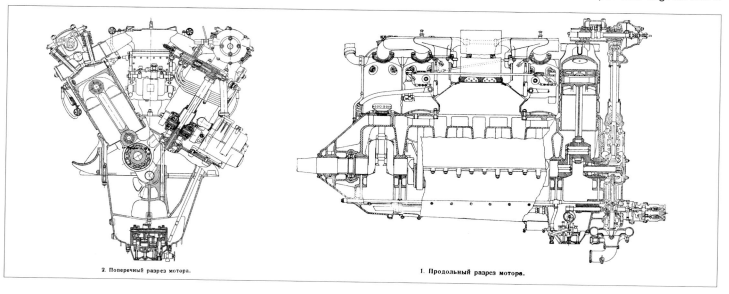

2. Поперечный разрез мотора.

1. Продольный разрез мотора.

prime concern. In late 1925 it was decided to enlist the assistance of leading aero-engine manufacturers from abroad. Contacts with various German aero engine companies led the Soviet side to give special attention to the offerings of the BMW company. The 600-hp BMW VI was of particular interest; this liquid-cooled Vee-12 engine was assessed as meeting the requirements of the Red Army Air Force with regard to both output and operational qualities. Two specimens of the new engine were ordered in Germany in 1925 and bench-tested by July 1926. The results were satisfactory, and negotiations with BMW were soon successfully concluded. On 14th October 1927 Aviatrest (to which the Soviet aircraft industry was subordinated) signed an agreement with BMW permitting the USSR to start licence manufacture of the BMW VI. Appropriate agreements were concluded with BMW's subcontractors supplying the engine's electric equipment and crankshaft.

The State Aviation Factory No. 26 in Rybinsk was chosen as the site for the licence manufacture of the German engine, which received the Soviet designation M-17; the production launch was achieved with the assistance of German engineers and workers. Preparations took more than two years; not until 1930 did the factory begin to turn out the M-17 in series. The number of engines produced rose from 165 in 1930 to 679 in 1931; the factory's output continued to grow. In the 1930s the M-17 became the most widely used Soviet aero engine – the production run of all M-17 versions totalled 27,534 units! Among the versions developed at Rybinsk was the boosted M-17F rated at 730 hp for take-off. The M-17 powered numerous types of Soviet aircraft. It was installed in the Polikarpov I-3 fighter, the Polikarpov R-5 and Tupolev R-6 reconnaissance aircraft, the Polikarpov TSh-2 and ShON ground attack aircraft, the Tupolev TB-1 and TB-3 bombers, the Beriyev MBR-2 flying boat, the Kalinin K-5, Putilov Stal'-3, Tupolev PS-9 and Laville PS-89 passenger aircraft and several other types. Some of these aircraft were also powered by imported BMW VI engines. There were also M-17 versions intended for use in tanks and for marine use.

In parallel with the licence production of the BMW VI, imported engines of this type were used in many Soviet prototype and production aircraft. The BMW VI was installed experimentally in a Tupolev R-3 (ANT-3), it powered the TB-1 (ANT-4) prototype, the R-6 (ANT-7) prototype, the Tupolev MDR-2 flying boat, the Polikarpov I-3 and D-2 (DI-2) prototype fighters, the R-5 prototype, the Polikarpov TB-2 bomber prototype, the Grigorovich MR-3 (MR-5) prototype fly-

ing boat, the Laville TOM-1 floatplane torpedo bomber, the I-7 fighter prototype, the Laville DI-3 fighter, the Tupolev TSh-1 and early series Polikarpov TSh-2 attack aircraft, the Chetverikov MDR-3 prototype flying boat, the TB-3 prototypes and early series aircraft, the early series MBR-2s. Some of these aircraft were powered by the more powerful BMW-VIZ version rated at 730 hp for take-off.

The M-17 served as a basis for the projecting of the more powerful M-34 engine designed by Aleksandr A. Mikulin, which was built in large numbers and powered many types of Soviet aircraft up to the early 1940s.

No other German engine repeated the success of the BMW VI in the USSR, but at least one type was purchased for evaluation. It was the 720-hp Junkers Jumo 4 diesel engine which featured two opposed pistons in each cylinder. Several examples of this engine were acquired from Junkers and bench-tested at the Central Aero Engine Institute (TsIAM – *Tsentrahl'nyy institoot aviatsionnovo motorostroyeniya*). In 1935 one Jumo 4 was installed in an R-5 reconnaissance aircraft which became a flying testbed designated ED-1; it was identifiable by its revised engine cowling contours and four-blade propeller. The rear cockpit was modified into two separate cockpits for two observers monitoring the behaviour of the engine. This aircraft performed nearly 200 flights, including a flight of 12 hours' duration. The engine was chosen for evaluation because of its low fuel consumption ensuring greater endurance and range. There were plans for acquiring a certain number of the Jumo 4 engine for installation in the military version of the Tupolev RD (ANT-25).

According to Shavrov, two Jumo 4 engines were installed in the RDs (presumably in the DB-1/ANT-36 military derivative of the RD). This assertion appears to be an error. In his book on Russian piston aero engines Vladimir Kotelnikov writes: *'It was planned to install a Jumo 4 in the record-breaking ANT-25 (RD), but successful development of the indigenous AN-1 diesel led to its use in the ANT-36 (RDD)'*. Indeed, in the summer of 1936 the AN-1 diesel (not the Jumo 4) was installed in a production example of the ANT-36.

Clandestine German flying school at Lipetsk

Soviet-German ties in the field of aviation and aircraft construction were not confined to co-operation with aircraft manufacturing companies. An important aspect of military co-operation between the two countries was the interaction of the Reichswehr and the Soviet military leaders; with regard to aviation matters it found its expression in the setting up of a clandestine German flying school in the USSR. The formal basis for this was provided by the secret agreement between the Red Army and the Reichswehr, which was concluded shortly after the signing of the Rapallo Treaty of 11th August 1922. This agreement permitted Germany to organise in the Soviet Union a number of centres for the testing of military hardware forbidden by the Versailles Treaty and for the training of German military personnel. The Soviet side was motivated by the desire to profit by German experience and know-how in the field of military technology.

The clandestine German flying school was set up at an airfield located at the north-western outskirts of Lipetsk, some 380 km

An aerial view of the flying school in Lipetsk where German airmen were clandestinely trained. The barracks are visible in the upper part of the photo.

Above: The flight line at Lipetsk with at least five Heinkel HD 17 biplanes.

(236 miles) south of Moscow. On 15th April representatives of the UVVS and of the German 'Special group' signed an agreement on the setting up of the school. The airfield was to be used jointly by German pilots and pilots of a Soviet air detachment. The Lipetsk aviation training centre was to provide train-

Above: D-2238, a Heinkel HD 45 operated by the flying school in Lipetsk.

Another Heinkel type operated by the school – the HD 46 parasol monoplane.

ing not only of the German flying personnel, but of Soviet pilots and aircraft technicians as well.

The first aircraft intended for the school were shipped from Germany via Leningrad in June 1925; these were Fokker D.XIII fighters. Fifty machines of this type were deliv-

ered to Lipetsk, according to some sources. At the same time the first German instructors and trainees arrived in the USSR – in utmost secrecy, of course. In addition to the Fokker D.XIIIs, the school had at its disposal several Albatros light trainers. The training of pilots for the German Luftwaffe was started on 15th July 1925. In 1926 the school widened the scope of its activities which came to comprise also the training of observers for reconnaissance aircraft and experimenting with aerial photography. The school's aircraft inventory was accordingly supplemented by eight Heinkel HD 17 two-seat reconnaissance aircraft, which were specially built for the Lipetsk school to an order from the Reichswehr. The school also operated several Junkers, Heinkel and Albatros trainers, as well as the Albatros L 76 and L 78 two-seat multi-purpose military aircraft built clandestinely for the Reichswehr. At the same time two Albatros L 69 trainers were sent back to Germany as obsolescent.

In the autumn of 1926 the Lipetsk school had at its disposal 52 aircraft, which comprised 34 Fokker D.XII and one Fokker D.VII fighters, eight Heinkel HD 17 reconnaissance aircraft and several Albatros trainers. These were supplemented by single examples of the Heinkel HD 21 and Junkers A 20 trainers and a single Junkers F 13 transport intended to cater for the needs of the school staff section.

The inventory of the school continued to grow. In late 1929 it comprised 43 Fokker D.XIIIs, two Fokker D.VIIs, six Heinkel HD 17s, six Albatros L 76s, six Albatros L 78s, one Heinkel HD 21, one Junkers A 20 and one Junkers F 13. In 1930 it was supplemented by single examples of the Heinkel HD 40, Junkers K 47, Dornier Merkur and Rohrbach Ro VIII Roland.

In addition to flying skills, the training programme of the school comprised

**German aircraft based at Lipetsk 1926-1933
(compiled by L. Andersson)**

Albatros L 69
Albatros L 76a
Albatros L 77v
Albatros L 78
BFW M 23c
Dornier B Merkur
Fokker D VII
Fokker D XIII
Heinkel HD 17
Heinkel HD 21
Heinkel HD 40 II
Junkers A 20
Junkers A 48 (K 47)
Junkers F13
Junkers W 33
Rohrbach Roland

Above: A Heinkel A 20 in landplane configuration operated by the Lipetsk school. The shape of the tail differs from the Soviet J 20 seaplanes.

Another aspect of the same A 20 ('9'). Note that the Junkers logo was carried on one side only and that a machine-gun has been installed in the rear cockpit.

**German aircraft types tested at Lipetsk
(compiled on the basis of information published by
L. Andersson and D. Sobolev)**

Albatros L 75d	trainer
Albatros L 76a	reconnaissance aircraft
Albatros L 78	reconnaissance aircraft
Albatros Al 84	two-seat fighter
Arado SD II	fighter
Arado SD III	fighter
Arado SSD I	fighter
Arado Ar 64	fighter
Arado Ar 65.	fighter
Dornier B Merkur	modified as bomber trainer
Dornier Do F/Do 11a	bomber
Dornier Do P	bomber
Dornier Do 10	two-seat fighter
Focke-Wulf A 40	reconnaissance aircraft
Focke-Wulf S 39	reconnaissance aircraft
Focke-Wulf W 7	two-seat reconnaissance aircraft
Heinkel HD 38a	single-seat fighter
Heinkel HD 45	reconnaissance aircraft
Heinkel HD 46	reconnaissance aircraft
Heinkel He 59a	multi-purpose twin-engined aircraft
Junkers A 35	modified as bomber trainer
Junkers G 24	emergency bombing aircraft
Junkers K 47	two-seat fighter
Rohrback Ro VIII	auxiliary bomber

weapons training in simulated aerial combat, as well as training in bombing techniques (something that was unthinkable in Germany controlled by the Allies). Yet another direction of joint effort of the Germans and the Soviet hosts at Lipetsk was experiments with the use of aircraft for chemical warfare. These experiments were conducted in 1926 and 1927 and included the use of the Albatros L 78 aircraft for testing various devices intended to disperse toxic substances. A Junkers A 20 and two Junkers F 13s also participated in such experiments in the Soviet Union during 1926 and 1927.

In the course of eight years while the Lipetsk flying school was in existence, 120 German fighter pilots received initial or advanced training there; furthermore, nearly 100 German observers were trained. The number of Soviet pilots and aircraft technicians trained there was more or less on a par with these figures.

Apart from the training of pilots, the Reichswehr activities at the Lipetsk school had another important aspect. In 1928 a special centre was set up at this flying school for the purpose of testing German military aircraft. From 1930 onwards this aspect, directly encouraged by the Soviet side, came to dominate the school's activities.

Between 1928 and 1931 nearly 20 types of German aircraft were tested at Lipetsk. These included the Arado SD II, Arado SD III, Arado SSD I, Arado Ar 64 and Ar 65 fighters, the Junkers K 47 two-seat fighter, the Dornier Do 10 two-seat fighter, the Heinkel HD 38 single-seat fighter, the Heinkel HD 45 and HD 46 and the Focke-Wulf S 39 and A 40 reconnaissance aircraft. The Arado SSD I was a floatplane which was temporarily fitted with a wheel undercarriage for the ferrying flight. A special seaplane station was set up in Lipetsk for the purpose of testing this machine, making use of a lake in the suburbs of the town. Some work was also conducted on multi-engined aircraft. It started with converting the three-engined Junkers G-24 and Rohrbach Ro VIII transports into bombers. These 'civil' aircraft were equipped with bomb racks, bomb sights and machine-guns in the workshops at Lipetsk. In 1929 the modified two-seat Junkers A 35 and the Dornier Merkur passenger aircraft were tested as bomber trainers. Somewhat later some 'real' bombers came to Lipetsk for operational testing. These included the twin-engined Dornier Do P, Do F and the Heinkel He 59 multi-purpose aircraft. Some of them failed to proceed beyond the prototype stage; others, such as the Ar 65, Do F and He 59, were adopted for service with the Luftwaffe (the name adopted for the German Air Force on 24th February 1932). The Soviet side tried to profit by these activities at Lipetsk for the purpose of gaining as much information as possible on the latest technical achievements of German aircraft designers. This goal was largely achieved, albeit suspicions were voiced that the German side was unwilling to share that kind of information to the full extent.

The German flying school at Lipetsk was closed down in the autumn of 1933. On the

Above: The German trainees of the Lipetsk school, 1928. Their last names are marked on the photo.

face of it, this could be ascribed to the deterioration in Soviet-German political relations after Hitler came to power. However, there is enough evidence indicating that the decision to close down the school was contemplated by the Reichswehr in 1932 and even as early as 1930 – ostensibly, on financial grounds. But it may be presumed that the main reason was the waning interest on the part of Reichswehr for this school due to the slackening of the restrictions on military activities on German territory. Germany was already in a position to train a sufficient number of pilots at home, as well as to conduct the development of military hardware.

On 15th August 1933 the Lipetsk air training centre was turned over to the Red Army Air Force. German aircraft based there were flown to Germany, with the exception of a number of obsolescent Fokker D.XIIIs (15 machines in one account, 'thirty or so' in another). At present the Lipetsk air base is an important training centre of the Russian Air Force.

Summing up, it can be presumed that the co-operation described above brought some positive results to both sides. In particular, it enabled the Soviet side to obtain, at least partially, acquaintance with new products of German aircraft design and get some insight into the German experience of aerial warfare. But it did not play any paramount role in the development either of the Luftwaffe or of the Red Army Air Force – basically, the two countries pursued the development of their military aviation independently of each other.

Soviet-German relations in the domain of aviation after 1933

Hitler's rise to power in Germany in January 1933 set off a marked worsening of political relations between the Soviet Union and Germany, which also had its detrimental effect on relations in other spheres. Economic relations between the two countries and the co-operation in military-industrial matters,

including aircraft construction, could not remain unaffected by these events. France and the USA replaced Germany in the role of the Soviet Union's main trade partners in the field of aircraft construction; in the following years up to 1939 this resulted in the acquisition of licences for the manufacture of a number of French and US aero engines and aircraft in the Soviet Union.

However, this turn of events was not due solely to Hitler's take-over. The relations between the Soviet Union and Germany had begun to cool even before 1933 on the background of the growing pro-Western orientation of Germany's policy. The slackening of restrictions imposed by the Versailles treaty enabled Germany gradually to start developing her military aviation at home, so that there no longer was a pressing need for Soviet assistance in these matters. The Soviet Union, for its part, also attained a position when it could confidently pursue its economic development basically on its own, with a minimum of help from outside.

It would be wrong to assume that all ties between the USSR and Germany in the field of aviation were severed after January 1933. On 10th May 1933 a group of high-ranking German officers headed by General von Bockelberg, responsible for the armament of the Reichswehr, came to Moscow at the invitation of Marshal M. N. Tukhachevskiy as a response to the latter's visit to Germany in 1932. During their visit to the USSR the Reichswehr officers visited a number of enterprises of the Soviet military industry, including TsAGI, aircraft factory No. 1 in Moscow and aero engine factory No. 29 in Zaporozhye. In 1934-35 negotiations took place on the purchase of two examples of the Heinkel He 70 high-speed mailplane and passenger aircraft. However, Hitler imposed a ban on this deal because this aircraft was regarded by RLM (the German National Ministry of Aviation) as a prototype for a prospective bomber. In 1936-37 prominent Soviet aviation specialists made business trips to Germany. These included aero engine designer Aleksandr A. Mikulin, chief of the Civil Air Fleet Chief Administration (GUGVF – **Glav**noye oopravl**en**iye grazh**dahn**skovo vozdooshnovo **flot**a) I. F. Tkachov, some specialists in aerodynamics from TsAGI and the Air Force Academy.

However, the trend was unmistakable – the close co-operation of the 1920s between the Reichswehr and the Red Army was a matter of the past. The civil war in Spain, which broke out in 1936, came to highlight, albeit indirectly, the fact that the air forces of the two countries could in due course of time become opponents – but more on this in the next chapter.

The German personnel of the school celebrates some festive occasion in the local casino.

Chapter 3

THE SPANISH CIVIL WAR AND WORLD WAR II

German Aircraft of 1936-1945 in the USSR

The Spanish Civil War (1936-1939)

In the second half of the 1930s, relations between the Soviet Union and Germany, as regards matters aeronautical, were largely confined to competition in the field of military air power, given the accelerated development of aircraft industry in the Third Reich, which had discarded all limitations imposed on military aircraft design and production by the Versailles Treaty. German aircraft manufacturers started producing new combat aircraft that were advanced enough to attract the attention of Soviet designers and Red Army Air Force commanders. Understandably, the latter were intent on acquiring examples of new German combat aircraft for the purpose of studying them. An opportunity for this arose when the civil war in Spain erupted.

The Spanish Civil War of 1936-39 was accompanied by the involvement of the Soviet Union backing the Republican Government, while National-Socialist Germany and Fascist Italy gave their support to the

Nationalist rebels led by Franco. The intervention of these opposing external forces found its expression, not least, in the participation of Soviet, German and Italian 'volunteer' pilots in the air war in Spain and in the supply of combat aircraft by these three countries to their respective Spanish protégés.

The Spanish Civil War became a proving ground for the combat aircraft developed by Soviet, German and Italian aircraft designers. The Soviet Union sent to Spain the Polikarpov I-15 biplane fighters and the latest Polikarpov I-16 monoplane fighters; these proved to be superior in speed to all their opponents, including the early models of the Messerschmitt Bf 109 fighter, during the initial phase of the conflict. However, during the final stages of the war they were confronted by the improved Bf 109E which outclassed the Polikarpov monoplane by a considerable margin.

It was during this military conflict that Soviet military specialists and aircraft

designers got their chance to study some of the German aircraft that took part in the air war in Spain. Several examples of German and Italian aircraft were captured by the Republican forces and were promptly shipped to the Soviet Union. In some cases the aircraft were severely damaged and could only be studied on the ground; in others cases the captured machines were in more or less serviceable condition and could eventually be test-flown and even pitted against Soviet types in mock combat. The captured aircraft included the Heinkel He 51B-1 and Messerschmitt Bf 109B-1 fighters; as for the bombers, the types acquired in Spain included the He 111B-1 and the Junkers Ju 52/3m.

The story of these captured machines is related below.

To sum up, the confrontation between the Soviet and German fighter aircraft during the Spanish Civil War, particularly during its final stages, revealed to the Soviet political and military leaders the painful fact of the

A large Soviet delegation visiting Heinkel Flugzeugwerke poses beside a He 111 coded H...+JA (W.Nr. 323); Ernst Heinkel himself is in the centre.

Above: Part of the Soviet delegation in Germany.

Achgelis helicopters (misidentified in some Russian sources as 'Focke-Wulf helicopters'), the Junkers Jumo 211 and Daimler-Benz DB 601 engines, Junkers diesel aero engines, numerous items of equipment and armament.

Between 25th October and 15th November 1939 a Soviet State Commission led by People's Commissar for Ferrous Metallurgy I. F. Tevosyan visited Germany. It examined a large number of industrial enterprises engaged in the manufacture of aircraft, aero engines, aviation equipment and armament. The delegation was shown a fairly large number of production (or allegedly series-produced) aircraft. These included the Heinkel He 100, Focke-Wulf Fw 187 and Fw 197, Messerschmitt Bf 109E and Bf 110 fighters, Junkers Ju 87, Ju 88, Heinkel He 111, Dornier Do 215 and Do 217 bombers, Blohm und Voss Bv 138 and Bv 141 flying boats, Henschel Hs 126 and Focke-Wulf Fw 189 reconnaissance aircraft, Heinkel He 115, Arado Ar 196 and Ar 198 reconnaissance floatplanes, Heinkel He 70 and He 116 passenger aircraft, the four-engined Fw 200 Condor transport, the Ar 79, Ar 96, Ar 199, Fw 44, Fw 58, Bücker Bü 181 and Bü 183 sports and training aircraft.

Commenting on the range of types shown, the leader of the 'aviation' part of the delegation, A. Goosev, said that the Germans were showing 'old stuff'. Albeit too categorical, this statement was true to some extent. According to an appraisal made by Russian aviation historian Aleksey Stepanov, eleven of the 17 combat types shown were not in squadron service or series production, or did not correspond to the declared mission type; only six types met these criteria. True, in the course of 1940 the figures were reversed; yet six of the types listed above never reached production and service.

Despite the outward friendliness and openness, the German side pursued its own ends, namely to misinform and intimidate the Soviet side with a show of German power while withholding information about the latest German aircraft, such as the Focke-Wulf Fw 190 fighter and the Heinkel He 176 and He 178 jet aircraft. At the same time the Germans actively promoted the He 100 – purportedly the most modern German fighter; in fact it was essentially an experimental aircraft that was not adopted for squadron service. Soviet specialists understood full well that the Germans had demonstrated some of the aircraft purely for the purpose of advertising and for exercising psychological pressure on the Soviet Union.

On 25th December Anastas I. Mikoyan, People's Commissar for Foreign Trade, submitted to K. Ritter, the head of a German economic delegation, the lists of orders made

Revival of co-operation with Germany (1939-1941)

As noted above, after 1933 Germany lost the status of the Soviet Union's main partner in the field of aircraft construction, ceding that role to France and the USA. Co-operation with Germany came virtually to a standstill. But the situation changed overnight in the late summer of 1939.

Relations between the Soviet Union and Germany entered a special phase after the signing of the Soviet-German Non-Aggression Pact (aka the Molotov-Ribbentrop Pact) on 23rd August of that year. This step undertaken by the Soviet government remains controversial to this day. The sudden

improvement of the political climate between the two countries had a direct impact on relations in other spheres. An agreement on trade and credits signed on 19th August 1939, in anticipation of the political treaty, marked a turning point in both economic and political relations. In exchange for the deliveries of Soviet raw materials to Germany the Soviet leaders obtained German consent to grant a credit amounting to 200 million Deutsche Marks and supply industrial equipment, non-ferrous metals and some specimens of aviation hardware to the Soviet Union.

As early as October 1939 the People's Commissariat of Defence drafted a 'shopping list' of German military hardware specimens to be purchased for evaluation. The aviation part of the list included the Messerschmitt Bf 109 and Heinkel He 112 fighters, the Dornier Do 215 and Heinkel He 118 bombers, various types of trainers, Focke

Soviet and German specialists together. As you see, the Soviet delegation included ladies.

by the Soviet side, including orders for aviation hardware.

On 11th February 1940 a Soviet-German economic agreement was signed in Moscow. It provided for exports of Soviet grain, oil and strategic raw materials to Germany in exchange for the deliveries of German industrial goods, including aircraft, to the Soviet Union.

In March 1940 a special Soviet commission charged with selecting and purchasing specimens of German military hardware was sent to Germany; it included a group of aviation specialists headed by Aleksandr S. Yakovlev, Deputy People's Commissar of Aircraft Industry. Among other things, the commission discussed with the German side a range of practical questions pertaining to the deliveries of German aircraft.

Under the terms of the agreement of 11 February the following aircraft were ordered:
• five He 100 fighters with surface evaporation cooling and five He 100s with traditional water cooling; only the five aircraft with evaporation cooling were delivered;
• five Messerschmitt Bf 109Es; all five machines of the E-3 subtype were delivered;
• five Messerschmitt Bf 110Cs; all delivered;
• two Junkers Ju 88 bombers; two A-1 models delivered;
• two Dornier Do 215 bombers; two B-1 models delivered;
• three Focke-Wulf Fw 58 trainers (B and C models); all delivered;
• Bücker Bü 131 Jungmann trainers; three Bü 131Ds delivered;
• Bücker Bü 133 Jungmeister trainers; three delivered.

Machines ordered but not delivered included a single Messerschmitt Me 209 record-breaking aircraft and two Focke-Achgelis Fa 266 helicopters.

In addition, the Soviet Union obtained two Fieseler Fi 156 Storch utility aircraft.

The aircraft listed above were supplemented in early 1941 by three Junkers Ju 52/3m transports and two Messerschmitt Bf 108 Taifun utility aircraft. All aircraft were purchased with a full complement of armament and equipment, including machineguns, cannon, bombs, gunsights and bombing sights, radio equipment.

The Research Institute of the Soviet Air Force (NII VVS – *Naoochno-issledovatel'skiy instit**oot** Voyenno-vozd**oo**shnykh seel*) was the main centre for the studying and testing of the German aircraft. The effort also involved the newly established Flight Research Institute (LII – **Lyot**no-is**sled**ovatel'skiy insti**toot**) formed on the basis of TsAGI' flight test department, TsAGI as such and the Bureau of New Technology (BNT – *Byuro **nov**oy **tekh**niki*) affiliated to TsAGI, as

well as the Central Aero Engine Institute (TsIAM – *Tsen**trahl**'nyy insti**toot** aviatsionnovo mot**or**ostro**yen**iya*) and other organisations. According to some estimates, the overall number of personnel in the Soviet aircraft industry involved in the study of German aircraft was in excess of 3,500 persons; it included specialists from three design bureaux, as well as pilots, engineers and technicians from the Red Army air units.

The German aircraft were test flown for the purpose of establishing their performance characteristics and for comparison with the new-generation Soviet aircraft. They were also thoroughly studied with a view to determining their technical advantages, as well as eventual vulnerabilities and deficiencies, in particular with regard to defensive armament and armour protection. Details in

the assessment of each type are described below. Generally speaking, the German aircraft received a high appraisal from the Soviet test pilots. That was in particular the case with the twin-engined aircraft (Bf 110, Do 215), which were found to have good controllability and fine handling qualities. Importantly, all German aircraft adopted for Luftwaffe service had a good stability margin; this enhanced flight safety and made the aircraft suitable for operation by pilots of less-than-average skill. In contrast, Soviet aircraft were very often inherently unstable (as was the case with the I-16) for the sake of greater manoeuvrability.

The study of the German aircraft also revealed that they were superior to Soviet aircraft as regards ease of maintenance and suitability for operation in field conditions.

Soviet aircraft industry representatives (the trio in the centre – left to right: V. K. Mikhin, Aleksandr S. Yakovlev and I. F. Petrov) examine s Dornier Do 215 during their visit to Germany in October 1939.

Above: Another scene from the same trip. The Soviet delegation examines a Heinkel He 100; test pilot Stepan P. Sooproon (centre) has just completed a flight.

Soviet specialists examine a Messerschmitt Bf 109E; I. F. Petrov is rightmost in this picture.

Lessons learned from the acquaintance with the German aircraft industry were discussed at several meetings held at NKAP between Soviet aircraft designers and representatives of the aircraft industry. At these meetings Nikolay N. Polikarpov and Aleksandr S. Yakovlev shared their impressions of the visits to Germany. Polikarpov, in particular, expressed the opinion that 'the German aircraft construction had made great progress and moved to the forefront of the world aircraft industry'. Highlighting the German achievements in the organisation of aeronautical research, design work and production process, they, by way of comparison, criticised the serious drawbacks and deficiencies that plagued the Soviet activities in these spheres. Yakovlev, in particular, was very eloquent in stressing the advantages and efficiency of the German approach to organising the work of design bureaux.

Many novel technical features found in German aircraft were introduced into the Soviet aircraft industry and incorporated in new models of Soviet aircraft. For example, self-sealing fibre fuel tanks were put into production instead of welded metal tanks; a two-stage centrifugal supercharger patterned on that fitted to the DB 601A engine was developed at TsIAM; the automatic dive recovery device of the Ju 88 was copied and later used on production Soviet dive bombers. Numerous minor improvements were also introduced, such as the tailwheel locking device for greater stability during the landing run, ejector exhaust stubs, easily detachable propeller spinners and others.

Most importantly, awareness of the need to bridge the technological gap with Germany caused the Soviet leaders to speed up the work on the development of new-generation combat aircraft, such as the Yak-1, MiG-1/MiG-3 and LaGG-1/LaGG-3 fighters that would be on a par with their German counterparts. Determined efforts were made to increase the tempo and volume of aircraft production and establish new production facilities for the manufacture of aircraft and aero engines.

Until recently, Russian historians were more or less unanimous in emphasising the positive effect of the study of German technology that spurred the activities of Soviet aircraft design bureaux and the improvement of production methods in the industry, as well as the preparations to meet the challenge from the Luftwaffe. However, some historians (notably Aleksey Stepanov) hold the opinion that these positive effects were, to a large extent, offset by the errors committed when evaluating German aircraft and especially the production potential of the German aircraft industry. Stepanov attaches special importance to the conclusions submitted by Deputy Chief of NII VVS I. F. Petrov who was a member of the Soviet Commissions visiting Germany in 1940 and in the spring of 1941. Petrov was personally tasked by Stalin with evaluating the production capacity of the German aircraft industry. On coming back from his visit to Germany in June 1940, to the dismay of Soviet political, military and industrial leaders, Petrov asserted that Germany was capable of producing three times as many aircraft per day as the Soviet Union, namely 70-80 aircraft versus 26 in the Soviet Union.

This assertion was erroneous; as it turned out later, at that moment the two countries were roughly on a par as regards the volume of aircraft production, but Petrov succeeded in convincing Stalin of the correctness of these calculations. The result was Stalin's directive requiring the aircraft industry urgently to double the output of aircraft. This, in the opinion of A. Stepanov, had a detrimental effect on the Soviet Union's preparations for war with Germany, which everybody considered to be imminent. Firstly, huge resources had to be spent on the construction of new aircraft factories; secondly, the growth of production increased the proportion of outdated types, such as the I-153 and I-16, in the Soviet Air Force inventory. This appraisal, however, is open to question. Nor was Petrov solely responsible for the misleading information, which also came from other sources. In the long run, the strenuous efforts directed at building up the aircraft industry's potential in terms of both quantity and quality did play their positive role in enhancing the country's defence potential.

The aircraft purchased in Germany in 1939-41 are described separately below.

The 'Baltic heritage' of 1940

In 1940 the three Baltic republics – Lithuania, Latvia and Estonia – were incorporated into the USSR in the rank of constituent republics (a status they retained until 1991 when they became independent states again).

Automatically, the materiel of these countries' air forces and air transport organisations was taken over by the appropriate Soviet authorities. It comprised a motley collection of imported and locally-designed aircraft, for the most part obsolete. These also included a handful of German-built aircraft: Junkers Ju 52/3ms and Henschel Hs 126s from Estonia, and Bücker Bü 131s from Lithuania. For details see the descriptions of individual types below.

War booty aircraft of the Great Patriotic War of 1941-1945

After the German invasion of the Soviet Union on 22nd June 1941 the question of studying the enemy's aircraft and gaining comprehensive information about their performance, their strengths and weaknesses became of paramount importance for the Soviet leaders and the Red Army command. This knowledge was a prerequisite for shaping the strategy and tactics of aerial warfare. Information gained through the testing of German aircraft purchased in 1940 was a valuable asset, but its value was of a passing nature since the German designers went on producing new, more advanced versions of these aircraft. Understandably, much importance was attached to capturing examples of the then-current versions of German combat aircraft for the purpose of testing them and drawing appropriate conclusions.

Despite the disastrous turn of events for the Red Army during the first months of the war, German aircraft began falling into the hands of Soviet forces from the very first days of the hostilities. In many cases the aircraft shot down by Soviet fighters or damaged by anti-aircraft artillery managed to force-land in Soviet-held territory; some of them suffered only minor damage and could be repaired and restored to airworthy condition. Such examples were evacuated from the front and delivered to NII VVS, which became the main centre for studying the captured aircraft (in addition to its main task – the development of new types of Soviet combat aircraft). Evaluation results were issued to the VVS command and were duly taken into account in the planning of operational activities and the development of air combat tactics.

Naturally, the testing of the captured enemy aircraft was not the only source of information about their performance and combat capabilities. Reports from Soviet airmen about the lessons learned in the course of aerial combat provided much valuable information for comparing the relative merits and deficiencies of Soviet and enemy aircraft and analysing the enemy's combat tactics. Yet the results obtained in studying captured aircraft were particularly valuable in assessing the technical aspect of the matter, even though the aircraft tested were sometimes well-worn and could not show the best of their performance. Information about the preponderance of the enemy aircraft over Soviet types served as an impetus for energetic efforts with a view to countering the disparity and ensuring an improvement in the performance of the Soviet aircraft. The study of the captured machines also provided the Soviet designers with the information on innovations in the German aircraft design which could be put to good use in improving the performance of Soviet combat aircraft.

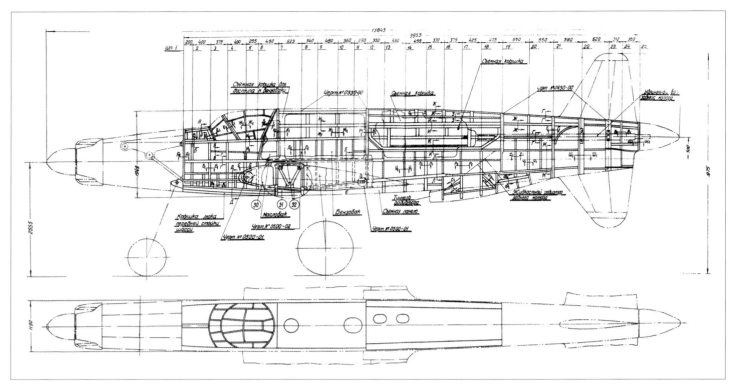

Above: A cutaway drawing of the Dornier Do 335A completed by Soviet specialists, with inscriptions and references to other drawings in Russian.

When the tide of the war was eventually turned and the German troops began to retreat under the onslaught of the Red Army, successful operations of Soviet troops were not infrequently accompanied by the capture of German airfields packed with assorted aircraft. Of course many of them were badly damaged, but there were also numerous cases when German aircraft fell into Soviet hands in airworthy condition. Such was the number of aircraft thus cap-

tured that some of them were pressed into service with the Soviet Air Force and (after the end of the war) with various Civil Aviation organisations. Single examples of German fighters and other combat aircraft were used by some VVS units for special operations. The types so used included the Messerschmitt Bf 109 and Bf 110, the Focke-Wulf Fw 190D, the Gotha Go 145 utility biplane, the Heinkel He 111, the Junkers Ju 88, the Ju 52/3m, the Dornier Do 24, the Fieseler

Fi 156, the Messerschmitt Bf 108, the Siebel Si 204 utility aircraft and others.

Listed below and described in some detail are the types of German aircraft obtained by the Soviet Union in various ways (captured, purchased or taken over) in the period between 1936 and 1945. They are divided into groups according to their basic roles: fighters, bombers, reconnaissance and attack aircraft, transport aircraft and assault gliders, general-purpose and training aircraft and helicopters, and arranged alphabetically within each group.

Fighters

Dornier Do 335A-1 and A-3 Pfeil single-seat fighter-bomber

At least one example of the unique Do 335 Pfeil (Arrow) push-pull fighter fell into the hands of Soviet troops during the last days of the war, together with many other types under development that were discovered at Oranienburg, Dallgow, Damgarten, Tempelhof and other places. It was found by two officers of the 812th IAP, Maj. Yegor Ye. Ankudinov and Capt. Aleksandr T. Tishchenko, while inspecting the premises of an aircraft factory at Oranienburg in April 1945. In their report they stated that they had found an aircraft *'of unusual appearance with propellers fore and aft and with antennas on the wings'*. It is presumably this machine that was despatched to the Soviet Union and delivered to BNT, a subdivision of TsAGI, where it was duly examined by spe-

This Focke-Wulf Fw 190A captured intact was displayed at one of the war booty exhibitions during the war (note the Sd.Kfz. 251 armoured personnel carrier in the background).

cialists. There is no evidence to indicate it was flight-tested. The aircraft in question was the Do 335A-3, which lacked armament.

The results of this examination, together with the captured technical drawings, formed the basis for a technical description of the Dornier Do 335A-1 and A-3 prepared by BNT in 1947 for distribution to Soviet design bureaux and research institutions. Summing up the description, its authors drew attention to the following special features of the aircraft: the unique design of the box-type wing spar; the ejection seat design incorporating a safety feature (ejection was impossible when the canopy was closed); the unusual tail unit design with vertical tail surfaces jettisonable with the help of explosive bolts in the event of an ejection or a belly landing. As for the fighter's overall concept, advanced as it was for a piston-engined machine, the advent of the jet age obviously made it devoid of any special value.

The Do 335 could still be seen in the hangar of BNT TsAGI in Moscow until the early 1950s, in company with the Me 163, Me 262, He 162 and He 100 fighters.

Focke-Wulf Fw 190 single-seat fighter and fighter-bomber (A-series)

The Fw 190 was not among the German aircraft purchased in 1940; in fact, the Germans treated this fighter, still under test at that time, as secret and declined to show it to Soviet specialists. Thus, the first acquaintance with this fighter was gained by Soviet pilots the hard way when they encountered it in combat during the war.

The wide-scale use of the Fw 190 on the Soviet-German front began in the autumn of 1942. Naturally, every possibility was used to obtain some knowledge of this aircraft.

On 16th January 1943 *Unteroffizier* Helmut Brandt of I./JG 54 'Grünherz' shot off the propeller blades of his Fw 190A-4 '2 Black' (W.Nr. 142310) due to a synchroniser malfunction during a dogfight and made a belly landing on the ice of Lake Ladoga. The fighter was urgently recovered by Soviet forces and transported to the rear and then transferred for testing to NII VVS. Eng.-Capt. P. S. Onopriyenko was appointed engineer in charge of the testing of this machine.

According to some reports, the damaged propeller was replaced by an airscrew from a Junkers Ju 87 at the 1st Repair Depot in Leningrad prior to transfer to NII VVS.

Top right: Focke-Wulf Fw 190A-4 '2 Black' (W. Nr. 142310) of I./JG 54 force-landed on the frozen Lake Ladoga on 16th January 1943 and was captured. Here it is seen after recovery.

Above right, centre right and right: The same machine following repairs; note that the yellow areas on the undersides have been overpainted. The aircraft was tested at NII VVS in this guise.

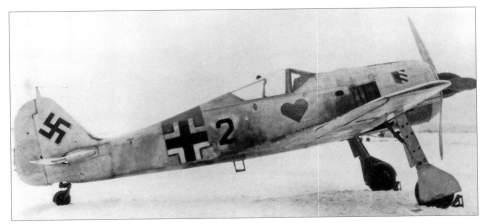

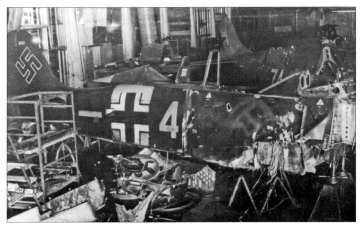

Above left: Fw 190A-4 W.Nr. 142310 undergoing repairs. Note the propeller blades shot off by the inboard wing cannons.
Above right: Another Fw 190A coded '4 Yellow' (W.Nr. 1185) undergoing repairs, with a Soviet Air Force Curtiss P-40C Kittyhawk in the background.

This particular machine was subjected to a lengthy and thorough study. Maj. Yuriy A. Antipov made 37 flights in it in late June 1943. These flights, in addition to determining the aircraft's performance, provided the data on engine acceleration capacity, manoeuvrability at different altitudes and operational reliability of various equipment. Antipov recorded a maximum speed of 610 km/h (379 mph) at 6,000 m (19,680 ft). He and other pilots who had flown the aircraft were dissatisfied with its speed and rate of climb, considering the Soviet Yak-9 and La-5 fighters to be superior in performance at altitudes up to 6,000 m.

On the other hand, they recognised that the Fw 190 had some indisputable advantages. Antipov found the German fighter's automatic engine control, superior equipment and structural strength especially commendable. He and his colleagues noted also the excellent all-round view from the cockpit with no distortion of objects within the field of view, good lateral controllability throughout the speed envelope and automatic switching of supercharger speeds during combat. The Fw 190 had very potent

Four stills from a cine film prepared by NII VVS showing a Fw 190A undergoing tests at the institute. The film was intended for training Soviet fighter pilots ('know your enemy'), hence the Luftwaffe marking reapplied rather crudely by hand (note the absence of individual identification numbers or unit insignia).

More stills from the same film.
Left: NII VVS technicians turn over the BMW 801 engine of the Fw 190A before a flight.

Above: The moment of engine start-up.

Above, right and above right: The aircraft takes off from Chkalovskaya AB. Note the 'green heart' emblem of JG 54 'Grünherz' beneath the cockpit and the traces of a unit badge on the engine cowling suggesting this is the same Fw 190A-4 W.Nr. 142310 as depicted on the preceding pages.

Above and right: The moment of landing gear retraction. Note the excessively large and lop-sided hand-painted swastika on the tail.

Above: Close-up of the engine cowling and propeller of the Fw 190A-4 tested at NII VVS.

Above right: This photo from the NII VVS materials has the parts of the cowling (fixed and detachable panels, tension locks, efflux gills etc.) marked on it.

Detail views of the Fw 190A-4 from the NII VVS report.

Upper row, left to right: The front end of the engine cowling, the 12-bladed engine cooling fan driven by reduction gear and the VDM variable-pitch propeller; the instrument panel; and the windshield with the Revi C/12D reflector gunsight behind it.

Centre row, left to right: The upper cowling panel with recesses for the barrels of the two fuselage-mounted 7.9-mm MG 17 machine-guns; the toggle latches of the lateral cowling panels; and the rear cowling panel opened to expose the breeches of the MG 17 machine-guns.

Lower row, left to right: The starboard wing root with the starboard 20-mm MG 151 synchronised cannon above the mainwheel well; the muzzle of the starboard 20-mm MG FF cannon; and the port wing cannons.

armament comprising a quartet of 20-mm (.78 calibre) cannons and a pair of synchronised machine-guns of the normal calibre; a 4.93-kg (10.86-lb) weight of fire was recorded by Antipov. The aircraft was stable in a dive, built up speed quickly, briskly performed half-rolls, easily banked first to one side and then to the other. Yet, the test pilots found the Fw 190 to be more difficult in handling than the Soviet Yakovlev and Lavochkin fighters.

Soviet specialists took note of many special features in the fighter's design. For example, the single engine control lever controlling both engine rpm and propeller pitch indisputably made piloting easier,

The machine-gun ammunition box.

ensuring faultless and fuel-efficient adjustment of the engine. Of much interest were such features as the engine cowling design incorporating an armoured front ring that provided space for the oil tank and oil cooler; scavenging the oil from the engine directly into the oil tank; and enforced cooling of the engine by means of a multi-bladed fan. Soviet designers, first and foremost Semyon A. Lavochkin who specialised in designing fighters with air-cooled engines, had an opportunity to evaluate these ideas and incorporate them to some extent in the subsequent versions of their aircraft.

Soviet specialists rated very highly the Fw 190's emergency cockpit canopy jettisoning system incorporating a pyrotechnical cartridge; it was considered to be superior to the systems used on the Bf 109 and the Curtiss P-40 Kittyhawk. Influenced by the study of the German achievements in this field, the Yakovlev OKB introduced a canopy jettisoning mechanism on the prototypes of the Yak-3 fighter in September 1943.

Useful knowledge was gained by studying the cockpit of the Fw 190, which boasted high-quality glazing that did not distort the view; the good ventilation ensuring high comfort for the pilot also earned praise (as

distinct from the La-5 with its inadequately ventilated and overheated cockpit).

In 1944 Fw 190A-4 WNr 142310 was displayed at the comparative exhibition of foreign and Soviet aircraft at BNT TsAGI.

Another example, Fw 190A-4 W.Nr. 2362, belonging to IV./JG 51, was test-flown at LII by many test pilots, including Mark L. Gallai and Aleksey N. Grinchik. They were critical – maybe, somewhat too critical – in their assessment of the fighter. The pilots considered the Soviet fighters to be more pleasant in handling; they found the cockpit of the Fw 190 to be too cramped, entailing excessive pilot fatigue in a long flight. On the plus side, they noted the simple landing procedure and the automatic tailwheel castoring lock connected to the elevator control. The latter feature attracted the attention of Soviet designers; a similar device was introduced by Aleksandr S. Yakovlev on his Yak-1M (the prototype of the future Yak-3) built in early 1943 and was incorporated in later production machines, drawing much positive comment from service pilots.

An Fw 190A-4/U3 coded '6 Black' (ex TH+ST?; W.Nr. 2367), also belonging to IV/JG 51, was also captured and tested at LII. Unlike '2 Black', which was in winter

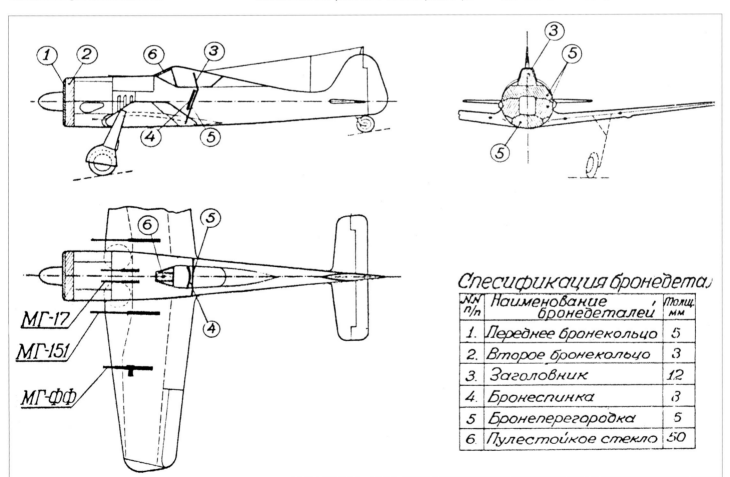

№ п/п	Наименование бронедеталей	Толщ. мм
1.	Переднее бронекольцо	5
2.	Второе бронекольцо	3
3.	Заголовник	12
4.	Бронеспинка	3
5	Бронеперегородка	5
6.	Пулестойкое стекло	50

Above: A Soviet diagram of the Fw 190A's armour protection (1. Forward armour ring, 2. Second armour ring, 3. Headrest, 4. Armoured seat back, 5. Armoured bulkhead, 6. Bulletproof windscreen), with the thickness in millimetres given in the table.

Above: Fw 190A-4 W.Nr. 142310 on the NII VVS hardstand (note the characteristic hexagonal pavement slabs of Chkalovskaya AB) with Soviet insignia applied in the course of the evaluation. The red stars are of the early type with no red/white outline.

Below: An upper view of the same aircraft. This example carried Soviet insignia on the tail and the wing underside only.

camouflage at the moment of capture, this aircraft was in standard summer mottle camouflage.

A book on German aircraft prepared in 1943 by NII VVS specialists cited the following performance for the Fw 190A-4, presumably on the basis of the testing conducted at that institute:

Focke-Wulf Fw 190A-4 performance

All-up weight, kg (lb)	3,989 (8,796)
Empty weight, kg (lb)	3,273 (7,217)
Engine power at take-off rating, hp	1,580
Maximum speed, km/h (mph):	
at sea level	510 (317)
at 4,000 m (13,120 ft)	565 (351)
at 6,000 m (19,685 ft)	610 (379)
at 9,000 m (29,530 ft)	581 (361)
Time to height, minutes:	
to 3,000 m (9,840 ft)	3.8 min
to 5,000 m (16,400 ft)	6.8 min
to 7,000 m (22,965 ft)	10.2 min
Service ceiling, m (ft)	10,500 (34,440)
Time to service ceiling, minutes	32
Range at 0.9 of max speed, km (miles)	552 (343)
Range in optimum conditions (at 395 km/h; 245 mph)	983 (611)

Interestingly, an Fw 190A-4 tested in Great Britain attained a speed of 643 km/h (400 mph) at 5,640 m (17,910 ft). The higher performance of the 'British' example may be due to the fact that the Fw 190A-4 was tested at NII VVS at nominal engine rating only, without using the MW-50 water/methanol injection system that had been introduced on that model for a brief engine boost.

In the overall assessment the Soviet specialists noted such advantages as the potent armament comprising four 20-mm cannons, the armour plating of the oil and fuel tanks, the use of an air-cooled engine (less vulnerable to combat damage) as distinct from the water-cooled one on the Bf 109, the rational design of the powerplant as a single package incorporating the engine with all its accessories, and a wide use of automation of control reducing the pilot workload. It was particularly noted that the pilot had to use only the throttle which was linked to a central engine control unit comprising the propeller pitch governor, automatic supercharger control, automatic fuel-air mixture

Top right: This front view shows well the Fw 190's wide wheel track.

Centre right: Three-quarters front view of Fw 190A-4 W.Nr. 142310 at NII VVS.

Above right: Three-quarters rear view, showing the cooling air efflux/engine exhaust gills.

Right: Rear view of the same aircraft.

Above and left: Two more views of Fw 190A-4 W.Nr. 142310 at NII VVS, this time on a grass airstrip. Note the well-weathered appearance of the aircraft and the wire aerial of the FuG 7a and FuG 25a radios.

control and automatic switching of supercharger speeds. It was stressed that the complete automation of engine control and armament functioning considerably eased the pilot workload in combat. Other positive features included light aileron control.

At the same time the Fw 190A-4 was considered overweight, its vertical manoeuvrability was found to be inadequate and horizontal manoeuvrability to be inferior to that of the best fighters. The Fw 190A-4 was considered inferior to the Bf 109G-2 as regards vertical speed and combat turns. Likewise, its speed was also found to be inferior to that of the Bf 109G-2 at all altitudes except at sea level. High elevator stick forces were also noted during aerobatic manoeuvres.

Further subtypes of the Fw 190 tested at NII VVS were the A-5 and A-8 models.

Fw 190A-5 W.Nr. 1154 captured in July 1943 was delivered to NII VVS for testing. This model featured additional armour plating (16 additional plates with a weight totalling 200 kg/440 lb were mounted on the

Left: These two Fw 190As discovered by Soviet troops at a German airfield have unusually bulbous propeller spinners and lack individual insignia, which suggests they might be decoys.

lower parts of the wing centre section and of the engine cowling). Two of the wing cannons were deleted. The testing revealed some improvement in performance. The aircraft attained a speed of 582 km/h (362 mph) at an altitude of 5,000 m (16,400 ft) and climbed to this altitude within 12 min. The actual performance must have been higher, since the machine under test suffered some malfunctions of the automatic adjustment of the fuel/air mixture. The Fw 190A-5 was deemed to represent a danger both for ground troops and for the Il'yushin IL-2 attack aircraft. Tests of this machine at NII VVS provided the basis for appropriate recommendations to AA units.

Two examples of the Fw 190A-8 (W.Nr. 682011 and W.Nr. 580967) underwent testing at NII VVS. The former aircraft had an ETC 501 bomb rack under the fuselage and was fitted with two 30-mm (1.18 calibre) cannons in the wings. It is presumably this machine that one source refers to as the cannon-equipped Fw 190A-8/R6 equipped with MK-108 cannons. This version had an impressive 9.74-kg (21.47-lb) weight of fire but was considered primarily intended for ground-attack and thus no match for the new Soviet dogfighters.

Tests revealed that this aircraft posed a serious danger to ground troops and attack aircraft of the Red Army. The activities of NII VVS were directed, among other things, at evolving the tactical methods of combating the Fw 190s used in the role of attack aircraft. The most modern fighters of the VVS – the Yak-3, Yak-9U and La-7 – flew test missions to intercept the two captured German machines.

The other Fw 190A-8 (W.Nr. 580967) is described in some sources as a 'lightweight' version, which had a fuel load of only 3,939 kg (8,685 lb) and an armament of two heavy machine-guns and two 20-mm Mauser cannons giving a 3.44-kg (7.58-lb) weight of fire. A maximum speed of 542 km/h (337 mph) at sea level and 642 km/h (399 mph) at 6,500 m (21,325 ft) was recorded. The climb time to 5,000 m (16,400 ft) was 5.4 minutes with a take-off weight of 3,986 kg (8,789 lb). Several mock combat sessions were staged at NII VVS in which the Fw 190A-8 was flown by many of the test centre's pilots. They were unanimous in the opinion that the German fighter could no longer claim superiority over its Soviet opponents.

Top right: Fw 190A-4/U3 '6 Black' (W.Nr. 2367) of IV/JG 51 undergoing tests at LII. Note the manufacturer's test code (TH+ST?) still carried on the wing underside and the yellow-painted undersides of the wingtips and engine cowling.

Centre, above and right: More views of '6 Black' in front of a hangar at LII. Note the low-visibility *Balkenkreuze* and the generally weathered finish.

Above: Fw 190A-8 W.Nr. 580967 undergoing tests at NII VVS in the winter of 1943-44. The aircraft represented the 'lightweight' version armed with two 20-mm Mauser cannons and two machine-guns.

Above: The aircraft was painted in two shades of grey. Note the late-style outlined Soviet insignia.

Three-quarters rear view of the same machine. Again, the stars were not applied to the wing upper surface.

Yuriy A. Antipov was the project test pilot at NII VVS for the Fw 190A-8, Fw 190A-4 and Fw-190A-5 versions. In one of the test flights his Fw 190A-8 entered a 'stubborn' spin from which Antipov could only recover at tree-top level. Other test pilots flying the Focke-Wulf fighter included Vasiliy Ye. Golofastov of NII VVS and LII test pilots Viktor L. Rastorgooyev, Aleksey N. Grinchik and Mark L. Gallai.

Various examples of the Fw 190 captured by Soviet forces are mentioned in liter-ature without indicating the subtype or iden-tity of the aircraft. For example, three exam-ples captured in 1943 included a machine acquired after a forced landing in the winter of 1943 at the North-Western Front, which was covered by the 6th Air Army com-manded by Maj.-Gen. Fyodor P. Poloonin. It was tested on site by an inspector of the VVS Headquarters, Col. N. G. Seleznev who arrived from Moscow for the purpose. Another Fw 190 was captured intact on the Southern Front in the summer of 1943 by Lt.

Semeyko of the 814th IAP, who, together with other pilots of his unit, forced the Ger-man fighter to land at a Soviet base. Yet another Fw 190 was flown to a Soviet AF base near Leningrad by fighter pilot Gustav Heuler who deserted to the Soviets in Sep-tember 1943. Of these three machines, the one tested by Seleznev was later ferried to Moscow and may well be one of the above-mentioned Fw 190s tested at NII VVS.

Focke-Wulf Fw 190D-9 fighter

Another version encountered by the Soviet forces during the closing stage of the war was the Fw 190D-9 (dubbed 'long-nosed Dora'). On this model the BMW 801D radial was replaced by a Junkers Jumo 213A 12-cylinder inverted-Vee liquid-cooled engine driving a VDM VS-111 variable-pitch wooden propeller. The resulting improve-ment of the powerplant's aerodynamics (the slimmer nose) and the greater engine power gave the new machine a speed and rate of climb superior to those of the Fw 190A.

An example of this model was delivered for testing to NII VVS after the end of hostili-ties. The Fw 190D-9 was tested at NII VVS at Chkalovskaya AB between 11th and 25th May 1945. During the State tests V. O. Mel'nikov acted as project engineer, with V. Ye. Golofastov as test pilot. The air-craft was also flown by A. G. Kochetkov, A. G. Proshakov, V. I. Khomyakov, L. M. Kuvshinov and V. G. Masich. The NII VVS test pilots stated in their reports:

'The Fw 190D-9 aircraft powered by the Jumo 213A liquid-cooled engine is inferior in its performance to Soviet fighters: the Yak-9U powered by the VK-107A engine, the Yak-3 powered by the VK-105PF-2 engine and the La-7 powered by the ASh-82FN engine.

Replacement of the air-cooled BMW 801 with the Jumo 213A liquid-cooled engine has resulted in an insignificant increase in the air-craft's maximum level flight speeds.'

To illustrate this appraisal, here are some comparative performance figures for the types mentioned. The maximum speed of the Fw 190D-9 at 5,000 m (16,400 ft) as recorded at NII VVS was 608 km/h (378 mph) without boost and 624 km/h (388 mph) with boost. The speeds attained at the same altitude by Soviet fighters were as follows: 672 km/h (418 mph) for the Yak-9U, 637 km/h (396 mph) for the Yak-3 and 634 km/h (394 mph) for the La-7.

In the opinion of leading specialists at NII VVS, the modified Fw 190D-9 W.Nr. 210251 could not wage combat on equal terms at low and medium altitudes against the Soviet Yak-3s, Yak-9Us and La-7s. The Focke-Wulf proved to be inferior to them in speed by at least 24 km/h (15 mph) at sea level and by more than 10 km/h (6.2 mph) at 5,000 m. A

Fw 190A-8/R6 W.Nr. 682011 under test at NII VVS in the winter of 1943-44. This view shows the ETC 501 centreline rack permitting carriage of an SC 500 bomb; the rack was mounted on a fairing to permit normal main gear retraction.

comparison of the horizontal and vertical manoeuvrability was not in favour of the German fighter either.

The Fw 190D-9 fighter participated in a mock combat session with the La-7, in which the Soviet machine displayed its complete supremacy. NII VVS test pilots Eng.-Col. A. G. Kochetkov, Lt. Col. A. G. Proshakov, Lt. Col. V. I. Khomyakov and Maj. V. Ye. Golofastov came to the conclusion that the new German fighter was no more a match for the La-7 than its predecessor, the Fw 190A-8. Entering the engagement head-on, the Soviet fighter succeeded in getting on the tail of the German machine after the third full

Above: This Fw 190D-9 (W.Nr. ...133) shared the flight line with three Fw 190F-8s when the airfield was overrun by the advancing Red Army (the location is unknown). Note the differently styled *Balkenkreuze* on individual aircraft.

Several captured Fw 190D-9s were pressed into service by the Soviet Navy/Baltic Fleet Air Arm. These machines were photographed at Marienburg in 1945. The nearest aircraft is W.Nr. 2...85 (the c/n is partly obscured by the star insignia). Surprisingly, none of the aircraft carries identification numbers....

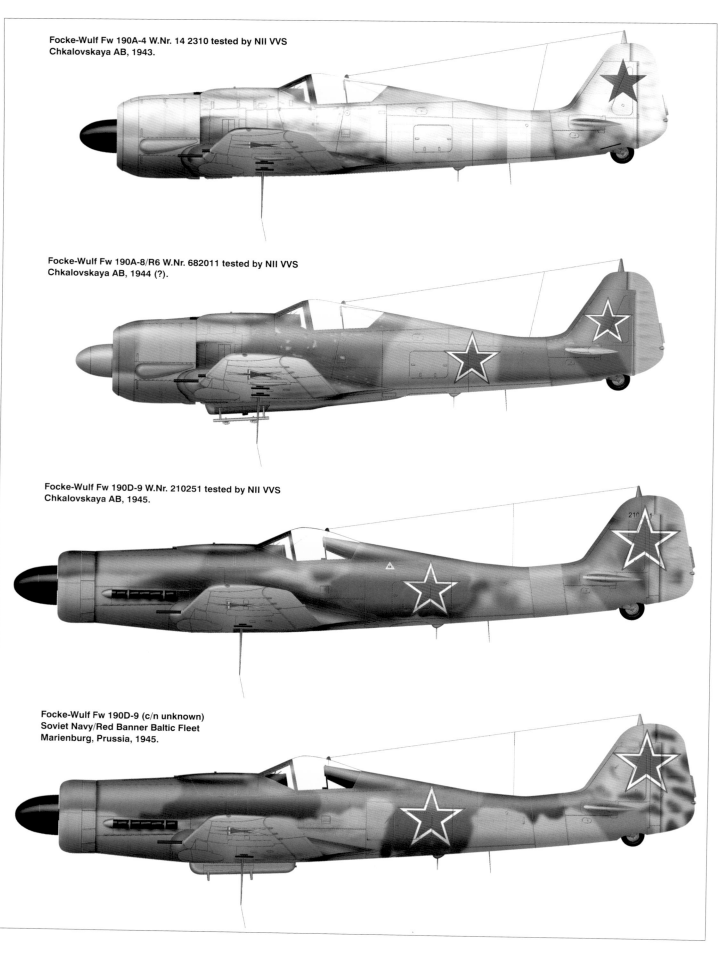

Focke-Wulf Fw 190A-4 W.Nr. 14 2310 tested by NII VVS
Chkalovskaya AB, 1943.

Focke-Wulf Fw 190A-8/R6 W.Nr. 682011 tested by NII VVS
Chkalovskaya AB, 1944 (?).

Focke-Wulf Fw 190D-9 W.Nr. 210251 tested by NII VVS
Chkalovskaya AB, 1945.

Focke-Wulf Fw 190D-9 (c/n unknown)
Soviet Navy/Red Banner Baltic Fleet
Marienburg, Prussia, 1945.

banking turn or after the second combat turn.

In fairness, it has to be mentioned that the Fw 190D-9's specifications, as cited by William Green in his book *Warplanes of the Third Reich* included a maximum speed of 426 mph at 21,650 ft (685 km/h at 6,600 m), while the maximum speed of the production La-7 was 658 km/h (409 mph) at 5,900 m (19,350 ft). It is possible that the Fw 190D-9 had failed to show its best performance at NII VVS because Soviet test pilots did not make use of the engine's contingency rating with injection of the water-methanol mixture.

The 'long-nosed Dora' also took part in the tactical evaluation of Tupolev's then-latest high-speed long-range bomber, the SDB (alias 'aircraft 63'). This machine was an adaptation of the prototype 'aircraft 103' (Tu-2) to accept Mikulin AM-39 liquid-cooled Vee-12 engines; it used many units and assemblies of the production Tu-2 bomber. It turned out that the Fw 109D-9 could attack the '63' bomber only from behind at small angles of fire because it had only a slight advantage in speed at altitudes of 6,000-8,000 m (19,680-26,240 ft).

Irrespective of the performance comparison, many technical features of the Fw 190 proved to be of value for Soviet specialists. Particularly interesting for the Soviet aircraft industry was the rational layout of the engine units and powerplant equipment, the high maximum admissible oil temperature on entry into the engine (130°C/266°F), the efficient design of the automatic device adjusting the coolant temperature, and the wide-chord wooden propeller blades of high efficiency. It was also noted that in the course of the tests conducted between 11th and 26th May 1945 all the units of the German fighter's special equipment functioned flawlessly. Much useful information was gained by studying the special unit of the FuG-16ZY radio that enabled the pilot to use the receiver of this radio in the radio navigation system.

The well-developed weapon control system was supplemented by the high quality of the bulletproof windscreen and by the efficient gunsight. As distinct from some Soviet machines fitted with a potent complement of weapons, simultaneous firing of all guns did not cause the sighting to be lost, and the recoil of the weapons was almost unnoticeable for the pilot. Cannons and machine-guns could be fired separately. Wide use of electrically actuated equipment items simplified the pilot's work.

The Fw 190D-9 was the only type among the captured German fighters to be adopted for service in the Soviet Air Force, albeit in small numbers. In the spring of 1945 a batch of factory-fresh Fw 190D-9s was captured at

Four views of Fw 190D-9 W.Nr 210251 that underwent evaluation at NII VVS in 1945.

Above: The spoils of war. Apart from a Junkers Ju 87D in the background, Fw 190A '17 Red' (W.Nr. 920415) is virtually the only intact Luftwaffe aircraft at this German airfield littered with wrecks (mostly of Fw 190s). The airfield has been overrun by the Red Army (note the two Yakovlev Yak-3 fighters).

Marienburg in East Prussia (now Malbork, Poland). These machines were taken over by a Fighter Aviation Regiment of the Red Banner Baltic Fleet Air Arm, as evidenced by

several pictures showing these aircraft in Soviet markings. According to another source, two fighter regiments of the Red Banner Baltic Fleet operated the type in

1945-46. Unfortunately, no details of their operational service are available.

It might be added as a postscript that four examples of the Fw 190 (subtypes unknown) were obtained by the Soviet Union from Sweden in the autumn of 1945. These were W.Nr. 739137 of I./JG 54, W.Nr. 682790 of 5./JG 54, W.Nr. 931484 and W.Nr. 584205 of III./SG 3 that had escaped to Sweden on 8th May 1945 but were 'extradited' to the USSR on 8th November of the same year. Their subsequent fate is unknown.

Heinkel He 51B-1 single-seat fighter
This biplane fighter, first flown in 1933, was operated in Spain in some numbers by the Legion Condor and the Nationalist air force. Initially it had some success in aerial combat but proved clearly inferior to the Polikarpov I-15 fighters which made their appearance in Spain. An example of the He 51B-1 was captured by the Republican side near Navalmoral on 24th February 1937, reportedly in damaged condition, and was sent to the Soviet Union for evaluation. In the USSR it was promptly delivered to NII VVS where it was given the 'disguise' designation of I-25.

The machine was returned to airworthy condition and then flight-tested by Pyotr M Stefanovskiy who conducted several mock dogfights against Soviet fighters, including the I-15. Stefanovskiy wrote in his evaluation report: *'The I-25 aircraft, despite its modest speed (515 km/h [319 mph]), can conduct active defensive combat against the M-25-powered I-16 fighters, the DI-6 and DI-6Sh fighters* (the latter two types were two-seaters, the Sh being an attack version – Auth.) *and gain success in the case of a sur-*

Above: The Baltic Fleet Fw 190D-9 flight line at Marienburg. The tail of the second aircraft in the row has been jacked up.

The same flight line from a different angle, with a Soviet Air Force Lisunov Li-2 or Douglas C-47 in the background. The light-coloured canopy on the nearest aircraft may be a replacement item.

This Heinkel He 51B-1 captured in Spain in 1937 was tested at NII VVS as the 'I-25'. The aircraft appears to be finished in silver dope and light grey. The top right picture shows the open cover of the radio bay.

prise attack against the SB, DB-3 and R-9 air-craft (bombers and reconnaissance aircraft – Auth.), but the I-25 cannot retain initiative during air combat. In a dogfight between the I-16 and the I-25 all the advantages are on the side of the former.' Thus, the He 51 was not considered to be a serious opponent by the Soviet pilots and specialists, unlike the more advanced Messerschmitt Bf 109 (see below).

A Russian publication asserts that two He 51 fighters were captured in Spain and sent to the USSR where they were tested at NII VVS; the version is identified as the He 51A. The latter is presumably an error (William Green makes no mention of the He 51A in Spain; *Flieger Revue* 6-1976 states that the Nationalists received 135 He 51B-1 fighters and 79 He 51C-1s from Germany, no He 51As being present in the comprehensive list of deliveries), while the mention of two aircraft needs confirmation.

Heinkel He 100 fighter

When the Soviet delegation was negotiating the purchase of German combat aircraft in early 1940, the Germans actively promoted the He 100, which they claimed to be the ulti-

Top left: One of the Heinkel He 100 fighters delivered to the Soviet Union is seen here parked at LII with the cockpit and engine under wraps.

Above left and left: The He 100 V6 undergoing tests at NII VVS in 1940. Note the ventral excess steam condenser of the engine cooling system.

Below: This view shows the alcohol vapour condenser in the upper rear fuselage serving the oil cooling system.

Top right/far right: The cockpit of the He 100.

Centre right: The He 100's two-section flaps.

Right: More alcohol vapour condensers were built into the wing and tail surface leading edges.

Far right: The cockpit canopy of the He 100.

Far right, bottom: A cutaway drawing of the rear fuselage structure.

Above: The cockpit of the Bf 109B-1 during initial tests in Spain (note the Republican Air Force red fuselage band) The absence of a rear armour plate on the canopy of the B version is clearly visible.
Above left: The engine cowling and distinctive chin-mounted water radiator of the Bf 109B.
Left: The Bf 109B's Junkers Jumo 210D engine with the cowling and propeller removed, showing the welded steel-tube engine bearer. Later versions had a cast engine bearer.
Below, centre and bottom: The same aircraft in the Soviet Union (pictured in front of the hangar at LII). All insignia have been removed. The ink stamp reads *Sekretno* (Classified).
Bottom left: The Bf 109B-1 parked at LII with the engine and cockpit under wraps.

In December 1937 a Nationalist Air Force Bf 109B-1 (serial 6-15) landed 'on the wrong side' of the frontline and was captured by Republican troops. The aircraft shared the fate of the He 111 bomber captured at about the same time (see the bomber section below). It was tested by the French technical commission in February 1938. The aircraft was subsequently shipped to the Soviet Union, where it was carefully studied during May-June 1938 at NII VVS at Chkalovskaya airfield. Engineer Tarakanovskiy was responsible for the testing of the Bf 109B-1 at NII VVS. Ground tests and examination of the aircraft revealed many technical points testifying to the high quality of the design and representing considerable value for the Soviet aircraft industry. In particular, some items of equipment were deemed to be of special interest. These included the oxygen system and associated

Top left, above left and left: The same aircraft at NII VVS in somewhat dilapidated condition.

The other photos on this page show close-ups of the fighter's armament, cockpit, powerplant and wheel wells taken during trials at NII VVS.

items; various electrical switching elements; the undercarriage and tailwheel design; the hydraulic systems.

Subsequent flight testing revealed such strong points as ease of handling and ease of servicing under field conditions.

The Bf 109B fighter was flown by test pilot Stepan P. Sooproon. In his evaluation report he wrote: *'The Messerschmidt-109 (sic) aircraft powered by the Jumo 210 engine is inferior in its performance to all high-speed fighter aircraft in the inventory of the Red Army Air Force'.*

The situation changed when an improved version, the Bf 109E powered by the 1,100-hp Daimler-Benz DB 601A, made its appearance in the Spanish skies. Its speed of 570 km/h (354 mph) and the potent armament comprising four MG 17 machine-guns (or two MG 17s and two 20-mm MG FF cannons in some versions) made it a formidable opponent for the I-15s and I-16s, which were outclassed in speed by a considerable margin. The Bf 109E also came to be tested in the USSR, but that happened later and under different circumstances.

Messerschmitt Bf 109E-3 fighter

Five Bf 109Es were purchased in Germany under the terms of the agreement of 11th February 1940. In May 1940 they were delivered in crates by train to Moscow (the construction numbers of two aircraft are known to have been 2734 and 2738).

The Bf 109E-3s powered by DB 601A engines were assembled at Moscow's Central Airport (Khodynka) under the supervision of NII VVS engineer Izrail G. Rabkin. The first of these was assembled by Rabkin and Ivan V. Zhulyov, an experienced engineer, virtually on their own, without assistance from the Messerschmitt representative who had come to Moscow for that purpose. The other aircraft were assembled together with the German engineer. Of the five machines, three were flown to NII VVS and tested there, while two assigned to LII. The testing at these two centres was conducted by test pilots Grigoriy Ya. Bakhchivandzhi, A. I. Filin, Mark L. Gallai, Aleksey N. Grinchik, A. I. Kabanov, A. S. Nikolayev, V. L. Rastorgooyev, Igor' I. Shelest, Stepan P. Sooproon, Ivan D. Seleznev, A. N. Zhuravchenko, Pyotr M. Stefanovskiy, A. I. Nikashin, A. G. Proshakov and others.

At NII VVS Rabkin was appointed project engineer for the testing of one of the three Bf 109Es; the flight test programme was to be completed within two weeks and thus had to proceed at a very strenuous tempo. The first stage of the testing of the two machines mentioned above (W.Nr. 2734 and W.Nr. 2738) took place between 29th May and 18th June 1940.

Four aspects of a Bf 109E-3 undergoing tests at NII VVS in late 1940.

The Bf 109E-3 tested at NII showed the following performance (with a 1,050-hp DB 601A and an AUW of 2,585 kg/5,700 lb): speed at sea level 440 km/h (273 mph); maximum speed at altitude 547 km/h (340 mph); rate of climb 6.3 m/sec (1,240 ft/min); service ceiling 10,000 m (32,810 ft); landing speed 129 km/h (80 mph). The speed of the Bf 109E exceeded considerably that of the Soviet standard fighters: the I-16 was almost 100 km/h (62 mph) slower and the I-153 biplane more than 100 km/h slower. The situation improved when the Bf 109E-3 was compared to the latest Soviet fighters then

Left: The same machine outfitted for spinning trials, with a spin recovery parachute on an outrigger. Note the elevator deflection sensor which was part of the test equipment.

undergoing tests – the Yak-1 developed a maximum speed of 592 km/h (368 mph), the LaGG-3 could do 605 km/h (376 mph) and the MiG-3 reached 628 km/h (390 mph) at 7,200 m. However, it was the Polikarpov machines that formed the bulk of the Air Force's fighter fleet at that time.

The armament and various systems of the German fighter were also studied carefully, as were all structural details, especially from the maintenance point of view. The armament of the Bf 109E was heavier than that of the Soviet fighters: in addition to machine-guns, the German fighter was equipped with two underwing 20-mm Oerlikon cannons. The weight of fire of the Bf 109E was 2.49 kg (5.48 lb), or more than double that of any contemporary fighter, including the I-200 (MiG-1) prototype.

Upon completion of testing one of the machines was dismantled for further technical study at NII VVS. One of the test centre's Bf 109E-3s was lost on 11th October 1941 when test pilot T. Chigarev crashed it during the evacuation of NII VVS to Sverdlovsk.

The Bf 109E was also tested at LII. The LII pilots flying this aircraft included Igor' I. Shelest, Ivan D. Seleznyov, Aleksey N. Grinchik, Viktor L. Rastorgooyev and Mark L. Gallai.

The Soviet test pilots generally had a very high opinion of the German fighter. They were particularly impressed by the ease of maintenance and attention to everything that might simplify the operation of the machine; it earned the laudatory description 'soldier's aircraft' (*samolyot-soldat*).

Messerschmitt Bf 109F fighter

Messerschmitt fighters came to be the most dangerous adversaries for the Soviet airmen after the German invasion in June 1941. During the four years of the Soviet-German war (the Great Patriotic War, as it was termed in the Soviet Union) the number of Bf 109 fighters of different models that had fallen into the hands of the Red Army reached quite impressive proportions; suffice it to say that several dozen of these machines were repaired by Soviet technicians and put into operational service! But that was the final result of a gradual process which began with

Top left and centre left: Two more pictures of a Bf 109E-3 at NII VVS taken at another time.

Left: The Daimler-Benz DB 601Aa engine (c/n 6376) and VDM variable-pitch metal propeller of the Bf 109E-3 with the cowling and the spinner removed. Note the MG 17 machine-guns.

Above: A Red Army ZiS-5 3-ton lorry is used to evacuate this captured Bf 109F-2 coded '7' which was downed by Soviet fighters.

the capture of single Messerschmitt machines and their study by Soviet specialists in an effort to supplement the knowledge gained by testing the examples acquired in 1940.

The captured machines were of different subtypes, not always indicated in the various sources. Of particular interest are the machines of the F and G series that were tested at NII VVS.

Apparently the first such aircraft, Bf 109F-2 W.Nr. 12766, was captured relatively intact near Tosno on 20th July 1941 when German pilot Lt. H. Raub, from I./JG 54, force-landed in Soviet-held territory. A few days later the captured machine took up its place at an exhibition of war booty in Leningrad.

The first Bf 109F to have been captured in reparable condition was flown by *Hauptmann* Rolf Pingel of JG 51. He made a forced landing in the Moscow Region in the autumn of 1941. After repairs by the 47th IAD based at Moscow-Tushino airfield, his aircraft was tested at NII VVS by A. G. Proshakov and others. The institute's armament specialists noted especially the new cannon firing through the propeller hub – a Mauser MG 151 whose calibre could be either 15 or 20 mm (0.59 or 0.78 in). Proshakov established the Bf 109F's maximum speed to be 510 km/h (316 mph) at sea level, 560 km/h (348 mph) at 2,750 m (9,020 ft), and 556 km/h (346 mph) at 500 (*sic* – 5,000?) m while he climbed to 5,000 m (16,400 ft) in 5.4 minutes. The service ceiling was 8,750 m (28,700 ft). (This story was related by Karl-Fredrik Geust on the basis of Russian materials unavailable to the authors of this book).

The enhanced performance of the F model caused NII VVS director Gen. Fyodorov to write in alarm to Aleksandr S. Yakovlev on 24th December 1941: 'Today we have no fighter equal to the Bf 109F!'

Yet, it was the Yak-1 that was deemed to be better suited (compared to the LaGG-3 and the MiG-3) for combat with the German

Above: Judging by the bent propeller blades, the Bf 109F-2 had made a belly landing and was then put on its undercarriage. These photos were probably taken near Stalingrad in the autumn of 1942.

Top and above: This captured Bf 109G was tested by Soviet specialists and then painted up in Luftwaffe markings for demonstration purposes.

Left and below left: Bf 109F-2 W.Nr. 9209 undergoing tests at NII VVS in March 1942. Above: The open canopy of the same aircraft, showing the rear armour shield.

machine, albeit it was inferior to the Bf 109 in speed and rate of climb at low altitudes. Here is the opinion of the Chief of the fighter section of NII VVS Mil Eng 1st rank A. N. Frolov who had analysed all available information on the Bf 109F. Frolov wrote in his conclusions: *'The enemy has an ascendancy in basic performance characteristics over all types of our new fighters up to the altitude of 2,000 m. Our machines have unsatisfactory field performance (in particular the LaGG-3). The take-off run is too long, and the tendency to veer to starboard makes it a complicated matter to take off in a formation and requires special attention during take-offs from short field airstrips. The high landing speed and long landing run also necessitate of extreme attention and require sufficient experience for calculating precisely the landing approach…'*

Further Bf 109s fell into Soviet hands during the Soviet counteroffensive near Moscow in December 1941. However, the opportunity to test the F model offered itself a little later, when Bf 109F-2 W.Nr. 9209 made a forced landing in Soviet-held territory on 22nd February 1942. After some repairs and initial testing by service pilots of the 47th IAD, it was eventually delivered to NII VVS and entered flight test in March 1942. The machine was thoroughly studied under the direction of Eng.-Capt. A. S. Rozanov. He noted that the Bf 109F had an advantage of 70 km/h (43 mph) in maximum speed at sea level over the Bf 109E, half of the increment being due to the greater power output of the DB 601N engine, while the other half was attained thanks to better aerodynamics.

It was established that the Bf 109 enjoyed an advantage in performance over Soviet fighters within the range of altitudes from sea level to 3,000 m (9,840 ft).

Soviet specialists paid special attention to the machine's operational qualities. They noted good access to all units of the engine, especially to the plugs, the rational arrangement of the cowling panels, and the use of automatic devices, in particular, for controlling the engine coolant and oil temperature, which considerably simplified piloting. The test results led to the conclusion that the new Bf 109 model was more convenient in operation than the new Soviet fighters.

At the same time the Soviet test pilots noted that the cockpit canopy of the Bf 109F-2 did not afford a sufficient view to the rear and thus made the fighter vulnerable to surprise attacks from the rear hemisphere.

A mock combat session was organised at NII VVS between the Bf 109F-2 and a Yak-1 (c/n 0511); it enabled the institute's specialists to draw up some recommendations for service pilots. It was believed that the Soviet fighters would enhance their chances of a victory by climbing to altitudes in excess of 3,000 m where the two machines allegedly were on a par. Later it was revealed that the Bf 109 was faster than the Soviet fighters at altitudes up to 6,000 m (19,680 ft) as well.

Soviet soldiers inspect a downed Bf 109F-4 of Stab I/JG 52 (W.Nr. 8419). This aircraft flown by Ofw. Karl Münz was shot down by AA fire near the village of Gredino, Stalingrad Front, on 8th January 1943.

The information gained by NII VVS pilots was made available to service pilots. However, the examination of the German aircraft was accompanied by numerous mistakes in assessments and factual information. For example, it was erroneously asserted that the Germans equipped their Bf 109s and Ju 88s with ski undercarriage for winter use, while in fact the German troops preferred to clear the airfields of snow and operate their aircraft on wheels all year round.

Somewhat later the NII VVS specialists obtained yet another example of the Bf 109F – this time a Bf 109F-4/R1 (W.Nr. 13043). This machine of I./JG77 was captured at the Southern Front north of Slavyansk on 22nd April 1942. A special team led by Mil. Eng. 1st Rank Stepanov studied the aircraft on the ground. Examination revealed the improvements introduced on this subtype: the more powerful DB 601E engine, the Zeiss optical gunsight, new oxygen equipment and the absence of an automatic device limiting the time of engine operation in the boosted mode. The engineers paid special attention to seeking out the vulnerable points of the aircraft. They came to the conclusion that the most vulnerable spot of the powerplant was the lower part of the cylinder banks – a single hit by a shell or incendiary bullet would cause a fire. The fighter's coolant radiators and oil cooler were not protected by armour, which also made them a suitable spot for aiming.

Information thus obtained was supplemented by the preliminary examination of the captured Bf 109F-4/Z conducted at about at the same time by specialists of BNT TsAGI. The specialists noted changes in the hydraulic system, in the layout of the carburettor cooling air duct, in the design of the carburettor air intake, as well as the use of a more powerful generator. Furthermore, the German designers had made provision for the use of a dust filter on the carburettor air intakes to cater for summer operations in steppe areas. Soviet engineers determined the speed of the fighter as 612 km/h (380 mph) at 6,400 m (21,000 ft).

Examination and testing of the captured German aircraft led to the conclusion that at that time the Messerschmitt fighters remained a potent adversary of the Soviet

Top right and above right: Bf 109F-4/R1 of I/JG 77 (W.Nr. 13043) was damaged and force-landed near Slavyansk, Southern Front, on 22nd April 1942. Here the captured aircraft is seen in dismantled condition in the process of being studied by Soviet specialists. The individual markings are painted out.

Right: The DB 601E engine of the same aircraft. Noteworthy items have been marked on the photo by the Soviet specialists.

Above and above right: The Soviet fighter ace Capt. P. T. Tarasov (812th IAP) climbs from the cockpit of Bf 109G-4/R6 ('2 White' (ex KJ+GH, W.Nr. 14997) and reports to a Soviet marshal. The aircraft flown by Uffz. Herbert Meissler of 7./JG 52 was downed on 28th May 1943. Note the 15 'kill' bars on the rudder.

Left: A Soviet airman poses with a captured Bf 109G-2 marked '212 Black', with a Bf 109E and a Junkers Ju 88 in the background.
Right: Another captured example of the Bf 109G-2. The *Balkenkreuze* on the wing underside appear to have been overpainted.

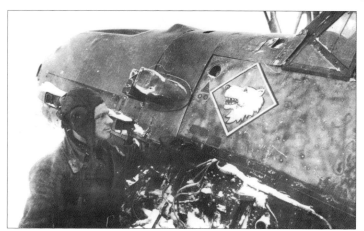

Left: A Soviet pilot examines a dismantled Bf 109 captured near Murmansk in 1942. It was the mount of Oblt. Franz Menzel, 5./JG 5 (the 'Polar Bear Squadron').
Right: This rear view shows the pilot's rear armour shield.

Two views of Bf 109F-2 '4 Yellow' (W.Nr. 12913) of 6./JG 52 put on display at the Central House of Aeronautics in Moscow in December 1941; the unit's *Tatzelwurm* emblem is visible on the cowling. Note Bf 110C-5 5D+BL (W.Nr. 2290) of 3(F)/31 in the background. Unfortunately these exhibits have not survived.

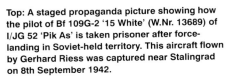

Top: A staged propaganda picture showing how the pilot of Bf 109G-2 '15 White' (W.Nr. 13689) of I/JG 52 'Pik As' is taken prisoner after force-landing in Soviet-held territory. This aircraft flown by Gerhard Riess was captured near Stalingrad on 8th September 1942.

Centre left: A damaged Bf 109F or early-model Bf 109G on display in a Soviet city park.

Top right: When the tide of the war had turned, a large display of captured German hardware was set up in Moscow's Central Culture & Recreation Park (Gor'kiy Park) in 1943 to boost public morale, remaining there until mid-1945.]Seven assorted Bf 109s are visible here.

The other pictures on this page were also taken at Gor'kiy Park in the summer of 1945.

Above: A Bf 109E in good condition.

Above right: A damaged Bf 109G-6 with the Krymskiy Most ('Crimean Bridge') suspension bridge in the background.

Centre right: The identity of this Bf 109G is not certain but could be W.Nr. 13547. The overpainted individual code is either '6' or '16'.

Right: This wrecked Bf 109G ('12 Yellow', W.Nr. 10110) belonged to I/JG 3 'Udet'. '10 White' in the background is a JG 54 'Grünherz' aircraft.

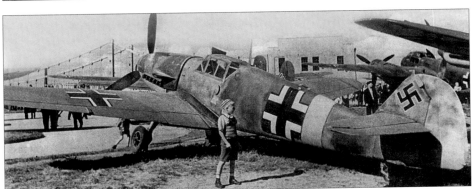

Above: Soviet pilots applaud the speech of their commander congratulating them on the mastering of the captured Bf 109.

Above: A captured Bf 109G-6 of JG 54 wearing temporary winter camouflage is seen at the 1st Aircraft Repair Plant at Siverskaya airfield, Leningrad, in the winter of 1943-44.
Below: A diagram from a Soviet manual showing the sectors protected by the Bf 109's cockpit armour.

pilots as they had been at the beginning of the war. To assess the situation better, a joint testing of Soviet fighters and the captured Bf 109F was conducted for comparison purposes in late May 1942. The Soviet types represented were the Yak-1, Yak-7B and LaGG-3 with boosted engines. The tests revealed an increase in the speed of the Soviet fighters amounting to 14-35 km/h (8.7-21.8 mph) at altitudes up to 4,000 m (13,120 ft). Mock combat conducted against the NII VVS machine (W.Nr. 9209) showed that *'The LaGG-3 and Yak-1 aircraft are inferior in their manoeuvrability to the Bf 19F at altitudes below 3,000 m. […] The speed and manoeuvrability in the vertical plane of the Yak-7B and the Bf 109F are virtually identical, but the Messerschmitt can maintain a lower minimum control speed and has greater lateral stability thanks to the availability of leading-edge slats…'*

Another Bf 109F-4, W.Nr. 7640, was captured intact near Chugooyev on 29th May 1942 after its pilot had lost his bearings and made a landing on the Soviet side of the frontline. A comprehensive test programme was drawn up but it was not put into effect. The reason was a request from the Allies who asked the Soviet side to supply a machine of that type as a replacement for a captured Bf 109 which had been lost in an accident in the USA. The request was granted, and the fighter was duly despatched to the USA where it underwent a complete test programme.

In 1943 TsAGI issued a report analysing handling qualities of several Allied fighters and the Bf 109F. The report noted that the Bf 109, *'thanks to the high engine output and*

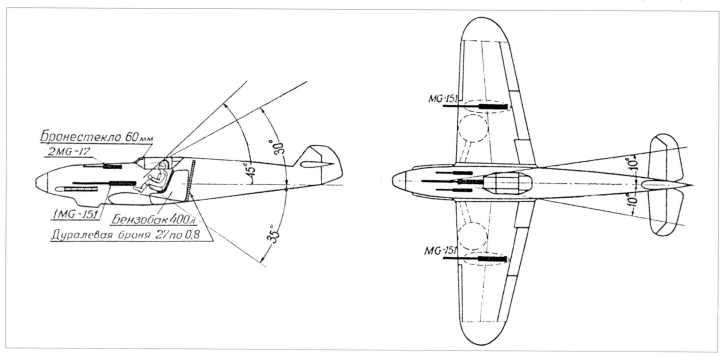

low all-up weight, rapidly gains altitude at a high angle of climb and is superior to all other machines in vertical speed'. In the overall assessment, the Bell P-39 Airacobra and the Bf 109F were singled out as the fighters with the best handling qualities. Yet, it was remarked that the Bf 109F, *'as compared to other aircraft, does not have a decisive advantage in manoeuvrability and handling qualities, which must be due to its relatively poor aerodynamic characteristics. [...] The banking turn, as compared to the Me 109E, has become more unpleasant and more complicated'.*

Messerschmitt Bf 109G-2

In the summer of 1942 the Germans started introducing a more advanced version of the Messerschmitt fighter – the Bf 109G-2 – into operational use on the Eastern front. Soon several such machines were captured by the Soviet troops, one of these being Bf 109G-2 W.Nr. 13529. The machine could not be evacuated to the rear and had to be studied on site. It was equipped with a new, more powerful engine type – the DB 605A. The engine was removed and bench-tested. The Soviet engineers estimated its take-off output at 1,600 hp (a take-off rating of 1,475 hp is cited in Western sources). With this engine the Bf 109G-2 had an advantage in speed over the Soviet fighters. Comparable Soviet Vee-12 liquid-cooled engines (the M-107A) were still very far from being operational.

In January 1943 NII VVS finally got an opportunity to study the Bf 109G-2 thoroughly. An example of the Bf 109G-2/R6 W.Nr. 13903 (of I./JG3), captured at Stalingrad, was delivered to the Institute and was subjected to testing under the direction of Eng-Capt A. S. Rozanov. Inspection showed that the new machine differed from the Bf 109F-2 W.Nr. 9209 tested earlier at NII VVS in having a more powerful DB 605F engine, and in being fitted with additional wing-mounted 20-mm MG 151 cannons, a bullet-proof windscreen and a duralumin plate of 18-mm ($0^{45}\!/_{64}$ in) thickness behind the fuel tank. This was, in Soviet parlance, the 'five-point' version of the Bf-109 (that is, armed with five guns). The fighter was flown by test pilots Col. Pyotr M. Stefanovskiy , Capt. A. G. Proshakov and Capt. A. G. Kubyshkin. The tests showed that the Soviet fighters had a hard time trying to wage war on equal terms with the Bf 109G (or *Gustav*). The advantages of the German machine included easier engine control, as well as a thorough sealing of all airframe joints and tight-fitting engine-cowling panels. Its rate of climb could be matched only by the proto-type Polikarpov I-185, and its service ceiling only by the MiG-3. At the same time the manoeuvrability of the 'five-point' *Gustav* in

Four views of Bf 109G-2 W.Nr. 14513 on test at NII VVS. The individual insignia are painted out but the crest of II./JG 53 'Udet' is still visible on the nose. The aircraft was brought down and captured after a dogfight on 19th March 1943. Here it is shown in 'three-gun Messerschmitt' form (with two 7.9-mm MG 17 machine-guns and one 20-mm MG 151 cannon). See also next page...

Above: The same aircraft in its original configuration as a 'five-gun' Bf 109G-2/R6 with a further two MG 151 cannons in underwing pods. The aircraft was captured on the Stalingrad Front and tested in this guise in March 1943 when the ground was still snow-covered.

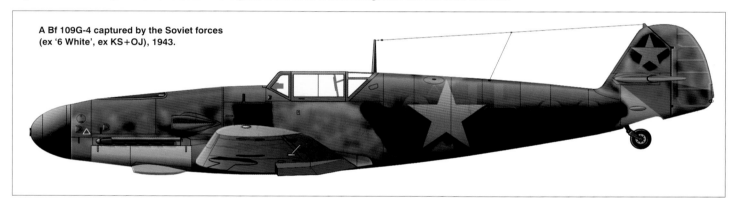

A Bf 109G-4 captured by the Soviet forces (ex '6 White', ex KS+OJ), 1943.

Four views of another Bf 109G-2/R6 (W.Nr. 13903) tested by NII VVS in 1943. Here the machine is crudely painted in Luftwaffe insignia for shooting an instructional film (note the lop-sided swastika and the identification number '2' on the rudder, which was absolutely uncharacteristic for the Luftwaffe).

Five views of the same aircraft in the colour scheme in which it was tested (note the '2' in the same position and the absence of a red star on the tail).

the horizontal plane was impaired by the installation of the underwing cannon pods, and most Soviet fighters could latch onto its tail after two or three full banking turns. Mock combat conducted at NII VVS between the Bf 109G-2/R6 and a La-5 showed that the Soviet fighter could tackle its opponent successfully. Yet, the German fighter remained a very formidable adversary, not to be taken lightly.

The test results obtained with the German fighters formed the basis for a number of recommendations as regards improving the performance of Soviet fighters. These included perfecting the external and internal aerodynamics, installing more powerful engines, such as the Klimov M-106 and the Shvetsov M-82 with direct fuel injection. The latter feature ensuring stable engine operation irrespective of the ambient temperature was prompted by the study of the DB 605 engine. Furthermore, it was found expedient to incorporate some devices similar to those used on the German fighter, such as the hydraulic supercharger drive and automatic control of its hydraulic coupling, the control stick with gun firing buttons on it, and so on.

A Bf 109G-4 (W.Nr. 19968) captured in May 1943 eventually reached NII VVS where it underwent testing. A bomb rack fitted under the fuselage indicated that this machine had been used in the fighter-bomber role. Its performance was impaired by the worn-out engine and by some aerodynamic imperfections (bulges on the wing upper surface to house the enlarged mainwheels and a fixed tailwheel instead of the earlier retractable one). In consequence, the machine did not attract much interest. In May 1944 this machine was pitted in mock combat against a new Soviet fighter, the Yak-3, which was about to start its service trials. It was a production machine (c/n 0906). In the opinion of the pilots and engineers of NII VVS, the Soviet fighter demonstrated its ascendancy over the opponent, especially in the vertical plane. Better aerodynamics and a lower power loading enabled the

Soviet fighter to get on the German fighter's tail after the very first combat turn. At altitudes up to 5,000 m (16,400 ft) the Messerschmitt machine was inferior in speed to the Yak-3 by some 30-40 km/h (19-25 mph).

In 1943 TsAGI issued a technical report on new German fighters analysing their mer-

its and drawbacks. Speaking of the various versions of the Bf 109, the report criticised the pilot accommodation as inconvenient and causing excessive fatigue; it noted the absence of rudder pedal adjustment. On the positive side, it noted the installation of various automatic devices relieving the pilot:

Above: Here, Bf 109G-2/R6 W.Nr. 13903 is seen in its initial test guise, retaining the temporary winter camouflage in which it was captured at Proleyka airfield near Stalingrad in January 1943. The '2' is already applied to the rudder. The main gear doors have been removed to prevent fouling by snow.

(automatic propeller pitch adjustment, automatic control of coolant and oil temperature).

The overall assessment given in the report asserted that the new German fighters (the Bf 109G and the Fw 190), *'albeit being quite up-to date in their performance and operational qualities, do not, nevertheless, represent anything exceptional and cannot ensure a decisive superiority over the British, US and Soviet machines'*.

However, it would be wrong to assert that the Soviet aircraft had reached overall superiority in performance over the German types by that time. In 1944 the main Bf 109 subtype used on the Eastern front was the Bf 109G-6 which had entered service with the Luftwaffe units in the summer of 1943. The new machine had a more potent fuselage-mounted armament. The usual 7.9-mm MG 17 machine-guns were replaced by 13-mm MG 131 heavy machine-guns mounted above the engine. In addition, the new

Left and above left: A Bf 109G-4 on test at NII VVS. The star insignia are carried on the wing undersurface only. The code '6 White' is retained but the Luftwaffe insignia, including the squadron badge, are painted out.

Opposite page: More views of the same aircraft, now with a star added to the tail. The delivery code KS+OJ is still carried on the wings.

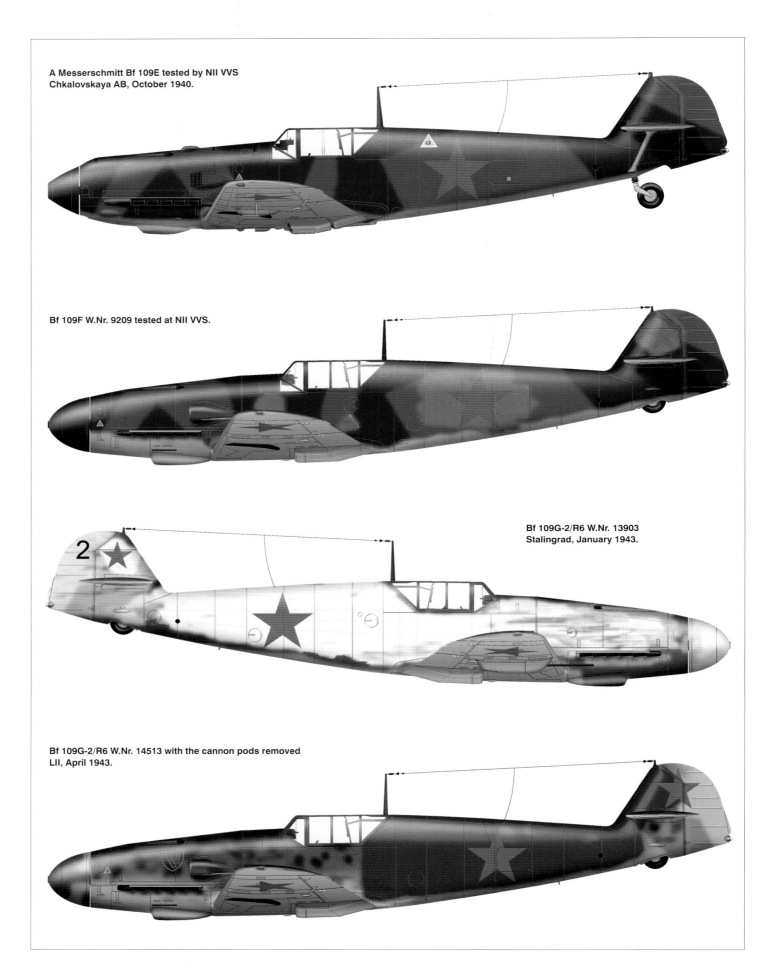

A Messerschmitt Bf 109E tested by NII VVS Chkalovskaya AB, October 1940.

Bf 109F W.Nr. 9209 tested at NII VVS.

Bf 109G-2/R6 W.Nr. 13903 Stalingrad, January 1943.

Bf 109G-2/R6 W.Nr. 14513 with the cannon pods removed LII, April 1943.

model had strengthened mainwheel legs and reverted to the retractable tailwheel. The DB 605 engine was boosted by means of fuel injection and water/methanol injection which helped raise the maximum speed at sea level to 530-545 km/h (329-339 mph) – an improvement of some 25-30 km/h (15-19 mph) over the G-4 model).

This information was obtained by interrogating German prisoners of war, but for some time could not be verified by testing a captured aircraft. The opportunity arose only at the closing stage of the war. In March 1945 pilots of the Fighter Division commanded by thrice Hero of the Soviet Union Aleksey I. Pokryshkin compelled a Bf 109G-6 to land on the territory held by Soviet troops (no information is available as to its further fate).

Finally, a few words should be added about the operational use of the captured Bf 109s in the Soviet Air Force. In the spring and summer of 1943 these fighters, as well as other types of captured aircraft, were widely used both in the rear and at the front. The number of Bf 109 fighters operated by the Soviet Air Force exceeded fifty. Available evidence indicates that they were flown by pilots of the 9th, 31st, 54th Guards Fighter Regiments and of some other air units. On 20th April 1943 a conference of pilots flying the Bf 109 was held at NII VVS, presided by General P. L. Losyukov. The participants exchanged opinions about the merits and deficiencies of these fighters. The captured machines flew different types of missions, ranging from leaflet dropping to surprise strafing attacks against enemy ground troops, in addition to instructional mock combat sessions staged in some air units.

Messerschmitt Bf 110C-4 (C-2) Zerstörer heavy fighter

The agreement of 11th February 1940 between Germany and the Soviet Union called for the delivery of five Bf 110Cs, which, according to some sources, were despatched in June (other sources indicate their arrival on 28th April 1940). The subtype delivered is indicated in some sources as Bf 110C-4, while Bf 110C-2 is mentioned elsewhere. In this case, too, the machines delivered were distributed for testing between NII VVS and LII. The NII VVS pilots who flew the Bf 110 included Pyotr M. Stefanovskiy and M. I. Tarakanovskiy; at LII the aircraft was flown by Aleksey I. Grinchik and Igor' I. Shelest, the latter reporting very good handling qualities.

The test results shown by the Bf 110C at NII VVS were recorded in the aforementioned book on German aircraft published by that test centre in 1943. In addition to a detailed description of the aircraft, the book contained a table of performance figures

Five aspects of Bf 110C-4 FO+XO (W.Nr. 3130) purchased in 1940 and tested by NII VVS.

established during the flight tests. The table is found on page 128 in abridged form:

Like the Bf 109E, the Bf 110C also received a high appraisal from the NII VVS test pilots. The assessment of the Bf 110C's handling qualities reads:

'The aircraft has good controllability, manoeuvrability and stability. It is capable of

Basic performance of the Messerschmitt Bf 110C-4 tested at NII VVS

All-up weight, kg (lb)	6,500 (14,330)	6,510 (14,350)
Maximum level flight speed, km/h (mph):		
at sea level	460 (285)	442 (274)
at 4,600 m (15,090 ft)	530 (329)	525 (326)
at 8,000 m (26,250 ft)	n.a.	471 (292)
Service ceiling, m (ft)	10,000 (32,810)	9,500 (31,170)
Take-off run with flaps set at 20°, m (ft)	300 (990)	370 (1,210)
Landing run with flaps set at 20°, m (ft)	450 (1,480)	340 (1,115)

Above: The cockpit of Bf 110C-4 FO+XO with the canopies open. Note the extended access ladder.

Above right and right: The nose of Bf 110C-4 FO+XO with the cowl removed, exposing the four MG 17 machine-guns and their ammunition boxes.

Below and bottom: Seen here in different seasons, this Bf 110C was one of the many captured aircraft on display in Moscow's Gor'kiy Park in 1943-45. The aircraft's code ends in a P (definiterly oversized).

a prolonged stable flight with hands off the stick.

The aircraft is simple in piloting and can be flown by pilots of average and less-than-average skill. The aircraft is capable of flying with one engine inoperative; the propeller of the inoperative engine can be feathered.

The aircraft is stable in a dive. The diving speed is built up quickly'.

One of the Bf-110s delivered from Germany in 1940 was fitted with an experimental 23-mm (.90 calibre) cannon designed by Yakov G. Taubin and M. N. Baboorin and used as a flying testbed.

After the outbreak of the war NII VVS took pains to continue operating the aircraft purchased from Germany in 1940, among them the Bf 110. As related by Dmitriy Sobolev, *'Bf 110 W.Nr. 3130 that was at the disposal of NII VVS took part in tests intended to determine the optimum flight path for fighters scrambling to intercept enemy reconnaissance aircraft (among these, the Bf 110s). It came to light that any delay of the take-off and any failure to use fully the performance capabilities of our fighters seriously impeded the successful fulfilment of the intercept mission even when the Bf 110 was flying at cruising speed'.*

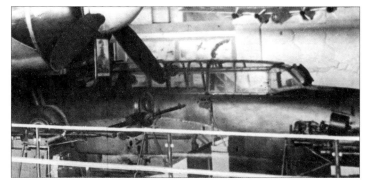

Left and above: The fuselage of Bf 110C-5 5D+BL (W.Nr. 2290) of 3(F)/31 on display at the Central House of Aeronautics in Moscow in December 1941. Below: A captured Bf 110 night fighter – apparently a Bf 110G-4d/R3. The two lower sections of the Liechtenstein radar array appear to be missing.

Messerschmitt Bf 110 fighter – captured aircraft

A number of Bf 110s of different models were captured on the Soviet-German front, some of them sufficiently intact to be restored to a flying condition. They were examined on site by personnel from service air units and, in some cases, flown by service pilots. There are no cases on record of any captured Bf 110 having been flight-tested at NII VVS, but specialists of this test centre studied later models of this fighter. Sobolev relates that *'among the battle-damaged twin-engined Messerschmitt fighters especially thorough study was conducted on the reconnaissance machine belonging to 3(F)/32, which had been captured on 13th September (1941) at the Bryansk Front. The Bf 110C-5 (W.Nr. 2290) differed from the C-2 model tested in our country before the war in having addi-*

Right and below: A cutting in a wood crammed with dead Bf 110s, including SP+GD, PN+CI and U5+EM, in April 1945. Note the highway in the background in the lower photo, which was apparently used as an airstrip when the grass runways became soggy in the spring.

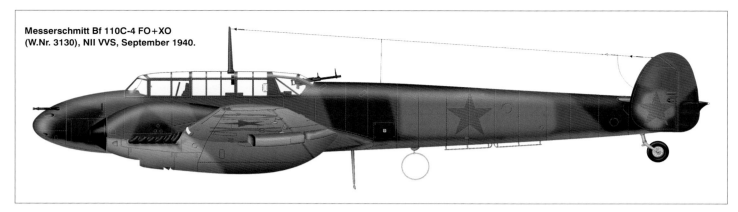

Messerschmitt Bf 110C-4 FO+XO
(W.Nr. 3130), NII VVS, September 1940.

tional armour protection for the crew, in having both MG-FF cannon deleted and in being fitted with the Rb 50/30 long-focus automatically operated camera for downward- forward photography. Quite probably, the concept of this conversion was put to good use when developing the reconnaissance version of the Pe-2.' This example of the Bf 110 was not test-flown, it was immediately sent for examination to the BNT TsAGI.

Of interest is the assessment of the Bf 110 presented in the book on German aircraft that was prepared by NII VVS in 1943. After a description of different versions of the fighter and its main mission types, the authors of the chapter on the Bf 110 state: 'The Me 110 did not gain wide acceptance in the role of a long-range fighter for bomber escort because of the relatively weak protection of the rear hemisphere and insufficient range.

The fixed forward-firing armament of the aircraft, comprising machine-guns and cannons, was regarded as fairly potent at the beginning of the war. Now, after the lapse of two years and the war entering its third year, this armament begins to be overshadowed even by some single-seat single-engined fighters. The rearward-firing small-calibre machine-gun does not ensure effective protection of the aircraft from fighter attacks from behind, from the upper rear hemisphere and the lower rear hemisphere.

The armour protection of the crew introduced already after the beginning of the war does not provide reliable protection against the weaponry of modern fighters'.

Like the Bf 109, its twin-engine stablemate was used operationally on some occasions by the Soviet air units. F. D. Tsykin states in his book on the history of the Soviet Long-Range Aviation (ADD): 'In some divisions (of the ADD – Auth.) there were captured German aircraft, mostly Me 110s, in which experienced and daring pilots repeatedly flew daylight and night-time 'free chase' missions in the enemy's rear. Their assumptions proved correct: the German anti-aircraft defence usually did not pay attention to the Messerschmitts. On the other hand, the crews of these aircraft suffered unmerciful treatment from our own anti-aircraft artillery on the way back to base.' An episode dealing with the Bf 110 is mentioned in the memoirs of M. Moisyuk and A. Khanayev. Major Opalev (from a Long-Range Bomber Regiment) mastered the piloting of a Bf 110 which had made a forced landing on Soviet territory after being damaged in combat. Flying this aircraft, he shot down the German ace Rudolf Sauker who also flew a Bf 110. Sauker was buried in the small town of Berestyanoye in the Bryansk Region. As related elsewhere (K.-F. Geust), the Bf 110 in

Above: This Messerschmitt Me 410A-3 was captured by Soviet troops in heavily damaged condition. The damage was probably inflicted by the retreating German forces.

Above: Soviet servicemen pose for a photo with a recently captured Me 410 (W.Nr. 420437).
Right: This Me 410A-2/U4 'tank buster' (3U+Z...) was on display in Moscow's Gor'kiy Park in 1945. The propeller blades are inscribed Iz Berlina (From Berlin).

question was flown by Lt. (SG) Vyacheslav G. Opalev and his co-pilot Yevgeniy Okorokov from the 750th AP DD (Long-Range [Bomber] Regiment; to become the 3rd Guards AP ADD on 18th August 1943). During their 'free chase' operations in the German rear, an unsuspecting Junkers Ju 88 had already been shot down on the first mission. Opalev flew approximately ten such clandestine missions in the Bf 110 before being shot down by 'friendly' AA fire at Tula. He was able to bail out, parachuting to safety, but was later killed in action in August 1943 near Kursk.

According to K.-F. Geust, a single Bf 110 was among the 18 German aircraft which were returned to the Soviet Union by Sweden in the autumn of 1945 at the demand of the Soviet government. This was a radar-equipped Bf 110G-4/R4 night fighter (G9+AA, W.Nr. 140655) of Stab/NJG which had force-landed at Trelleborg, Sweden; it was delivered to USSR in dismantled condition in November 1945.

Messerschmitt Me 209 experimental aircraft

The Me 209, the prototype of which was flown in 1938, was an experimental high-speed aircraft of small dimensions powered by a Daimler-Benz DB 601 engine. With this machine Messerschmitt AG managed to win back the world speed record, which had previously been established by Heinkel with the He 100. The agreement on the purchase of German aircraft by the Soviet Union signed on 11th February 1940 contained provisions for the delivery of a single Me-209 within twelve months (15 months, according to other sources). Aviation historian Dmitriy A. Sobolev notes that the German side never delivered this aircraft in spite of the contract.

Messerschmitt Me 410 Hornisse two-seat heavy fighter

An example of the Me 410 Hornisse (Hornet) twin-engined fighter was test-flown at GK NII VVS at the very end of the Second World War. This machine was captured at one of the enemy's airfields. There are slightly differing accounts as to the origin of the aircraft. According to one of them, an example of the Me 410 was ferried to the Soviet Union by A. I. P'yetsukh, a pilot who fought in the Polikarpov U-2LNB light night bomber during the war. In the spring of 1945 P'yetsukh, together with his colleagues, assembled one airworthy example of the Me 410, making use of subassemblies of several damaged examples, and ferried it to Moscow. Another report identifies the aircraft as Me 410B-2/U4 (W.Nr. 130379) belonging to II./ZG26. This aircraft was captured in East Prussia in the spring of 1945. Yet another

Above: Me 410B-2/U4 W.Nr. 130379 captured in Eastern Prussia in the spring of 1945 was extensively tested at NII VVS. This view shows the 50-mm BK 5 cannon.

Three more aspects of Me 410B-2/U4 W.Nr. 130379.

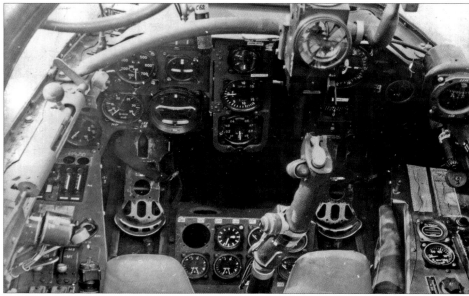

Above: The BK 5 cannon with the cowling removed, exposing the U-shaped magazine.
Above left: This view of the FDSL-B131 lateral barbettes shows how the MG 131 machine-guns could be brought to bear on a higher-flying target.
Left: The cockpit of the Me 410B.

account generally similar to the P'yetsukh version speaks of Western Poland where several Me 410s were discovered at an abandoned airfield in February 1945. An unnamed bomber pilot, together with his technician Konstantin Shoomskiy, received an order to restore one aircraft of this type to airworthy condition for the purpose of ferrying it to Moscow. They moved to this airfield situated near the town of Bednary and selected a machine which had suffered less damage than the others (the damage appeared to be limited to a broken instrument panel). They enlisted some help from a Pole, Zbyszek by name, who turned up at the airfield. He translated for them the German inscriptions on the instrument panel. Both of the aircraft's engines had to be overhauled, revealing a number of damaged parts; the repairs took some two weeks.

Upon completion of the repairs the Me 410 was test-flown at the same airfield; a little later, NII VVS test pilots arrived and took charge of the machine. Still retaining Luftwaffe markings, the Me 410 was flown to

Moscow, accompanied by a Yak-9 fighter. *'We ferried the aircraft to Moscow, after which I returned to my regiment. At that time it was already taking part in combat actions near Berlin'*, wrote the pilot in conclusion. (The story, narrated in the first person, was published by the Russian magazine *Vokrug sveta* (Around the World) in December 1966 with Pechnikov as the author, but this appears to be the name of a journalist, while the hero of the story may well have been P'yetsukh.)

The Me 410B-2/U4 (W.Nr. 130379) was tested at GK NII VVS . Here, again, there are some discrepancies in the available information. One report states that the machine ferried by P'yetsukh was submitted for testing at GK NII VVS in June 1945, and the testing was conducted in the course of one month. Another report says that the Me 410 was test flown at GK NII VVS 'at the very end of the Second World War' and the test report was signed on 15th May 1945, shortly after Victory Day. Obviously, the same aircraft is referred to here.

The Me 410B-2 mentioned above was armed with the 50-mm (1.96 calibre) BK 5 cannon. Russian aviation historian S. Kolov has questioned the correctness of the Me 410B-2 designation as applied to this particular example. According to the test report the machine tested at NII VVS was powered by DB 603A engines; this engine type was characteristic of the Me 410A subtype, while the Me 410B was powered by DB 603G engines of greater output. Hence, in Kolov's opinion, the machine tested should in fairness be designated Me 410A-2. Furthermore, the subtype armed with the BK 5 cannon was designated in the Luftwaffe as Me 410A-2/U4, and that is the designation which is applicable in this case. Kolov remarks, though, that the machine tested at NII VVS differed from the standard Me 410A-2/U4 in having a reduced complement of forward-firing armament supplementing the 50-mm cannon: only a pair of forward-firing 20-mm (.78 calibre) MG 151 cannons and one 13-mm (.51 calibre) MG 131 machine-gun, while the standard complement included two MG 151 cannons and two 7.92-mm (.31 calibre) machineguns. Kolov's interpretation is corroborated by the fact that the Me 410B-2/U-4, which also had the BK 5 cannon differed from the Me-410A-2/U4 not only in the engine type but also in having the standard combination of forward-firing cannons and machineguns replaced by a pair of 30-mm (1.18 calibre) MK 103 cannons. (K.-F. Geust must have followed this logic when he captioned a picture in his book as 'the Me 410A-2/U4 being tested at NII VVS'.)

However, in all further references to the mentioned test report the B.-2 subtype des-

Above: An intact Heinkel He 177 Greif bomber captured by the Soviet Army.

Citing this information, historian Dmitriy A. Sobolev does not say anything about the actual delivery of these aircraft, but it appears obvious that these orders were not fulfilled before the German invasion of the Soviet Union in June 1941. Occasional references in literature to a He 111 allegedly delivered to the USSR in 1940-1941 are presumably based on a misunderstanding.

Heinkel 111H-6 and Heinkel 111H-11 bombers

A number of He 111 bombers of different models were captured on the Soviet-German front in the course of the war; some of these aircraft were briefly studied on the sites where they crashed or force-landed; others were repaired and transported to test centres where they were test-flown; still others were even used operationally for special missions.

Several He 111s were among the aircraft captured in December 1941 in the course of the Soviet counteroffensive near Moscow. More machines of this type were captured at Pitomnik airfield west of Stalingrad in early 1943. Of these, two examples were restored to airworthy condition and ferried to NII VVS for testing. One of them was a He 111H-6, delivered to NII VVS at Chkalovskaya on 24th February 1943. The testing had no chance to proceed normally: after the third flight one of the engines went unserviceable. The testing of the second machine – a He 111H-11 – was more successful. Its fairly worn-out engines were replaced by motors removed from another example of the bomber. In May 1943 this aircraft duly completed the test programme.

The test team (engineer Maj. G. V. Gribakin, project test pilot Lt. Col. G. A. Ashitkov) was not particularly impressed by the aircraft's performance. In their opinion, the He 111H-11's maximum speed, rate of climb and service ceiling were very low for 1942, despite the installation of boosted Junkers Jumo 211F-1 engines rated at 1,350 hp for take-off. The German bomber proved to be inferior to its Soviet counterpart, the IL-4, in speed, range and rate of climb (time to 5,000 m/16,400 ft).

On the other hand, the He 111 had certain advantages, including the considerably improved protection from fighter attacks. This was achieved by increasing the number of weapon positions and by using the MG 131 heavy machine-gun and the semi-flexible MG FF cannon, as well as by the installation of collimator sights instead of simple bead sights and by other measures.

The armour protection of the He 111H-11 was found to be insufficient with regard to area and plate thickness for protection against large-calibre bullets and shells. Yet, the armour plates covered the most vulnerable units of the powerplants and crew stations, thus increasing the aircraft's survivability.

A feature of the He 111 that attracted the attention of Soviet engineers was the use of feathering propellers. The results of the examination of this device on the He 111 prompted the introduction of such propellers (the VISh-61IF-1 model) on a new version of the IL-4, which was under test at NII VVS concurrently with the Heinkel bomber. On the whole, the He 111 proved to have handling qualities that were in many respects superior to those of the IL-4 (the latter suffered from longitudinal instability, a tendency to pitch down when the flaps were deployed, and other deficiencies). Coupled with the advanced air navigation and radio communication equipment, this made the He 111 a bomber to reckon with.

In mid-1943 the Soviet command decided to put to good use the numerous He 111 aircraft captured at the fronts. By that time a total of 25 He 111s had been captured, 16 of them being airworthy. Among the examples with known identities were He 111H-16 W.Nr. 8182 and He 111H-6 W.Nr. 160291. There were plans for converting the 132nd Bomber Air Regiment (CO A. S. Khlebnikov) to the He 111, but an order to that effect was cancelled in August 1943 and the unit subsequently operated Tu-2

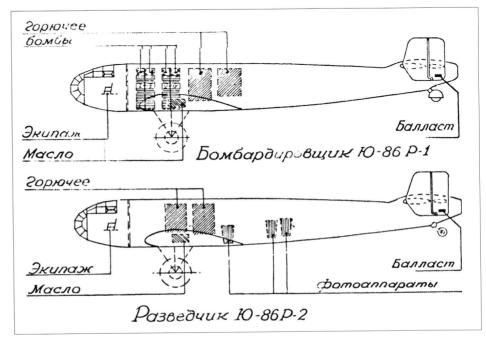

A NII VVS diagram comparing the internal layouts of the Junkers Ju 86R-1 bomber and the Ju 86R-2 reconnaissance version.

bombers. Operational use of the captured He 111 was a matter of top secrecy, so there is little documentary evidence on that score.

Several He 111 bombers of different subtypes were displayed at a war booty exhibition which opened in Moscow's Central Culture & Recreation Park (aka Gor'kiy Park) in June 1943.

Heinkel 177 Greif heavy bomber
At least two He 177 Greif (Vulture) bombers are known to have fallen into Soviet hands. One made a belly landing after being damaged in action (supposedly in mid-1943), while the other one was captured intact. Unfortunately no further information is available.

Junkers Ju 52/3m bomber – see transport aircraft section

Junkers Ju 86 bomber
The Russian aviation historian Vladimir Kotel'nikov states that the Ju 86 bomber was among the German aircraft delivered to NII VVS from Spain in 1937-1938, along with the He 51, Bf 109B, Ju 52/3m and He 111B. He does not dwell on how the Ju 86 was obtained or state the aircraft's sub-type and identity, merely remarking that the Ju 86 was too badly damaged to be reassembled, and the NII VVS personnel had to make do with studying its units and subassemblies. Another historian, Dmitriy A. Sobolev, adds the following:

'The [Soviet] military especially liked the Jumo 205 diesel engines installed in the Ju 86 bomber. In its specific fuel consumption and power-to-displacement ratio the German diesel aero engine was noticeably superior to the main Soviet engines – the AM-34, M-25 and M-85. NII VVS even recommended that the Jumo 205 be placed in production at one of our engine plants.'

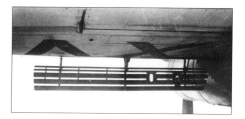

Top left: This Junkers Ju 88A-0 coded WL+008 was reportedly one of the two sold to the Soviet Union in 1940.

Second, third and fourth from top: This Ju 88A-1 was delivered to the Soviet Union with the civil registration D-AXVM.

Above: The port dive brake of D-AXVM.

Left and far left: The port Junkers Jumo 211B engine and annular radiator of the Ju 88A-1.

Top: Iosif V. Stalin (centre) and other top Soviet government officials inspect the recently opened war booty exhibition in Gor'kiy Park in July 1943.
Above: Two Ju 88As of KG 1 in winter camouflage, V4+DL and V4+IL, apparently captured near Stalingrad in the winter of 1942-43.
Top right: A Ju 88S-3 captured by Soviet forces.
Above right: The wreckage of Ju 88A-5 F6+AK (W.Nr. 880285) displayed at a railway station in Moscow in 1941.
Right: A captured Ju 88A-15 with a ventral weapons pannier.

According to various sources, five examples of the Ju 86D-1 bomber were delivered to Spanish Nationalists in late 1937; the example studied at NII VVS may have been one of them.

Junkers Ju 88A-1 (Ju 88K-1) four-seat level- and dive-bomber

Soviet experts had an opportunity to examine the Ju 88 dive-bomber during the visit of a Soviet delegation to Germany in November 1939; the pilot and designer V. Shevchenko, a member of the delegation, was even given a chance to fly the machine. The delegation was very much impressed by the aircraft, which was later included into the list of types to be purchased in Germany.

In keeping with the agreement of 11th February 1940 the Soviet Union was to receive two (some sources say three) Ju 88s from Germany. In most sources, including official Soviet documents, they are identified as Ju 88 A-1s; Lennart Andersson, though, chooses to call them Ju 88K-1, this being an export designation for the Ju 88A-1. He states that two Ju 88K-1s were delivered in

Junkers Ju 88A-4 D-AXVM NII VVS, 1940.

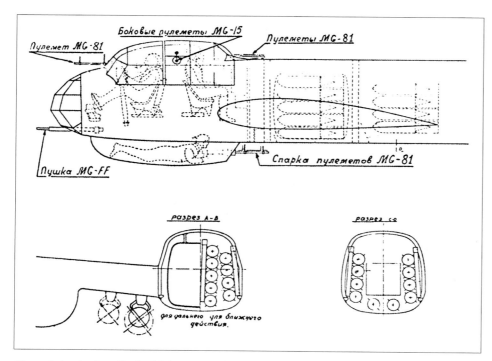

Above: A drawing from the Soviet documents showing the offensive and defensive armament of the Ju 88. Note how the small bombs carried internally are arranged around the fuselage fuel tank.

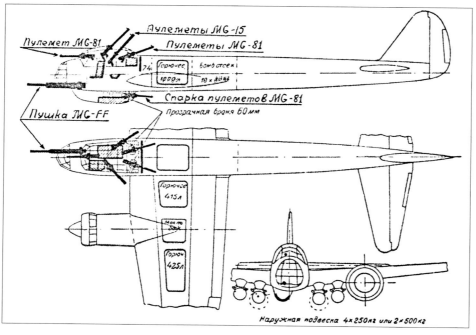

One more diagram showing the location of the defensive weapons ('what to beware'), fuel tanks and external bomb load ('where to aim').

April 1940; these were registered D-AXVL and D-AXVM (c/ns 0885023 and 0885025 respectively). They were tested at NII VVS and LII by Igor' I. Shelest and others. K.-F. Geust, however, claims that the two aircraft were of the Ju 88A-0 subtype, and identifies the example tested at LII by Shelest as WL+008 (this code is discernible on a photo of the machine).

The two Ju 88A-1s (or Ju 88K-1s, if you prefer) were delivered on 28th April 1940, taking off from Königsberg together with a

pair of Do 215s and landing at the Central airfield in Moscow. In early May one of the Ju 88s was ferried to NII VVS and subjected to comprehensive testing. In the course of 20 days a team comprising engineer Strizhevskiy, pilot Doodkin and navigator Akopyan succeeded in fulfilling almost the entire programme, but on 28th May a ground incident occurred – a leaky fuel pump caused a fire in the starboard engine. The fire was quickly extinguished, but the machine had become unserviceable.

In July the Chief of NII VVS endorsed a report on the results of the testing. This report stated, among other things, that the Ju 88 could be classed as a modern aircraft, albeit its aerodynamics were marred by the external bomb racks, dive brakes and the ventral 'bathtub' for a gunner under the forward fuselage. Despite these aerodynamic deficiencies, the aircraft had a good turn of speed thanks to efficient streamlining of the fuselage and tail unit (there were no dorsal or ventral turrets and the tailwheel was retractable), to the use of ejector exhaust stubs, as well as the good surface finish, including the use of flush riveting. The test pilot was satisfied with the aircraft's stability around all three axes; the aircraft was easy to control in turbulent air.

The accommodation of all crew members together in one cockpit earned praise – the test team noted that this permitted the crew to communicate directly. The view from the pilot's and navigator's workstations was deemed 'simply marvellous'.

It was duly noted that the designers of the Ju 88 had taken pains to ease the pilot workload in every possible way; for this purpose they introduced a number of automatic devices. For example, upon extension of the airbrakes the aircraft entered a dive automatically. After bomb release the elevator trim tab was automatically deflected, and the Junkers automatically recovered from the dive; at the same time, a g-limiter was switched on. On take-off after the lapse of 60 seconds the engines automatically went from boost to maximum rating; when the aircraft reached a certain altitude the second speed of the two-speed superchargers was switched on automatically. The oil temperature, the fuel-air mixture and the pressure at the carburettor air intake were regulated automatically, depending on the air density. An autopilot was provided. This kind of 'catering' was something the Soviet pilots could only dream of, even after the war!

A commendable property of the Ju 88 was its ability to fly without problems with one engine inoperative.

Performance characteristics established during testing at NII VVS (for an AUW of 12,300 kg/27,120 lb) included a maximum speed of 365 km/h (227 mph) at sea level and 445 km/h (277 mph) at 5,600 m (18,370 ft). Time to 5,000 m (16,400 ft) was 18 minutes; a service ceiling of 7,400 m (24,270 ft) and a range of 2,345 km (1,457 miles) at 3,000 m (9,840 ft) were recorded. The speeds were very close to those indicated for the A-1 version in present-day Western sources, while the ceiling and range were even in excess of the figures published now.

After the study of the Ju 88 conducted at NII VVS and LII, some of its technical fea-

Two Mistel combinations captured by Soviet troops. The upper photo shows a Mistel S 1 (Ju 88A-4 + Bf 109F); the stills from a cine film on the left depict a Mistel S 2 (Ju 88G-1 + Fw 190A-8). Both Misteln are in training configuration (without warheads).

tures was incorporated by Soviet aircraft designers into their machines. Moreover, such was the impression produced by the Ju 88A-1 that the VVS and NKAP top officials came to a firm conclusion that a similar aircraft was urgently needed for the Soviet Air Force. This, in the opinion of some researchers, prompted the decision to convert the Petlyakov '100' (VI-100) high-altitude fighter into a dive-bomber that later became the famous Pe-2. Many features of the Pe-2 were similar to those of the Ju 88 –

the characteristic dive brakes and the reference lines on the cockpit glazing to assist bomb aiming. One of the Ju 88s purchased in Germany was used in the USSR as a flying testbed for developing various units for the Pe-2. In July 1940 Captain Koval'chuk tested different versions of the automatic dive recovery device on this Ju 88. In fact, on 27th June 1940 the Soviet government issued a directive calling for copying the Ju 88's dive recovery device by the Soviet industry; Plant No. 213 was tasked with its manufacture.

In addition to the dive-bomber version, Soviet experts had an opportunity to examine the Ju 88C heavy fighter (Zerstörer, in German terminology). This version was intended for the support of ground troops and for combating the enemy's heavy bombers. To increase speed, the aircraft was stripped of all external appendages and provided with a streamlined forward fuselage; the navigator's cockpit was replaced

by an installation comprising two cannons and two machine-guns. An example of this aircraft was shown to a group of senior officials of the People's Commissariat of Aircraft Industry (NKAP) which visited Germany in February-April 1941. It was led by I. F. Petrov; other members of the group were aircraft designer Artyom I. Mikoyan, test pilot Stepan P. Sooproon and aircraft factory representatives A. V. Maksimov and Ye. V. Rodzevich. The demonstration took place on 24th-25th March during a visit to the plants of Junkers AG.

During the war the Ju 88s purchased in 1940 were included, together with other German aircraft tested at NII VVS, into a special reconnaissance unit manned in part by Spanish pilots who had arrived in the Soviet Union after the Spanish Civil War. During the training conducted in the Urals region one of the Ju 88s crashed on take-off, the crew suffering injuries.

Above: A Soviet serviceman proudly poses with a Ju 188D captured in Germany.
Right: Another Ju 188 on display in Gor'kiy Park in the summer of 1945.

Junkers Ju 88A-4, A-5, A-6 bomber (wartime captured aircraft)

The Ju 88 bomber and multi-purpose aircraft was used by the Luftwaffe in large numbers on the Eastern front, so it is hardly surprising that quite a few of the Junkers Ju 88s of different models (notably A-4, A-5 and A-6) were captured by Soviet troops in the course of the war. The first acquisition was made as early as 23rd June 1941, when a Ju 88A-5 (W.Nr. 8260) belonging to II./KG 1 force-landed on a sand beach of the Gulf of Riga coast after being hit by AA fire. Examination conducted on the spot by teams of experts provided materials for preparing an illustrated manual intended to familiarise the VVS units with this machine, particularly with its defensive armament and armour plating.

On the following day, Ju 88A-6 W.Nr. 2428 of KG 54 'Totenkopf' (Death's head) fell into the hands of Soviet troops near Kiev. According to the German version of the event, it made a forced landing after being hit by ground fire. Soviet official sources claimed that the crew had defected to the Soviet side (some memoirs indicate that the crew spoke in a propaganda broadcast addressed to German troops).

On 8th July 1941 Ju 88A-5 W.Nr. 4341 of KG 1 'Hindenburg' landed 120 km (74.5 miles) from Lake Chudskoye.

In July 1941 a Ju 88A-5 coded F6+AO (W.Nr. 880285) made a forced landing near Istra, Moscow Region. Five days later it was put on display in the centre of Moscow.

In 1944 a Ju 88A-4 of KG 30 'Adler' (Eagle) force-landed near Murmansk. These are only a few examples.

Surprisingly, no attempt was made to conduct a thorough study or testing of a captured Ju 88 at NII VVS. In the opinion of D. A. Sobolev, this may be partially explained by the fact that in the spring of 1942 the British press published materials on a Ju 88A-6 that was captured and tested by the British. This information was brought

to the knowledge of Soviet specialists who could thus appraise the differences between the Ju 88A-1 tested in the Soviet Union before the war and the later model. Furthermore, on 8th February 1943 the Soviet intelligence service supplied Moscow with the latest information from Dessau where one of the main Junkers factories was situated. This intelligence contained details about the modifications introduced on the Ju 88F-4 which the Luftwaffe was using operationally on the Eastern front This version had improved handling properties, a weapons load increased by some 600 kg (1,310 lb) and bulged rear glazing of the cockpit which permitted a more effective use of the defensive armament.

In 1943 NII VVS summed up the results of analysing all available information on the Ju 88 in a report that was included in the aforementioned book on German aircraft types. The chapter on the Ju 88 contained a description and analysis of the Ju 88A-1, presumably based on the testing at NII VVS. However, no assessment of this version was given. This description was followed up by a similar description of the Ju 88A-4 (main differences from the A-1) and the Ju 88A-6 (main differences from the A-4). A short description was given of the Ju 88C-6 and Ju 88D-1 versions, followed by brief mentions of the Ju 188 and Ju 288 derivatives. A special part of the report was devoted to the aircraft's vulnerable spots.

The conclusions referred broadly to all the versions described. The authors noted that the Ju 88 had been conceived as a dive bomber, but in the course of the war with the Soviet Union it had largely lost its significance in this role due to high losses to enemy fighters and AAA, and *'now it is widely used as a usual medium bomber for level-flight bombing in daytime and at night'*. Noting some design features associated with the dive-bomber role, the authors of the report mentioned, in particular, the excellent view for the pilot enabling him to aim accurately during the diving attack. Progressive improvement of the aircraft with regard to enhancing its performance, defensive capabilities and survivability, was noted. The changes involved the installation of more powerful engines and, in particular, the improvement of the defensive armament, which came to comprise nine machine-guns (on the A-6 version) instead of three. However, this measure was assessed by Soviet specialists as being of dubious effectiveness because of the small calibre of the rearward-firing machine-guns. Furthermore, the crew complement remained the same and some crew members had to man three machine-guns, to the detriment of the overall effectiveness of the armament.

A passage in the assessment read: *'The armour plating of the aircraft is inadequate, because armour protection is provided only for the crew, yet with the exception of the navigator who has no protection. The armour has small thickness, ranging from 5 to 8 mm, and does not provide adequate protection even from 7.62-mm bullets…'*

The report further stated: *'The Ju 88 is used by the Luftwaffe mainly in its A-6 version. Due to the Ju 88A-6's poor performance, to the use of small-calibre machine-guns for protecting the rear hemisphere and to inadequate armour protection this aircraft is easily shot down by our fighters. As a rule, the Ju 88A-6 bombers are provided with fighter cover when flying daytime missions'.*

Junkers Ju 88 Mistel flying bomb

The various German aircraft captured by the Soviet forces on German territory in the spring of 1945 included a few examples of the *Mistel* (Mistletoe) weapons system. This was a composite aircraft in which a heavy aircraft (in this case, the Ju 88 bomber) was used as a flying bomb – a pilotless aircraft with a large shaped-charge warhead replacing the cockpit section. It was guided to the target by a single-seat fighter temporarily attached to it 'piggy-back' by struts and then disengaged during the final run-in. A photo published by K-F. Geust in one of his works shows a Mistel S1 (a trainer version of the Mistel 1) captured in eastern Germany being inspected by Soviet personnel. That particular combination consisted of a Junkers Ju 88A-4 and a Messerschmitt Bf 109F.

No detailed information is available on the extent of studies which may have been conducted on Mistels by Soviet specialists. A Russian author dealing with the Mistels in a magazine article refers only briefly to this subject, saying: *'After the war captured Mistels were studied and tested in the USA, France, Britain and the USSR. Specialists came to the conclusion that this weapon had no potential for further development. The only thing that really captured the attention of engineers was the sight with the help of which the lower component of the Mistel was set and maintained on the attack heading. Subsequent development of guided weapons followed the option of creating dedicated unmanned aircraft and missiles'.*

Junkers Ju 188 bomber

Several examples of this bomber were captured in the course of the war. One of them was exhibited in Gor'kiy Park in Moscow.

Junkers Ju 388L (L-1) three-seat photo reconnaissance aircraft

This machine is described here together with the Ju 88 bomber and multi-purpose

---

Opposite page, far left: Four views of the Junkers Ju 388L-1 tested at NII VVS in the winter of 1945-46. The photos show the high aspect ratio wings, the ventral pannier accommodating cameras and an extra fuel tank, and the same 'eye' design of the cockpit's front glazing as seen on the Ju 188.

Top right: Soviet specialists examine the Ju 388L.

Second from top: The port BMW 801TJ engine.

Third from top: One of the cameras housed in the ventral pannier.

Fourth and fifth from top: The FA 15 powered tail barbette with paired MG 131Z machine-guns and its PVE 11 periscopic sight.

The lower row of pictures shows the Ju 388's instrument panels (pilot's instruments, radio equipment controls and flight engineer's station).

aircraft, of which it was the ultimate development. A single example of the Ju 388L (some sources give the subtype as L-1) was tested at NII VVS in 1945-46. No information is available on the origins and identity of the aircraft.

Tests of the Ju 388L in the USSR gave the Soviet specialists the opportunity, albeit belatedly, to evaluate the ultimate results of the evolution of the Ju 88/Ju 188/Ju 388 twin-engined multi-role aircraft. This aircraft was the first among those delivered to NII VVS to be powered by supercharged BMW 801TJ engines. The second rated altitude of the engine was 11,800 m (38,700 ft); pressure cabins and other high-altitude equipment allowed the crew to operate at altitudes in excess of 12,000 m (39,360 ft). The pilot, Col. I. P. Piskunov, assessed the longitudinal stability of the Junkers as insufficient and found its handling to be more complicated in comparison with the Pe-2 and the Tu-2. Unfortunately, it proved impossible to test the Ju 388 at high altitudes because both engines broke down after 18 hours of operation (there was no possibility to determine the overall engine life).

Upon completion of extensive testing associated with the aircraft as such, the Ju 388L was used for other purposes. In 1948-1950 it was used for towing experiments with the DFS-346 supersonic research aircraft which underwent development in the Soviet Union under the EF-346 or simply '346' designation (see Chapter 5).

Karl-Fredrik Geust makes an interesting remark on the 'Soviet' Ju 388 which, together with numerous other ex-German aircraft, took part in the Aviation Day display on 18th August 1945. The captured Messerschmitts and Focke-Wulfs flew mock com-

Top and right: This Arado Ar 196 used by the Soviet Border Guards was refitted with a Shvetsov ASh-62IR radial driving a VISh-21 propeller (both taken from the Lisunov Li-2 transport) in 1946 when the original BMW 132K radial ran out of engine life.
Centre and above right: Bulgarian Navy Ar 196s taken over by Soviet forces after the liberation of Bulgaria in 1944, seen on Lake Chaika.
Above: An Ar 196 painted overall silver in service with the Soviet Navy in 1946.

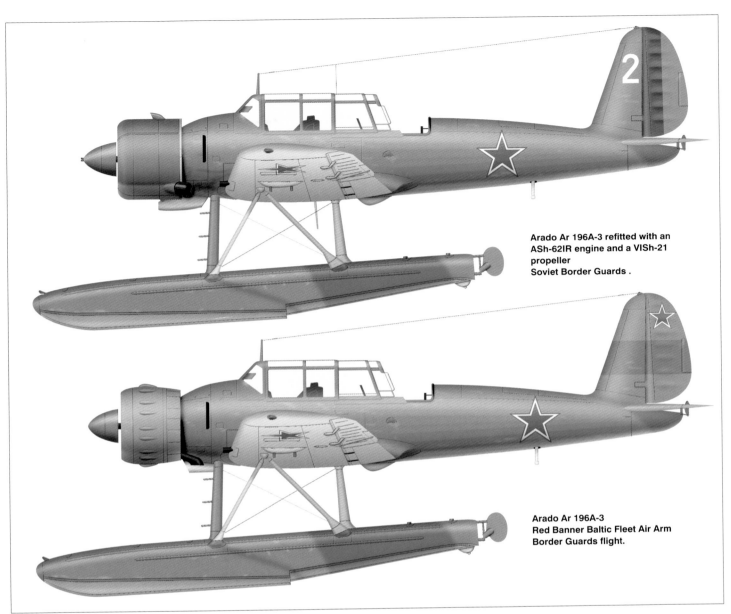

Arado Ar 196A-3 refitted with an
ASh-62IR engine and a VISh-21
propeller
Soviet Border Guards .

Arado Ar 196A-3
Red Banner Baltic Fleet Air Arm
Border Guards flight.

bat against Soviet fighters, naturally now performing as the 'losing party' (the 'bad guys' have to lose in the end, you know), while Maj. I. Piskunov *made an especially impressive performance, simulating a force-landing of a Junkers 388 shot down by Soviet fighters'*.

Reconnaissance and attack aircraft

Arado Ar 196 reconnaissance seaplane

A certain number of Arado Ar 196 twin-float reconnaissance seaplanes was acquired by the Soviet Union and put into service with the Soviet Naval Aviation. These machines came from different sources. One example of the Arado 196A-3 was obtained from Finland. According to the Finnish aviation historian Karl-Fredrik Geust, it was one of the three examples which had been given on loan to the Finnish Air Force by the Luftwaffe

(flown by Finnish crews, but in the original German colours). The machine in question, coded A3+AC, was used by the Finnish Air Force during the so-called Lapland War against the retreating German forces in northern Finland. It was given the unofficial

Finnish civil registration OH-PMK. The German origin of this aircraft attracted the attention of the Allied (that is, Soviet) Control Commission supervising the fulfilment of the armistice conditions; as a consequence, the machine was withdrawn from service with

A Blohm & Voss BV 138C flying boat captured in Ventspils, Latvia, in May 1945. Note the Soviet officer on the shore.

an Ar 196A-0 or Ar 196A-1. Although this example had been in operation for ten years and was considerably worn out physically, it was modified by a team led by A. P. Golubkov at the request of the command of the Navy. [...] The aircraft was refitted with an ASh-62IR engine driving a VISh-21 propeller (a powerplant of the Li-2 transport). It was accordingly fitted with new engine cowlings, a new oil tank and a new engine mount. Further modifications included the installation of a Soviet-made oil cooler, of fire suppression equipment, of a GSK-1500 generator and a 12-A-30 storage battery. The aircraft was provided with an instrument panel with Soviet-made navigation and flight instruments. The gunner/radio operator's cockpit was fitted with twin 7.62-mm [Degtyaryov] DA-2 machine-guns.

There are reasons to presume that the 'rejuvenated' Ar 196 went on to serve in the Naval Aviation until 1953.'

Top: Soviet soldiers examine a pair of abandoned Focke-Wulf Fw 189A artillery spotting aircraft.
Above: Fw 189A H1+KL of Aufkl.Gr.(H) 12 was captured at Pitomnik airfield, Stalingrad, in February 1943.

the Finnish troops in November 1944 and eventually dismantled and delivered to the Soviet Union on 16th March 1945.

Yet another source was Bulgaria. Russian historians note that, following the liberation of Bulgaria by Soviet forces, the Arado Ar 196 floatplanes which had served in that nation's air force were transferred to the USSR for use by the Soviet Navy. The number and identity of these aircraft is not stated.

The Ar 196s remained in Soviet service until the early 1950s. At least one Ar 196 was fitted with a Soviet-made Shvetsov ASh-62IR nine-cylinder radial to extend its service life. An account by N. Soiko published in Russia in 1996 states that State acceptance trials of an Ar 196 thus modified were completed at Institute No. 15 of the Soviet Navy in August 1951. *'Judging by the armament complement, this was an early production machine –*

Blohm & Voss BV 138C long-range maritime reconnaissance flying boat

An example of the twin-boom three-engined Blohm & Voss BV 138C flying boat was captured in Ventspils, Latvia, in May 1945, as evidenced by a photo published in a book by Russian aviation historians. No information is available on the identity of the aircraft (except the letter D – part of the aircraft's code – just visible on one of the fuselage booms) and its subsequent fate.

Focke-Wulf Fw 189 Uhu short-range reconnaissance/artillery observation aircraft

This twin-engined reconnaissance aircraft occupies a special place among the Luftwaffe aircraft that fought on the Eastern front. The Fw 189's German sobriquet was *Uhu* (Owl), but to the Soviet troops it was universally known as the **rama** (frame, or window-frame) due to its twin-boom layout.

The fuselage nacelle of the Fw 189 had an exceedingly large glazing area. As these photos show, the conical rear portion of the glazing incorporating the rear machine-gun mount could swivel to increase the field of fire of the rear MG 81 machine-gun.

Above: The forward fuselage of Fw 189A U2+RB (W.Nr. 2345) captured in Latvia in May 1945 as a stripped-out hulk.
Above right: Soviet soldiers are intrigued by the curious sideways-retracting tailwheel of the Fw 189. This example appears to be intact.

When this seemingly innocuous slow-flying aircraft appeared over the positions of the Soviet troops, one might with a fair degree of certainty expect that this would soon be followed by a German bomber raid or an artillery attack. The Fw 189 was very effective in its tactical reconnaissance and artillery spotting ('bird dog') role, not least thanks to its unorthodox layout which provided the crew with an excellent field of view.

A number of Fw 189s were among the German aircraft captured during the Soviet counteroffensive on the Stalingrad Front. An example of the Fw 189A-2 was flight tested at NII VVS. In March 1944 the institute published a new book called *German Aircraft at NII VVS* containing the performance figures and descriptions of the main aircraft types used by the Luftwaffe. Here is how this book explained the effectiveness of the operations undertaken by Fw 189 crews: *'The excellent visibility afforded by the aircraft lessens the chances for a fighter to make a surprise attack. [The aircraft's] high manoeuvrability enables the gunners to get ready for repelling the attack, once the attacking aircraft has been noticed in time. During a turn the pursuing fighter will all the time be within the field of fire of its* (the Fw 189's – Auth.) *aft-firing weapons'.*

Flight testing of the Fw 189A-2 conducted by NII VVS yielded the following performance. The maximum speed was 300 km/h (186 mph) at sea level; the machine

Top. The hulk of Fw 189A U2+ZB (W.Nr. 2274) sits alongside U2+RB. Both aircraft belonged to I./NAGr 5.
Above: Still wearing its original unit badge, an Fw 189A in Soviet markings sits on a snowbound airfield.

These stills from an instructional film prepared by NII VVS show the crew climbing into an Fw 189A. The swivelling tailcone is in the neutral position. Note the absence of an individual code beside the *Balkenkreuz* revealing that the Luftwaffe markings are fake.

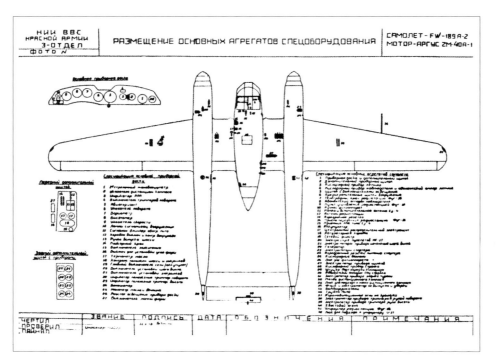

Above: A diagram from the NII VVS documents illustrating the placement of equipment on the Fw 189A-2. Interestingly, the engine type is stated as 'Argus 2M-410A-1' (the '2' means two engines), not As 410A-1.

Top and above: The Fw 189A-2 tested by NII VVS is seen here in Soviet markings. Note the gust lock clamping the rudder mass balance.

Top right: The Fw 189A-2 taxies at Chkalovskaya AB in fake German insignia.

Second from top: The fuselage nose and engine nacelles. Note the Luftwaffe squadron badge on the engine cowling.

Centre right: The starboard Argus As 410A-1 engine with an Argus automatic variable-pitch propeller (the so-called *Einheitstriebwerk* – standard powerplant).

Above right and right: The dorsal gunner's station with an MG 81 machine-gun.

Left: The breech of the starboard forward-firing MG 17 machine-gun in the wing root.

Above and above right: The pilot and the observer climb into the cockpit.
Right: These stills from the NII VVS film show the institute's Fw 189A-2 in flight.

climbed to 5,000 m (16,400 ft) in 25 minutes and had a service ceiling of 6,750 m (22,140 ft). The take-off run was 460 m (1,510 ft) and the take-off distance up to an altitude of 25 m (82 ft) was 1140 m (3,740 ft). Some of these figures compare unfavourably with figures from other sources (William Green) indicating a maximum speed of 217mph and a service ceiling of 23,950 ft.

It was noted that the aircraft was easy to fly and could be operated by average-skilled pilots and even by pilots with less-than-average skills. Assessing the aircraft's design, Soviet engineers singled out the fuselage nacelle as the most interesting feature of the airframe. They noted the excellent view forward, to the sides and downwards afforded to the pilot, as well as a good view for the navigator and the rational design of his rotating seat enabling him to slide back, turning through 140° to man the defensive gun installation. However, the absence of a seat back was considered a drawback. It was also noted that placing the navigator beside the pilot enabled them to communicate freely during flight, facilitating the fulfilment of the combat mission. The test conclusions stated that the Fw 189's twin-boom configuration was one of the best suited for a tactical reconnaissance and artillery observation aircraft. Operational experience gained at the front also assessed as confirming the wisdom of selecting this layout for the type of mission stated above.

A detailed study of the Fw 189A-2 was undertaken at NII VVS by Maj. M. S. Dmitriyev. Among other things, he noted the high degree of comfort provided for all crewmembers. This included a well-chosen arrangement of the navigation instruments and radio; the seating of the pilot and the navigator side-by-side, which enabled them to communicate without an intercom; and the efficient cabin heater. The NII VVS specialists were also impressed by the excellent radio equipment (the FuG-17 VHF radio).

An Fw 189A was displayed at the war booty exhibition in Moscow's Gor'kiy Park in the summer of 1943.

Among the Fw 189As that fell into Soviet hands one may mention the six aircraft that were flown to the Soviet side by Slovak pilots who defected from Isla in eastern Slovakia to L'vov on 31st August 1944. Two Fw 189As of Stab 1./NAGr 5 – U2+ZB (W.Nr. 2274) and U2+RB (W.Nr. 125345) were reportedly turned over to the USSR by Sweden after arriving in Bulltofta, Sweden, from Latvia on 8th May 1945. However, there is evidence that they were captured in Latvia as hulks and that U2+RB was actually W.Nr. 2345.

Top and above: This almost complete Henschel Hs 126A was on display in Moscow's Gor'kiy Park in February 1942 along with other war booty.

155

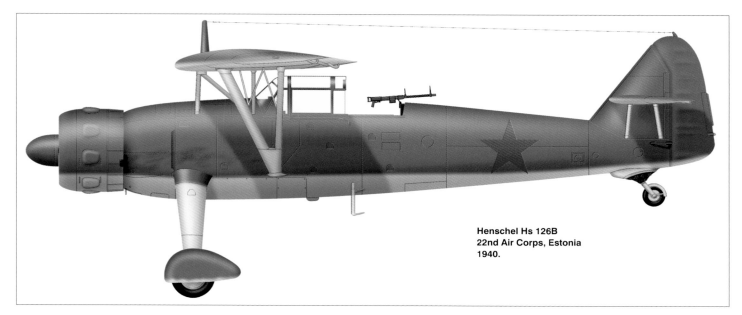

Henschel Hs 126B
22nd Air Corps, Estonia
1940.

Above: Hs 126 P2+DL was captured in damaged condition during the Battle of Stalingrad. Note the yellow-painted undersides of the outer wings. The wheel spats were often removed in service.

This Hs 126 (V7+1K) was shot down over Murmashi airfield near Murmansk on 9th February 1942. Note the inscriptions: 'Landing light; pilot's armoured seat back; fuel tank; camera; armoured bulkhead'.

Soviet designers were obviously impressed by the operational success scored by this reconnaissance machine, attributing this success in no small measure to its layout. Indirect evidence of this is provided by the fact that this layout was used in the Soviet Su-12 reconnaissance aircraft

built in prototype form by the Sukhoi design bureau in late 1947. It was, however, a much larger and heavier aircraft powered by two 1,850-hp Shvetsov ASh-82FN 14-cylinder radials (there was also a similar, but smaller RK project based on the use of two 1,000-hp ASh-62 engines). The Su-12 was an excel-

lent aircraft, but the onset of the jet age made its service entry pointless.

Heinkel He 114A-2 reconnaissance floatplane

This two-seat twin-float sesquiplane powered by a 960-hp BMW 132K nine-cylinder radial was used by the Luftwaffe and by the Romanian Air Force in small numbers. At least two He 114A-2s were captured; in 1946 they were displayed at a war booty exhibition in Kiev.

Henschel Hs 126B-1 reconnaissance aircraft

A small number of aircraft of this type was supplied to Estonia shortly before its incorporation into the USSR. According to some sources, the Estonian Air Force received 12 Henschel Hs 126B-1 reconnaissance aircraft (c/ns 3917-3928), other sources speak of 'at least five aircraft'. In the autumn of 1940 they were assigned to an air unit attached to the 22nd Territorial Corps of the Red Army (the corps was formed on the basis of what was left of the Estonian Army); the aircraft were based at Jägala. According to some sources, after the German invasion of the Soviet Union on 22nd June 1941, the Aircraft Squadron of the 22nd Corps was ordered to retreat to Russia on 27th June with its few serviceable aircraft (the most potent being a handful of Avro Ansons and Hs 126s). A number of aircraft are reported to have been flown to Russia; all others were burned and destroyed.

Yet, according to K-F. Geust, at the end of July 1941 three Hs 126 were still available at Jägala, and one of them was chosen for an operation in the German rear. Maj. A. V. Koronets (CO of the Baltic Fleet Air Arm's 71st AP) *flew the aircraft to Ülemiste (in the vicinity of Tallinn) and, starting on the*

next day, he made a number of reconnaissance flights without any trouble. This Hs 126 was obviously destroyed when the Soviet forces retreated from Tallinn on 27th August 1941'.

Further examples of this type were captured during the war at different sectors of the Soviet-German front. Several Hs 126s were among the machines captured during the Soviet counteroffensive near Moscow in December 1941. Later a few more examples were captured in the Stalingrad area.

A technical description of the Hs 126 can be found, together with the descriptions of other German aircraft types, in the manual prepared by NII VVS in 1943. It is not clear whether this description was based in any way on the examination of the captured aircraft. Soviet aviation specialists analysed the Hs 126 and stressed the following points in their overall assessment. The aircraft's layout (strut-braced high-wing monoplane/ parasol) gave the crew a good view (important for a reconnaissance aircraft); the armament comprising one fixed forward-firing machine-gun and one flexible machine gun in the rear cockpit was weak and quite insufficient for the aircraft's protection; armour plating was unsatisfactory with regard to armour thickness and sectors of enemy fire. On the plus side, mention was made of the availability of a smoke screen laying device and a glider-towing hook.

Henschel Hs 129 single-seat close-support and anti-tank aircraft

Soviet specialists took much interest in this twin-engined attack aircraft which, at least in theory, could pose a serious threat to Soviet tanks. After the British had studied the armament and weapon load of an Hs 129 shot down in the Middle East, the danger this aircraft posed for armoured vehicles became apparent.

An opportunity to study this type offered itself in August 1942 when Soviet AA artillery shot down a Hs 129B armoured attack aircraft in the vicinity of Rzhev. The heavily damaged machine made a forced landing near the village of Chashnikovo. However, it was not before December that the aircraft's description could be compiled. By then Soviet intelligence had succeeded in obtaining sufficiently comprehensive data from German sources on the aircraft's development history and on its initial versions.

A notable feature of this single-seat machine was its completely armour-plated forward fuselage and the highly survivable structure of the fuselage and the wings. Also of note was the offensive armament comprising one 30-mm MK 101 cannon under the fuselage and two MG 151 cannons in the wing root fillets (on the Hs 129B-2/R2).

Top and above: Henschel Hs 129B-2 ??+TQ (W.Nr. 141537) of 13(Pz)/SG 9 was destroyed by the retreating Germans at Wagrowiec near Poznań, Poland, on 22nd January 1945 to stop it from falling into Soviet hands.

Above: Soviet officers survey another sabotaged Hs 129B-2/R2 at Wagrowiec; the C on the nose suggests it was coded ??+CQ. The 30-mm MK 101 cannon under the belly is well visible.

A Hs 129B at a German airfield seized by Soviet forces.

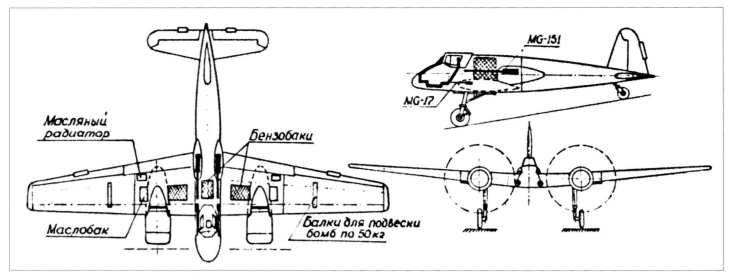

Масляный радиатор
Бензобаки
Маслобак
Балки для подвески бомб по 50 кг
MG-151
MG-17

Above: This diagram prepared by NII VVS shows the Hs 129B's cockpit armour, the location of the weapons, and 'soft' spots (the fuel tanks and the oil coolers).

Left: This somewhat incomplete Hs 129B-1 was delivered to NII VVS.

Below left: Soviet troops succeeded in capturing an example of the extremely rare Henschel Hs 130 reconnaissance aircraft.

A Henschel Hs 129B-1 was assigned to the NII VVS test centre (it is not clear whether this was the same machine or some other example). When analysing the Hs 129, Soviet aviation specialists took note of the following design features: the single-pilot crew which precluded providing defensive armament for the rear hemisphere; the armoured capsule enclosing the pilot; the twin-engine layout ensuring good visibility for the pilot; the existence of a tank-busting version equipped with a 30-mm MK 101 cannon; lack of armament for the protection from the rear and absence of view to the rear, making the aircraft easy prey for fighters attacking from behind; insufficient armour plating making the aircraft vulnerable to ground fire, including small arms fire.

Assessing the aircraft's handling, they regarded the machine's tendency to veer to port during take-off and landing as a major deficiency that complicated the conversion training of pilots. Judging by a report compiled at NII VVS, the MK 101 cannon was assessed by Soviet specialists as insufficiently effective against tanks; a conclusion was made that the Hs 129 had failed to justify the hopes pinned on it as an anti-tank aircraft. This was viewed as the reason for the development of the Junkers Ju 87G armed with two 37-mm cannons. Thus, the overall assessment (as of 1943) was rather uncomplimentary. Later Russian historians differ in their views on the effectiveness of the Hs 129 and its handling qualities, at least one of them sticking to the opinion that this aircraft was underestimated.

An example of the Henschel Hs 129, apparently in good condition, was among the numerous German aircraft shown at a big war booty exhibition that opened in Moscow's Central Culture & Recreation Park at the end of June 1943.

Henschel Hs 130A high-altitude reconnaissance aircraft

The Henschel Hs 130A high-altitude reconnaissance aircraft developed from the Hs 128 is known to have existed in the A-0 and A-0/U6 versions. There is no evidence that it was used operationally, albeit some sources say it was built in small numbers. An example of this aircraft (exact identity is unknown) was captured on a German airfield in 1945, as evidenced by a picture from Russian sources. The aircraft's subsequent fate is unknown.

Junkers Ju 87 Stuka attack aircraft

Before the war this aircraft, despite its formidable reputation in Europe, was derided by the Soviet military as 'antiquated, slow aircraft, very vulnerable to our fighters and having a very low speed'. However, the wide and sufficiently successful employment of the Stuka on the Eastern front prompted a change of attitude and motivated attempts to study this aircraft. The opportunity for this soon offered itself. Quite a few Stukas fell into the hands of Soviet troops. In the course of the battle of Stalingrad at least 15 intact Ju 87Ds were discovered at airfields after the surrender of Field Marshal von Paulus' troops. One of them was a Ju 87D coded JJ+HJ (W.Nr. 2481) of I/St.G2, which was captured on 30th December near Kotel'nikovo. In January 1943 a Ju 87D-3/Trop. (W.Nr. 2754), supposedly a StG 77 aircraft, was captured near Stalingrad. It was delivered to NII VVS and underwent lengthy repairs before its first flight there in early July 1943. (Some sources refer to the example tested at NII VVS in 1943 simply as a Ju 87D-3, others claim it was a Ju 87D-1.)

The flight testing generally corroborated the previous rather unflattering assessments

Top: A damaged Junkers Ju 87D-3 dive bomber coded ??+L? at an airfield in Germany overrun by the Red Army in January or February 1945.
Centre and above: Another Ju 87D-3 (??+B?) at the same location.

Above: This Ju 87B coded A?+HC stood on its nose after hitting a pothole on landing – without even damaging the propeller. It was in this undignified attitude that it was captured.

Left: A Ju 87D-3 of the Romanian Air Force's 6th Dive-Bomber Group seized at Khersones on the Crimea Peninsula, the Ukraine, in 1944. The meaning of the '5a' on the rudder is not known.

Below left: Iosif V. Stalin (rightmost) examines a Ju 87D in the war booty display in Gor'kiy Park, July 1943.

of this aircraft. Despite the considerable changes introduced into the design of the 'Dora', the most salient characteristic features of the machine were retained. These included the fixed undercarriage, the external airfoil flaps and ailerons, the stabiliser bracing struts. However, the aerodynamics of the aircraft were considerably improved, the fuel capacity and the carrying capacity of the bomb racks were increased, and more potent defensive armament was fitted. Soviet armament specialists took some interest in the Ju 87D-3's cockpit armour plating and some details of the powerplant, albeit they found it to be 'inadequate' and inferior to that of the IL-2 attack aircraft.

Assessing the Ju 87, Soviet specialists noted some features of the aircraft associated with its dive bomber role. These included the installation of dive brakes; an automatic dive recovery control device; a raised cockpit canopy affording good view and facilitating the aiming in a bombing attack; special bomb displacement gear preventing the propeller from being hit by the centreline bomb. The Soviet engineers showed interest in the German EZ-4 radio compass, the latest model of an altimeter, and the design of the 'howling siren' used by the Ju 87 during a diving attack to intimidate the enemy on the ground. Actually, it was recommended that a test batch of similar sirens be manufactured by one of the factories producing equipment for the aircraft industry. Soviet specialist also noted the provision for a glazed hatch in the floor of the Ju 87's cockpit which facilitated weapons aiming in a diving attack; it was recommended that a similar glazed hatch be incorporated into Soviet dive bombers.

In the summer of 1944, during the offensive in Belorussia, Soviet troops captured one more Ju 87D (W.Nr. 7986) supposedly belonging to I./SG 1. No information is available as to its airworthiness and eventual flights.

Soviet aircraft engineers showed much interest in the anti-tank version of the Ju 87. An example of this version, Ju 87G-1 W.Nr. 1097, was shot down in the vicinity of Bryansk in March 1943. It proved impossible to salvage it, and engineers had to satisfy themselves with studying the 37-mm BK 3,7 anti-tank cannons, which were removed from the machine and delivered to the Research & Test Range for Aircraft Weapons (NIPAV – *Naoochno-ispytatel'nyy poligon aviatsionnovo vo'oruzheniya*). The BK 3,7 differed very little from the standard German Flak 18 anti-aircraft cannon; the cannons had an ammunition complement of 12 rounds each and were carried in underwing pods instead of the usual underwing bomb racks. One cannon, complete with the gun mount, weighed 473 kg (1,042 lb). The cannon's high muzzle velocity – 1,170 m/sec (3,883 ft/sec) – made it possible to take aim

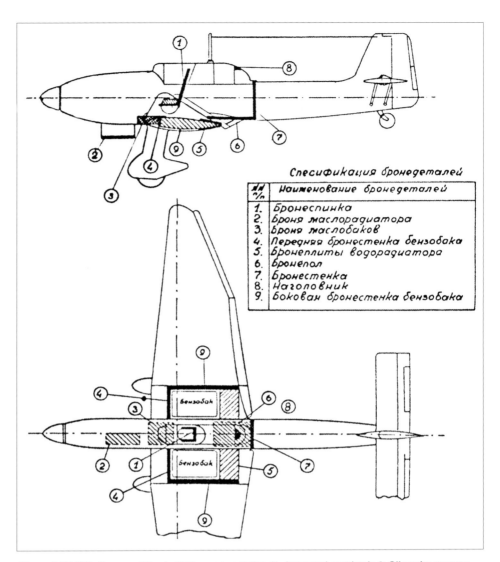

Above: A NII VVS diagram of the Ju 87D's armour plating (1. Armoured seat back; 2. Oil cooler armour; 3. Oil tank armour; 4, 9. Fuel tank armour; 5. Radiator armour; 6. Floor; 7. Bulkhead; 8. Head protector).

and fire its rounds against tanks at a distance of up to 800 m (2,640 ft).

As revealed by the pilot of the downed Ju 87G-1, only experienced pilots could efficiently operate the anti-tank version whose handling became much more difficult after the installation of the heavy cannons at some distance from the aircraft's axis.

Junkers Ju 87D-3 W.Nr. 2754
NII VVS.

Far left: Ju 87D-3 W.Nr. 2754 (ex ??+A?) undergoing tests at NII VVS in 1943. The aircraft carries a 250-kg bomb on the centreline. As usual, NII VVS studied the aircraft thoroughly, photographing every detail.
Left column, top to bottom: The Junkers Jumo 211J-1 engine and the Junkers VS 11 variable-pitch propeller; the bulletproof windscreen; the port armour-plated coolant radiator; and the main gear units with wheel spats and slipstream-driven dive-bombing sirens for scaring the enemy.
Centre column, top to bottom: The port wing MG 17 machine-gun; the aft-firing MG 81Z paired machine-gun; the tail unit; and the radio dial.
Right column, top to bottom: Aspects of the aircraft; the pilot's seat (note dive bombing reference lines on the canopy) and instrument panel.
Below: Three stills from a NII VVS film showing Ju 87D-3 W.Nr. 2754 on take-off and in cruise flight.

The testing of the German 37-mm cannon may have speeded up the Il'yushin Design Bureau's work on an improved 'tank buster' version of the IL-2 equipped with 37-mm Nudel'man/Suranov NS-37 cannons after the less-than-successful trials of a version with Shpital'nyy Sh-37 cannons of identical calibre. Soviet engineers conducted comparative trials of the 37-mm cannons produced in the USSR, Germany and the USA. The tests showed that the Flak 18 had a somewhat greater armour-piercing capacity than the NS-37 thanks to its greater muzzle velocity, but it was almost twice as heavy as the Soviet weapon and its rate of fire was 1.5 times slower than that of the NS-37.

It is of interest to take a look at the assessment of the Ju 87 as presented in an account prepared by NII VVS in 1943 (making no direct reference to the testing of cap-

tured aircraft). Describing the aircraft and its versions, the authors of the analysis pay special attention to the Ju 87G-1 anti-tank version produced in 1943 and fitted with two 37-mm cannons. Although the cannon had a rate of fire of up to 70 rpm, its immature design did not permit firing the weapons in bursts and only single shots could be made at two-second intervals, the authors noted. They also stressed that the installation of the cannon had appreciably affected the manoeuvrability and had made entering a dive more difficult. In consequence, instead of diving, the aircraft made its attacks in a shallow descent at an angle of 10-12°.

Assessing the defensive armament of the Ju 87 as 'weak' and the armour protection as inadequate, the authors of the analysis noted that, due to these deficiencies, the aircraft could be used in combat only with fighter cover. The version with the 37-mm anti-tank cannons with its inferior speed and manoeuvrability and reduced armour was even more vulnerable than the standard version. The aircraft was generally assessed as obsolete.

Transport aircraft and assault gliders

Arado 199 four-seat combat search and rescue floatplane

A single example of this aircraft was shot down over the Kola Peninsula in 1943; its wreckage was recovered after the war. Although this aircraft was not tested or studied in the USSR, it merits being mentioned here because of its unique story.

Two examples of the Arado Ar 199 four-seat floatplane were specially outfitted as combat search and rescue (CSAR) aircraft intended to support the operations of German aviation in the North. One of these machines was assigned to the Luftwaffe's 5. *Luftflotte* which was tasked with destroying Soviet aircraft at airfields on the Kola Peninsula and in North Karelia, bombing the port of Murmansk and disrupting Soviet communications in the Barents Sea. The Ar 199 was indispensable in ensuring the rescue of German pilots shot down in that area. It was always at the ready to be sent to the emergency site where it would alight on a nearby lake or river (which were in abundance) and pick up the pilot in distress. The aircraft was

repeatedly observed by Soviet troops and got the nickname *seraya stervyatnitsa*, which may be translated as 'grey buzzard' or 'grey carrion-eagle'. On one of these missions the Ar 199 had the misfortune of encountering a flight of Soviet fighters; the latter promptly attacked, whereupon the damaged floatplane came down on a small nameless lake some 10 km (6.2 miles) from Lake Urdozero. Two airmen from the 5th Independent GVF (Civil Air Fleet) Air Regiment of the 7th Air Army flying a Shavrov Sh-2 light amphibian were sent to the site to examine and destroy the aircraft. They managed to alight on the water nearby the downed floatplane and, having examined it with all due precautions, discovered two dead crewmembers in the cockpit. The Soviet airmen took all the documents they could find from the German aircraft and then used hand grenades to make it unsuitable for further operation.

Much later, forty years after the end of the war, a search group of the Aeroflot's Leningrad Civil Aviation Directorate/Murmansk United Air Detachment headed by Pavel Konovalov discovered the wreckage in the midst of impenetrable forests and swamps. The machine was in a sorry state: the airframe was riddled with bullets, the engine and floats torn off, and the cockpit canopy and cabin doors missing. The wreckage was recovered with the help of a helicopter which lifted and transported it on a sling to Murmansk-Murmashi airport. This is the story told by M. Golovenkov, an Aeroflot veteran, in a press article in December 1991. The subsequent fate of the wreckage is not known.

Arado 232B-0 medium-range general-purpose transport

An example of the Ar 232B-0 four-engined transport was captured by Soviet troops near the village of Karmanovo some 150 km (93 miles) west of Moscow on 4th September 1944. The aircraft is identified in some sources as K1+ZX (W.Nr. 110017) of I./KG 200; other sources describe it as one of the machines of Trsp. Fl. St. 5 which operated a special flight for the *Oberbefehlshaber der Luftwaffe* (Luftwaffe C-in-C), performing special missions over Soviet territory from bases in Finland and Norway. This transport had taken part in Operation *Zeppelin* undertaken by the Germans – an attempt to assassinate Stalin. The operation was a failure; the machine was extensively damaged on landing (which turned out to be a crash-landing) and the German commando group disguised as Soviet officers was arrested, as was the crew of the aircraft.

The wreckage was inspected on site by Soviet specialists. They took special note of the unusual undercarriage arrangement

Above and above right: The wreck of Arado Ar 232B-0 K1+ZX (W.Nr. 110017) near Karmanovo.
Left: This view of the landing gear explains how the Ar 232 got its nickname, 'Millipede'.

which, in addition to a retractable tricycle landing gear, included 11 pairs of small non-retractable idler wheels along the fuselage centreline. This multi-wheel undercarriage, which had earned the Ar 232 the nickname *Tausendfüssler* (Millipede), was intended to support the machine when it was lowered on its fuselage to permit direct loading or unloading from a truck bed (the main gear oleos could be compressed during load-ing/unloading and then extended again hydraulically so that the idler wheels lifted clear of the ground for take-off). An additional advantage was the possibility of taxiing on the idler wheels on unprepared surfaces. One more feature that proved of interest was the hydraulically operated forward dorsal turret with one 20-mm MG 151 cannon; it featured semi-automatic training of the weapon.

Dornier Do 24T air-sea rescue and transport flying boat

A single example of the Dornier Do 24 three-engined flying boat served with the Soviet Polar Aviation during the first post-war years. Russian sources identify the aircraft as the Do 24T (the version powered by BMW-Bramo 323R-2 Fafnir radial engines), albeit a British magazine once reported it as a Do 24K (the initial version powered by Wright R-1820-F52 or R-1820-G102 Cyclone radials). Exact information on the origins of the aircraft is not available; in several Western sources it is surmised to be the machine that fled to Sweden on 9th May 1945 from Ventspils, Latvia, and was returned from Sweden to the USSR on 14th August 1945. This aircraft had served with *Seenotstaffel* 50 and borne the code 5W+BU (WNr 42).

According to historian Vladimir Kotel'-nikov, the Do 24T initially served with the aviation subdivision of the Ministry of Interior where it carried the registration X-662 (that is, Kh-662 in Cyrillic characters). As he presumes, it was this machine that was trans-

A Dornier Do 24T flying boat seen in Igarka (on the Yenisey River in Western Siberia) in 1947. The aircraft (possibly ex 5W+BU of Seenotstaffel 50, W.Nr. 42) was 'extradited' from Sweden on 14th August 1945.

ferred to the Moscow air detachment of the Polar Aviation where it was reregistered H-473 (Cyrillic for N-473). Until the end of 1948 the aircraft sat idle at Zakharkovo airfield. On 19th October 1948 the Do 24T suffered damage to the planing bottom during beaching; it was repaired but was eventually struck off charge in the first half of 1950. Actually the registrations should have been applied as CCCP-X662 (= SSSR-Kh662) and CCCP-H473 (= SSSR-N473). However, the only available photo of the Soviet Do 24T shows this aircraft in Air Force markings, with no civil registration visible.

Some details on the Soviet service of this machine are to be found in the memoirs of T. F. Yeryomenko, a Polar Aviation pilot. He recalls that in 1946, a year after the end of the war, he was appointed crew captain of a flying boat of which he took charge at the Khimki water aerodrome (on the Khimki Reservoir north of Moscow). It turned out to be a Dornier Do 24. The crew took pains to study the aircraft very carefully, whereupon it was test-flown in the Khimki area. In late June 1946 the machine set off on its eastward flight, the destination being Krasnoyarsk, a city in West Siberia. Upon arrival there the aircraft was met by senior officials of the Noril'sk Air Transport Detachment (Noril'sk, a town situated beyond the Arctic Circle in West Siberia, was an important nickel mining centre).

The Do 24T was intended to maintain regular flights between Krasnoyarsk and Noril'sk, operating from water aerodromes on the Yenisey and Valyok rivers respectively. Its mission was to transport passengers (the nickel plant employees and local hunters who went south for their vacations, as well as specialists and actors from Moscow) and to deliver various supplies, including fruit and vegetables, for the population of Noril'sk. This was an air service of vital importance for the functioning of the northern mining town. The operation of the Do 24 posed some problems, mainly connected with the absence of original spare parts. These were overcome by different means including the use of equipment items from Soviet aircraft instead of the German ones. At one stage the flights had to be suspended because of the failure of some small gears in the propeller automatic pitch mechanism. With the onset of the winter seasons the aircraft was beached and underwent checks and repairs.

The Do 24T was flown by a crew comprising A. Rogachov, M. Dresvyanskiy, A. Chimerov, T. Yeryomenko, Ya. Sukhachov and A. Kuznetsov. (A Western source mentions Matvey I. Kozlov as one of the pilots who had flown this aircraft.)

Above: Focke-Wulf Fw 200C-3/U2 Condor F8+OW of I./KG 40 (W.Nr. 0034) was captured at Pitomnik airfield near Stalingrad in February 1943. Here it is seen in Soviet insignia during tests at NII VVS.

Above: The same aircraft in Gor'kiy Park in Moscow in 1945. Note the supports placed under the outer wings as a public safety precaution.

A Soviet Army officer shows the preserved Fw 200 to a group of enlisted men during an excursion to the war booty exhibition.

Above: A panorama of the aircraft display in Gor'kiy Park in 1943, showing the Fw 200C-3/U2 as originally displayed (without supports) in company with a He 111B, a He 111H, an Fw 189A-2, a Ju 87D-3, a Hs 129B-2 and so on. Large-calibre bombs are arranged beside the Condor.

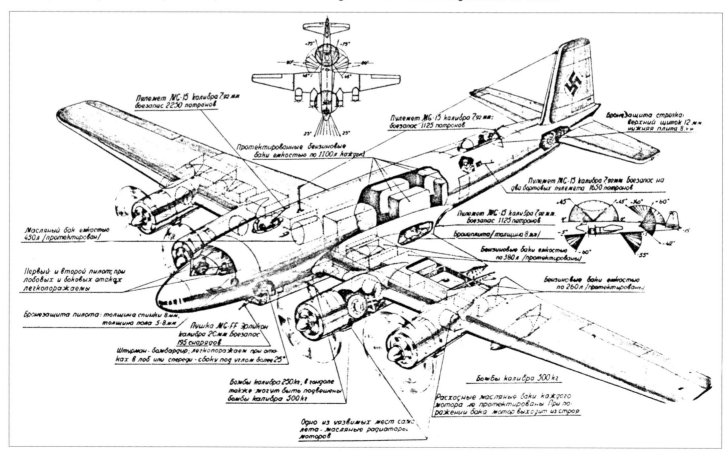

This cutaway drawing completed by NII VVS shows the Fw 200's armour protection, the fuel tanks, the defensive machine-gun positions and their field of fire.

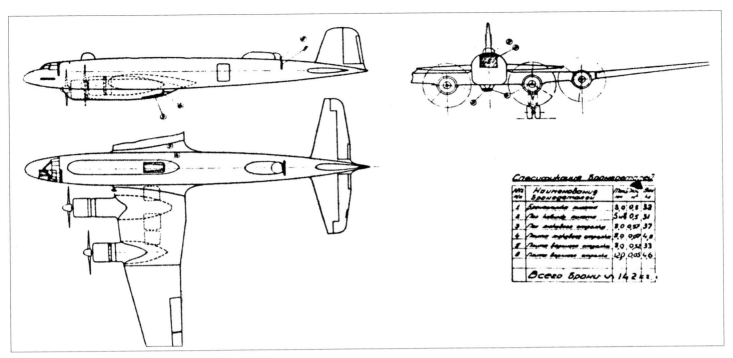

Above: One more Soviet drawing specifying the placement and thickness of the Fw 200's armour shields.

Focke-Wulf Fw 200 Condor maritime reconnaissance, bomber and transport aircraft

Several examples of the Fw 200 Condor were captured at the Soviet-German front by the Red Army. One of them was an Fw 200C-3 coded F8+OW (W.Nr. 0034), captured near Stalingrad. This machine representing a maritime reconnaissance/bomber version of the basic transport aircraft was sent to NII VVS where it arrived in April 1943. (In one account its subtype is stated as C-3/U2 and the former operator as KG 30. Yet another account identifies the machine delivered to NII VVS as an Fw 200C-4 belonging to KG 40, but the NII VVS documents speak of an Fw 200C-3.)

Eng.-Maj. G. V. Gribakin was appointed engineer in charge of the testing, with Col. A. I. Kabanov as project test pilot.

The machine tested at NII VVS in 1943 was powered by four BMW-Bramo 323R-2 engines, for which the NII VVS report gives a take-off rating of 1,000 hp and a nominal rating of 775 hp at 4,200 m/13,780 ft (as compared to the nominal rating of 940 hp at 4,000 m/13,120 ft according to German official data). No use was made of the MW-50 water/methanol injection system that raised the take-off rating to 1,200 hp.

The flight tests at NII VVS in 1943 provided the following results. Maximum speed at nominal engine power was 387km/h (240 mph) at 4,200 m and 342 km/h (212 mph) at sea level. Time to 5,000 m (16,400 ft) was 11.6 minutes and the service ceiling 6,480 m (21,260 ft). The take-off run on a paved runway was 630 m (2,070 ft); the take-off dis-

tance to an altitude of 25 m (82 ft) was 1,180 m (3,870 ft). The performance is valid for an all-up weight of 20,000 kg (44,090 lb), including a fuel load of 4,100 kg (9,040 lb). Interestingly, these performance figures are higher than those quoted for the Fw 200C-3/U4 by William Green in his well-known book *Warplanes of the Third Reich* – possibly because they were obtained at a lower AUW than the normal figure of 21,693 kg (47,833 lb).

The assessment of the Fw 200C formulated at NII VVS was worded as follows:

'Analysis of these data shows that the aircraft does not possess the requisite characteristics for a modern bomber. Its speed and service ceiling are too low. A considerable increase of AUW resulting from the installation of armament, armour plating and additional fuel tanks precluded an improvement in performance that might come from a certain increase in engine power. [...]

Testing of the captured Fw 200C-3 aircraft at NII VVS has revealed the following handling characteristics: [...] On take-off the

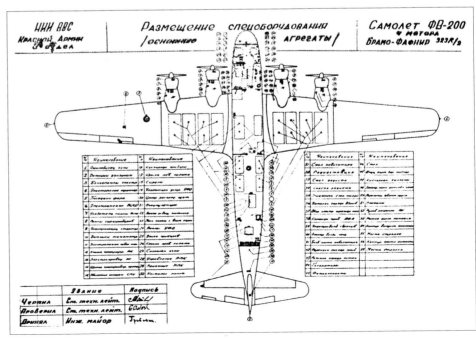

This diagram from the NII VVS documents shows the placement of the Fw 200's equipment items.

Head of page: Fw 200C-3/U2 W.Nr. 0034 in Soviet markings during tests at NII VVS in April 1943.
The other pictures on this page are stills from an instructional film prepared by NII VVS, with the aircraft painted up in Luftwaffe markings again for the occasion.
Upper row: The Fw 200's tail unit and No. 1 engine.
Above and above right: The radio aerials on the fuselage roof and a view of the radio operator's station.
Right-hand column: Views of the forward fuselage and engines. The latter were located high, requiring a tall access ladder. The photo on the right shows the entry door and the dorsal gunner's blister.

a) the external suspension of bombs, because the Fw 200C-3 can carry internally only a bomb load of 1,000 kg [2,200 lb], while the remaining bomb load – up to 2,800 kg [6,170 lb] – is carried externally;

b) the under-fuselage nacelle with forward- and rearward-firing gunner's stations.

3. Defensive fire protection of the aircraft is poor because of the small calibre of the weapons used. […]

4. The armour protection of the aircraft is unsatisfactory […]

5. The Fw 200C-3 aircraft is very vulnerable. The most vulnerable spots are:

a) the fuel tanks occupying a large area in the wings and fuselage;

b) the crew;

c) the unprotected service oil tanks in the engine nacelles.

The aircraft's low performance, high vulnerability and low effectiveness of the defensive fire restrict its combat use.'

The Condor was assessed as being inferior to the He 111 as regards cockpit visibility, simplicity of handling and reliability of the powerplant.

Drawing a comparison between the Condor and its Soviet four-engined counterpart, the Pe-8 powered by four AM-35A engines, Soviet engineers came to the conclusion that the Pe-8 was considerably superior in maximum speed, service ceiling, the number and location of gun turrets and the weapon calibre.

At the same time, some features of the Fw 200 were found to be of practical interest for Soviet aircraft designers. They included a very simple and reliable thermal de-icer, advanced and well-manufactured radio equipment, sighting devices for low-level bombing. After the completion of the testing in late April 1943 all these devices and gadgets, as well as the EZ-2 radio direction finder, the Dorenz instrument landing system, Askania homing stabiliser, Bauer-Sperry artificial horizon, Patin remote-indicating electric magnetic compass, were transferred to appropriate scientific research institutes for detailed study and practical use.

The same example of the Condor was displayed at the war booty exhibition in Moscow in June 1943.

Several more Condors formerly operated by Deutsche Lufthansa in airliner configuration were captured near Berlin in the spring of 1945. At least three Fw 200s, after repairs at a factory in Krasnoyarsk, were assigned to the Polar Aviation. They were to be used in the Soviet Far North regions, carrying out ice surveillance for the Arctic shipping routes. Known registrations include [CCCP] H-400, [CCCP] H-401 and [CCCP] H-500 (that is, N-400, N-401 and N-500 in Cyrillic characters; no prefix was applied).

Left column, top to bottom: The dorsal observation blister; the dorsal and waist gunner's positions, and the Fw 200 in flight.
Right, top to bottom: The No. 3 BMW-Bramo Fafnir 323 engine; the faired bomb rack and retractable landing light under the port wing, and the front end of the ventral gondola with a 20-mm MG 151 cannon.

aircraft has a tendency to swing to port. To counter this tendency, the pilot has to use differential engine power because the rudder alone is insufficient. […] The aircraft accelerates well and is controlled easily. In flight a good trim is achieved and the aircraft can be flown with hands off the rudder control. Stick forces during manoeuvring are considerable. […] The landing is simple. […]

Despite the aircraft's large size, the crew compartment in the forward fuselage is cramped, which hampers the work of the crew in flight. This affects especially the navigator/bomb-aimer. […] On the whole, with

regard to the ease of handling, the aircraft can be rated as a machine of average complexity.'

The overall assessment reads, in part:

'2. The conversion by the Germans of the Fw 200 passenger aircraft into a bomber is a compromise solution, and a not quite successful one. The shortage of high-output air-cooled engines during the conversion of the aircraft for military use necessitated the installation of the Bramo Fafnir engines with which the Fw 200 has inferior performance.

The aerodynamics of the aircraft are worsened by:

Top: CCCP-H401, one of the three Polar Aviation Fw 200Cs. The aircraft retains basic Deutsche Lufthansa colours. Note that the CCCP- prefix is carried on the wings only and the registration is applied to the fuselage as H-401.
Top right and above: H-500 (that is, CCCP-H500), the fourth Condor transferred to Polar Aviation. Note the large Polar Aviation logo on the nose.
Right: Another Polar Aviation Fw 200C (identity unknown).

H-400 was flown by Mikhail A. Titlov, the pilot who had ferried this machine from Berlin to Moscow in April 1946. He flew the Condor for three months. The flight from Khatanga to Moscow via Igarka on 13th December 1946 was his last flight in this aircraft; two of the engines quit en route and the aircraft was damaged beyond repair in the ensuing crash-landing in the Baydaratskaya Guba bight (69° 20'N, 67° 30'E). The crew and passengers (totalling 21 persons) were unhurt, subsequently being rescued by a Douglas C-47 piloted by N. L. Syrokvasha and Valentin I. Akkuratov, who landed safely on the ice in the vicinity of Titov's Condor. Fw 200 H-401 had a short service career, too.

In 1948 the example registered H-500 was reengined with Shvetsov ASh-62IR radials at plant No. 23 (Moscow-Fili) when the original engines went unserviceable; in this guise it was known as the MK-200 (*modifitseerovannyy Kondor* – modified Condor). This unique aircraft, too, was unlucky. On 14th February 1950 the MK-200 was jacked up for landing gear checks at Zakharkovo airfield and the jacks collapsed, resulting in damage to the oil coolers. The aircraft was repaired; yet, on 23rd April 1950 it crashed at Yakutsk while landing in a stiff wind, suffering severe damage to the port main gear unit, wings and engine nacelles. This time it was declared a write-off.

Gotha Go 242 assault and transport glider

The Gotha Go 242 glider utilising a twin-boom configuration was among the numerous German aircraft captured at Stalingrad after the famous battle near that city. In the course of war on the Soviet-German front Gotha gliders were used near Leningrad, Demyansk, Moscow and over other battle areas. This sturdy and reliable glider was superior in some respects to similar Soviet machines; it featured a partially armour-plated pilot's seat and a wide range of electrically powered equipment items.

The Go 242 was studied closely by Soviet specialists; it may well be that some lessons learned from that study helped improve the quality of Soviet assault gliders built during the war. What is certain, however, is the way the German know-how embodied in the Go 242 was put to good use by Soviet designers after the war. The well-known Soviet aircraft designer Yevgeniy G. Adler who worked for many years in Aleksandr S. Yakovlev's OKB-115 recalled in his memoirs how he was tasked with designing a transport glider that came to be known as the Yak-14. The OKB had no previous experience of designing such gliders, and Adler hit upon the idea of procuring some sort of an 'analogue' that might serve as a source of inspiration. He learned that a captured Go 242B-2 assault glider (coded TE+UL) was being kept in storage in Naro-Fominsk, not far from Moscow. To quote Adler:

'At first glance this glider had nothing in common with our Yak-14, but only at first glance. In effect, the similarity was quite substantial: approximately the same cargo-carrying capacity, single-spar strut-braced wings, the welded steel-tube structure of the fabric-covered fuselage, a similar way of mating the fuselage and the strut-braced wings.

There were also quite a few differences, yet the Gotha glider served for us as a sort of a tuning fork which enabled us to strike the right chord from the outset. Of particular interest was the fuselage mainframe to which the wings and the undercarriage were attached. We copied it outright. As for the skid undercarriage, we chose to ignore it, bearing in mind the peace-time conditions in which it was important to ensure good mobility on the ground and make the glider reusable.'

Junkers Ju 52/3m bomber

The Ju 52/3m is famous first and foremost as a rugged and dependable transport aircraft. However, it was also adapted for the bomber role, and it was in this capacity that it was used in Spain. An example of the Ju 52/3m bomber (information on the exact version and identity of the aircraft is not available) was captured in Spain by the Republican side from the Nationalist forces and was sent to the Soviet Union, where it was tested by NII VVS in 1937-38 under the disguise designation DB-29 (*dahl'niy bombardirovshchik* – long-range bomber). Test pilot Pyotr M. Stefanovsky performed 93 flights in this machine, according to his memoirs (193, according to a different source). The machine, as Stefanovskiy recalls, was powered by three 'Hornet BMW' engines (that is, Pratt & Whitney Hornet radials manufactured under licence as the BMW 132).

Curiously, the captured Ju 52/3m bomber (alias DB-29) was used for mock combat with the Il'yushin DB-3 bomber during the closing stage of the latter's service trials. Il'yushin OKB historian Yuriy A. Yegorov remarks that, *being superior in speed to the German bomber, the DB-3 conducted the combat aggressively and kept making attacks in a fighter-like manner'*.

The testing described above was only the start of the 'career' of this Junkers transport-turned-bomber in the Soviet Union – it had its sequel in 1940 and during the war, as well as during the first post-war years (see the following chapters).

Junkers Ju 52/3m transport (taken over from Estonia)

When Estonia became a Soviet republic in 1940, the Estonian airline AGO had in its inventory two Ju 52/3ms, ES-AGO and ES-AUL. They were taken over by Aeroflot and subsequently operated by the Baltic department of Aeroflot from September 1940 onwards.

Junkers Ju 52/3m transport (deliveries from Germany)

By 1940-41 Soviet aviation specialists had already had a chance to get acquainted with the Ju 52/3m both in its transport version (Deruluft aircraft and machines obtained

Right: A Junkers Ju 52/3m g4e See or g6e See floatplane used by an Arctic expedition in 1947. Note the Consolidated Catalina in the background.
Below: This Ju 52/3m displayed in a Soviet city park had been captured during the Battle of Stalingrad. The meaning of the emblem on the fuselage nose (a G in a circle) is unknown.
Right: Posing for a group photo with 'Auntie Ju' used as a freighter after the war.

CCCP-Л59, a demilitarised ex-Luftwaffe Ju 52/3m g7e used as a freighter by Aeroflot, is loaded at Ufa, Bashkiria, in 1945. Note the faired-over dorsal gun position and the addition of a Soviet-made RPK-10 direction finder with a small loop aerial aft of the flightdeck.

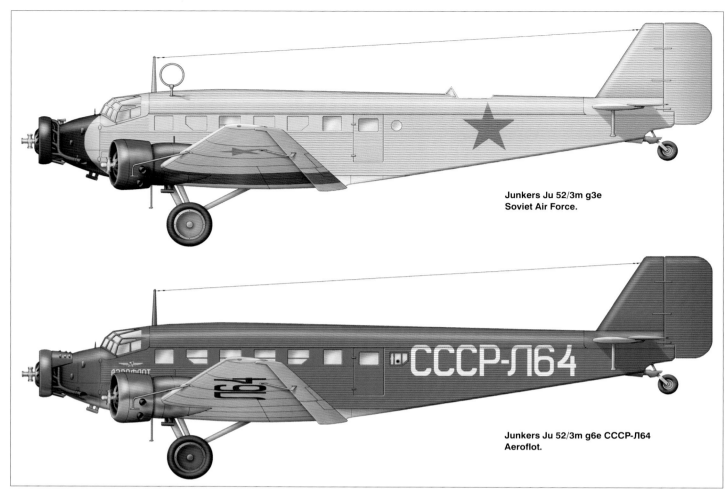

Junkers Ju 52/3m g3e
Soviet Air Force.

Junkers Ju 52/3m g6e CCCP-Л64
Aeroflot.

from Estonia) and bomber version (Spanish war booty). Ten Ju 52/3ms in airliner configuration were ordered in Germany in 1940; of these, only three were delivered in early 1941. In February-April of that year a delegation of high-ranking NKAP officials headed by I. F. Petrov paid a visit to Germany (the last of its kind). One of the goals of the visit was to take delivery of the aircraft that had been ordered earlier. In the course of the two-month tour over the country the Soviet specialists visited many factories, performed acceptance flight tests and took delivery of three Ju 52s, as well as two Me 108s. The identities of the three Ju 52s and their further fate are unknown.

Describing this visit, historian Dmitriy A. Sobolev notes that the Soviet delegation displayed particular interest for a Ju 52/3m converted into a flying testbed for testing aero engines. The development engine was installed in the fuselage nose instead of the No. 2 BMW 132. In case of need it could be shut down and the aircraft could continue flight on the power of the standard Nos. 1 and 3 wing-mounted engines. This type of testing was very useful for the 'fine tuning' of a new powerplant. Obviously impressed by this engine testbed, members of the aviation group in the delegation asked their hosts

that five of the ten Ju 52/3ms ordered be equipped in a similar way. The Junkers company agreed to modify only one aircraft, but not earlier than by October 1941. Needless to say, this order was never fulfilled.

Junkers Ju 52/3m transport aircraft (war booty after June 1941)

Assessing the Ju 52/3m during the war, specialists of NII VVS ascribed the wide use of this aircraft in the Luftwaffe to the following strengths of this type: simplicity of the design permitting it to be manufactured without the use of highly skilled labour; good operational qualities, such as high reliability and maintainability; a spacious cabin with easy access for loading and unloading; good field performance and simple handling permitting the aircraft to be piloted by crews of less-than-average skill and operate from semi-prepared airfields; and, last but not least, the ability of the airframe to absorb a lot of battle damage. At the same time they noted the generally obsolescent design having low performance and insufficient defensive armament, which entailed heavy losses during combat operations and imposed limitations on the type's operational use.

Dozens of Ju 52/3m transports were captured at different sectors of the Soviet-

German front. In particular, a large number of these aircraft fell into Soviet hands after the Battle of Stalingrad and the surrender of the encircled German troops there. Some of the aircraft were quite new, while others needed repair or were only usable for spares. Repairable examples were dealt with by GVF repair shops in early 1943 under the supervision of the Civil Air Fleet Research Institute (NII GVF – *Naoochno-issledovatel'skiy institoot Grazhdahnskovo vozdooshnovo flota*), then based at Zakharkovo airfield near Moscow. The personnel of an aircraft repair shop led by engineers A. Protopopov and P. Kozlov returned more than 80 Ju 52/3ms to airworthy status. The plants repairing the Junkers transports were the GVF repair shops Nos. 401, 403 and 405, plus plant No. 243 in Tashkent, Uzbekistan, which concentrated on refurbishing the BMW 132 engines of the Battle of Stalingrad war booty.

In the late spring of 1943 Aeroflot started using the Ju 52/3m for transport tasks on its routes. For obvious reasons the aircraft were operated in the rear areas of the Soviet Union (east of the Moscow meridian); even so, in the early days of Soviet Ju 52 operations several aircraft came close to being shot down by 'friendly' anti-aircraft fire! For example, the type served the Molotov (now Perm') – Kuibyshev route in the summer of 1944; it also found use on the Sverdlovsk (now Yekaterinburg) – Krasnoyarsk and Kuibyshev (now Samara) – Alma-Ata services. Starting in 1944, captured Ju 52/3ms were delivered to detachments of Civil Aviation in Western Siberia and elsewhere. Some aircraft were refitted to passenger configuration, others retained the cargo layout.

Known registrations include CCCP Л-23 (= SSSR L-23), CCCP Л-27 (which crashed in April 1946), CCCP Л-35, CCCP Л-37 (which crashed near Asha on 24th October 1943 en route from Ufa to Chelyabinsk), CCCP-Л54 (which crashed on 3rd February 1949), CCCP-Л58, CCCP-Л59, CCCP-Л64 and CCCP Л-68. These aircraft were in regular airline service, as indicated by the Л operator designator (meaning *leeneynyy* [*samolyot*] – aircraft in airline service – and denoting the Main Directorate of the Civil Air Fleet (GU GVF – **Glahv**noye oopravl**en**iye grazh**dahn**skovo voz**doosh**novo **flot**a). CCCP-Л64, CCCP Л-68 and five other examples were assigned to Aeroflot's Turkmenian Directorate, which used them since 1944 for carrying sulphur. One of the four aircraft was lost in a crash on 15th March 1945 when attempting a forced landing on two engines.

At least one machine, [CCCP] H-380, saw service in the Polar Aviation branch.

Top: A Ju 52/3m sits in the middle of the war booty aircraft exhibition in Gor'kiy Park (1943). A second example is visible in the background.
Above: A Soviet Air Force Ju 52/3m in overall olive green camouflage.
Top right: Another Aeroflot Ju 52/3m freighter, CCCP-Л64, is offloaded after delivering a cargo of fertiliser to a Central Asian airfield. Unlike CCCP-Л59, it shows no trace of a dorsal gun position.
Above right: Small cargoes are loaded into an Air Force Ju 52/3m from a GAZ-MM 1.5-ton lorry.
Right: This example serving as a backdrop for a publicity photo wears a civil-style colour scheme.

Above: A silver/black Ju 52/3m g3e pictured at Chkalovskaya AB during trials. Note the dorsal gunner's position with a small windshield.

Another Ju 52/3m studied in detail by NII VVS and used for shooting the customary instructional film.
Left column, top to bottom: Three views of the aircraft at rest, and a close-up of the ring-mounted dorsal MG 15 machine-gun.
Centre column, top to bottom: A ground crewman uses a special pole with a loop at the end; the centre BMW 132 engine; and the starboard side of the cargo cabin with the cargo door open (looking aft).
Right column, top to bottom: The starboard side of the fuselage, showing the three-segment cargo door; the port side with the entry door open; and the port side of the cabin, looking aft.

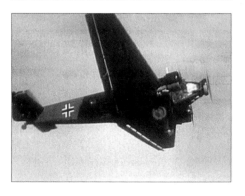

with Shvetsov ASh-62IR radials; it is not known if the project was implemented.

In addition to transport tasks, the type was used for other duties. For example, at LII the Ju 52/3m served as a glider tug, towing the experimental *Sokol* (Falcon) and *Oryol* (Eagle) transport gliders piloted by Igor' I. Shelest and the Tsybin KTs-20 gliders piloted by Viktor L. Rastorgooyev. The Ju 52/3m glider tug was piloted by Aleksey N. Grinchik and Nikolay V. Gavrilov who had developed the methods of towing. In 1942 a Ju 52/3m was modified into a 'flying laboratory' for TsAGI by the designer Vasiliy V. Nikitin.

Junkers Ju 252 general-purpose medium transport

The Ju 252 was a scaled-up derivative of the highly successful Ju 52/3m transport, retaining its three-engined configuration but incorporating such concessions to modernity as a retractable tailwheel undercarriage and normal smooth metal skin instead of the precursor's corrugated skin.

A single Ju 252 fell into the hands of the Soviet forces at the end of the war (no information is available as to the circumstances of the acquisition or to the subtype and identity). This machine was sent to the Soviet Union where it was tested at about the same time as the Dornier Do 217M (late 1945/early 1946). The machine proved to be a flying testbed: the Nos. 1 and 3 engines were the type's standard Junkers Jumo 211F radials, while the nose-mounted engine was the prototype Jumo 222A mounted on a snout-like adapter. According to D. A. Sobolev, subsequently the '222' engine was replaced by Soviet piston engine prototypes which were tested in various modes of operation in the air (no information is available on the types tested). Interestingly, somewhat later one of the Petlyakov Pe-8 four-engined bombers was converted into a similar engine testbed by modifying its forward fuselage for the installation of a fifth engine – an ASh-82 radial which underwent development test flying. (In some publications this particular machine is misidentified as a Ju 352.)

Soviet specialist took note of a useful feature incorporated in the Ju 252: the aircraft was provided with a large cargo hatch in the lower rear fuselage, which was very convenient for the loading of bulky cargoes. The hatch was closed by a hydraulically powered vehicle loading ramp known as the *Trapoklappe*; when opened, the ramp lifted

Other non-airline examples were operated by the Ministry of Interior's auxiliary flights and the Ministry of Fisheries (three were in service in 1949). Ju 52/3m CCCP-И511 (that is, SSSR-I511) was operated by a branch of the Ministry of Aircraft Industry (MAP). On 7th February 1948 it crashed fatally near Beloyarsk in poor weather when all three engines died after the carburettor inlets had been blocked by ingested snow. The type was even used for transport duties by the Soviet Air Force.

The Ju 52/3m transports used by Soviet transport organisations included at least one example of the floatplane version – the Ju 52/3m g4e (See) or Ju 52/3m g6e (See). An aircraft of this type was ferried from Germany in the summer of 1945 and was used by an Arctic expedition led by Avgevich in 1947.

The type was quite popular with the Soviet pilots; despite being slow and unwieldy, it was easy to fly and could stand up to a lot of abuse. On the other hand, the Ju 52/3m suffered from spares shortages, as the locally made substitutes were naturally of lower quality than genuine spares. Various Soviet-made components, such as magnetos, carburettors, wheels and skis, were used to keep the transports operational. The skis were of several models; one type was even specially developed by NII GVF and first fitted to CCCP Л-23. The BMW 132 engines suffered from the dusty environment in the Central Asian republics; hence redesigned carburetor inlets and air filters devised by NII GVF were fitted. There was even an attempt to reengine a Ju 52/3m

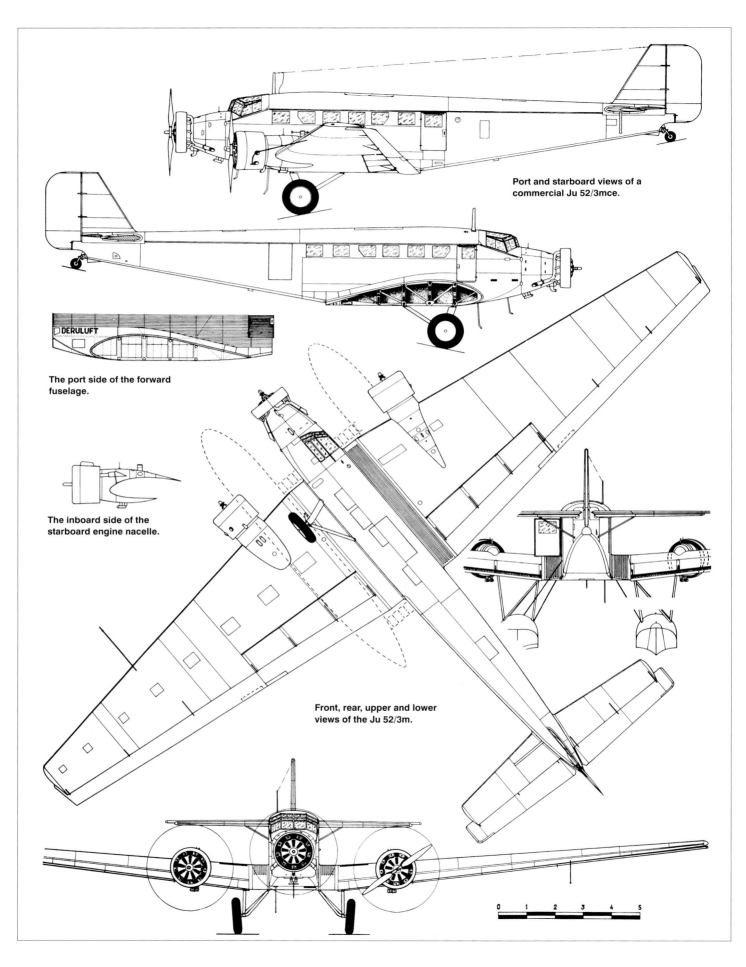

Port and starboard views of a commercial Ju 52/3mce.

The port side of the forward fuselage.

The inboard side of the starboard engine nacelle.

Front, rear, upper and lower views of the Ju 52/3m.

DERULUFT

0 1 2 3 4 5

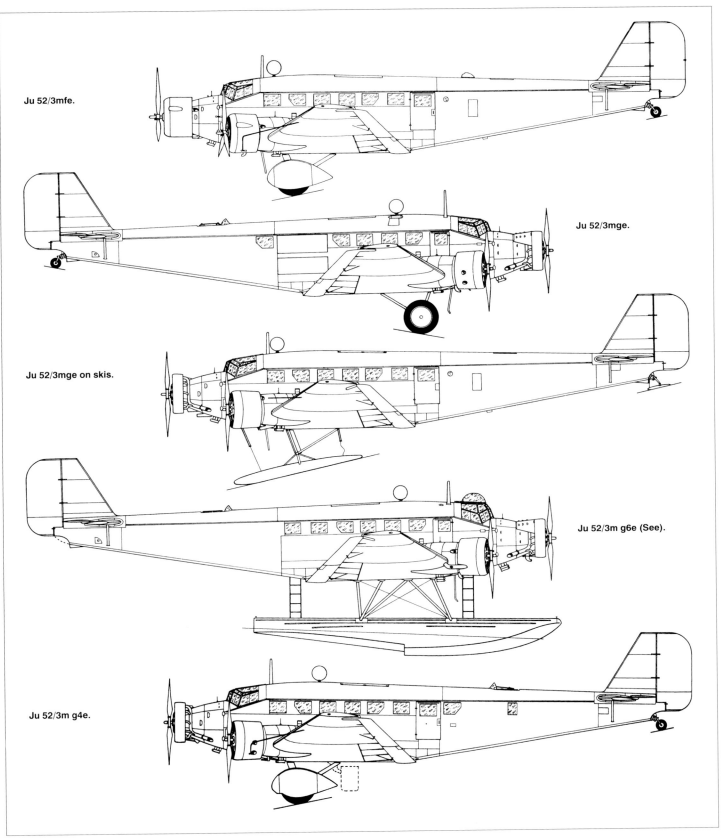

Ju 52/3mfe.

Ju 52/3mge.

Ju 52/3mge on skis.

Ju 52/3m g6e (See).

Ju 52/3m g4e.

the fuselage into a horizontal (line of flight) position. This rear-loading concept was eventually used on Soviet transport aircraft featuring a tricycle undercarriage and an upswept rear fuselage, the first of these being the Antonov An-8.

Junkers Ju 352A-1 general-purpose medium transport

The Ju 352A-1 was yet another large three-engined transport aircraft with a family lineage going back to the Ju 52/3m; it was basically similar to the Ju 252, with some dif-

ferences in the airframe structure, power-plant and armament.

There are some conflicting statements in various publications as to this aircraft being among the German types acquired by the Soviet Union immediately after the end of

Above: Seen here at Prague, this Junkers Ju 352A-1 wears Soviet insignia but is operated by a Czechoslovak Air Force unit that was in the Red Army Air Force structure until July 1945, as indicated by the CzAF roundel on the nose.

Above left, left and below left: This Junkers Ju 252 captured by the Soviet forces was used by NII VVS as an engine testbed. Here it is seen with its first development engine, a Junkers Jumo 222A, in the No. 2 position.

Bottom left: Close-up of the Jumo 222A installation on a long adapter.

Below: Test equipment in the cabin of the Ju 252.

the Second World War. Indeed, photos exist showing a white-painted Ju 352 with Soviet stars on the wings and tail, but they represent a Czechoslovak aircraft temporarily carrying Soviet insignia (together with a Czechoslovak Air Force roundel on the forward fuselage side). In one publication this photo is provided with the following caption: *'One of the few Ju 352A-1 transports to survive the W.W. II, and originally operated by the so called Grossraum-Transportgruppe, the example illustrated left was completely refurbished in Czechoslovakia. In 1946, it was presented by the Czechoslovak Air Force to the Soviet Air Force, and flown to Moscow carrying a Tatra 8 car as a gift from the Czechoslovak Government to Josef Stalin'.*

However, accounts published in the Czechoslovak magazine *Letectvi a Kosmonautika* (Aviation & Spaceflight) do not seem to bear out this statement. The story presented in this source is as follows. After the end of hostilities in May 1945 the Czechoslovak Air Units previously forming part of the Red Army became the backbone of the renascent Czechoslovak Air Force. Among its units was the Training and Transport Unit (*Cvičná a dopravná skupina*), which operated a motley collection of ex-Luftwaffe aircraft that had been found on former German airfields in the country. The biggest among

these was the three-engined Ju 352A-1 which was abandoned by the Germans at Prague-Ruzyně airport. As early as 9th May 1945 it was prepared by Czechoslovak technical personnel for the first flight, which was performed by a crew comprising test pilot F. Kládek from the Letov aircraft factory and technician Růžička. Several further flights followed, whereupon the Ministry of National Defence decided that the aircraft needed an overhaul. That work was accomplished at the Letov aircraft factory in co-operation with other factories based at Ruzyně. The work took some time, and the aircraft was first flown again in July 1945. The aircraft received Soviet insignia (red stars), as did all the other aircraft of the Training and Transport Unit of the 1st Composite Air Division that formed part of a large Red Army unit until 20th July 1945.

On 26th July 1945 the Tatra automobile factory informed the Czechoslovak Ministry of National Defence of the intention of the factory personnel to send a Tatra limousine to Moscow as a gift to Iosif Stalin. Permission was requested to use the Ju 352A-1 for delivering the car to Moscow. Permission was granted, and on 22nd August 1945 this aircraft took off for Moscow, carrying the car and three attendants. An accompanying delegation travelled in a Ju 52/3m aircraft. After a number of refuelling stopovers the two aircraft arrived at Moscow-Vnukovo airport, and the gift was duly handed over to the Soviet side. An account of this event published in *Letectvi a kosmonautika* does not mention anything about the Ju 352 also being handed over as a gift – one may surmise that it returned to Czechoslovakia, although this is not stated explicitly either. Anyway, the event took place in 1945, not 1946, as stated elsewhere.

Another account in the same magazine describes the doings of the Ju 352A-1 as follows: this machine was registered OK-JUE (W.Nr. 100023). (It is not mentioned whether the aircraft ever carried that registration visibly; at any rate, no pictures of the Ju 352 wearing this registration are available – *Auth*.) Between September 1945 and February 1946, when it was withdrawn from use, this aircraft made three flights to Moscow, carrying Gen. Ludvik Svoboda, then a group of 18 Czechoslovak officers enrolled in Soviet military schools, and finally a car for the Czechoslovak ambassador (a version of events somewhat differing from the one in the preceding account). From the last-mentioned flight – which was its last flight altogether – it returned on 24th February 1946, after suffering some technical troubles.

Soviet/Russian sources do not shed any light on this aircraft.

Junkers W 34 transport aircraft

This small transport aircraft, which first flew in 1924, was not imported into the USSR during the pre-war period, as distinct from its direct relative, the Junkers W 33. The W 34 differed from the latter type primarily in being powered by a radial engine instead of a liquid-cooled Vee-12 engine. Despite its obsolescence, the W 34 was used by the Luftwaffe on the Eastern front, and several examples were captured by the Soviet forces. There was one Junkers W 34 among the 26 Slovak aircraft that defected to the Soviet side in a mass exodus on 31st August 1944. A picture exists of a W 34 in Soviet Air Force insignia.

Junkers W 34s were among the captured German aircraft that were pressed into service with Soviet organisations and were operated by them in the early post-war years. In particular, three examples were operated by the GVF in Latvia, Kazakhstan and Moscow (specifically, as a trainer at NII GVF). At least four machines of this type were used by agencies within the People's Commissariat of the Interior (later Ministry of the Interior) framework. Two W 34s in MoI service were lost in accidents in 1946. In early 1947 a single W-34 remained in the inventory of the aircraft detachment assigned to the Ministry of Forestry.

Messerschmitt Me 323 Gigant heavy transport (powered assault glider)

Soviet specialist had an opportunity to study captured examples of the huge Me 323 powered assault glider. Fitted with six French Gnôme-Rhône 14 radials, this derivative of the Me 321 unpowered assault glider was used by the Germans for the delivery of supplies to a large grouping of German troops surrounded by the Soviet forces in Kurlandia (Latvia) in the second half of 1944.

Soviet specialists took pains to analyse the characteristics of this impressive machine. When inspecting one of the battle-damaged Me 323s, the Soviet engineers noted the huge dimensions of the cargo hold, good armour protection of the crew cockpit, the unusual design of multi-wheel undercarriage, and the defensive armament comprising 7.92-mm MG 15 machine-guns installed in numerous positions.

Siebel Si 204D transport aircraft

Among the captured German aircraft used in the Soviet Union during the first post-war years, the Siebel Si 204 transports were especially numerous. Lots of these aircraft were captured by the Soviet troops during the final stages of the war. Immediately after the end of hostilities the captured Si 204s underwent repairs at the Avia factory in Czechoslovakia. This aircraft had been produced in that country by the BMM and Aero factories since 1943, as well as in France, no production capacity being available for this type in Germany. After the war, Si 204 production continued in Czechoslovakia for local needs, the aircraft receiving the post-war local designation C-103 (later changed to C-3). However, the captured machines in Soviet service (presumably Czechoslovak-built) retained their German designation. Czechoslovak sources have published pictures of a Si 204D sporting Soviet Air Force insignia and coded '20 Black'. The pictures were captioned 'Aero C-103 (Siebel Si 204D)'. However, there is no evidence to suggest that machines of post-war manufacture were delivered to the Soviet Union.

Initially the captured machines were mostly operated by the Red Army; the headquarters of many regiments and divisions stationed in Germany used the Siebels as liaison aircraft. Fairly often their presence was not reflected in documents because they were considered an 'extra to the main course' – that is, to the normal complement of aircraft. Later they were duly taken on charge and some of them moved to Soviet territory. The Si 204 was a prized mount among Soviet airmen on account of its reliability and versatility. One such machine was flown by Vasiliy I. Stalin, the son of Iosif Stalin, who commanded the aviation of the Moscow Military District.

The machines in Soviet service were all Si 204Ds. A Soviet flight manual issued in 1946 contained a description of the Si 204D-0 and D-1, the engine type being indicated as the Argus AS41 (other sources identify the engine as As 411). The Si 204D was intended for transporting seven to nine passengers; with the cabin seats removed, they could carry cargo. Its avionics and equipment rendered it usable as a conversion trainer for long-range bomber crews. The aircraft's electrics and radio equipment permitted instrument/night flying.

The Si 204D-1 differed from the D-0 version in having a revised equipment fit. The most important change, as stated in the manual, was the *'provision of electrically actuated refuelling and some alterations in the location of instruments'*.

The specifications for the Si 204Ds from the Soviet manual are given on page 182.

A Soviet soldier inspects the burnt-out hulk of a Messerschmitt Me 323A Gigant transport at an airfield overrun by Soviet forces.

Above and above right: Several Siebel Si 204D utility transports were operated by the Soviet Air Force. This one was flown by Vasiliy I. Stalin, son of the Soviet leader, who was Commander of the Air Force of the Moscow Military District.

Above: A Soviet Air Force Si 204D (alias Avia C-3) in standard olive drab finish. Contrary to normal practice, there are no star insignia on the fins..

The Si 204D also saw service with the Soviet civil aviation. For starters, one example was tested at NII GVF in 1945. The type came in handy because at that time Aeroflot had no machine to fill the gap between the two classes of aircraft used in big numbers – the big Li-2s and Douglas C-47s, on the one hand, and the small Po-2s, on the other.

In civil aviation the Si 204Ds were used in areas ranging from the Far North to the southernmost mountainous regions of Tajikistan. The first among the civil departments to receive the Si 204 was the Polar Aviation directorate (GU SMP), which began taking delivery of the captured aircraft in the summer of 1945. Nine machines of this type were ferried from Germany by the crews of GU SMP's Moscow-based detachment between June and August 1945. Two of these remained in Moscow, the other seven were sent to Krasnoyarsk (in West Siberia) where they were modified to suit the operating conditions in northern areas, including operations on skis.

As early as 1945, the Si 204s started their operations in the North. A machine registered [CCCP] H-370 (that is, N-370 – again with no country prefix) was assigned to the Chukotka Air Detachment but stood idle most of the time because it had not been

Right: This Soviet Air Force Si 204D wears an unusual white or light grey overall finish.
Above: A civilian Si 204D performing feeder services on Aeroflot's routes is pictured in Khorog, Tajikistan, in the Pamir Mountains. Note the overpainted Luftwaffe insignia on the wings and tail.

adapted for operations in cold climates. In September 1946 it was sent back to Moscow for modification. On the other hand, new deliveries took place. By April 1947 the Polar Aviation had nine Si 204s on strength, including [CCCP] H-379, [CCCP] H-398, [CCCP] H-408, [CCCP] H-409 and [CCCP] H-414.

Operations of the Si-204Ds in the North were plagued by several incidents and fatal crashes; these involved the machines registered H-379, H-414, H-408 and others. This led to the conclusion that the German aircraft, after all, were ill-suited for operations in the North. The Si 204 had not passed special cold-weather tests. As a result, in 1948 the Polar Aviation, which by that time had 12 Siebels in its inventory, withdrew them from use. The aircraft were for the most part transferred to other organisations (see below).

The Si 204 made its appearance on Aeroflot routes somewhat later than in the Polar Aviation. The GVF (Civil Air Fleet) was primarily interested in using the Si 204s in the Pamir Mountains of Tajikistan. One machine was taken on loan from GU SMP and underwent operational trials in the course of a month, whereupon the aircraft was returned to the Polar Aviation. Obviously, the results of the trials were satisfactory, since the Chief of the Civil Air Fleet requested that the VVS should transfer 20 captured machines for airline operations. A small number of Si 204s was transferred to

Above: This example operated by the Soviet Polar aviation (Aviaarktika) looks like a Si 204C with the initial stepped nose. However, it may also be a locally modified Si 204D.

Aeroflot in 1945, supplemented by further deliveries in 1946 and 1947; they were used on local routes in Tajikistan, Armenia, Azerbaijan and Uzbekistan. A single Si 204 (the last to be obtained by Aeroflot) was supplied in 1948. However, even before that Aeroflot had begun to phase out the German machines due to an influx of 'demilitarised' Li-2s and C-47s from disbanded SovAF transport units that obviated the need for the captured materiel. In 1949 Aeroflot terminated operation of the Si 204 and all remaining examples were struck off charge by the end of the year.

The Si 204s operated by some other state agencies lingered on in service for a somewhat longer period. The agencies in question were the Ministry of Aircraft Industry (five machines as of 1st October 1947), the Ministry of Interior and the Main Directorate of Hydrometeorological Service). The latter received ten Si-204s from the Polar Avi-

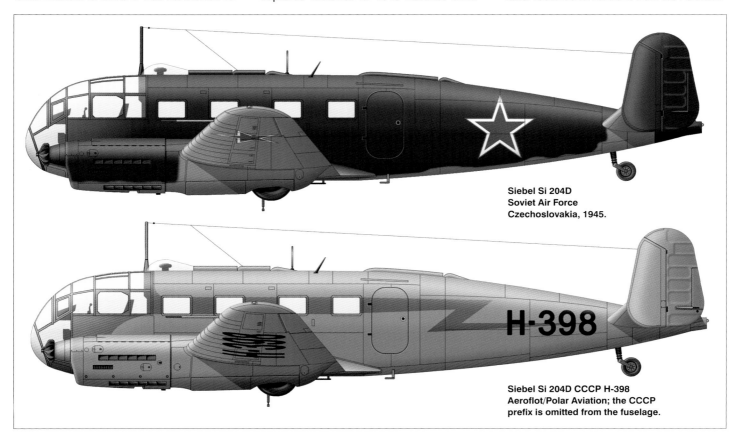

Siebel Si 204D
Soviet Air Force
Czechoslovakia, 1945.

Siebel Si 204D CCCP H-398
Aeroflot/Polar Aviation; the CCCP
prefix is omitted from the fuselage.

Specifications of the Siebel Si 204D from the Soviet flight manual of 1946

Normal all-up weight, kg (lb)	5,600 (12,345)
Maximum AUW, kg (lb)	5,800 (12,790)
Empty weight, kg (lb)	4,000 (8,820)
Payload, kg (lb):	
at normal AUW with 450 kg (990 lb) of fuel	950 (2,090)
at maximum AUW with 450 kg of fuel	1,100 (2,425)
at normal AUW with a maximum fuel load	560 (1,230)
Maximum speed at 2,600 m (8,530 ft), km/h (mph)	347 (215)
Cruising speed, km/h (mph)	280 (174)
Maximum cruising speed at 2,000 m (6,560 ft), km/h (mph)	315 (195)
Range at 280 km/h with 1-hour fuel reserves, km (miles)	1,250 (776)
Service ceiling, m (ft):	
at an AUW of 5,400 kg (11,900 lb)	7,250 (23,790)
at an AUW of 5600 kg	6,850 (22,470)
Landing speed, km/h (mph)	130 (80)

A Hungarian Air Force Arado Ar 96 liaison aircraft captured in the winter of 1942-43.

ation in 1948; they were reregistered CCCP M-351 through CCCP M-360 (M being the designator generally reserved for local authorities; the tie-up with the previous registrations is not known). Only five of them remained in service by April 1950, and by the late spring of 1950 all but one had been written off.

Finally, in 1947 a single Si 204 was transferred from the Polar Aviation to the Selkhozaerosyomka agricultural survey agency sorting under the Ministry of Agriculture. The machine received a new registration, CCCP Ф-274 (= SSSR F-244, the F

standing for foto and being the operator designator of photo mapping aircraft, normally operated by the Aerogheodeziya trust of the Chief Directorate of Geodesics and Mapmaking). By early 1951 there were no longer any Si 204s in operation in the USSR.

Utility and training aircraft and helicopters.

Arado Ar 66 trainer
According to the Russian aviation historian D. A. Sobolev, a few Ar 66 training biplanes were among those captured at airfields and air strips. They could be brought to a serviceable condition after minor repairs. No infor-mation about their use by the Soviet troops or testing at flight test centres is available.

Arado Ar 96 trainer
These is photo evidence that at least one Ar 96 trainer used by the Hungarian Air Force for liaison duties was captured on the Soviet-German front.

Bücker Bü 131 Jungmann trainer
Three examples of this two-seat aerobatic biplane were delivered from Germany in 1940 under the terms of the agreement signed on 11th February of that year. This aircraft, first flown in 1934, was used as a primary trainer by the German Luftwaffe. The aircraft was tested at NII VVS and at LII where it was flown by Mark L. Gallai, Aleksey N. Grinchik, Igor' I. Shelest and others. Shelest, in particular, performed advanced aerobatics, including prolonged inverted flight, in the Jungmann. The NII VVS test pilots who flew the Bü 131 included the female test pilot Nina I. Rusakova.

Some sources identify one of the three imported machines as a Bü 131D-2

A few examples of the Bücker Bü 131 used as liaison aircraft were captured by Soviet troops at different sections of the Eastern front. An example of this type was included in the display of captured German equipment in Moscow's Central Culture & Recreation Park in 1944-45.

Bücker Bü 133 Jungmeister trainer
Three examples of this machine, which was basically a scaled down Bü 131, were likewise imported in 1940. They were tested by Igor' I. Shelest, Viktor L. Rastorgooyev, Aleksey N. Grinchik, Sergey N. Anokhin and other LII and NII VVS test pilots. No information is available as to the test results.

When Lithuania became part of the Soviet Union in 1940, three of the Lithuanian Bü 133D aircraft were taken over by the Soviet armed forces. They were used by a

A Bücker Bü 131 trainer on display at the war booty exhibition in Gor'kiy Park in 1943. The plaque behind it tells the visitors how much hardware the Nazi invaders had lost during the three years of hostilities.

Above: In contrast, this Bü 131D-2 was acquired in 1940 for evaluation. It is seen here at LII. Right: The same machine at NII VVS. The fin bears the inscription 'Bücker Jungmann'.

reconnaissance air squadron of the 29th Infantry Corps.

Bücker Bü 181 Bestmann utility aircraft

Several examples of the Bücker Bü 181 Bestmann utility aircraft were captured by Soviet forces during the final stage of the war and impressed into service with Red Army units. One such machine coded '13 White' and wearing Soviet Air Force insignia was seen flying in the Prague area after the liberation of the Czechoslovak capital in May 1945. Another Bü 181 wearing the tactical code '2 White' on the fuselage behind the red star was seen at the NII GVF civil aviation test centre at Zakharkovo. It is not known whether it was subjected to testing or merely served as a utility machine or a personal 'hack' for the needs of the test centre.

In 1947 three Bü 181s were among the aircraft assigned to the Ministry of Forestry, together with a single Junkers W 34. The aviation department of the ministry was disbanded shortly thereafter; the ultimate fate of these aircraft is not known.

Fieseler Fi 156 Storch utility, reconnaissance and observation aircraft

Two Fieseler Fi 156 Storch utility aircraft were delivered to the USSR from Germany in 1939-40. The first one was presented as a gift by Reichsmarschall Hermann Göring to the Soviet delegation which was touring the German industry in 1939. Presumably it was the aircraft that, according to Lennart Andersson, was flown to Moscow via Kaunas, bearing the German registration D-IXWO. The other one was apparently purchased in 1940 together with many other aircraft types.

Stalin was so impressed by the short take-off and landing capabilities of the Storch that he gave express orders for a similar aircraft to be produced by the Soviet aircraft industry. The task was entrusted to Oleg K. Antonov, the future famous aircraft designer, who at that time worked at Aleksandr Yakovlev's OKB-115. Antonov was appointed chief designer of a small design

Top and above: Bücker Bü 181 Bestmann '2 White' at Zakharkovo airfield (seat of NII GVF – the Civil Air Fleet Research Institute), with a Li-2 and a Junkers W 34hau in the background.

Another Soviet Air Force Bü 181. In defiance of superstition the machine is coded '13 White'.

Above: A Fieseler Fi 156C Storch coded 8U+CC (or 8U+CG?) captured in its earthen revetment.

Left: Two more captured Fi 156Cs, DH+ML and ??+A?, tied down to prevent storm damage at a German airfield.

Right: The first prototype Antonov OKA-38, the Soviet derivative of the Fi 156, in the assembly shop of plant No. 23 in Leningrad on 14th September 1940. The longer nose housing the Soviet MV-6 engine is clearly visible, as are the larger wheels. The first prototype was built in an observation/liaison version known as SS.

Below right: This view shows the shape of the OKA-38's vertical tail, which differed from the German original. Note the slats on the underside of the elevators increasing their efficiency at high angles of attack.

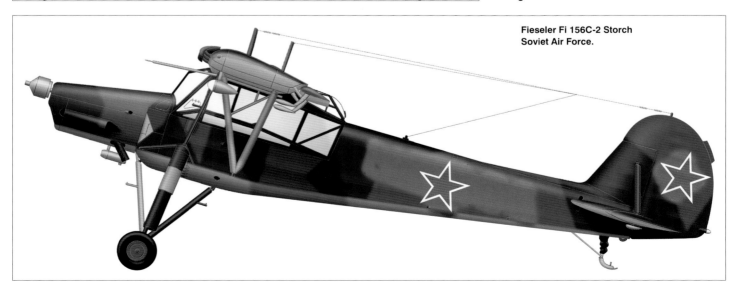

Fieseler Fi 156C-2 Storch
Soviet Air Force.

Above: A Soviet Air Force Fi 156C equipped with skis demonstrates its short take-off capability, climbing away at a high angle of attack.

Right: Another captured Fi 156C on a compass swing platform in Czechoslovakia in 1945.

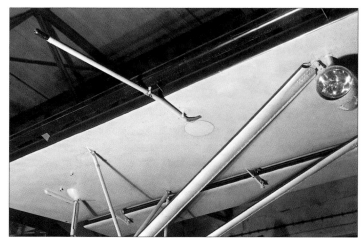

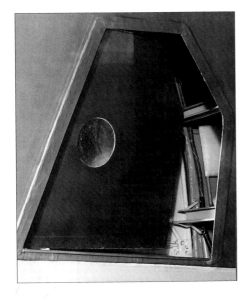

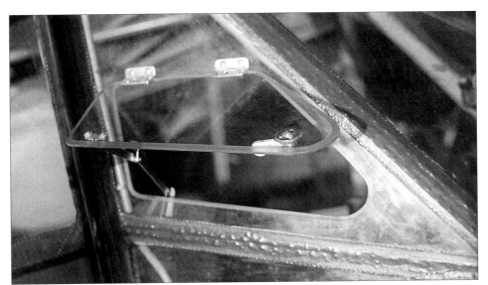

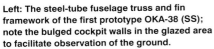

Left: The steel-tube fuselage truss and fin framework of the first prototype OKA-38 (SS); note the bulged cockpit walls in the glazed area to facilitate observation of the ground.

Far left, below: The port side of the fuselage of the second prototype OKA-38, alias 'aircraft No. 2', representing the medical version. The upward-opening door of the stretcher compartment (incorporating a small circular window) and the two stretchers are visible.

Far left, bottom: The instrument panel of the OKA-38.

Below left: The port wing of the OKA-38, showing the bracing strut, the full-span fixed leading-edge slat, the landing light and the pitot tube.

Bottom left: The starboard side of 'aircraft No. 2'. The ambulance version had flat fuselage sides and a much smaller glazing area.

Above: The emergency exit on the starboard side of the ambulance version's fuselage. Its shape was dictated by the design of the fuselage truss.

Above right: The starboard direct vision window.

Right: Overall view of the OKA-38's cockpit. The seat is not yet installed. Note the hand crank and chain drive of the flap extension mechanism.; note also the aileron trim handwheel.

Overleaf:
Three views of the first prototype OKA-38 in front of the hangar at LII. The six exhaust stubs of the MV-6 engine offset to starboard are visible; the engine cooling air intake is offset to port. Note the three aerial masts on the fuselage and the wingtips. The aircraft was painted olive drab with blue undersides and wore no insignia.

Page 189:
Three more views of the same aircraft. Interestingly, the OKA-38 (SS) was tested with smaller wheels of the same type as fitted to the Fieseler Fi 156.

bureau at Plant No. 23 in Leningrad to which one of the Storchs was sent to serve as a pattern aircraft. Antonov arrived in Leningrad in March 1940 and set about preparing the construction of the prototype of the Fi 156 copy which was given the designation OKA-38 (after the initials of Oleg Konstantinovich Antonov). It was also given the Russian name *Aïst* (Stork). Interestingly, having examined the pattern aircraft, Antonov discovered that the German designers had made use of the R-II wing airfoil developed by the Soviet aerodynamics specialist Pyotr P. Krasil'shchikov.

Two prototypes were built. The first of them, intended for liaison and artillery spotting duties, received the service designation SS (*samolyot svyazi* – liaison aircraft). Outwardly it was very similar to the German aircraft, the main difference being the shape of the engine cowling – the OKA-38 was pow-

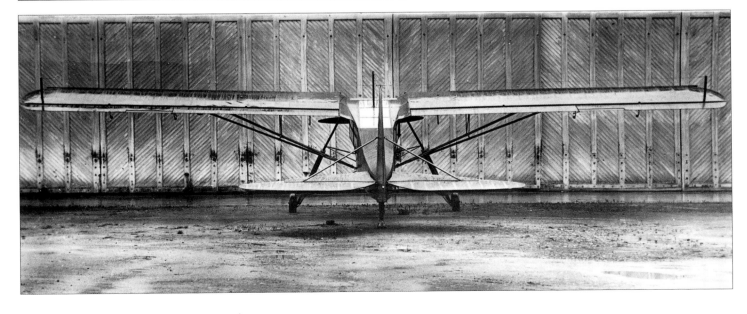

Above: A Soviet Air Force Fi 156 on skis during tests in the Soviet Union; the engine cowling is under wraps.
Below: This view of the second prototype OKA-38 ('aircraft No. 2') gives a comparison of the two types' silhouette. The stencilled inscription on the fuselage side reads *Podnimi zakrylki* (Raise the flaps), reminding the pilot to retract the flaps before opening the door of the stretcher compartment.

ered by a Soviet MV-6 inverted in-line engine (a licence-built derivative of the Renault Bengali 6) instead of the original Argus As 410C inverted-Vee 12-cylinder engine. The second prototype was an ambulance version accommodating three wounded persons (two stretchers and one wounded or a medical attendant on a seat); it was referred to simply as Aircraft No. 2. The air-

craft successfully passed State Acceptance tests at NII VVS and was launched into series production at Plant No. 465 in Kaunas, Lithuania. In March 1941 Antonov was appointed chief designer of this plant and went to Kaunas where production quickly got under way, several machines being completed by mid-June. However, on 22nd June the town of Kaunas and Plant No. 465

were bombed by German forces, and all the SS aircraft were destroyed. The work on the OKA-38 never resumed. Antonov returned to Moscow and became deputy Chief Designer in Yakovlev's OKB.

According to Czechoslovak sources, in 1941 German forces captured several uncompleted OKA-38 aircraft in the vicinity of L'vov, Western Ukraine (it is not stated

Above: Another view of the Fi 156 depicted on the opposite page, showing the Soviet insignia on the wing undersurface.
Below: This Fi 156 wearing a German civil registration was probably D-IXWO – the one presented by Hermann Göring in 1940. Note the fully deployed flaps and drooped ailerons. The background appears to have been retouched away by military censors.

how they ended up there). They were duly finished and then handed over to the Slovak Air Force. As of 30th July 1943, six of these aircraft, designated ŠS-6, were assigned to a flying school in Trenčianske Beskudice.

The other Fi 156 delivered from Germany served with NII VVS as a liaison aircraft; it was flown by Pyotr M. Stefanovskiy, Aleksandr S. Nikolayev, Stepan P. Sooproon and other test pilots. The aircraft was still operated by the institute in 1942. Interestingly, it was in the Fi 156 that Capt. Grigory Bakhchivandzhi, a NII VVS test pilot, arrived at a test site in the Urals to take up the testing of the Bereznyak/Isayev BI-1 rocket-powered interceptor in 1942.

During the war years a number of Fi 156s were captured by Soviet troops; they must have belonged to different subtypes, including the Fi 156C. Serviceable examples were used operationally as courier aircraft by the Soviet Air Force. For example, Maj. Gen. Yevgeniy Ya. Savitskiy, Commanding Officer of the 205th IAD (Fighter Division), – he went on to become Commander of the Air Defence Force's fighter element after the war – used an Fi 156 as his personal hack.

Top and centre: The first prototype OKA-38 during manufacturer's flight tests in the winter of 1940-41. Interestingly, the propeller spinner is missing.
Above: Three-quarters rear view of 'aircraft No. 2'.

So did the commissar (senior political officer) of the 812th IAP (Fighter Regiment) Maj. Timofei Ye. Pasynok; he flew a Storch found at the former Luftwaffe base at Sochaczew, Poland, in January 1945. Cases were known when Soviet POWs escaped in Storchs stolen from Luftwaffe bases. For example, Nikolay Loshakov of the 14th Guards IAP escaped from Ostrov with Ivan Denisyuk as passenger in 1943; on 4th October 1943 the ADD (Long-Range Aviation) pilot Arkadiy Kovyazin escaped from Riga-Spilve in a Storch, landing at Lipovka 50 km (31 miles) north-west of Rzhev.

In August 1945 the Soviet Union obtained four Fi 156 Storchs from Sweden. These were the machines that had escaped to Sweden from Latvia in early May 1945. According to K.-F. Geust, their identities were as follows: PV+ZZ (of 14./Fl.Verb.G. 2, W.Nr. 5323); KC+LJ (W.Nr. 5044); U2+OB (of Stab I./NAGr 5); and KP+GI. What happened to these machines after the transfer to the USSR is not known. What *is* known is that at least one Fi 156 was operated by Aeroflot. It must have been one of the six Fi 156s, including CCCP-Л556, that were received by the Civil Air Fleet (GVF) in 1946. They were all assigned to the Latvian Independent Air Detachment. CCCP-Л556 crashed on 27th June 1946 due to pilot error, killing the pilot and the two illegal passengers. The remaining Storchs were grounded pending investigation. Later one of these machines went to NII GVF where it was tested and then used as a trainer.

In April 1990 the British magazine *FlyPast* published a picture of a Fi 156 in Soviet Air Force markings captioned *Fi 156 Storch on a compass circle in Czechoslovakia, where it was found*. This may well have been an aircraft belonging to a SovAF unit stationed in Czechoslovakia in May 1945, or to a Czechoslovak air unit which had been a part of the Red Army and wore Soviet insignia for a short while after the capitulation of Germany.

Flettner Fl 282 Kolibri helicopter

First flown in 1939, the Flettner Fl 282 Kolibri (Hummingbird) was a single/two-seat helicopter intended for artillery spotting, liaison and reconnaissance; it utilised an unconventional layout with side-by-side intermeshing rotors and aircraft-type tail surfaces. Its development, including operational trials, resulted in a fairly reliable machine suitable for practical use. At the end of the war the Fl 282 entered quantity production; however, due to the critical situation at the fronts and allied bombing raids only 22 machines were produced.

An incomplete Fl 282 was discovered in Germany after the end of hostilities; together

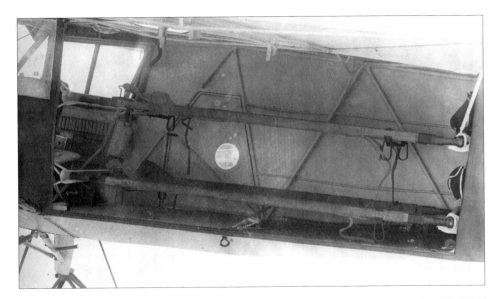

Top: 'Aircraft No. 2' with the stretcher loading door open, showing the emergency exit door on the starboard side.
Centre and above: 'Casualties' are loaded into 'aircraft No. 2' during trials. The OKA-38 offered much more convenient stretcher loading than the Fi 156D, the medical version of its German progenitor.

193

One more view of 'aircraft No. 2' with the stretcher loading door open; note the retaining brace.

with the Focke-Achgelis Fa 233 described below, it was despatched to the Soviet Union and assigned to LII where it arrived in dismantled condition. It was decided to reassemble the helicopter and test it. Nikolay Smorodin was appointed engineer responsible for the re-assembly, which was eventually completed, despite a number of difficulties.

After a few tethered flights conducted in the winter of 1947 the helicopter made its first free flight at the hands of test pilot V. V. Tezavrovskiy. The first flight was accompanied by a mishap – during the take-off a gust of wind caused the helicopter to bank and one of the rotor blades struck the ground, shattering on impact. Fortunately, the pilot was not hurt and the machine suffered no further damage. A new set of rotor blades had to be manufactured before testing could resume. The tests went on under the supervision of Dokuchayev who replaced Smorodin as project engineer. With new rotor blades the Fl 282 performed

several more flights. The test pilots were generally satisfied with the machine, which proved docile and easy in handling. However, the complexity of the intermeshing rotor layout prevented this configuration from gaining a foothold in Soviet helicopter design practice. The OKB-329 helicopter design bureau led by Mikhail L. Mil' opted for the single-rotor layout in its first product, the Mi-1, and stuck to this layout ever since. Another major helicopter designer, Nikolay I. Kamov, gave his preference to the co-axial layout. (In contrast, the intermeshing rotor layout found use in the USA, being adopted by the Kaman company.)

Focke-Achgelis Fa 266 helicopter
Two Focke-Achgelis Fa 266 twin-rotor six-seat helicopters were to be delivered to the Soviet Union under the agreement concluded with Germany on 11th February 1940. The Fa 266 was a civil version of the Fa 223, which was completed in August 1939. The delivery of the Fa 266 was slated

for 1941, but never took place; as historian D. A. Sobolev noted, *'the Me-209 aircraft was not delivered to the USSR, nor were the helicopters designed by the Focke-Wulf company* (sic) *that had been included into the list of purchases for 1941'*. (Sobolev had obviously mixed up Focke-Achgelis and Focke-Wulf – *Auth.*)

Focke-Achgelis Fa 233 helicopter
The Fa 233 helicopter featuring a twin side-by-side rotor layout was first flown in August 1940; it proved to be a successful machine, and plans were in hand for its mass production. However, these plans were frustrated by Allied bombing raids which twice forced the Focke-Achgelis company to restore its production facilities wiped out by enemy bombs. As a result, only eleven machines were assembled and flown, while 37 nearly completed helicopters burnt down on the assembly line.

After the end of hostilities an incomplete example of the Fa 233 was discovered in Germany. Together with the Flettner Fl 282 described above it was delivered to the Soviet Union and made airworthy by the end of 1946. Thereupon the Fa 233 was transferred for examination and study to the OKB led by Ivan P. Bratukhin which was also engaged in the designing of helicopters featuring a side-by-side rotor layout. Unfortunately, no details about the testing are available.

Focke-Wulf Fw 58 Weihe trainer
In 1940 three Fw 58 Weihe (Harrier) trainers were delivered to the Soviet Union among the German aircraft purchased for the purpose of study under the terms of the 11th February 1940 agreement between Germany and the Soviet Union. The delivery took place in May 1940; the machines in question were Fw 58B-2 D-OXWR (c/n 2754) and Fw 58C-2s D-OXWS and D-OXWT (c/ns

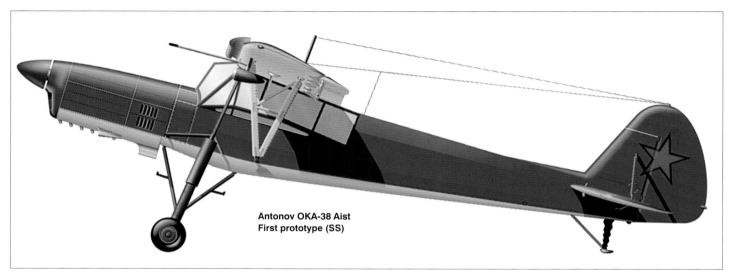

Antonov OKA-38 Aist
First prototype (SS)

Four views of the Flettner Fl 282 Kolibri helicopter captured by the Soviet forces and tested in the Soviet Union.

3547 and 3548). The two subtypes fulfilled different roles and were rather different outwardly. The Fw 58B was intended for the training of gunners/bomb-aimers, navigators, radio-operators and for night and instrument flying. The Fw 58C featuring dual controls was intended for training the pilots of twin-engined aircraft and radio-operators, as well as for practising night and instrument landings.

In the summer of 1940 the Fw 58s were tested and thoroughly studied at NII VVS

and at LII where they were flown by Igor' I. Shelest and other pilots. At NII VVS the team in charge of the testing comprised Mil. Eng. 3rd Class Yas'kov as project engineer, Maj. Pokrovskiy and Mil. Eng. 1st Class K. Kalinets as project test pilots, Lt (SG) Gorbunov as project navigator, Mil. Eng. 3rd Class I. Khvostovskiy as project engineer in charge of the powerplant, and Mil. Eng. 1st Class S. Avakimyan as project engineer in charge of the equipment. The NII VVS pilots performed 63 flights in the Fw 58B-2, log-

ging 35 hours and 50 minutes in all; 112 flights totalling 32 hours 35 minutes were made in the Fw 58C. In their conclusions the test pilots stated that the aircraft *'fully meets the requirements for training navigators, gunners, radio-operators, bomb-aimers and pilots of twin-engined aircraft'*.

In general, the Focke-Wulf trainer received a very high appraisal, especially with regard to the convenience for the crew, stability and controllability. The report stated: *'In its performance this aircraft is on a*

This Hungarian Air Force Focke-Wulf Fw 58B-2 liaison aircraft was captured at an airfield near Voronezh in February 1943. The damage to the wing suggests the aircraft had been sabotaged by its own troops as they retreated.

Three views of Fw 58B-2 W.Nr. 2754 bought from Germany in 1940. The aircraft still wears the delivery registration D-OXWR along with Soviet Air Force insignia.

par with the UT-3 (Yakovlev's twin-engined trainer – Auth.). *But it is very simple in handling and can be flown by pilots of less-than-average skill'.* The report further stated: *'The aircraft has good longitudinal and lateral stability in all flight modes and with all payload options. It can be flown hands-off. [...] The* *hatches for the inspection of units and control linkages are flush with the skin and convenient in operation'.* The test pilots liked the spacious navigator workstation of the Fw 58. It provided accommodation for two persons (a trainee and an instructor), which was especially convenient for training bomb-aimers. Soviet airmen especially took note of the fact that the navigator's cabin was well protected from the slipstream and the navigator could work without wearing flying goggles.

The conclusions made by the Soviet test pilots and engineers were as follows:

Above and right: Close-up of the starboard Argus As 410 engine and fixed-pitch wooden propeller of Fw 58B-2 D-OXWR. The letters on the photos are Roman, suggesting they were applied by the Germans, with explanatory notes, for the benefit of the Soviet customer.

Top and above: Fw 58C-2 W.Nr. 3547 bought from Germany in 1940 also wore a delivery registration (D-OXWS) along with Soviet insignia.

'1 The Focke-Wulf Fw 58 aircraft powered by two Argus 10C engines is superior to indigenous similar-mission aircraft as regards its multi-purpose capability, simplicity in handling, crew comfort and stability.

2. […] Convenient location of the equipment units and the presence of an instructor on board undoubtedly enhances the quality of the training and helps make it shorter.

3. It is expedient to provide our flying schools with aircraft of a similar type in two versions, which must additionally be fitted with an aerial camera, armament installations and equipment adopted in the Red Army Air Force'.

It might be added that the performance characteristics of the Fw 58 obtained in tests at NII VVS proved to be fully in accordance with the data supplied by the manufacturer and even exceeded them.

According to Sobolev, 'The study of the German twin-engined Fw 58 featuring a side-

Three more views of D-OXWS. The Fw 58B and Fw 58C differed markedly in their fuselage design.

by-side seating of the crew resulted in A. S. Yakovlev being asked to modify the UT-3 (twin-engined) trainer aircraft so as to incorporate similar seating arrangement. A project of a UT-3 version having a wider cabin was prepared on the eve of the war, but failed to reach the hardware stage before the outbreak of hostilities'. Here it must be added that in 1941 a new version of the UT-3 trainer was developed at Plant No. 47 in Leningrad under the direction of Yevgeniy G. Adler. It featured rearranged crew seating: the trainee and the instructor were seated under a common canopy, the instructor being placed aft of the trainee and offset to starboard for better forward view; the glazed nose cabin was deleted. This alteration may well have reflected the lessons learned from testing the Fw 58. The new version proved quite successful but was not put into production because of the turmoil caused by the outbreak of the war.

Curiously, during the war Fw 58C-2 W.Nr. 3548 was experimentally flown by NII VVS with a ski undercarriage for the purpose of verifying the suitability of German machines for that type of operations. The Red Army commanders did not know that the Luftwaffe had opted for clearing snow-covered airfields so as to ensure operating its aircraft on wheels all year round.

During the war, several further examples of the Weihe were captured and used by the Soviet Air Force. A Hungarian Air Force Fw 58B-2 was captured near Voronezh in February 1943. One Fw 58 was displayed at the war booty exhibition in Moscow in the summer of 1943. Another Fw 58 was among the German aircraft obtained by the Soviet Union from Finland after the armistice of 19th September 1944. This was a machine coded NH+OI which was loaned by the Luftwaffe to the Finnish Air Force (Ilmavoimat) in 1943 and flown by a Finnish crew, but in Luft-

waffe colours. After the Finnish-Soviet armistice, the Fw 58 was used for a while in the 'Lapland War' against the retreating German troops in northern Finland, wearing both the Ilmavoimat serial FH-1 and the unofficial civil registrations OH-PMS. Later it was impounded by the Allied (read: Soviet) Control Commission supervising the fulfilment of the armistice conditions, and was used by this commission for some time before being despatched to the Soviet Union (according to K.-F. Geust, to whom we owe this story, rumour has it that the aircraft was destroyed by fire before reaching the Soviet Union!).

In 1947 the Soviet Ministry of Aircraft Industry had at its disposal two Fw 58s. By 1st January 1950 only one of them remained in the inventory; it was withdrawn from use in the first quarter of that year.

Gotha Go 145 primary trainer

First flown in February 1934, the Gotha Go 145 was a very successful primary trainer biplane built in large numbers both in Germany and (under licence) in Spain and Turkey. Several examples of this aircraft fell into the hands of the Soviet forces during the war. For example, two Go 145s and one Fi 156 were captured by the Red Army after rupturing the front towards Kalach on 23rd November 1942. These machines were used by the Germans as light night bombers. It should be noted that the use of small training aircraft in the role of light night bombers was pioneered by the Red Army, which used the Polikarpov U-2LNB (Po-2) biplane efficiently for night harassment air raids against German troops since the autumn of 1941. A year later the Germans, in turn, used trainers in a similar role. Thus, in the opinion of Soviet specialists, the mentioned examples of the Go 145 represented an attempt by the Germans to make use of the Soviet know-how. The captured machines were studied under the direction of Eng. Maj. Abroshchenko.

Naturally, it was interesting for the Soviet specialists to compare the way in which the Gotha and Polikarpov training biplanes had been adapted to their new role. The two machines had much in common: a similar layout and all-up weight, low-output engines driving wooden propellers. There were some differences, however. As a rule, the Go 145s flew their missions with a single pilot and without machine-guns; they carried a bomb load of up to 120 kg (265 lb) on two bomb racks and their speed at sea level reached 200 km/h (124 mph). On the other hand, the U-2VS aircraft (*voyskovoy standartnyy* – standard military version) flew their missions with two crew, dropped 300 to 350 kg of bombs on the enemy, not infrequently

Above: Gotha Go 145 trainers PF+NJ and BJ+?O (W.Nr. 2468) captured near Kalach on 23rd November 1942.

Another view of the same two aircraft, with a Fieseler Fi 156C coded ?B+?? in the background.

supplementing this with a burst of the flexible machine-gun; their speed normally did not exceed 130 km/h.

Some captured Go 145s were used for special missions in the enemy's rear. As related by the Finnish historian Karl-Friedrich Geust, a Latvian pilot, J.Kirsteins of the night ground attack unit NSGr 12 (the personnel being Latvian volunteers) defected to the advancing Soviet forces in Lithuania in a Gotha Go 145 on 24th July 1944. The aircraft was later used by two Latvian pilots of the Soviet Air Force, Lt. (SG) Nikolais Vulfs and Lt. Pavels Elvins (of the 1st Latvian NBAP) for a special task over German-occupied Latvia on 22nd August 1944. The operation involved dropping an open letter from the imprisoned General-Feldmarschall Friedrich von Paulus addressed to Feldmarschall Ferdinand Schörner (CO of Armeegruppe Nord), urging him to capitulate honorably. Vulfs and Elvins were decorated with the Order of the Red Banner for their special mission.

Heinkel He 115 general-purpose and torpedo bomber floatplane

Several examples of the Heinkel He 115 twin-float seaplane previously operated by the Finnish Air Force or by the Luftwaffe in Finland ended up being captured by Soviet troops or transferred to the Soviet Union from Finland under the terms of the Soviet-

Finnish armistice treaty signed on 19th September 1944. We owe the details of this story to Karl-Friedrich Geust.

One of the aircraft in question was an ex-Royal Norwegian Air Force He 115A-2 wearing the very appropriate Ilmavoimat serial HE-115; it was used to transport Finnish long-range patrols beyond the frontline into

One more captured Gotha Go 145. Following the example of the Soviet Air Force, the Luftwaffe adapted the trainer for the light bomber role (note the bomb racks under the fuselage).

Above: This Messerschmitt Bf 108 Taifun was among the German aircraft purchased in 1940.

In contrast, this Bf 108 came from rather unlikely quarters, being one of the Imperial Japanese Army aircraft captured by Soviet troops at Chanchung, Manchuria in 1945.

the Soviet East Karelia. This aircraft was W.Nr. 3038, No. 156 (F.50) of the Norwegian Naval Air Force, and was flown to Petsamo by a Norwegian pilot who escaped from Tromsø on 8th June 1940 after the capitulation of the Norwegian forces in the Far North. The aircraft was interned in Finland and was subsequently taken over by the Finnish Air Force. This aircraft was captured on one of its missions on 4th July 1943 when it force-landed in Soviet territory after being fired upon by Soviet troops. The crew were taken POW. On 3rd October 1943 a Finnish long-range patrol saw this aircraft dismantled at a railway station (there is no information as to the subsequent fate of the aircraft – *Auth.*)

In the spring of 1943 the Finnish Air Force received two more He 115s on loan from the Luftwaffe. One of them was evacuated by the Germans in September 1944 after the Finnish-Soviet armistice, while the other one, coded 6H+BK, was used by the Finnish Air Force during the 'Lapland War', this time transporting Finnish long-distance patrols into the German rear! At the end of September it received both the Finnish military serial HE-116 and the unofficial out-of-sequence civil registration OH-PMJ. The German origin of the seaplane, however, was not lost on the Allied Control Commission, and on 22nd November 1944 HE-116/OH-PMJ flew to Santahämina, Helsinki, where it was dismantled. On 16th March 1945 the aircraft was delivered to the

Soviet Union (as were an Ar 196 and an Fw 58) where its traces are lost.

Another He 115, 8L+IH of 1./Kü.Fl.Gr. 906, fell into the hands of the Red Army on 22nd October 1942, when it flew out from Pälläjärvi, Hirvas, in East Karelia to bring home a long-distance patrol consisting of Estonian volunteers in the Finnish Army. This aircraft was flown by an all-Luftwaffe crew. The crew and the leader of the Abwehr (German military intelligence service) operation who flew out as a passenger were intercepted by the NKVD security police upon landing at Lake Yungozero; a shootout ensued in which the Germans were killed. The aircraft, however, suffered only minor damage to the port engine and was inspected by Soviet military personnel on site. Nothing further is known about the fate of this aircraft.

Klemm Kl 35 trainer, sports and liaison aircraft

This small two-seater externally resembling Yakovlev's UT-2 trainer was also among the German aircraft captured during the war. At least one example was in operational use after the war; in 1947 it formed part of the inventory of aircraft used by the Ministry of Aircraft Industry.

Messerschmitt Bf 108 Taifun liaison, training and sports aircraft

Two examples of the Bf 108 Taifun (Typhoon) four-seat aircraft were ordered by the Soviet

Union in late 1940 and delivered in 1941. A delegation of Soviet high-ranking officials and aviation specialists took delivery of these aircraft, together with three Ju 52/3ms, when visiting Germany in February-April 1941. These light aircraft, used for liaison, training and sports, were tested at Soviet flight test centres – LII and NII VVS.

The aircraft was deemed sufficiently interesting to merit the preparation of a special technical description which was issued at BNT TsAGI in 1941 (in this document the machine was designated Me-108B). Its authors stated that the aircraft was used in Germany for the training of fighter pilots, notably those converting to the Bf 109; the side-by-side seating of the trainee and the instructor 'considerably reduced the training time and enhanced the quality of training'. (Nevertheless, the training of fighter pilots in the Soviet Union continued to be based on the use of tandem two-seat trainers for decades to come). The Bf 108 attracted the attention of Soviet engineers not least due to the fact that it was regarded as a forerunner of the Bf 109 fighter with regard to general layout, basic outline of the airframe and a number of aerodynamic and structural features.

Judging by the BNT description, the Bf 108s acquired by the Soviet Union were powered by the 200-hp Argus As 10C engine. The aircraft's performance at an AUW of 1,380 kg (3,050 lb) included a maximum speed of 300 km/h (186 mph) and a cruising speed of 265 km/h (165 mph), a service ceiling of 4,800 m (15,740 ft); time to 4,000 m (13,120 ft) was 21.6 minutes with a variable-pitch propeller (presumably this data was determined during testing at NII VVS or LII).

One of the two Bf 108s was flown, among others, by Aleksey N. Grinchik of LII. One Taifun was used as a liaison aircraft by Pyotr M. Stefanovskiy of NII VVS in 1942 when he was dispatched to the aircraft factory at Omsk in Siberia to test the '110' (I-110) fighter prototype designed by Dmitriy L. Tomashevich.

Photo evidence exists that a Bf 108 belonging to the Imperial Japanese Army was captured by the Soviet troops at Chanchung airfield, Manchuria, during the Soviet-Japanese war in the summer of 1945.

Russian historian D. A. Sobolev mentions the Bf 108 among the captured German aircraft that were pressed into service with Soviet organisations during or after the war. A single Taifun was in the air fleet of the Ministry of Aircraft Industry; it was withdrawn from use in the first quarter of 1950.

Chapter 4

TESTING OF CAPTURED GERMAN JET AIRCRAFT

and turbojet engines in the Soviet Union 1945-1947

During the war, especially in its final stage, the Soviet military and political leaders became painfully aware of the fact that the German aircraft industry had by far out-stripped the Soviet aircraft industry in the development of turbojet engines and jet air-craft. Before the war, a lot of pioneering research had been made in the Soviet Union in the field of rocket propulsion, and some steps had been undertaken as regards development of rocket-powered aircraft. Liq-uid-fuel rocket motors became the main direction of Soviet research and develop-ment in the field of jet propulsion. This was exemplified by the BI rocket-powered point-defence interceptor designed by Aleksandr Ya. Bereznyak and Aleksey M. Isayev under Viktor F. Bolkhovitinov's direction, which first flew in May 1942. However, attempts to develop it to a production standard ran into problems and the project was eventually abandoned. Several similar projects – Andrey G. Kostikov's '302' interceptor and Nikolay N. Polikarpov's *Malyutka* (Little one) – did not even reach the hardware stage.

Soviet aircraft designers experimented with rocket motors and ramjets, using them as boosters for piston-engined aircraft, but this line of development eventually proved to be of little use. As for turbojet engines, the very promising work that had been started in the late 1930s by Arkhip M. Lyul'ka, who developed the first Soviet turbojet engine, had to be suspended after the German inva-sion in June 1941. It resumed in 1942, but under the harsh conditions of the Soviet wartime economy it was impossible to give it a scope that would immediately produce practical results in the shape of turbojets suitable for installation in production aircraft. Thus, at the end of the war the Soviet lead-ers were faced with a situation when Ger-many and the Soviet Union's allies – the USA and Great Britain – had put turbojet-powered fighters into production and were using them operationally, while the Soviet Union had to make do with attempts to improve the performance of Lavochkin and Yakovlev fighters with the help of rocket or ramjet boosters.

Understandably, the Soviet Union, as well as its allies, was extremely interested in gaining access to German jet propulsion

technology. The defeat of Germany opened up the possibilities of obtaining specimens of German jet aircraft and engines, as wells of acquiring technical drawings and other documentation on various advanced proj-ects. Needless to say, all of the Allies, includ-ing the Soviet Union, strove to obtain as much of these valuable assets as possible. Examples of German jet-powered aircraft were captured by Soviet forces in the course of their offensive operations on the territories of Germany, Austria and Czechoslovakia during the final months of the war. After the end of hostilities further specimens of war booty were discovered in aircraft factories and research centres that happened to be within the Soviet occupation zone.

As a result, after the war Soviet special-ists had at their disposal a considerable number of captured German aircraft of assorted types; some of them represented major advances in aeronautical design, while others were of a more conventional nature. Some of these aircraft were tested or studied at NII VVS, LII and TsAGI. Naturally, it was the jet-powered aircraft that were the most interesting objects for testing and studying. The types tested in the USSR included the Messerschmitt Me 163 rocket-powered interceptor, the Me 262 and Heinkel He 162 jet fighters, the Arado Ar 234 jet bomber. There were also several types which were brought to the Soviet Union as incomplete or damaged examples unsuit-able for flight testing; these were studied by engineers on the ground. All these types are described below individually in alphabetical order. Finally, many other types were stud-ied solely on the basis of captured docu-

ments, but this is generally beyond the scope of this book.

Of the German aircraft tested in the USSR it was the Me 262 that influenced the development of Soviet jet-powered aviation to the greatest extent; more limited was the influence produced by the acquaintance with such types as the Arado Ar 234, Me 163 and He 162. It must be admitted that the study of German experience in the field of jet propulsion and turbojet-powered aircraft design was truly of great importance for the Soviet aircraft industry. Examination and testing of the German hardware, coupled with the analysis of documents on the results of aerodynamic research in the field of high subsonic and supersonic speeds provided a lot of useful knowledge to Soviet designers and production engineers and considerably facilitated initial steps in the manufacture of jet aircraft and their intro-duction into service.

Especially important in this respect was the use and study of German turbojet engines (this subject is treated separately at the end of this chapter).

Arado Ar 234B Blitz jet bomber

The German combat jets tested by Soviet specialists included the Arado Ar 234 Blitz (Lightning) bomber. Several aircraft of this type were found at Ribnitz-Damgarten (between Rostock and Stralsund) by a team of Soviet engineers which in the spring of 1945 was sent to Germany for the purpose of spotting and recovering aircraft and other aviation materiel that would be of value to the Soviet aircraft industry. In March 1945 the team discovered an uncoded Arado Ar

The Arado Ar 234C was the second German four-turbojet bomber. This Ar 234C-1 is seen in Germany after being captured by Soviet troops. This aircraft was not tested by Soviet specialists, though.

Three views of an uncoded Arado Ar 234B-2 (W.Nr. 140355) undergoing tests at Püttnitz, Germany, in late 1945. Note the extremely narrow wheel track and the ETC 530 shackles for additional bombs (or solid-fuel rocket boosters) under the engine nacelles. The object above the cockpit is a rear-view periscope.

234B-2 (W.Nr. 140355) that had made a forced landing. This was the twin-engined version powered by Jumo 004 turbojets. For various reasons it was impossible to send it to Moscow by rail or by ship. A decision was taken in Moscow to test the aircraft on site, prepare it for a positioning flight and then ferry it, with several stopovers, to the Soviet Union. A special team from NII VVS, led by Col. Pyotr M. Stefanovskiy, was sent to Germany to take charge of this matter; the team also included NII VVS Chief Engineer Izrail G. Rabkin and bureau test pilot A. G. Kubyshkin. (Stefanovskiy writes in his memoirs that the team was sent in March 1946, but that must be a mistake; Dmitriy Sobolev states that the events described here took place in 1945.)

The aircraft was quickly repaired at the aircraft repair plant in Ribnitz. However, during the very first flight performed in April 1945 one of the two Jumo engines became inoperative. The team returned the aircraft to flyable condition again and continued the flight tests. As the runway in Damgarten proved to be too short for take-offs with a full AUW, A. G. Kubyshkin ferried the machine to the test centre in Rechlin. There, too, the available gravel runway was too short. Nevertheless, in January-February 1946 Kubyshkin performed five flights on the Arado bomber. This brief period of flight tests revealed the engines' low reliability. On two occasions one of the turbojets cut in flight and then caught fire; fortunately, the machine landed safely in both cases.

Stefanovskiy relates how on one of these occasions Kubyshkin saved the aircraft from an imminent crash by a narrow margin. He was performing a flight in the airfield area when one of the engines caught fire, forcing an immediate return. To make matters worse, the main landing gear units would not extend normally, and Kubyshkin had to make use of the emergency extension system, having no time to deploy the flaps. Suddenly he realised that the machine was almost above the runway, there was no

Above: The aftermath of an in-flight fire in the starboard Jumo 004B engine of Ar 234B-2 W.Nr. 140355.

choice but to make a touchdown with a considerable overshoot. The machine was still carrying an almost full fuel load, and wheel brakes alone would not stop it within the remaining short stretch of the runway. Fortunately, Kubyshkin had the presence of mind to make use of the aircraft's brake parachute – as the first among Soviet pilots to do so. The bomber came to a halt just a few dozen metres from the wood adjoining the end of the runway.

The aircraft was repaired and Kubyshkin resumed testing, making several flights at full AUW from a newly restored paved runway. The mentioned engine troubles prevented the Arado bomber from being ferried to the NII VVS, but the test pilots succeeded in establishing some of the performance characteristics.

The handling qualities of the Ar 234B-2 received a less favourable assessment from

Kubyshkin in comparison with the Me 262. He noted that take-off and landing were complicated due to the narrow wheel track; wheel brake efficiency was poor and it was hard to keep the aircraft on a straight course at the beginning of the take-off run. The concluding part of the Ar 234B-2's test report stated that the aircraft's field performance did not permit operations with a full payload from normal-length runways without the use of rocket boosters on take-off and a brake parachute on landing. In general, the NII VVS chiefs considered the Ar 234 to be a less mature aircraft than the Me 262. Yet, many of its novel technical features, such as the brake parachute and the turbojet powerplant and fuel system, were undoubtedly of much interest for the Soviet design bureaux/

According to Russian sources, after the war two captured Ar 234s, of the B and C subtypes, were despatched to the USSR

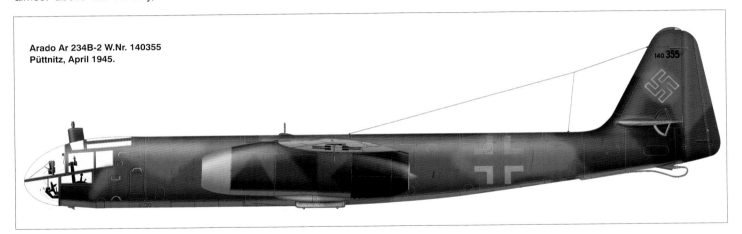

Arado Ar 234B-2 W.Nr. 140355
Püttnitz, April 1945.

where they underwent comprehensive study (one of the machines was thoroughly examined at BNT). Studies conducted at BNT, supplemented by captured German materials, formed the basis of a technical description of the Ar-234B-2 issued by BNT in 1947. The authors of the document noted in particular the excellent view forward, to the sides and downwards afforded by the extensively glazed cockpit and further enhanced by the L-shaped control column; the spacious cockpit was easily accessed by the pilot. The rearward view, afforded only by a periscope, was deemed insufficient. The use of booster rockets at take-off and of the brake parachute during landing, reducing the take-off and landing run by 40 to 50%, were mentioned among the notable design features. Soviet specialists noted the external location of all bomb racks. This feature led to some deterioration of performance but made it possible to increase the volume of the fuselage fuel tanks – an important asset for a bomber. At the same time they noted that the entire volume of the fuselage was occupied by fuel, mainwheel wells and various items of equipment (sometimes rather heavy). The same applied to the outer wings carrying the engines and, in some cases, bombs or rocket boosters. This distribution of masses, in the opinion of Soviet experts, increased the aircraft's moments of inertia relative to its main axes, impairing the bomber's manoeuvrability.

Soviet engineers showed considerable interest for the novel features incorporated in the Ar 234B-2's undercarriage. Stowing the mainwheels in the fuselage was deemed justified for high-wing aircraft and mid-wing aircraft with thin wings. On the other hand, it was noted that this undercarriage layout resulted in a narrow wheel track, which impaired the aircraft's controllability during taxiing and increased the danger of flipping over during a lateral drift landing (in a crosswind). The NII VVS pilots who tested the Ar 234 confirmed that the machine was difficult to steer on take-off and landing; they had to use differential thrust to keep the machine on course because the narrow track made the application of wheel brakes insufficiently effective.

In 1946 one of the captured aircraft was restored to airworthy condition and was used at LII for testing brake parachutes.

Russian aviation historian Nikolay Vasil'yev has unearthed some interesting details relating to the 'Soviet chapter' of the Ar 234 story. As was the case with the Me 262, the Soviet military made their plans concerning the Ar 234. After all, this was the only jet bomber of the Second World War that had been almost fully developed to operational status. In 1946, in keeping with a

Government directive, a design bureau (OKB) was set up at plant No. 458; it was headed by Igor' V. Chetverikov, a designer known for his MBR-5/Che-2 flying boat. This small team of designers was tasked with developing a single-seat bomber whose performance was to include a maximum speed of 750 km/h (466 mph) at an altitude of 5,000 m (16,400 ft), a service ceiling of 12,000 m (39,360 ft), a range of 1,600 km (999 miles) with a normal bomb load of 1,000 kg (2,205 lb), and a maximum bomb load of 1,500 kg (3,307 lb). The machine was projected in two versions: with four BMW 003 engines and two Jumo 004s.

In 1946 an advanced development project was submitted to the Soviet Air Force (referred to euphemistically as 'the customer'). Contrary to expectations, the Air Force demanded a revision of the project: the single-seat bomber was to be turned into a multi-seat machine and fitted additionally with flexible defensive weapons. However, MAP (the Ministry of Aircraft Industry) did not share the opinion of the VVS, and further work on the project was terminated.

Another source, presumably referring to the same project, states that in 1946 Chetverikov was working on a bomber powered by for BMW 003s. The work was officially sanctioned by a Government directive dated 20th June 1946 and terminated by a Government directive dated 30th November 1946.

Bachem Ba 349B Natter single-seat semi-expendable interceptor

It was asserted at one time that this vertically launched rocket-propelled target-defence interceptor was among the German aircraft captured by the Soviet forces. For example, in November 1956 the *RAF Flying Review* magazine (Vol 12 No. 3) wrote: *'Three Natters were shipped to the USSR, and the first Ba 349B which had been sent to Thuringia as a prototype for production in a factory there fell into Russian hands'.*

However, available Soviet and Russian sources related to the captured German aircraft make no mention of this rocket-propelled interceptor.

Interestingly, William Green in his fundamental book *The Warplanes of the Third Reich* does not mention any 'Soviet' Bachem Natters either. He states: *'A total of 36 Natter interceptors was actually completed at Waldsee of which 25 were flown, although only seven of these with pilots, and in April 1945, ten A-series Natters were set up at Kirchheim, near Stuttgart, to await the arrival of U.S.A.F. bombers. In the event, Dipl.-Eng. Bachem's ingenious weapon was never to be blooded in action for Allied tanks arrived in the vicinity of the launching site*

before the expected bombers, and the Natters were destroyed on their ramps to prevent them from falling into enemy hands'.

In any case, one thing is certain: although Soviet designers did engage for some time in the design of rocket-powered aircraft and carefully studied German experience in this field, the Ba 349 failed to provide inspiration for any Soviet project sharing the same configuration.

DFS 346 – see '346' (Siebel 346) in Chapter 5

Focke-Wulf Ta 183 swept-wing jet fighter project

This swept-wing jet fighter developed by the Focke-Wulf company represented a significant advance in aerodynamics as compared to the straight-wing jet fighters produced by other German designers; yet it failed to reach the hardware stage by the time Germany was defeated. This type deserves mention here because of the allegations, at one time current in Western publications, to the effect that the design of the famous Mikoyan MiG-15 fighter owed much to this project of Professor Kurt Tank. Such assertions must be regarded as gross exaggerations, to say the least. True, the Soviet Union did benefit from the results of the German research into the aerodynamics of swept wings – as did the Allies thanks to the captured German documentation, for that matter. The study of these materials may have played an important role in the virtually simultaneous emergence of such aircraft as the MiG-15 and its US counterpart – the North American F-86 Sabre. Moreover, according to a Russian researcher referring to some 'reliable evidence', a set of wings of this fighter was discovered by Soviet troops in the building of the Reich Ministry of Aviation (RLM) in Berlin. Yet, a close comparison of the MiG-15 with the available drawings of the different Ta 183 project versions reveals too many major differences for the MiG-15 to be regarded as merely a 'reworked Ta-183'. The MiG-15 contains no more of the German fighter's design than any other jet fighter of the late 1940s with a nose air intake and

Above right: An early project configuration of the Heinkel He 162 with a butterfly tail and two Jumo 004 or Heinkel HeS 11 turbojets above and below the fuselage. The nose gear unit was cunningly designed to stow above the lower engine. Note the drop tanks.

Right: Another project version of the He 162 with forward-swept wings and two HeS 11 engines; note the semi-recessed bomb on the centreline. These drawings were coped by Soviet specialists from German originals, hence the comments in Russian.

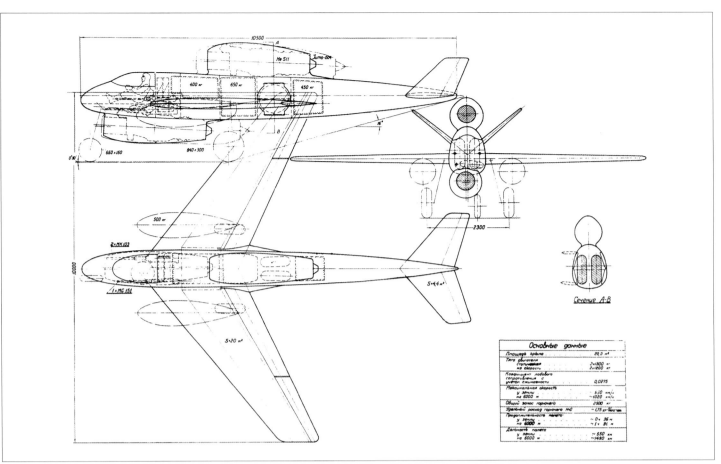

Сечение А-В

Основные данные		
Площадь крыла		20,0 м²
Тяга двигателя		
статическая		3×1300 кг
на скорости		2×1200 кг
Коэффициент лобового сопротивления с учётом сжимаемости		0,0275
Максимальная скорость		
у земли		~650 км/ч
на 6000 м		~1020 км/ч
Общий запас горючего		2500 кг
Удельный расход горючего №0		~1,75 кг/кг·час
Продолжительность полёта		
у земли		~0÷36 м
на 6000 м		~1÷31 м
Дальность полёта		
у земли		~550 км
на 6000 м		~1490 км

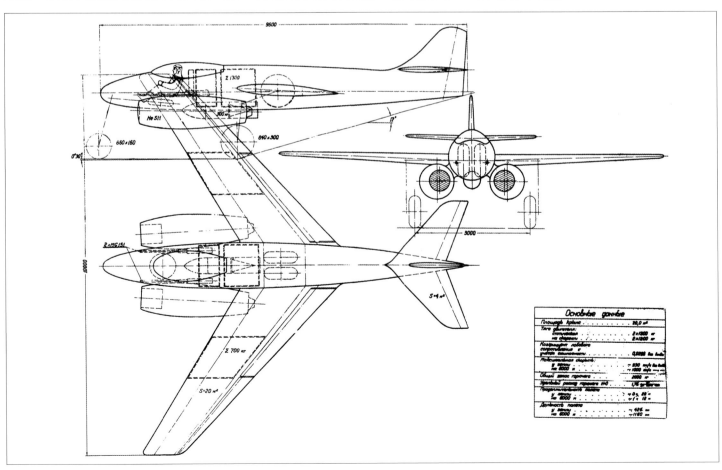

Основные данные		
Площадь крыла		20,0 м²
Тяга двигателя:		
статическая		2×1200 кг
на скорости		2×1800 кг
Коэффициент лобового сопротивления с учётом сжимаемости		0,0266
Максимальная скорость:		
у земли		~630 км/ч
на 6000 м		~1000 км/ч
Общий запас горючего		2000 кг
Удельный расход горючего №0		1,75 кг/кг·час
Продолжительность полёта		
у земли		~0÷19 м
на 6000 м		~1÷19 м
Дальность полёта		
у земли		~425 км
на 6000 м		~1160 км

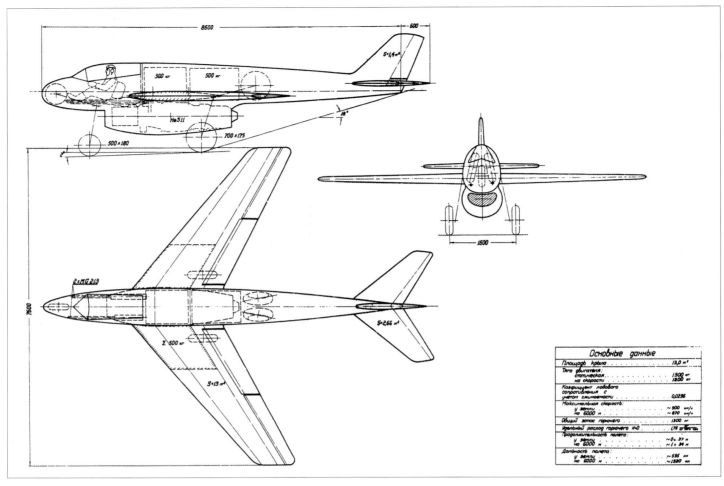

Above: One more preliminary design project configurarion of the He 162 built around a single HeS 11. Again, the drawing was copied by Soviet specialists when the captured German materials were studied after the war.

swept wings, which became a classic feature of jet-powered aviation.

Heinkel He 162A-2 single-seat interceptor

The Heinkel He 162A turbojet-powered fighter (known as the *Volksjäger* – 'People's Fighter') entered production in early 1945 and was even committed to action on a limited scale on the Western front. It was powered by a BMW 003 turbojet located atop the fuselage so that the exhaust jet passed between the twin tails. Soviet specialists got hold of several machines of this type. There are some discrepancies in Russian sources as to their number and condition. According to one account, by the end of 1945 there were seven He 162 fighters in the Soviet Union, only one of them being airworthy. Another source states that as many as eight machines were captured. Of these, three severely damaged examples were placed at the disposal of NII-1 (Jet and Rocket Propulsion Research Institute); one non-airworthy aircraft was delivered to Plant No. 155 (home of the Mikoyan OKB). A further four machines, three of which lacked engines, were allotted to the NII VVS test centre at Chkalovskaya AB.

Of these eight examples, up to five could be returned to flying condition. However, it appears that this idea was abandoned, and instead two examples of the He 162A-2 model armed with two 20-mm (.78 calibre) MG-151 cannons were assembled by German workers under the control of Soviet

Left: The remains of at least three He 162As destroyed by an air raid at an airfield that was later overrun by Soviet troops.
Right: A production He 162A captured intact by Soviet troops. The aircraft appears to be painted silver overall and devoid of markings.

specialists at a plant in Rostock from the available stock of units and assemblies. The machines were despatched to the USSR, followed by ample technical documentation. The two machines were assigned for study and testing to LII in Ramenskoye; of these, one example was test-flown in the spring of 1946. This machine was coded '02 Red' and sported red star insignia.

By then Soviet specialists knew that, along with some good properties, the He 162 had shown poor directional stability, insufficient longitudinal stability at high speeds and a tendency to drop a wing at high angles of attack. Some improvements had been introduced by Heinkel but had failed to cure the machine's handling deficiencies completely. Before the first flight at LII the technical commission imposed a number of restrictions concerning the speed, G loads and the all-up weight. For example, the maximum speed at altitudes up to 4,000 m (13,120 ft) was not to exceed 700 km/h (435 mph). On 8th May 1946 test pilot Gheorgiy M. Shiyanov made his first flight in the He 162. It was followed by two more flights (according to another source, Shiyanov made his first three flights in the He 162 in the winter of 1946, followed by two more flights on 8th and 13th May). The evaluation report stated: *'According to the pilot's assessment, the aircraft has a low margin of longitudinal stability, the lateral stability being close to neutral. In the directional channel the aircraft handles unpleasantly due to the lack of stability and excessive rudder authority'.* The report also noted the very long take-off run, which amounted to 1,350 m (4,430 ft) even with the all-up weight reduced by 9.6% as compared to the normal value. Further testing was terminated, the main reason being the excessive length of the take-off run.

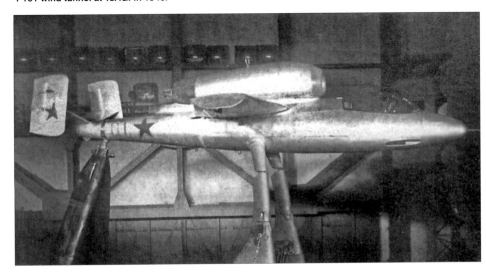

Above and below: '01 Red', one of two He 162s test flown in the Soviet Union, undergoing tests in the T-101 wind tunnel at TsAGI in 1946.

After this, one He 162A-2 was transferred to TsAGI for testing in the T-101 wind tunnel and another machine was partially dismantled for detail study at BNT TsAGI The results of this study were presented in a technical description of the He 162A-1 and A-2 issued by BNT in 1946. The authors of the report came to the conclusion that the fuselage

Left and right: These stills from a documentary film prepared by GK NII VVS show Soviet military specialists examining two different He 162As captured in non-flying condition.

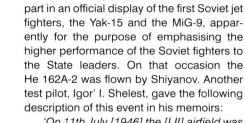

Above left and above: Front and rear views of He 162A '01 Red' undergoing flight tests at LII in 1946.

Left and below left: Two more views of the same aircraft. The dark-coloured rear section of the engine nacelle may originate from a different example.

Bottom left: The aircraft carried the old LII badge (the letters ЛИИ incorporated into an aircraft silhouette) on the starboard fin above the star.

On 11th July 1946, the He 162A-2 took part in an official display of the first Soviet jet fighters, the Yak-15 and the MiG-9, apparently for the purpose of emphasising the higher performance of the Soviet fighters to the State leaders. On that occasion the He 162A-2 was flown by Shiyanov. Another test pilot, Igor' I. Shelest, gave the following description of this event in his memoirs:

'On 11th July [1946] the [LII] airfield was being readied for demonstration flights of three jet aircraft – our two firstlings, the MiG-9 and the Yak-15, and, for comparison, of the captured He 162. [...] By the arranged hour the top officials of the Ministry of Aircraft Industry had arrived. All other flights were immediately cancelled, and the personnel who happened to be free from duty climbed to the roof of the hangar to gain a better viewing position. The guests – the Minister M. V. Khrunichev, his deputies P. V. Dement'yev and A. S. Yakovlev, Chief Designer A. I. Mikoyan – went to the runway where they would observe the flights near the starting point.

Gheorgiy Shiyanov was the first to take off in his Heinkel machine. The small jet took off after a long run, as though it were pressed down by a heavy burden: placed atop the fuselage, behind the cockpit, was the engine which, from afar, looked like a barrel.

Having stayed airborne for a few minutes, Shiyanov made a stealthy approach from the side of the nearby river and landed.' (It was on that occasion that the first prototype of the MiG-9 fighter suffered a crash, killing test pilot Aleksey N. Grinchik.)

Close examination of the airframe and equipment of the He 162 revealed many interesting design features. Of special inter-

structure did not have any special features associated with the installation of a turbojet engine, but some units and subassemblies merited attention. In particular, they noted the streamlined shape and small cross-section of the fuselage, the forward location of the cockpit affording a good view to the pilot; a novel feature was the cartridge-fired ejection seat. The TsAGI specialists noted with interest the integral fuel tanks incorporated into the all-wooden (!) wing structure, as well

as the unique method of adjusting the tailplane incidence in flight by deflecting the entire fuselage tailcone up and down. The He 162A-2 was also used at BNT for studying the nozzle of the fighter's BMW 003 turbojet featuring an electrically actuated translating centrebody. Despite certain deficiencies, the nozzle control system was found to be effective in ensuring the optimum gas flow and in easing the pilot workload.

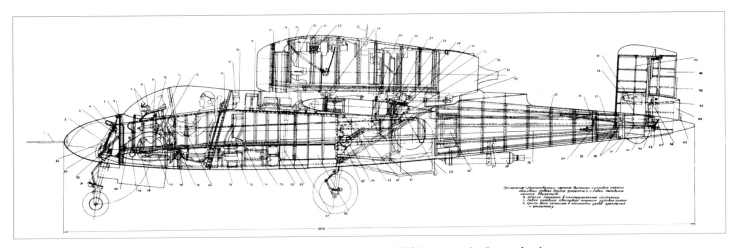

Above: A Russian cutaway drawing of the He 162's fuselage and vertical tail. Note the JATO booster under the rear fuselage.
Below: This Russian drawing shows the thickness of the skin panels. The dorsal skin panels aft of the engine are made of steel; the nosecone, main gear doors and access panels are made of plywood.

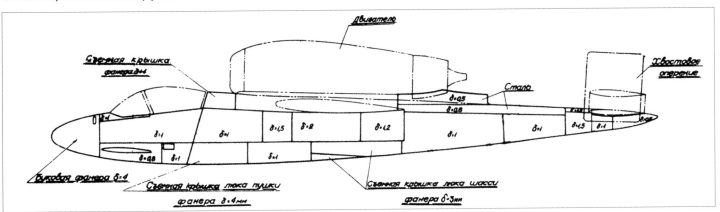

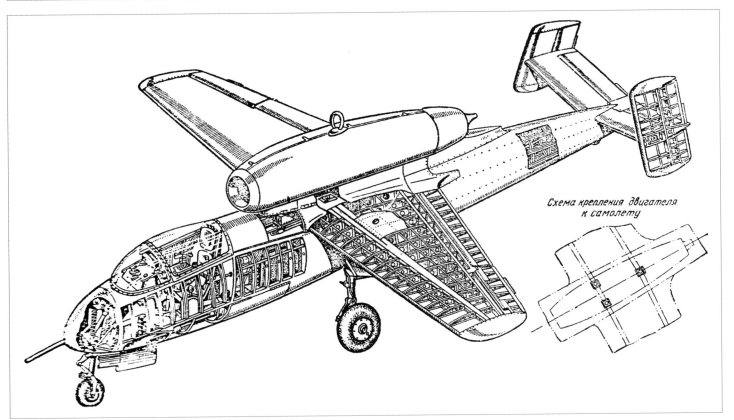

A three-dimensional cutaway drawing of the He 162. Interestingly, the wingtip fairings are conventional (not downward-canted). The scrap view shows the location of the engine attachment fittings.

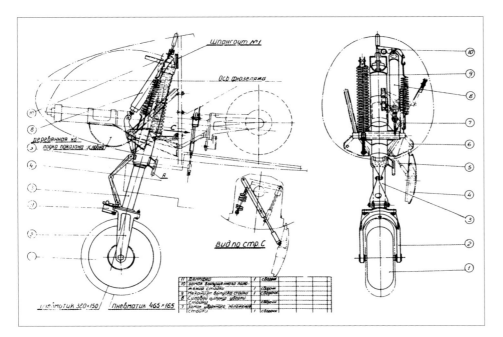

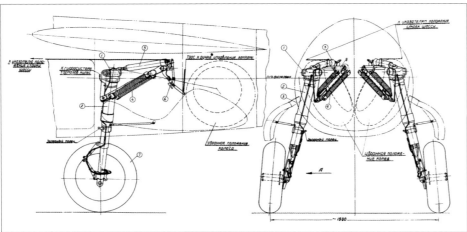

Top and above: These drawings from Russian documents on the He 162 illustrate the design of the nose and main gear units. Note that the nose gear oleo swivels around the middle.

He 162A '01 Red' in front of one of LII's hangars at Zhukovskiy with the cockpit canopy open.

est was the ejection seat, which was copied by Soviet designers for their first jet fighters. The ejection seat from the He 162 was used by Pavel O. Sukhoi on the Su-9 fighter (the first aircraft to bear this designation – the twin-engined *izdeliye* K prototype).

The unorthodox layout of the He 162 did not catch on in the Soviet Union, but there was at least one attempt to produce a Soviet analogue of this machine. In the spring of 1947 the OKB-153 design bureau led by Oleg K. Antonov started, as a 'private venture', the development of a light interceptor which was obviously inspired by the He 162, while not being a direct copy of the German machine. The fighter was named 'Salamander', repeating what was believed to be the name of the German fighter (in fact, Salamander was a code name for the He 162 programme but not for the fighter itself). Antonov's fighter shared with its German predecessor such features as unswept wings, the dorsally mounted engine and the twin-fin tail unit. The choice of this layout, according to Antonov, was dictated by the need to avoid thrust losses in long inlet ducts and jetpipes, since the fighter was to be powered by the German Jumo 004 or its Soviet copy (the RD-10) whose thrust rating was rather modest. In detail design, however, the fighter differed appreciably from the He 162: the wings had slight leading-edge sweep and an unswept trailing edge (on the German fighter it was vice versa) and the stabilisers had no dihedral. The engine nacelle extended as far back as the tail unit; the cockpit, which was placed close to the wing leading edge, featured car-type doors *à la* Bell P-39 Airacobra. The aircraft had a potent armament of three cannons and was envisaged as a front-line air defence fighter; the dorsal position of the engine was expected to prevent ingestion of pebbles when operating from semi-prepared runways.

However, the study of captured materials on the He 162, including flight test films, led Antonov and his colleagues to conclude that this type could not be used effectively as a combat aircraft. As a result, the 'Salamander' project was abandoned. (Information on the Antonov project was first published in the *Illustrated Encyclopedia of Aircraft of the Antonov ANTK* by Vyacheslav M. Zayarin and Konstantin G. Udalov.)

The He 162 could still be seen in the hangar of BNT TsAGI in Moscow until the early 1950s, in company with the Me 163, Me 262, He 100 and Do 335 fighters.

Heinkel 280 single-seat interceptor/fighter-bomber

The He 280 was a twin-engined jet fighter first flown on 5 April 1941; several prototypes underwent development testing until early 1943. In late April – early May 1945 three damaged He 280 fighters with Heinkel HeS 8A turbojet engines were discovered by a group of Soviet engineers which was sent by the People's Commissariat of Aircraft Industry (NKAP – *Narodnyy komissariaht aviatsionnoy promyshlennosti*) to Austria for the purpose of inspecting the Heinkel factories in Vienna and its suburbs. The examples captured by the Red Army were the He 280 V3 (coded GJ+CB), He 280V6 (NU+EA) and He 280 V9 (NU+ED). Several HeS 8A turbojets were also captured. Not one of the captured He 280s was restored to airworthy condition. However, the fighter was inspected very thoroughly – the airframe structure was carefully studied and analysed. The results of these studies, together with the information obtained from the design manual prepared by the company (Baubeschreibung He 280) formed the basis for a technical description of the He 280 aircraft which was compiled by the BNT TsAGI and published in 1947 in its issues Nos. 339 and 354 (airframe and undercarriage respectively). It is not known whether these aircraft were transported to the Soviet Union or were examined on site.

The assessment given to the He 280 by Soviet specialists was positive in some respects. They noted the good aerodynamics of the machine, the interesting design of the levered-suspension main landing gear, the efficient mechanical link between the flaps and the horizontal tail that changed the stabiliser incidence in concert with flap deployment, good access to cannons and armament units, an effective ejection system and a number of other interesting design features. However, these advantages were to a large extent outweighed by the fact that the airframe design was ill suited for production. It was concluded that *'the absence of a definite system in the location of various units […] increases the overall time of the aircraft's final assembly and makes considerably more complicated the production process of the airframe manufacture'*.

On the whole the He 280 was assessed as 'outdated'. However, it should be borne in mind that the prototype He 280 was first

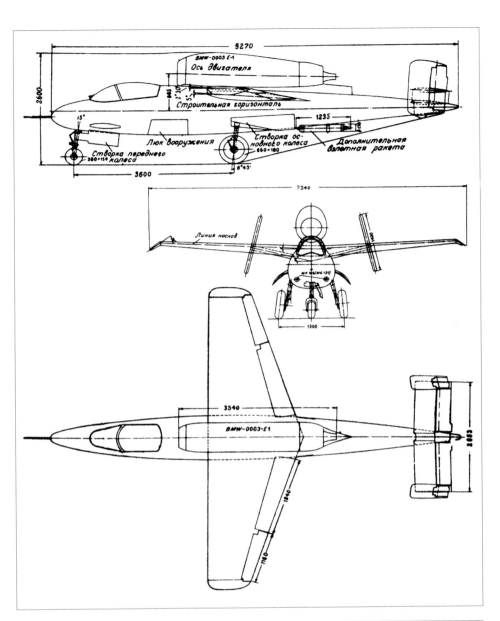

Top right: A three-view drawing of the He 162 from the Soviet documents showing the aircraft's dimensions. The side view shows the fuselage waterline and the engine axis, the rocket booster, and the cannon bay cover.

Above right: Three-quarters rear view of the BMW 003 engine, showing the movable nozzle centrebody.

Right: Another view of the uncowled engine, showing the engine accessories and the attachment points.

Top, centre and above: '02 Red', the other He 162A-2 tested by LII. It is seen here on a snow-covered field at Zhukovskiy in 1946. Again, the LII emblem is carried on the tail.

flown as early as April 1941 when it was undoubtedly ahead of any contemporary fighter; its failure to progress to full development and operational service use was largely due to causes beyond the Heinkel company's control.

Heinkel He 343 jet bomber

The Heinkel He 343 bomber powered by four wing-mounted turbojets was externally very similar to the Arado Ar 234 V6 prototype (the sole example with four engines in individual nacelles) but featured a conventional retractable wheel landing gear instead of skids. A prototype was under construction but was still incomplete when the hostilities ended. A group of Soviet engineers inspecting Heinkel's factories in Vienna, Austria, discovered parts of the fuselage and wings of the He 343 bomber there, along with several other aircraft.

There is no evidence as to the subsequent fate of these parts. It is highly unlikely that they were despatched to the Soviet Union. Nor is it known to what extent they were examined and studied on site, or to what extent the technical drawings and other German documents on this aircraft were studied and used by Soviet specialists.

Some historians call attention to the external similarity between the He 343 and the Il'yushin IL-22 bomber. Undeniably, the general arrangement of the IL-22 strongly resembled that of the Heinkel He 343, but, apart from this, there was very little in common between the two machines. Just like the Su-9 (izdeliye K) was not a copy of the Me 262, the IL-22 was by no means a copy of the He 343, having no structural commonality with the German machine. Obvious external differences include different forward fuselage shapes (the flightdeck of the IL-22 was faired completely into the fuselage contour); the Soviet bomber had a completely different tail unit with a tail gunner's station in addition to a dorsal turret (the He 343 had no defensive armament at all). The IL-22's powerplant arrangement with four Lyul'ka TR-1 turbojets in individual nacelles resembled the arrangement used on the German aircraft, but differed in having more pronounced short pylons with the engines placed ahead of the wings instead of adhering to the wing underside – akin to

Two views of a dismantled He 162A serving as an instructional airframe at BNT TsAGI. Unusually, the aircraft has ordinary wingtips, not downward-canted ones.

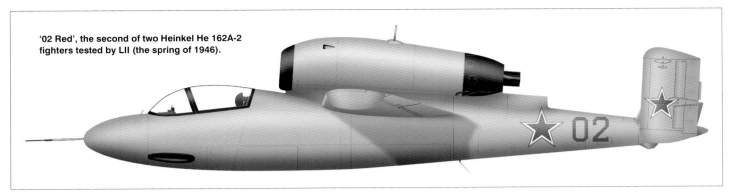

'02 Red', the second of two Heinkel He 162A-2 fighters tested by LII (the spring of 1946).

what is common practice nowadays. The main undercarriage units stowed in the fuselage forward of the wings, not aft of them. Thus, it would be a gross exaggeration to claim (as some historians do) that the Il-22 was 'almost identical to the He 343 project'.

It might be added that the actual performance of the IL-22 was somewhat inferior to the estimated performance of the He 343. This was, no doubt, due to the Soviet bomber's greater all-up weight resulting from the installation of defensive armament.

Henschel Hs 132 single-seat dive-bomber and attack aircraft

An example of the Henschel Hs 132 light jet bomber was captured by the Soviet troops, presumably after the capitulation of Germany. This was a single-engined aircraft powered by a BMW 003A-1 engine which was placed atop the fuselage in a manner similar to the He 162; also similar was the twin-fin tail unit. An unusual feature of the aircraft was the prone position of the pilot.

According to William Green, a series of six prototypes of the Hs 132 was ordered in 1944; two of these were to be A-series and four B-series aircraft. The Hs 132A, for which the Hs 132 V1 and V2 were to serve as prototypes, was a dive bomber powered by a BMW 003A-1 turbojet, whereas the Hs 132B was to be a ground attack aircraft powered by a Junkers Jumo 004B-2. *'By the spring of 1945, the prototype construction was well advanced, and the Hs 132 V1 was being*

readied for initial flight trials. The V2 and V3 were 80 and 75 per cent complete respectively, and the remaining three prototypes were in final assembly, but before trials could begin, the factory was overrun by Soviet forces.'

Thus, judging by the engine type, the example which fell into the hands of the Soviet specialists must have corresponded to the A-series dive bomber configuration. Some sources refer to it as 'one of the three examples built by the Henschel company'; the other two, according to unofficial information quoted in a Soviet source had crashed on take-off (which contradicts the information cited by W. Green). The example obtained by the Soviet specialists had not

been completed – it lacked the wings, the vertical tails and the undercarriage, being intended for static tests. It was delivered to BNT TsAGI, where it was carefully studied. The results of this examination, coupled with the description prepared by Henschel Flugzeugwerke AG (*Einmotoriges Nahkampfflugzeug Hs 132*) were used for compiling a technical description of this aircraft for the benefit of Soviet design bureaux and production engineers. The authors of the BNT report, apart from noting the unorthodox pilot position, specially mentioned the 'unusual' design of the elevator of wooden construction which was almost entirely filled with vertically placed corrugated stripes of plasticised veneer bonded to plywood walls.

Above right: The incomplete Hs 132 (fuselage, engine nacelle and horizontal tail) was studied by TsAGI's Bureau of New Technologies (BNT).
Left and right: Close-up of the Hs 132's cockpit, showing the bulletproof windscreen for the prone pilot.

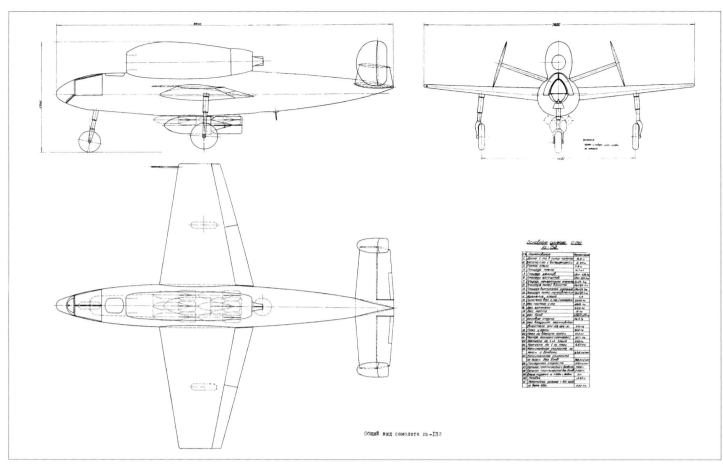

Общий вид самолета Hs-132

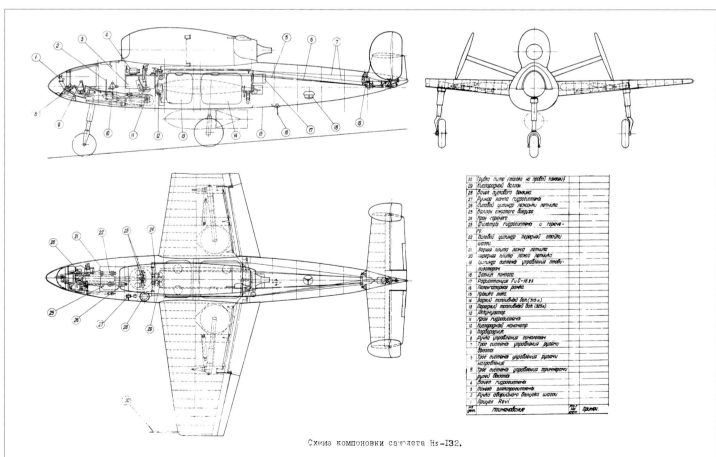

Схема компоновки самолета Hs-132.

214

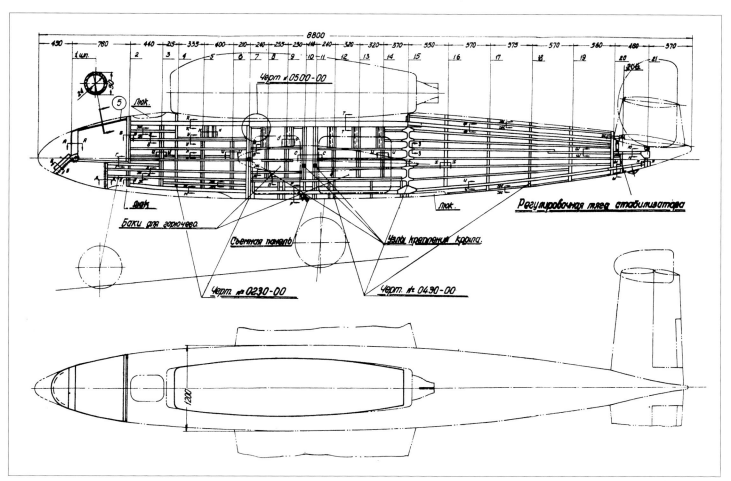

Above left: A three-view drawing of the Hs 132 bomber completed by Soviet specialists, with a table of specifications in Russian. Note the alternative external stores – four 100-kg bombs in tandem pairs or one 500-kg bomb.

Left: A Soviet cutaway drawing of the Hs 132, showing the location of the fuel tanks in the centre fuselage.

Above: A drawing of the bomber's fuselage structure with frame enumeration and references to other drawings.

Right: A drawing of the cockpit section. The Revi bomb sight was located ahead of the bulletproof windscreen.

Junkers Ju 287 – see EF 131 in Chapter 5

Messerschmitt Me 163 Komet single-seat interceptor

Several Me 163 rocket-propelled interceptors were captured by Soviet troops in the weeks and months following the capitulation of Germany. ('More than 20 Messerschmitt Me 163s and Me 262 jet-powered fighters were captured by Soviet forces at Oranienburg, Dallgow and Tempelhof in April-May 1945', according to K.-F. Geust). In July 1945 a dismantled Me 163 was loaded aboard a Li-2 transport in Statgart (not to be confused with Stuttgart) to be transported to the Soviet

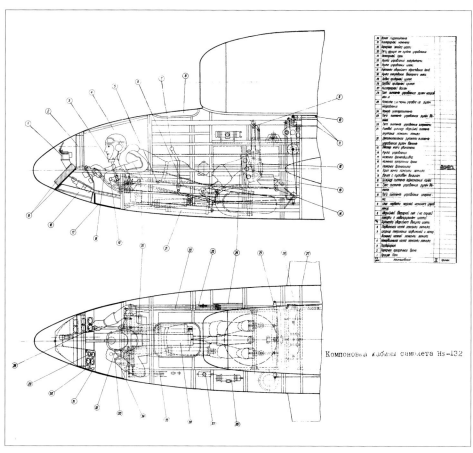

Above: A captured Messerschmitt Me 163B Komet interceptor in Soviet insignia undergoing tests at GK NII VVS. Here the aircraft is still in 'as-was' condition (with no test equipment).

Upper row and right: The Me 163's take-off dolly and the main landing skid; the latter has an electrically actuated lock for the dolly's U-shaped axle.
Left: Close-up of the extended main landing skid with the dolly detached. The skid fairing is removed, exposing wiring and pipelines.
Opposite page: Typically of NII VVS, faired deflection angle sensors forming part of the test equipment were fitted to the Me 163B's control surfaces during the trials. Note the added dorsal Venturi tube and the propeller-like vane on the nose driving the generator.

217

Opposite page, left row: Mark L. Gallai dons his flight helmet and climbs into the Me 163B's cockpit for a test flight. Note the faired-over gun ports in the wing roots. The bottom picture shows the same aircraft as it is towed to altitude by a Tu-2 bomber. Note where the towing line is attached.
Right row: The Me 163B is towed aloft by the Tu-2. The dolly is jettisoned at fairly high altitude to stop it from striking the aircraft on the rebound.
Above: A cutaway drawing showing the location of the Walter HWK 109-509 rocket motor in the Me 163's fuselage.
Above: The HWK 109-509's combustion chamber (indicated by the arrow) is at the extreme rear, with the steam/gas generator and turbo pump unit at the front.

Union; seven more machines of this type were loaded onto a train near the airfield of Oranienburg. By the end of 1945 there were ten Me 163 fighters in the Soviet Union; of these, seven were in the Me 163S two-seat training version (*Schulflugzeug*). However, of all the mentioned machines only one Me 163 was in airworthy condition; the others either required complicated repairs or were not flyable at all.

At least two (possibly three) Me 163s were flight-tested in the Soviet Union; several others were used for static testing and studies on the ground. The tests had to be restricted to flights in glider configuration, powered flight being impossible because the special fuel for the Walther HWK 109-509 liquid-fuel rocket motor was unavailable. Examples prepared for flight testing included a single-seat Me 163B (flown at NII VVS) and a two-seat Me 163S flown at LII. In the latter case, one of the test pilots entrusted with the testing of the machine was Mark L. Gallai. His Me 163S (dubbed *Karas'*, crucian, by Soviet pilots because of its fish-like shape) was towed on a long cable behind a Tu-2 bomber piloted by his colleague Igor' I. Shelest to the necessary altitude and then released. The Me 163S was also flown by the LII test pilots Yakov I. Vernikov and A. A. Yefimov. In gliding flight the heavy machine proved rather sluggish; coupled with the high sink rate, this demanded considerable skill on the part of the test pilot. Gallai performed a series of successful flights in the Me 163S, studying the aircraft's behaviour in different flight modes. He recalled later that the Me 163's descent prior to landing was very rapid and steep; the slightest error in flaring out for landing was fraught either with impacting the ground at an excessive sink rate, or with losing speed at a height of a few metres, with an ensuing stall. To solve the problem, Gallai opted for a steeper descent at greater

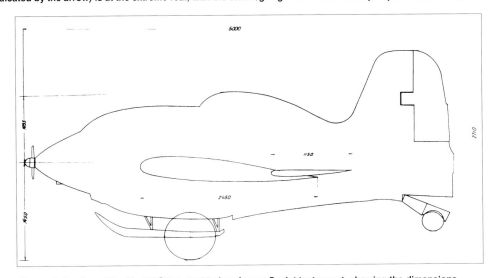

Above: A drawing of the Me 163S two-seat trainer from a Soviet test report, showing the dimensions.

horizontal and vertical speeds – a seemingly illogical decision. Yet, it was precisely the greater margin of speed that enabled Gallai to begin flaring out in advance, with the aircraft still dozens of metres above the ground, when no minute precision in handling was required. When the aircraft was quite close to the ground, the pilot merely had to perform a 'second-stage flareout' by further reducing the already modest speed, touching down without problems. This method, Gallai wrote, was 're-invented' later

The Me 163S in TsAGI's T-101 wind tunnel. Attachment struts had to be installed under the wings for this purpose. Note the fairing closing the rocket motor nozzle.

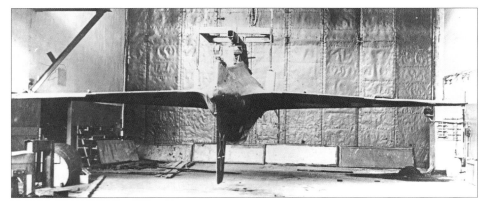

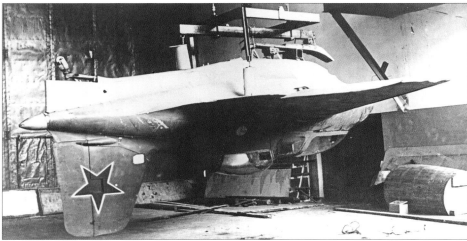

Top left: The Me 163S hangs inverted in one of TsAGI's shops during static tests.

Above left, left and below left: Three more views of the Me 163S during static tests at TsAGI. The aircraft is suspended from a special frame by the struts on which it had been mounted in the wind tunnel. Note that the fairing of the tailwheel strut and the tyre have been removed.

Top: The Me 163S trestled at TsAGI. This view shows the tandem canopies with a transparent section in between.

Above: The Me 163's wings had a strong leading-edge sweep and fixed leading-edge slots over much of the span.

for dead-stick emergency landings of supersonic jet fighters.

Still, one of Gallai's unpowered flights ended in a crash landing. He was testing the stability of the machine at various CG positions. In that flight the CG was moved forward by 2-3% MAC, the engineers overlooking the fact that on a tailless aircraft (such as the Me 163) the elevator moment arm was reduced by half as compared to the normal layout. After lift-off the aircraft proved to be very nose-heavy, and Gallai had to apply full back stick to maintain normal level flight. During the landing the lack of stick movement margin resulted in a heavy touchdown, the aircraft being damaged beyond repair. (Gallai was able to continue the gliding flights in another Me 163 three weeks later.)

Despite the difficulties noted, the LII test report stated that *'the rational choice of the aerodynamic layout and structural features of the tailless aircraft makes it possible to ensure for it sufficiently good characteristics of longitudinal and lateral stability, as well as the controllability in the field of subsonic flight speeds. This testifies to the possibility of using this layout as one of the possible design configurations of a high-speed aircraft'.*

At NII VVS a single-seat Me 163B (possibly W.Nr. 191952) was tested by Vladimir Ye. Golofastov, with Ivan P. Piskunov piloting the Tu-2 towing aircraft and Nikolay N. Borisov acting as project test engineer. Golofastov's experience with the Me 163 included a dramatic episode in which the take-off trolley failed to detach itself from his aircraft due to a malfunction in the release mechanism. Golofastov was advised of the situation by the Tu-2 crew when his aircraft had reached an altitude of 1,000 m (3,380 ft). It had taken some time and fairly risky manoeuvres to tackle the situation: the slackened towing cable got entangled with the trolley, and when the Tu-2 pulled the cable taut the Me 163 flipped over, flying in an inverted position. Slackening the cable again permitted Golofastov to restore the normal flight attitude by applying ailerons. Eventually he succeeded in getting rid of the unwelcome burden and landed successfully after a 45-degree dive. In all, Golofastov made 17 flights in the Me 163; the required tests were performed during a 5-minute dive from an altitude of 6,000 m (9,680 ft) to 2,000 m (6,560 ft).

As stated by D. Sobolev, the mentioned test flight led Golofastov to the conclusion that that the Me 163 single-seat tailless fighter had behaved in the unpowered flight, with regard to handling, in a way similar to the fighters of the conventional layout. In performing the basic aerobatic figures the machine was virtually in no way different from other fighters. It may be safely presumed that the results of the testing of the Me 163 were duly studied by the leading Soviet design bureaux; yet, the whole concept of a rocket-powered point-defence interceptor was abandoned at an early stage by the Soviet Air Force, and the influence of German experience in this field on the Soviet aircraft industry was thus fairly limited.

It remains to be mentioned that a Me 163S was subjected to static tests at TsAGI, while a Me 163S coded '94 White' (the one tested by M. Gallai at LII) had previously been used for wind tunnel tests. An example of the Me 163B, with some skin

**Top and upper centre: The Me 163S sits on the snow-covered LII airfield in Ramenskoye in take-off configuration.
Lower centre and above: These views show the Me 163's distinctive planform and the span of the leading-edge slots. The Me 163S gained the serial '94 White' during the trials.**

Top, centre and above: More views of Me 163S '94 White' on the snow-covered LII airfield in Ramenskoye in take-off, flight and landing configuration. Note the LII badge on the tail.

panels stripped off to expose the structure, was exhibited at BNT TsAGI. An example of the Me 163 was preserved at BNT, together with some other German aircraft, until the early 1950s.

Messerschmitt Me 262 Schwalbe/Sturmvogel fighter/bomber

Fighter pilots of the Red Army Air Force had their first encounters with the Me 262 jet fighter in the spring of 1945 over Germany.

On several occasions they engaged combat with these fighters and even emerged victorious on several occasions. Stepan A. Krasovskiy, CO of the 2nd Air Army at the end of the war and later Air Marshal, recalls in his memoirs that getting to grips with the Me 262 was no simple matter for Soviet pilots, given the German fighter's marked advantage in speed. *'We trained pilots for the special mission of waging combat against these aircraft. In our Air Army (2nd Air Army – Auth.) the first victory over a jet fighter was gained by the airmen of the 2nd Guards Attack Air Corps commanded by General S. V. Slyusarev. A Me 262 was shot down by escort fighters as it tried to attack a group of IL-2 strike aircraft.'* Often cited is the victory of the Soviet ace Ivan N. Kozhedoob who downed a Me 262 in the spring of 1945. Victories in encounters with these jet fighters were claimed by Markveladze, Kuznetsov, Sivko and some other pilots of the 16th Air Army. Several Me 262s were reported shot down by the gunners of the IL-2s belonging to the 2nd Guards Attack Air Corps. Yet, it was obvious that the Me 262 was a really tough opponent

An opportunity to study thoroughly this advanced aircraft 'live' presented itself shortly before the end of the hostilities; the first machines of this type fell into Soviet hands during the closing months of the war. Several Messerschmitt Me 262 turbojet-powered fighters were captured by Soviet troops during March-May 1945 on the territory of Germany and Austria. According to some sources, by the end of 1945 there were three Me 262 in the USSR, of which only one example was in an airworthy condition. Other sources speak of four examples. According to N. Vasil'yev, four examples of the Me 262 were delivered to the Soviet Union in a damaged condition. Three of them were assigned to aircraft industry enterprises, while the fourth (W.Nr. 110426) was sent to NII VVS.

On 30th March 1945 NII VVS received Me 262A-1 W.Nr. 110426, which arrived in dismantled condition from Schneidemühl. The machine was damaged and had to be repaired at a prototype construction plant at Chkalovskaya airbase. A. G. Kochetkov was appointed project test pilot for the machine; his first flight in the Me 262 took place on 15th August 1945. In the subsequent

: Me 163S '94 White' being towed to altitude. Note the sensor pertaining to the test equipment on a tripod-like structure ahead of the rear cockpit, which is vacant in this case.

months he performed in all 12 flights for the purpose of establishing performance characteristics of the machine and evaluating its handling. The latter point was of special importance, bearing in mind the reports about certain dangerous properties of the aircraft. The testing of the Me 262 performed by German pilots was accompanied by several fatal accidents caused by the aircraft's tendency to enter an uncontrollable dive at high speeds.

This propensity of the machine also manifested itself during the testing in the Soviet Union. In his last flight in the Me 262 Kochetkov had to resort to an extreme muscular effort in order to recover from a dive at high altitude. At an altitude of 1,000 m (3,280 ft) and a speed of 800 km/h (497 mph) his aircraft began to lower its nose… Kochetkov pulled the stick back, but the machine went on diving, and when the speed reached 850 km/h (529 mph) the pilot had to pull the stick with both hands, the stick force being in

Above: This Me 163B ended up at TsAGI's BNT as a cutaway instructional airframe. Note that the main skid is retracted here.

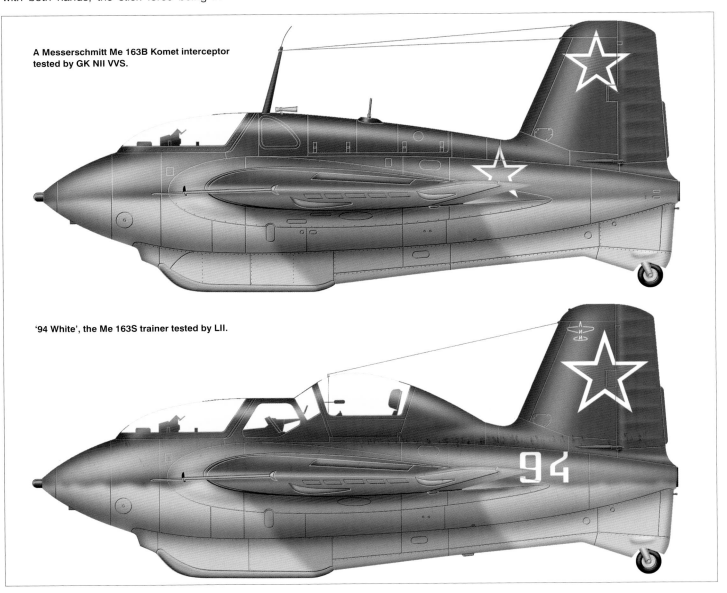

A Messerschmitt Me 163B Komet interceptor tested by GK NII VVS.

'94 White', the Me 163S trainer tested by LII.

Four views of Me 262A-2 (or A-1) WNr 110426 during trials at GK NII VVS (note the distinctive hexagonal pavement slabs at Chkalovskaya AB) in late 1945. The cannon ports have been faired over, and the unpainted air intake assembly suggests the port engine has been replaced.

excess of 24 kg (53 lb). He managed to take one hand off the stick and throttle back the engines. When the speed dropped to 700 km/h (435 mph), the control forces came back to normal. According to Dmitriy A. Sobolev, test pilot F. F. Demida was killed in similar circumstances on 17th September

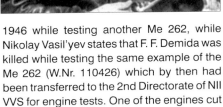

1946 while testing another Me 262, while Nikolay Vasil'yev states that F. F. Demida was killed while testing the same example of the Me 262 (W.Nr. 110426) which by then had been transferred to the 2nd Directorate of NII VVS for engine tests. One of the engines cut

Top left and right: Stills from a documentary film prepared by GK NII VVS, showing a Me 262A being repaired prior to the tests, with technicians crawling all over it. Here the starboard engine cowling is being fitted. This was probably a different example (note that the cannon port is not yet blanked off).
Second row, left and centre: The nose cap is reinstalled as a technician standing in the empty cannon bay gives instructions.
Third row, left and centre: Test pilot A. G. Kochetkov climbs into the cockpit of a Me 262A.
Above and left. Kochetkov climbs out and signs the flight assignment after the mission.
Right-hand column (rows 2, 3 and 4): The same Me 262A (W.Nr. 170063?) taxies at Chkalovskaya AB.
Right: The Me 262A's port engine belches fire during a ground run. The cowling appears to be removed.

Top and above: Four photos of the Me 262A depicted on the previous page as it takes off on a test flight. Again, the cannon ports have been faired over.

on take-off and the machine slammed into the ground near the village of Kishkino. This version of the story is repeated by K.-F. Geust who also states that Demida was killed on 17th September 1946 in the same aircraft as the one flown by Kochetkov; however, he asserts that *'according to Western sources this Me 262 was W.Nr. 170063 of Ofw Helmut Lennartz, JG 7, who crash-landed at Kolberg in April 1945'*…

The Me 262 was also flown by other pilots, including test pilot Pyotr M. Stefanovskiy. Apart from noting the mentioned 'perfidious' behaviour at high speeds, they gave a generally positive assessment of the aircraft's handling qualities, stating, in particular, that 'conversion to aircraft of this type

will present no difficulties, given the correct approach to the training of pilots'. On the negative side, they noted the German fighter's poor take-off performance, which necessitated the use of long runways (up to 3,000 m/9,840 ft) or the use of take-off boosters.

The testing conducted at NII VVS revealed the following performance characteristics of the Me 262: a maximum speed of 780 km/h (485 mph) at sea level; 850 km/h (528 mph) at 7,000 m (22,960 ft); time to 5,000 m (16,400 ft) was a mere 4.2 minutes. According to William Green, the Me 262A-1a attained a speed of 827km/h (514 mph) at sea level and 869 km/h (540 mph) at 6,000 m (19,685 ft). These figures exceeded by far

the performance characteristics of the best Soviet fighters powered by piston engines.

Photos exist of two different single-seat examples of the Me 262A-2 in Soviet markings; the photos show both of them had the guns removed and the gun ports blanked off with metal plates. One of them is the example tested at NII VVS; the other one may well be one of the examples placed at the disposal of MAP (no details on its identity and testing are available). The existence of this second single-seater is mentioned by Nikolay Vasil'yev who states that *'the second example of the Me 262 was restored at Plant No. 482 under the supervision of Vladimir M. Myasishchev in December 1945'*. Further on he states that in April 1946 *'one of the three Me 262s placed at the disposal of MAP was airworthy, another one underwent static tests and the third one was sent to plant No. 481 in Syzran' for conversion into a two-seat variant'*.

The two-seat version of the Me 262 was also tested in the USSR. According to Sobolev, it was the Me 262B-2 experimentally modified by German engineers into a night fighter. In this configuration it was equipped with a radar, the second cockpit being stripped of the second set of controls and outfitted with instruments presenting the information from the radar. Soviet engineers did not test this machine in its intended night fighter role. Instead, they recommended using it for the training of pilots

A two-seat Me 262B undergoing tests at GK NII VVS in September 1946. Some researchers list this aircraft as a Me 262B-2 night fighter which had the radar removed.

converting to jet aircraft. A photo exists of a 'Soviet' Me 262 two-seater without the characteristic *Hirschgeweih* (Stag's antlers) nose-mounted radar antenna array. One may surmise that this was the Me 262B-2 night fighter mentioned by Sobolev, after the modifications effected at Plant 482 (as related by Vasil'yev).

An interesting chapter in the 'Soviet episode' of the Me 262's history is associated with the plans for putting this aircraft into production in the USSR. The idea arose among Soviet specialists engaged in the testing of the German fighter who were obviously very much impressed by the high degree of perfection achieved in the course of the Me 262's prototype development. The concluding part of the test report read in part: *'The Council of People's Commissars (that is, Government) of the USSR shall be approached with a proposal that a batch of the Me 262 aircraft be manufactured without introducing any changes, both in the single-seat and the two-seat versions, for the purpose of the speediest conversion training of pilots in the service units of the VVS and for investigating the aerodynamic problems, associated with high flight speeds.'*

This proposal soon became an object of controversy. The Air Force command gave its support to the idea, which also seemed initially to find favour with Stalin who personally took an interest in the matter. The

Ministry of Aircraft Industry initially also voiced its support for this proposal. As related by N. Vasil'yev, on receiving the first results of the captured fighter's flight tests, Deputy People's Commissar of Aircraft Industry Pyotr V. Dement'yev wrote a letter to Gheorgiy M. Malenkov, Vice-Chairman of the Council of People's Commissars, which read in part:

'To shorten the time of studying and mastering the production of turbojet engines and aircraft, NKAP considers it expedient to start series production of the Me 262 jet aircraft powered by two Jumo 004 turbojet engines. [...]

Manufacture of the aircraft can be organised at plants No. 381 in Moscow and No. 292 in Saratov. Chief designer Myasishchev has been tasked with studying the structure of the Me 262, preparing the technical drawings and adapting the aircraft to accept our armament and equipment; he has already started this work. Chief Designer [Vladimir Ya.] Klimov has been tasked with studying the Jumo 004 engines...'

As mentioned above, the second example of the Me 262 was restored at Plant No. 482 under the supervision of V. M. Myasishchev in December 1945. Having studied the machine, he reported to Dement'yev in August 1946 that *'the Me 262 can be modified for series manufacture with the all-up weight reduced by 580 kg [1,280 lb] by sim-*

plifying the armament and equipment. Furthermore, while retaining fully its good performance, it will be fitted with a certain amount of new equipment associated with jet engines and mastered in production by the [Soviet] industry'. (N. Vasil'yev suggests that the example restored at Plant No. 482 may have been the Me 262C which was used as a testbed for testing the Jumo 004 and BMW 003E-1 engines at LII in 1946).

There were plans for subsequently increasing the aircraft's performance by equipping it with an afterburning version of the RD-10 (the Soviet version of the Jumo 004 – S.K.) or turbojets designed by Arkhip M. Lyul'ka, as well as by improving the wing aerodynamics. It was expected that the maximum speed would reach 900 km/h (559 mph) with the former powerplant and 960 km/h (596 mph) with the Lyul'ka engines. The take-off run with and without rocket boosters would be 500/800 m (1,640/2,620 ft) respectively with afterburning RD-10s and 450/650 m (1,480/2,130 ft) with the Lyul'ka engines. The range would be 800 and 750 km (496 and 465 miles) respectively.

Vasil'yev goes on to state: Despite all the efforts of the VVS and NKAP, the Me 262 was never placed in production in the Soviet Union. The reasons for this may appear clearer from the following. According to Sobolev, plans were in hand for manufacturing a batch of reverse-engineered Me 262s;

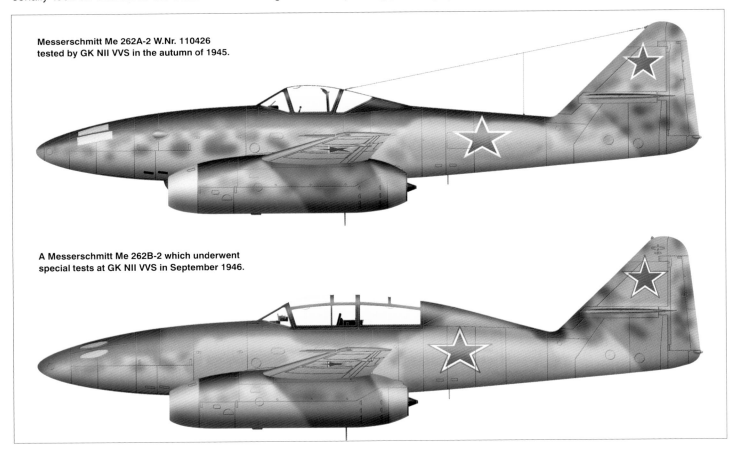

Messerschmitt Me 262A-2 W.Nr. 110426 tested by GK NII VVS in the autumn of 1945.

A Messerschmitt Me 262B-2 which underwent special tests at GK NII VVS in September 1946.

Above: A dismantled V-1 (Fieseler Fi 103) 'flying bomb' captured by Soviet forces in Germany.

yet they never materialised. NKAP (later MAP – Ministry of Aircraft Industry) was singularly unenthusiastic about putting into effect the decision to manufacture a batch of 'Soviet Messerschmitts' (despite Dement'yev's letter quoted above – *Auth*.). Eventually the idea fell into oblivion because the focus of attention had shifted to the construction of the new Soviet Yak-15 and MiG-9 fighters which were described as 'superior' to the German design (in actual fact, only the MiG-9 could claim an edge in performance over the Me 262).

The famous aircraft designer Aleksandr S. Yakovlev, who at that time also held the post of deputy People's Commissar of Aircraft Industry, recalls in his memoirs that the idea of putting the Me 262 into series production in the USSR was discussed at a meeting presided by Stalin. In the course of discussion Stalin asked Yakovlev about his opinion of this fighter. Yakovlev, according to his memoirs, answered that he was dead against putting that aircraft into production because he considered it to be a poor-qual-

ity machine, difficult in handling and notorious for a number of fatal accidents it had suffered in Germany. If adopted in the USSR, it would, in Yakovlev's opinion, discourage Soviet pilots from mastering jet-powered aircraft. Furthermore, allocating all the resources to copying a German machine would seriously prejudice the development of original Soviet designs and be damaging to indigenous Soviet jet aircraft technology. K.-F. Geust comments on this by saying that 'Stalin's decision was in line with Yakovlev's proposal, concentrating the efforts on developing Mikoyan's MiG-9 and Yakovlev's own Yak-15 jet fighters which were considered more promising than the Me 262'. He also asserts that *the Me 262 controversy led to the dismissal (and later imprisonment) of [People's Commissar of Aircraft Industry Aleksey I.] Shakhurin'*, although other sources give different reasons for this imprisonment.

Yet, there was one Soviet fighter which, at least outwardly, looked like a close relative of the German machine. It was the Su-9 designed and built by OKB-134 under the

supervision of Pavel O. Sukhoi. Like the Me 262, it was powered by two Jumo 004 engines located under the wings and featured the same basic aerodynamic layout. A layman might be excused for mistaking it for a copy of the German fighter – which, in fact, it was not. Closer scrutiny reveals there was no structural commonality between the two machines, apart from the similar engine installation. The fuselage of the Su-9 had an oval cross-section, as distinct from the triangular section of the Me 262; the straight wings featuring equal taper with rounded tips were quite unlike the moderately swept wings of the Messerschmitt; the rounded outline of the vertical tail of the Su-9 did not resemble the angular contours of the German machine and so on. But, of course, there is no point in denying a certain influence which, in particular, manifested itself in placing the cockpit amidships (as distinct from, say, the Gloster Meteor which likewise had the engines mounted on the wings but had the cockpit positioned well forward). The Su-9 was equipped with an ejection seat

This complete V-1 was put on display in a city park in Kiev along with other captured German hardware in the summer of 1945.

Above: This V-1 was captured complete with its ground handling dolly.

which was a copy of the seat developed by German engineers for the He 162. The Su-9, incidentally, had quite acceptable performance characteristics, including a top speed of 885 km/h (549 mph), a service ceiling of 12,800 m (41,990 ft) and a range of 1200 km (745 miles). It was clearly superior to the Yak-15 and only slightly inferior in maximum speed to the MiG-9, while being free from some problems that plagued the latter machine. Nevertheless, the Su-9 was not put into production; its outward resemblance to the German fighter may have played a certain role in this.

Interestingly, Miroslav Balous, a Czech author, asserts it was Pavel O. Sukhoi who had been charged with preparing a preliminary study of the necessary preparations for putting the Me 262 into production (that is, the adaptation of the German design to Soviet production standards, Soviet materials and equipment items etc.). Instead, Sukhoi came up with a proposal for a design of his own, as related above. Compare this with the reference above to Myasishchev as the designer tasked with preparations for the series production of the Me 262.

Me 263 (Junkers Ju 248) rocket-propelled interceptor

This interceptor started its life as the Messerschmitt Me 163D, embodying considerable redesign compared to the basic Me 163B model. While retaining the latter's wings, it featured an entirely redesigned and much larger fuselage affording increased fuel tankage and stowage space for a retractable tricycle undercarriage (the latter feature was intended to improve the aircraft's mobility on

Above: One more V-1 that fell into Soviet hands.

the ground radically). The project was transferred for further development to the Junkers organisation at Dessau where it was redesignated Ju 248.

Coded DW+PA, the Ju 248 V1 was completed at Dessau early in August 1944; plans had been prepared and approved by the RLM for series production of the interceptor, but the RLM insisted that the designation Ju 248 be discarded in favour of Me 263, since the aircraft was essentially a Messerschmitt design. According to W. Green, the prototype was captured intact by Soviet forces and sent to the Soviet Union where considerable interest in rocket-powered target-defence interceptors had been displayed. *'The design bureau supervised by Artem Mikoyan and Mikhail Gurevich was*

The 10X 'flying bomb', one of the Soviet derivatives of the V-1. The markings on the fuselage are noteworthy.

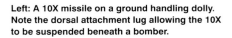

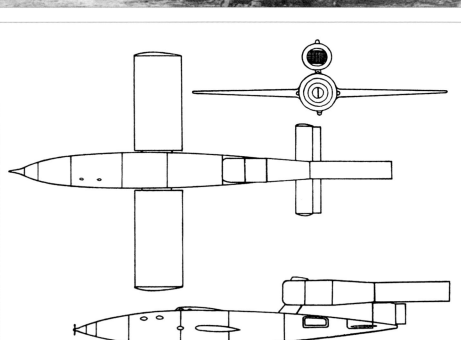

Above: A three-view drawing of the 14X.
Upper right: A 10X equipped with a pair of solid-fuel rocket boosters (1949).
Right: A 10X is launched from a Type 1 sloping launch ramp (1946).
Below: This Petlyakov Pe-8 powered by Shvetsov M-82 radials was used as a weapons testbed after the war, carrying a 10X missile under the fuselage.

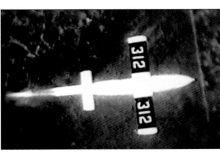

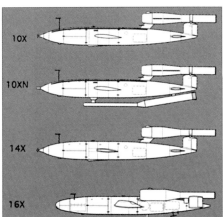

Left-hand column: This sequence of stills from a GK NII VVS documentary shows the Pe-8 'mother ship' carrying a 10X missile marked '404'. The missile's pulse-jet engine is ignited while the missile is still attached, belching tremendous flames, whereupon the weapon is released. The bottom photo depicts a different example marked '312', which is seen from the bomber a few seconds after release.

Centre column, top to bottom: An artist's impression of the 14X missile which was evolved from the 10X. The assembly line at plant No. 51 with at least eight substantially complete 14X missiles. An artist's impression of the 16X missile with two engines and twin tails. A 16XA Priboy missile (the early version with a pointed nose) on a ground handling dolly. Initial-production 16X missiles in the final assembly shop (the one nearest to the camera still lacks the warhead). A comparison of the 10X, the ground-launched 10XN, the 14X (note the thinner wings) and the 16XA (version 2).

Right-hand column, top to bottom: A desktop model of the 10X on a trailer-mounted launcher; a 10X being launched from a ramp; a desktop model of the 10X; and a desktop model of the 16X, showing the tail surfaces and the rear supporting struts of the engines.

allocated the task of developing the Me 263 for Soviet use, but, possessing limited experience in the use of wing sweepback and dubious of the lack of horizontal tail surfaces, Mikoyan and Gurevich discarded these features, marrying the fuselage of the Me 263 to new unswept wings of thin section and slightly swept horizontal tail surfaces which were attached to the tip of the vertical surfaces. Designated I-270 (izdeliye Zh), this Russo-German melange was flown in 1946 but was abandoned after limited testing.'

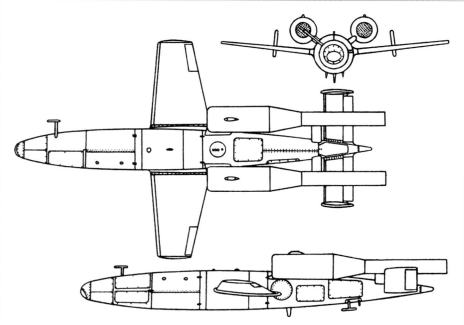

Available Soviet/Russian sources shed no light on the studies of the Me 263 in the Soviet Union; there is no evidence to suggest that it was flight tested. In describing the Mikoyan/Gurevich I-270, Russian sources generally avoid any mention of the German aircraft, albeit at least two publications concede that the German technological influence did play a part in the I-270's design. It should be stated, though, that the fuselage of the I-270, while bearing an external resemblance to that of the Me 263, was in fact designed anew to match the Soviet RD-2M-3V liquid-fuel rocket motor developed by Leonid S. Dooshkin and Valentin P. Glushko. The I-270 failed to progress beyond the experimental stage, the Soviet military having abandoned the idea of putting rocket-powered interceptors into operational service.

Fieseler Fi 103 (V-1) 'flying bomb' and Chelomey's cruise missiles

As described elsewhere in this book, the Soviet Union benefited from German experience in the design of unmanned winged missiles, notably the Fieseler Fi 103, for the development of a manned aircraft, the Ju 126 (EF 126) which was one of the types evolved by German engineers for Soviet customers after the war. However, the unmanned version proper, also known as the V-1 (*Vergeltungswaffe Eins* – reprisal weapon No. 1), also provided inspiration for similar Soviet projects which deserve being mentioned here, albeit the book basically deals only with manned aircraft.

In 1944 the Soviet political and military leaders received information about German aerial attacks against London involving the use of V1 pilotless winged missiles powered by pulse-jet engines. As a consequence, the

Top and above: This Tu-2 was converted into a weapons testbed which served for the initial tests of the 16XA missile. Note the very limited ground clearance of the missile.

Above: An early 16XA missile has just been dropped by the Tu-2 testbed.

Top, centre and above right: This sequence shows the separation of the Priboy missile.

Left: One of the prototype 16XA missiles marked 0123 is seen from the bomber a few seconds after separation.

Right: A 16XA missile in cruise flight.

People's Commissariat of Aircraft Industry was tasked with creating similar pilotless weapons. An appropriate resolution was issued by the State Defence Committee. The practical work on developing an unmanned flying vehicle similar to the V-1 was entrusted to the Central Aero Engine Institute (TsIAM – *Tsentrahl'nyy institoot aviatsionnovo motorostroyeniya*) where one of its leading engineers, Vladimir N. Chelomey, had been working since 1942 on the design of pulse-jet engines. In 1944 the first Soviet engine of this type, the D-3, was built and tested. In the late summer of 1944 Chelomey completed a preliminary design of an unmanned winged missile powered by the D-3 pulse-jet. The project was assigned the designation 10X (the X is presumed to be Roman, although there is a Cyrillic X transcribed as Kh in English. The Kh transcription is used for the designations of modern Soviet/ Russian missiles, but in this text we shall stick to X). In September 1944 Chelomey was appointed Chief Designer and director of Plant No. 51 previously led by the late Nikolay N. Polikarpov. With this plant as his production facility, Chelomey set about the implementation of his projects.

The work on the 10X received a new impetus when Chelomey was provided with incomplete examples of the V-1 (Fi 103) obtained from Britain or captured on the territory of Poland. According to some sources, Soviet troops advancing through Poland captured an example of the Fi 103 which had failed to explode on impact (it may have been a test vehicle launched from the island of Usedom in the Baltic Sea where development work on the Fi 103 had been conducted). The unmistakable influence of this acquisition can clearly be seen in the virtually identical general layout and basic aerodynamic features of the German weapon and the 10X, as shown by available pictures and drawings. Like its German prototype, the Soviet unmanned vehicle featured a cigar-shaped fuselage with pointed ends, short wings of rectangular planform and a pulse-jet located above the rear fuselage, its jetpipe resting on top a short fin-and-rudder assembly acting as the rear pylon of the engine nacelle. However, it was not a case of copying the German design wholesale. Some items of equipment incorporated in the 10X stemmed from Soviet series production (for example, the gyroscopic devices used in the missile's AP-4 autopilot).

The first prototype of the 10X was built before the end of 1944, and the first example from an initial production batch of 19 machines was completed at Plant No. 51 on 5th February 1945. Of these, seventeen missiles were assigned for flight testing which involved the use of three Petlyakov Pe-8

four-engined bombers converted into carrier aircraft. The testing took place between 20th March and 25th June 1945 in the desert areas of Central Asia. Its successive stages included the checking of release procedures and guidance systems, determining the missile's flight performance and, finally, evaluating its combat effectiveness in attacks against simulated targets at a test range.

While the speed and range of the 10X met the specifications, the reliability of this weapon left much to be desired. Of the 66 examples launched from the carrier aircraft during the tests, 44 entered automatically sustained guided flight. Of the 18 machines used to test guidance precision only five reached the target defined as a square measuring 20x20 km (12x12 miles) at a distance of 170 km (106 miles) from the release point.

Some 300 cruise missiles of the 10X type were built before the end of the Second World War. They were used for further testing with a view to enhancing the precision and reliability of the weapon. Close to 200 of them were used during the State acceptance trials conducted between 15th December 1947 and 20th July 1948. The machines tested in 1948 differed from the 1945 models in having the German-type wings and horizontal tail replaced by those of Soviet design and in being fitted with pulse-jets of greater thrust. The 1948 model showed a considerable improvement over the 1945 predecessor, the probability of hitting the target being raised to 88% as against the earlier 36% (in the case of the V-1, according to Soviet documents, it was 70%).

Despite the generally satisfactory results, Commander-in-Chief of the Soviet Air Force Air Marshal K. A. Vershinin voiced his opposition to service introduction of this weapon, the performance of which, in his opinion, fell short of the day's standards. Thus, the 10X was never adopted by the Red Army.

Vladimir N. Chelomey's design bureau developed several improved versions of the 10Kh. For example, the version referred to as '30' featured wooden rectangular wings fitted with ailerons; three examples known as 10DD had greater fuel capacity and, accordingly, greater range (the DD probably stood for **dahl'neye deystviye** = long range). The 10DD could be launched either from a carrier aircraft or from a ground launcher. In parallel, work proceeded on improved types of pulse-jet engines. One of these was the D-5 engine delivering a thrust of 420 to 440 kg (926-970 lb). As early as 1944 Chelomey started projecting the 14Kh cruise missile, to be powered by this engine. Greater thrust, coupled with aerodynamic refinement of the

fuselage, was expected to endow it with a considerably greater speed. In 1946 twenty examples of the 14X were manufactured; ten of them passed trials at a test range in 1948, again with the Pe-8 as a carrier aircraft. A boosted version of this missile attained a speed of 825 km/h (513 mph), a marked improvement as compared to 620 km/h (385 mph) of the 10X. Aerodynamically it differed from the 10Kh in having revised forward fuselage contours and tapered wings instead of rectangular ones. A variant of this model, referred to as '34', featured rectangular wooden wings fitted with ailerons.

In early 1947 the design bureau based at Plant No. 51 was tasked with designing several new unmanned aerial vehicles; one of them was the 16X cruise missile subsequently modified as the 16XA. The original 16X project dated back to 1945 and was based on the use of a single D-6 pulse-jet. Later the project was thoroughly revised and incorporated two D-3 pulse-jets located at the sides of the rear fuselage, the jetpipes protruding aft above the tailplane fitted with endplate fins. The project programme envisaged developing initially a variant featuring autonomous guidance, to be followed by a radio-controlled version. In the latter case, the development of the associated remote control equipment proved to be an arduous task defying the originally set time limits.

By the end of 1947 five 16X prototypes were manufactured; a single example of the Tu-2 bomber was converted into a carrier aircraft and fitted with suspension and release devices. Six 16XAs, renamed *Priboy* (Surf) by that time, were subjected to preliminary flight testing in the period between 22nd July and 25th December 1948. Five of them were equipped with the pneumatically actuated autonomous guidance system affording stabilisation in two planes, while the sixth machine featured an electrically actuated autonomous guidance system affording stabilisation in three planes. In the course of the tests the D-312 pulse-jet mounted on these examples displayed a tendency to cut at flight speeds of 720-775 km/h (447-482 mph). To remedy this, the D-3 pulse-jets were replaced by the more efficient D14-4 units which were capable of sustained running within the entire range of speeds between 300 and 1,000 km/h (186-620 mph). Machines powered by these engines attained a speed of 872 km/h (542 mph).

The Priboy missiles powered by D14-4 pulse-jets and equipped with an autonomous guidance system successfully passed joint manufacturer's tests/State acceptance trials in 1952. However, their satisfactory performance characteristics were marred by insufficient reliability and target hitting precision. This precluded the introduction of these weapons into service. Further development and testing was suggested by the Air Force; however, on 19th February 1953, at the initiative of Lavrentiy P. Beriya (the then Minister of the Interior who also supervised several important weapons development programmes at government level), work on Chelomey's cruise missiles was terminated and his design bureau and Plant No. 51 were disbanded.

Prior to that decision one more unmanned aerial vehicle was under development in Chelomey's design bureau. Designated 10XN and intended for use by ground troops as a strike weapon (hence the N for *nazemnyy poosk* – ground launch), this missile was powered by the newly-developed D-16 pulse-jet. The testing conducted during the winter of 1952-1953 revealed, on the one hand, insufficient reliability of the weapon; on the other hand, it displayed marked advantages as compared to other cruise missiles in the same class, holding the promise of low cost in large-scale production, simple maintenance, considerable strike efficiency and so on. The testing was interrupted by the abovementioned decision to disband the OKB, a decision which many regarded as unwarranted.

Very soon the political events in the country led to a drastic change in the situation. Lavrentiy Beriya was ousted from power and arrested. In 1954, after repeated pleas addressed to Gheorgiy M. Malenkov (one of the new Communist Party and Government leaders), Vladimir Chelomey succeeded in obtaining permission to resume work on his missiles. He was placed at the head of a Special Design Group which a year later was reorganised as OKB-52. The development work on the 10XN went on for another three years and was accompanied by the introduction of various modifications and new pulse-jet models. The results could not be described as an unqualified success; finally, the Ministry of Defence and the State Committee for Aviation Technology (GKAT, the former Ministry of Aircraft Industry) came to a joint conclusion that the 10XN did not meet modern combat weapon requirements. It was decided to use the production examples already manufactured only for training purposes in the Air Force and the Air Defence Forces.

Summing up, it has to be stated that the work based to a large extent on the use of the Fieseler Fi 103 technology did not result in the appearance of entirely successful Soviet cruise missiles in the first post-war years. Yet, this work did provide the design bureau led by Chelomey with much experience which was later put to good use in developing fully successful weapon systems, notably anti-shipping missiles.

***

As distinct from the German jet aircraft described above, the captured German turbojet engines were not merely tested and studied. They powered the first generation of Soviet jet fighters and thus played an enormous role in the introduction of jet technology to Soviet aviation. The events were as follows.

In 1945 the State Defence Committee (GKO – *Gosoodarstvennyy komitet oborony*) adopted a resolution 'On the measures for studying and mastering the German jet technology'. As far as engines were concerned, this document tasked the People's Commissariat of Aircraft Industry and a number of plants subordinated to it with the following specific measures:

Chief of the Central Aero Engine Institute (TsIAM – *Tsentrahl'nyy institoot aviatsionnovo motorostroyeniya*) Polikovskiy was to ensure the study of all the practical work and materials on the Jumo 004, BMW 003 and Heinkel turbojet engines obtained from DVL and the Junkers, Heinkel and BMW design bureaux;

Chief of the All-Union Institute for Aviation Materials (VIAM – *Vsesoyooznyy institoot aviatsionnykh materiahlov*) Tumanov was to ensure the study of the properties of the materials used in German turbojets and liquid-fuel rocket motors;

Chief Designer Klimov and Director of aero engine plant No. 26 Balandin were to study the Jumo 004 engine, copy it and place it into series production;

Chief Designer Kolosov and Director of aero engine plant No. 16 Lukin were to study the BMW 003 turbojet, copy it and place it into series production.

As early as August 1945 the Junkers Jumo 004, BMW 003 and Heinkel HeS 8A turbojets were bench-tested at NII-1 and TsIAM, and Plants Nos. 26 and 16 were tooling up for the manufacture of test batches of the Jumo 004 and BMW 003 engines.

The 'Soviet career' of the latter two type is described below in some detail, including the development undertaken in the USSR and their use in Soviet production and prototype aircraft.

Above: The RD-10F (*izdeliye* YuF), an afterburning version of the Junkers Jumo 004B.

Starboard side view of the *izdeliye* YuF on a transport dolly. The engine was developed by the Lavochkin OKB for the '150F' and '156' experimental fighters. The afterburner is clearly visible.

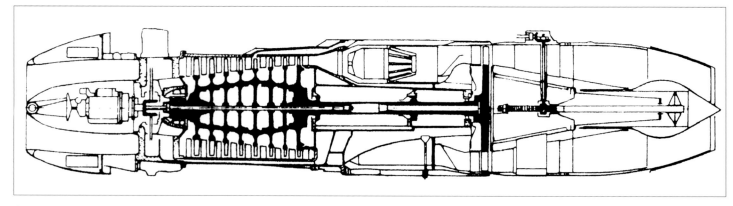

Above: A cutaway drawing of the RD-10, the Soviet reverse-engineered version of the basic non-afterburning Jumo 004B.

Junkers Jumo 004

In 1945 the aero engine design bureau led by Vladimir Ya. Klimov started preparations for organising the manufacture of the Jumo 004B-1 axial-flow turbojet. Its Soviet copy was designated RD-10 (*reaktivnyy dvigatel'* – jet engine) or *izdeliye* Yu. ('Yu' is the last-but-one letter of the Russian alphabet and is a reference to Yumo, the pronunciation of Jumo.) The RD-10 had the following parameters: static thrust 900 kgp (1,985 lbst); length 3,935 mm (12 ft 11 in); diameter 810 mm (2 ft 7 57/64 in); weight 720 kg (1,590 lb). Soviet engineers sought to improve the German engine, which was not sufficiently reliable and had a low service life. Early batches of the RD-10 had a TBO of 25 hours; later batches had the TBO raised to 50 hours. An improved version of the RD-10 with a TBO extended to 50 hours was designated RD-10A.

In an effort to increase the RD-10's thrust, Soviet engine designers opted for providing this engine with an afterburner. This work was done simultaneously by the Yakovlev and Lavochkin aircraft design bureaux (OKB-115 and OKB-301) in cooperation with TsIAM and the Merkoolov engine design bureau respectively. Several versions of the afterburner-equipped RD-10 eventually emerged, often referred to collectively as the RD-10F (the F suffix stood for

forseerovannyy – uprated). For further details see below.

In 1946-1949 the RD-10A/RD-10F engines were manufactured at Plant No.26 in Ufa (now called UMPO, the Ufa Engine Production Association). In late 1946 Vladimir Ya. Klimov, who headed the design bureau at Plant No.26, was transferred to Leningrad. His duties as Chief Designer at Plant No.26 were taken over by his deputy, Nikolay D. Kuznetsov who thus also 'had a finger in the pie' as regards the manufacture of the Jumo 004 in the USSR, before being transferred, in his turn, to another plant in Kuibyshev. The production run totalled 59 engines in 1946, 447 in 1947 and 833 in 1948. (Some sources assert that the RD-10 was built until 1953.)

The Jumo 004 engines captured in Germany and imported into the USSR, as well as their Soviet copy, the RD-10 (RD-10A), were used in several types of Soviet aircraft. These include the Yakovlev Yak-15 'taildragger' fighter and its Yak-17 derivative with a tricycle undercarriage, both of them being a straightforward adaptation of the piston-engined Yak-3 fighter to accept a turbojet engine. The Yak-15 and Yak-17 featured a pod-and-boom configuration; they were brought out in 1945-1946 and built in series, together with the Yak-17UTI two-seat trainer, the production totalling 710 machines of all

versions. These fighters had modest performance and were soon phased out from the inventory of the Soviet Air Force, but their importance should not be underestimated – they introduced the jet age into the Soviet aviation and helped train pilots who soon converted to newer and more advance types, such as the MiG-15.

Yet another Yakovlev type powered by the Jumo 004 (RD-10) engine was the prototype Yak-19 fighter which, as distinct from the Yak-15/Yak-17, was a 'clean sheet of paper' design. It featured an engine buried in the rear fuselage and breathing through a nose air intake – the layout that became classic for the first-generation jet fighters in the USSR and elsewhere. The Yak-19 was powered by an uprated version of the RD-10 that had been developed by the Yakovlev OKB in collaboration with TsIAM in 1946. It was equipped with an afterburner in the jet-pipe extended by 2.6 m (8 ft 6²³⁄₆₄ in), bringing the overall length of the engine to 4,036 mm (13 ft 3 in). Some sources identify the afterburner-equipped RD-10 developed for the Yak-19 as RD-10A (albeit this designation is also known to denote the RD-10 with an extended service life), other sources designate it as RD-10F, still others call it RD-10FK (for *forsazhnaya kamera* – afterburner). Tests showed that the translating cone adjusting the nozzle area, as originally

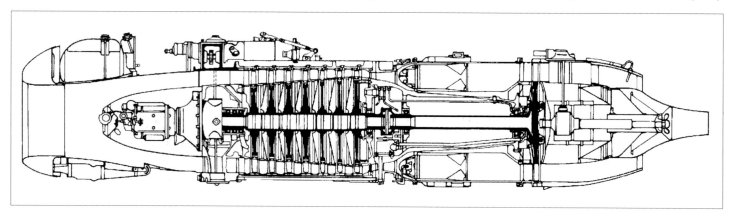

A cutaway drawing of the RD-20, the reverse-engineered BMW 003C.

designed by the Germans, could not withstand the increased exhaust gas temperature in the afterburner. Hence the nozzle cone was discarded and replaced by externally actuated clamshell doors or 'eyelids' regulating the nozzle section. The engine thus modified underwent flight tests on a North American B-25 Mitchell converted into an engine testbed. Initially the thrust of the engine with afterburner was 1,010 kgp (2,230 lbst). Its further development, known as RD-10FKS, had the thrust increased to 1,060 kgp (2,340 lbst) and the engine length to 4,300 mm (14 ft 1¼ in).

The testing of the Yak-19 prototypes conducted in 1947 showed a maximum speed of 904 km/h (488.64 mph) at 5,000 m (16,400 ft) with afterburner. Yet, it was also revealed that the afterburner was useless in combat because of unreliable operation, cooling problems and the cumbersome igniting procedure. The RD-10F engine was assessed by NII VVS test pilot Sergey N. Anokhin as outdated, unreliable and insufficiently powerful. The Yak-19 was not built in series.

OKB-301 led by Semyon A. Lavochkin also made use of the Jumo 004 and the RD-10 on its first turbojet-powered fighters built in 1946-1947. These were the '150', '152', '156' and '160' machines (often referred to as La-150, La-152 etc. in various publications). Like the Yak-15 and Yak-17, these were single-engined designs based on the pod-and-boom configuration. However, they were not adaptations of a piston-engined fighter to a turbojet powerplant, but totally new designs featuring from the outset nosewheel undercarriage and, in the case of the '150' (La-150) – a forward location of the cockpit. These machines were not built in series, but they served for experimenting with the use of reheat in turbojets (in all the mentioned types) and of swept wings (in the '160').

In an effort to boost the performance of the '150' and the '152', Lavochkin's OKB resorted to equipping both machines with a modified version of the RD-10 (Jumo 004B) engine. Developed by the Lavochkin OKB in co-operation with the OKB led by I. A. Merkoolov; it also bore the designation RD-10F, like the variant developed in the Yakovlev OKB. The engine incorporated an afterburner which increased the thrust by 20-25% in take-off mode and by 60-100% in cruise flight. The maximum thrust delivered by the RD-10F attained 1,100 kg (2,425 lb). It had an overall length of 4,600 mm (15 ft 1 in); 18 examples of the engine were built.

The '150' fighter equipped with this engine was designated '150F'; the use of the afterburner increased its speed by some 100 km/h. As for the '152' fighter, it was re-

Above and below: A standard RD-20 with a profiled air intake lip and a forward-mounted oil tank.

Above and below: This RD-20 has a modified inlet assembly (probably designed for mating with a long inlet duct).

engined with the RD-10F and renamed '154'. A further version of the '152' received the RD-10F-2 turbojet and was renamed '156'. Thanks to the improved afterburner, the RD-10F-2 engine delivered a thrust of 1350 kg, ensuring a speed increase of 127 km/h with the afterburner turned on. All these machines had straight wings.

The RD-10F-2 engine was used by Lavochkin once more on the '160' experimental fighter which shared the pod-and-boom configuration of its predecessors, but differed in having sweptback wings. In the course of flight testing conducted in mid-1947 it attained a maximum speed of 970 km/h (603 mph) in horizontal flight at 5,000m (16,400 ft) and was the first among Soviet fighters to attain a speed of Mach 0.92, or 1,050 km/h (653 mph) in a shallow descent at the same altitude. (The engine was referred to as RD-10YuF in some sources – probably in error, this being a combination of RD-10 and *izdeliye* YuF. The designation '160' was also applied to a project of a fighter powered by two wing-mounted Jumo 004 engines, but it was abandoned at an early stage.)

Later fighter designs by Lavochkin were based on the more powerful Rolls-Royce Nene I and Rolls-Royce Derwent V centrifugal-flow turbojets and their Soviet RD-45 and RD-500 derivatives.

Two RD-10 engines were used to power the Su-9 (*izdeliye* K) fighter developed by OKB-134 under Pavel O. Sukhoi. This fighter, featuring the same basic layout as the Me 262 but having nothing in common structurally with the German fighter, proved to be a sound design with quite good performance for its powerplant, but the advent of the MiG-15 prevented the Su-9 from entering production.

There were three fighter projects based on the use of the Jumo 004 (RD-10) engine. Of these, two projects were developed in the OKB led by Oleg K. Antonov (then called OKB-153). One of them, dubbed 'Salamander', was a single-engined fighter similar in layout to the Heinkel He 162 with its dorsally-mounted turbojet; the other, designated 'M', was a delta-wing fighter powered (in its initial project version) by two Jumo 004 engines buried in the wing roots. They did not reach the hardware stage. Two Jumo 004 engines were envisaged for Mikoyan's I-290 fighter project study (see below under the BMW 003 heading).

German turbojet engines were to be used in three early Soviet bomber projects. One of these was the Sukhoi Su-10 (*izdeliye* E) high-speed day bomber, work on which was started in 1946. The initial version of the project envisaged the use of six RD-10 turbojets arranged in a rather unorthodox fashion: four engines flanked the centre fuselage, being placed above and below the wing roots; two more engines were attached to the sides of the lower forward fuselage. One more project study provided for suspending the engines under the wings in two clusters of three engines each. In the course of projecting this powerplant was abandoned in favour of installing four more powerful Lyul'ka TR-1 engines in vertically staggered pairs on the wing outer panels. In this configuration the aircraft was completed as a prototype, but never tested.

The other project was the DSB-17 (VM-24) bomber developed in 1945-1946 by OKB-482 led by Vladimir M. Myasishchev. This was a high-speed day bomber (with the RB-17 reconnaissance version) powered, in one of the project configurations, by four Jumo 004 engines in vertically paired clusters under the wings. The project was terminated at the stage of detail design when Myasishchev's design bureau was closed down in early 1946. Prior to that, Myasishchev had studied the possibility of a straightforward adaptation of the Pe-2I piston-engined heavy fighter which, in the Pe-2I-RD version, was to be powered by two Jumo 004 engines. The project was not proceeded with.

Finally, as mentioned elsewhere in this chapter, in 1946 the OKB led by Igor' V. Chetverikov started designing a bomber based on Arado Ar 234 technology; it was to be powered by two Jumo 004 or by four BMW 003 engines. The work on this project was terminated at an early stage.

BMW 003

The BMW 003A turbojets were launched into series production manufactured at Plant No. 16 in Kazan' (now called KMPO – the Kazan' Aero Engine Production Association) under the direction of Chief Designer S. D. Kolosov (mis-stated as D. V. Kolesov in some sources). The initial Soviet version designated RD-20 had a take-off thrust rating of 800 kgp (1,760 lbst). It differed slightly from the German original in the location of the accessories. The BMW 003 engines and their Soviet copies were used in only one, but important fighter design. That was the MiG-9 (I-300, *izdeliye* F) fighter developed by Artyom Mikoyan and Iosif Gurevich.

Actually, the MiG-9 was preceded by early project studies of fighters sharing the Me 262's basic layout with two turbojets under the wings. One of them, the I-260 (which, like the Su-9, bore the manufacturer's designation *izdeliye* K), was to be powered by two BMW 003s. Another one, the I-290 (*izdeliye* Z), had a powerplant comprising two more powerful Jumo 004 engines. These projects were abandoned in favour of the I-300 which was powered by two captured BMW 003A-1 engines located in the fuselage in a pod-and-boom configuration. Initial production machines were equipped with the RD-20 Series A-1 engines which were actually captured BMW-003s refurbished in the Soviet Union. Later production machines were equipped with the RD-20 Series A-2 engines manufactured by the Kazan' aero engine plant No. 16, with a time between overhauls of 25 and 50 hours. They were followed by the RD-20B engine having a TBO of 75 hours.

Captured examples of the BMW 003A-1 powered the prototype MiG-9UTI (FT-1) two-seat trainer version of the MiG-9.

Boosted BMW 003C engines delivering a thrust of 1,050 kgp (2,315 lbst) were developed by German engineers in the USSR until eventually this task was taken over by Plant No. 16. In early 1947 these engines were installed in the I-307 (*izdeliye* FF) version of the MiG-9 which made its first flight on 24th May 1947 and eventually attained a speed of 950 km/h (590 mph) – a 40-km/h (25-mph) increase over the production MiG-9 (*izdelye* FS). The Soviet reverse-engineered version of this engine produced at Plant No. 16 was the RD-20F (*for**see**rovannyy* – uprated). The thrust augmentation was achieved by increasing the fuel feed, raising the turbine temperature and increasing the turbine rpm. The RD-20F delivered a maximum thrust of 1,000 kgp (2,205 lbst). It was later redesignated RD-21 (some sources treat the RD-21 as a further development of the RD-20F). Two such engines were installed in the MiG9-2RD21, and then in the MiG-9M (I-308, *izdeliye* FR). The RD-21 delivered a maximum thrust of 1,050 kgp (2,315 lbst). The boosted engines gave the aircraft a maximum speed increase of some 55 km/h (34 mph), as well as greater vertical speed. Yet the versions powered by the RD-21 were not built in series. Seven examples of the RD-21 were built.

The MiG-9, like the Yak-15 and Yak-17, gained the distinction of being one of the first turbojet-powered fighters to enter service with the Soviet Air Force, 602 examples being built.

The BMW 003 engines (or their Soviet-built versions) were also to power a four-engined bomber designed by Chetverikov (see above).

In addition to the straightforward adaptation of German production turbojets for manufacture in the Soviet Union, attempts were made to develop improved versions the Jumo 004 and BMW 003 engines within the system of German-staffed design bureaus set up initially on the territory of the Soviet occupation zone and then transferred to the Soviet Union (see next chapter).

Chapter 5

SOVIET-CONTROLLED GERMAN DESIGN BUREAUX

in Eastern Germany and in the USSR (1945-1954)

German-staffed aircraft design bureaux in the Soviet occupation zone (1945-1946)

The previous chapter dealt with the testing of captured German jet aircraft and turbojet engines conducted by Soviet specialists at flight test centres, scientific institutions, design bureaux and production factories. This testing was supplemented by careful study of the captured materials, including design descriptions of aircraft, project documentation and scientific reports from German research institutions.

This, however, was only part of the huge effort intended to draw the fullest advantage of the experience accumulated in Germany in the field of jet-powered aviation. The Soviet Union, as well as its allies (the USA, Great Britain and France), attached much importance to recruiting German aviation specialists. The idea of using their skills and knowledge in the interests of furthering the development of jet-powered aviation in the Soviet Union was first floated in the summer of 1945. Rank and file engineers from aircraft factories were available for recruiting in fairly large numbers, but the highly prized top-ranking specialists were not so easy to come by, given the competition among the Allies. The Western powers, which initially occupied some parts of the future Soviet occupation zone, were in a better position to recruit German specialists and succeeded in getting hold of many prominent scientists and designers, such as Ludwig Prandtl, Betz, Busemann, Georgi, Ernst Heinkel, Alexander Lippisch, Eugen Sänger, Flettner and others.

The story of the Soviet attempts to enlist the services of Professor Kurt Tank, Technical Director of the Focke-Wulf company, in the development of jet aircraft technology in the USSR, is of considerable interest. Several accounts on this subject differ in detail. Professor Kurt Tank was offered the opportunity to work for the Soviets after the war and continue the development of his jet aircraft projects. However, the negotiations with him brought no result.

An account of the events related by Dmitriy A. Sobolev is as follows.

In early September 1946 a meeting took place in Berlin between Kurt Tank and Olekhnovich, the chief of OKB-1, one of the German-staffed design bureaux set up by the Soviet authorities in Eastern Germany

(to be described below). Tank enquired about the possibility of being employed in this OKB. Having received a positive answer, he asked that one more meeting be arranged with him two or three days later, and asked for a certain sum of money that he would use to recruit specialists from his group. Two or three days later a second meeting with Tank took place; he said that by 20th-23rd September he would be able to assemble a group of eight to ten persons and would arrive in the Soviet zone with this group. A sum of 10,000 German marks was handed to him on that occasion. After that, Kurt Tank never turned up in the Soviet zone. As is well known, in late 1946 he went to Argentina where he was engaged in designing jet aircraft for Juan Peron's government.

Another version of the story is given in a comparatively recent press article by Col. (Ret.) V. I. Trembachov devoted to Grigoriy Tokayev (a Soviet expert in aerodynamics who defected to the West in 1946 and became a prominent expert in rocketry and space research). In 1945 Tokayev was included into the State commission tasked with finding, examining and selecting German materials and hardware pertaining to aviation and rocket technology. Tokayev objected to compulsory methods in engaging the services of German designers and refused to go the Western occupation zones in search of Professor Tank and Professor Sänger. Yet, yielding to the pressure from his superiors (Stalin had expressly demanded that Kurt Tank be found), he had to take up that task and actually succeeded in getting Tank's consent to work with Soviet specialists and to arrive in Berlin for negotiations. However, at that junction Marshal V. D. Sokolovskiy, Commander-in-Chief of Soviet Occupation Forces in Germany and Chief of Soviet Military Administration in Germany, gave an order that Kurt Tank be arrested and sent by plane to Novosibirsk. Tokayev did not conceal his indignation at this order, whereupon he was instructed to leave for Moscow 'to be assigned new duties'. This ominous circumstance prompted his decision to flee immediately to the British sector of Berlin and take up residence in the West. It remains to be guessed whether the possibility of a forced deporta-

tion had come to Kurt Tank's knowledge and could explain his failure to bring his negotiations with Soviet representatives to completion, as related by Sobolev.

Despite the lack of success in the case of Kurt Tank and some other personalities of the same magnitude, the Soviet authorities did succeed in enlisting the co-operation of some prominent aeronautical engineers and scientists. To mention but a few, they included Professor Günter Bock, former director of DVL (Deutsche Versuchsanstalt für Luftfahrt); Dr. Brunolf W. Baade, who had been responsible for prototype construction at the Junkers company; Dr-Ing. Alfred Scheibe a leading engine specialist of the Junkers company; Siegfried Günter, former chief of the projects department of the Heinkel company; Dipl.-Ing. Hans Wocke, responsible for the development of the Ju 287 bomber; Dipl. Ing Friedrich (Fritz) Freytag, a specialist in aerodynamics; Dr. G. Bockhaus, former chief of the aerodynamics department of the Junkers company; Dr. Karl Prestel, Oberingenieur, former department chief of BMW-Werke Spandau/Neu Stassfurt; Dipl. Ing. Hans Rössing; Ferdinand Brandner, former technical director of a Junkers engine factory, and others.

The matters proceeded as follows. On 27th June 1945 People's Commissar of Aircraft Industry Aleksey I. Shakhoorin wrote to the Communist Party Central Committee, advocating the setting up of special organisations in the Soviet occupation zone in which German scientists and engineers would work under Soviet supervision and conduct aeronautical research and design work for the Soviet Union. He asked that the matter be brought to Stalin's attention. Shakhoorin's suggestions were approved at the highest level and put into practice. At the time this letter was written, only 17 German engineers and scientists were helping Soviet specialists to study the German aviation hardware. In the course of the following several months more than one thousand specialists from various German firms and institutions were recruited for this work. They were organised into groups set up in Berlin, Dessau, Leipzig, Halle, Stassfurt and Rostock. The groups, which were called OTBs (*Osoboye tekhnicheskoye byuro*, Special

Above: Dr. Brunolf W. Baade, head of the German desaign team at OKB-1 where several models of jet bombers were developed.

technical bureau), were headed by representatives of Soviet aircraft factories and research institutions. Initially the work of these organisations was largely restricted to compiling reports answering the questions put by Soviet institutions. When it became apparent that most of the OTBs were in possession of test and experimental equipment and highly qualified specialists, representatives of the special directorate of NKAP

came up with a proposal that the German specialists be used for rebuilding and developing further the German jet aircraft and jet engines, work on which had not been completed by the end of the war.

In pursuance of this proposal the OTBs were reorganised into design bureaux (OKBs, in Russian parlance) dealing with the design of aircraft, engines and equipment. The biggest of these was the aircraft OKB set up in Dessau at a former Junkers factory. The OKBs in Dessau, Halle, Stassfurt and Berlin were to become the centres for the development of jet-propelled aircraft and jet engines.

The 'Soviet-German' OKBs supervised by Soviet specialists conducted their activities in utmost secrecy, since their existence ran counter to the decisions adopted by the Allies at the Yalta Conference of 1945 which forbade any military production on the territory of Germany after the end of the war.

On 17th April 1946 the Soviet Government issued a resolution assigning specific tasks to these OKBs. As regards aircraft, the tasks boiled down to the following:

The Dessau-based OKB-1 headed by Brunolf Baade was to finish the construction of the Junkers Ju 131 jet bomber prototype powered by six Junkers Jumo 004 engines by September 1946; it was to complete detail design of the Ju 132 jet bomber powered by six Jumo 012 engines and submit the engineering project by December 1946; furthermore, it was to complete the construction of the Junkers Ju 126 attack aircraft

Above: Dipl. Ing. Hans Rössing (second from right), head of OKB-3, who supervised the further development of the DFS 346 aircraft in the USSR.

powered by the Jumo 226 pulse-jet engine with a view to flight-testing this machine in the USSR in May-June 1946. The mentioned aircraft were often referred to as EF 131, EF 132 and EF 126 (EF = *Entwicklungsflugzeug*, development aircraft).

The OKB led by B. Baade bore the brunt of the aircraft design work. According to the plan for 1946, this design bureau was to build five EF 126s, four EF 131s and to com-

A working conference in Baade's office. Left to right: Bockhaus, Karl-Heinz Wolf, Hans Wocke, Johannes Haselof, Brunolf Baade, Freundel, Johannes Hoch. The subject is the '131' (EF 131) bomber, a drawing of which can be seen on Baade's desk.

plete design work on the EF 132; construction of the latter's prototype was slated for 1947. All this was a continuation of the work conducted at the Junkers company in 1944-45 when the company was engaged in projecting the Ju 126 and testing the Ju 287 (a prototype for the EF 131).

The first prototype, designated EF 131 V1 (V = *Versuchsmuster* – development article), was completed in Dessau in August 1946 and submitted for flight testing on 16th August; however, the flight testing was not conducted in Germany. In September the aircraft was disassembled and sent to the USSR for testing at LII.

In May-June 1946 the Dessau-based OKB completed five examples of the EF 126 attack aircraft. Its initial testing was conducted in the unpowered glider configuration. On 21st May 1946 the EF 126 V1, with the German pilot Mattis at the controls, crashed on landing, presumably owing to a misjudged approach pattern. The testing was resumed on other prototypes, but it did not last long – in September 1946 the EF 126 V2, V3 and V4 were disassembled, crated and sent to the USSR where the testing was to continue.

The Halle-based OKB-3 (former OTB-3) headed by Hans Rössing was tasked with

Above: German specialists share a banquet table during a festive occasion.

Above and below: German designers visit the wind tunnel test section at TsAGI.

completing the detail design of the Siebel Si 346 (DFS 346) experimental supersonic aircraft. The first prototype of this aircraft was completed at Halle on 29th September 1946 and submitted for ground testing. The engine section of this OKB was working on the liquid-fuel rocket motors for this aircraft. However, the absence of the necessary fuel components for these engines prevented them from being tested; for the same reason it was impossible to start flight testing of the Si 346.

German-staffed engine design bureaux in the Soviet occupation zone

German specialists in the field of aero engine design worked under Soviet supervision in three organisations: the engine section of OKB-1 in Dessau, OKB-2 in Stassfurt, and the engine section of OKB-3 in Halle.

The Dessau-based OKB staffed by former Junkers personnel was tasked with

Above right and right: German designers discuss the general arrangement of a new jet aircraft developed by OKB-1.

developing, building and testing the boosted version of the Jumo 004B jet engine (variously designated in different sources as Jumo 004C and Jumo 004F) and the more powerful Jumo 012 turbojet. Furthermore, the OKB was to rebuild the Jumo 224 diesel engine. These activities are described in detail below under separate engine headings.

The OKB-2 based at Stassfurt was organised on the basis of the BMW factories and was tasked with the development, prototype construction and testing of the BMW 003C – and with the development of the more powerful BMW 018 turbojet (likewise described below.)

Finally, the engine section of the Halle-based OKB-3 was intended to manufacture the Walter 109-509 liquid-fuel rocket motor for the Si 346 (DFS 346) aircraft. The work was hampered by a shortage of skilled specialists many of whom had been recruited by the Western allies and resettled to the USA or Great Britain. By the autumn of 1946 seven Walter HWK 109-509 motors were assembled at OKB-3; they had a thrust of 1,700 kgp (3,750 lbst). In addition, two examples of the modified HWK 109-510 version rated at 2,000 kgp (4,410 lbst) were completed. BMW specialists on the staff of OKB-3 produced technical drawings of the BMW 3395 liquid-fuel rocket motor with a thrust of 1,200 kgp (2,650 lbst) which was to be used as a booster in combination with the BMW 003C. Construction of a prototype was started. The same specialists were also engaged in projecting the BMW 3390C rocket motor with a design thrust of up to 4,000 kgp (8,820 lbst). These engines were not tested by the time when these design bureaux, together with the aircraft OKBs, had to wind up their activities on the German soil and be relocated a long way eastwards.

Deportation of German specialists. German aircraft design bureaux in the USSR

As early as April 1946 the Soviet authorities took a decision to transfer the German-staffed design bureaux engaged in aircraft construction from Germany to the Soviet Union. The setting up of these design bureaux was clearly a breach of the pledge to destroy the German military industry which was adopted by Iosif V. Stalin, Franklin D. Roosevelt and Winston Churchill at their meeting in Yalta in February 1945; the transfer was intended to prevent the possible political complications.

The idea of using German designers in the Soviet Union was called into question by some specialists, including the well-known designer Aleksandr S. Yakovlev. He recalled in his memoirs how this matter was discussed at a meeting presided by Stalin in April 1946. The then-Minister of Aircraft Industry Mikhail V. Khrunichev and Yakovlev as his deputy voiced their doubts as to the wisdom of using the German engineers employed at aircraft plants in Eastern Germany. They pointed out that this would entail disclosing to the German specialists the secrets of the latest Soviet research conducted in scientific institutions, which, in their opinion, was unacceptable; on the other hand, the activities of the German specialists could not be of any real use unless they were given access to the current scientific research and experiments.

However, these doubts were disregarded; the decision on the transfer was put into effect on 22nd October 1946 when some seven thousand German specialists in different branches of defence industry were put on the trains and sent to the Soviet Union. Aviation specialists were distributed between four factories in the Moscow region (Plants Nos. 1, 51, 456 and 500) and one factory in the vicinity of Kuibyshev (now renamed back to Samara) in the Volga region – Plant No. 2. Of these, experimental plant No. 1, located in the settlement of Podberez'ye, some 100 km (62 miles) north of Moscow, became the place of residence of two aircraft design bureaux – OKB-1 headed by Baade and OKB-2 headed by Rössing. Three plants (Nos. 2, 456 and 500) hosted the German specialists engaged in aero engine design, while Plant No. 51 became a temporary 'home' to those dealing with aviation equipment.

Prototype aircraft and engines on which the German specialists had worked in Germany were also delivered to the Soviet Union and sent to the appropriate plants. These included two examples of the EF 131 bomber (a flying prototype and a static test airframe), the third flying prototype of the EF 126, the Siebel Si 346 rocket-powered aircraft, and several examples of each of the following engine types: Jumo 004C; Jumo 012; BMW 003C; BMW 018; Walter HWK 109-509. The Siebel aircraft was sent to TsAGI for wind tunnel tests; three of the seven BMW 003C engines were delivered to Mikoyan's OKB-155; the rest of the hardware was distributed to the Plants No. 1 at Podberez'ye and Plant No. 2 near Kuibyshev.

* * *

Described below in alphabetical order are the types of aircraft which were developed by German specialists in the special design bureaux set up by Soviet authorities. This section is followed by a similar description of engine types.

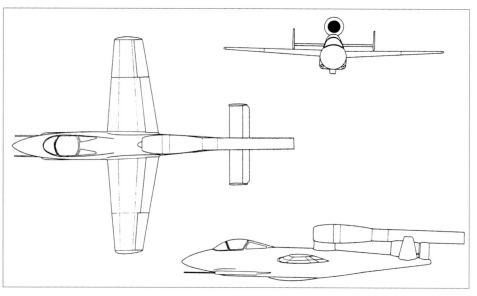

A three-view of the projected Junkers EF 126 pulse-jet powered interceptor. Note the long cannon barrels and the landing skid.

Aircraft

Junkers EF 126 (Ju 126) pulse-jet-powered attack aircraft

When the Soviet authorities set up design bureaux staffed by German engineers in the Soviet occupation zone, OKB-1 at Dessau was tasked, among other things, with projecting an attack aircraft proposed by Junkers engineers. In the documents of OKB-1 it was referred to as the EF 126, albeit the designation Ju 126 was also used. The EF 126 design was based on the Fieseler Fi 103, better known as the V-1 'flying bomb' (*Vergeltungswaffe* – 'reprisal weapon') – to be precise, the manned version known as the Reichenberg which was provided with a cockpit immediately ahead of the pulse-jet engine.

The project developed by Junkers engineers differed from the Fi 103/Reichenberg in many respects. Like its progenitor, the EF 126 was a very small single-seat aircraft with straight wings. However, the latter were new, featuring marked taper and large flaps inboard of the ailerons; in contrast, the 'flying bomb' had constant-chord wings with full-span ailerons. The single fin and rudder assembly supporting the Fi 103's engine nacelle was augmented by large trapezoidal endplate fins at the tips of the horizontal tail; the engine itself was moved forward so that the forward support pylon was located almost amidships. The cockpit, too, was moved forward to improve the pilot's field of view over the nose and the forward fuselage housed a pair of 20-mm (.78 calibre) cannons flanking the cockpit. The aircraft was fitted with a landing skid. The aircraft was to be launched from a catapult with the help of solid-fuel rocket boosters. Estimated performance of the EF 126 included a speed in excess of 700 km/h (435 mph), a service ceiling of 7,200 m (23,620 ft) and a range of 320 km (199 miles).

Work on the machine commenced in October 1945. According to the plan for 1946, OKB-1 was to build five EF 126 prototypes. In May 1946 the first prototype (EF 126 V1) was completed, followed by a further four machines by late June. The V1 was fitted with an Argus 014 engine yielding a thrust of 350 kgp (772 lbst), while the other four prototypes were powered by its Junkers Jumo 226 derivative rated at 500 kgp (1,100 lbst).

Initially the EF 126 was tested as a glider towed by a Ju 88. On 21st May 1946 the EF 126 V1 crashed while performing its second landing on that day. After a steep approach and an initial touchdown the aircraft bounced 8-10 m (25-33 ft) into the air, then touched down again with strong starboard bank. The starboard wing struck the

Above: A large model of the EF 126 undergoing wind tunnel tests. Note that the wings appear to be positioned lower than on the actual aircraft.

One of the EF 126 prototypes seen during tests; a ventral cover is opened, providing access to the cannon bay. The 'thimble' on the nose is the generator's ram air turbine fairing. Note the wingtip skids.

ground and broke; the machine rolled inverted and disintegrated, killing its German pilot Mattis (as mentioned above).

The tests continued after some modifications to the wing airfoil on the remaining four machines. The pulse-jet engines proved very capricious, and the attempts to ignite them in flight were unsuccessful; ground runs of the engine often ended in the engine casing burning through. Also, construction of the launch catapult was taking longer than expected and the required booster rockets were unavailable. A special commission arriving from Moscow for the purpose of inspecting the OKB-1 was uncomplimentary in its assessment of the EF 126, noting its inadequate armament, the absence of armour protection and small fuel load which made it difficult to use the machine as a mass-produced attack aircraft. Nevertheless, the work on this project went on, the prototypes being used for developing the pulse-jet technology and the techniques of catapult-assisted take-off and landing on a skid. In September 1946 the EF 126 V2, V3

and V4 were dismantled and despatched to the USSR for further testing which was to take place at LII. They were accompanied by a set of Jumo 226 pulse-jets (two engines per aircraft).

A group of some 30 German specialists and pilots took part in the testing at LII, which was also conducted initially in glider mode. The first such flight was performed by the EF 126 V5 on 16th March 1947. A total of 12 short flights were made by the V3 and V5 examples in 1947 without igniting the engines. Five powered flights followed in the autumn of 1947. At the same time testing of the pulse-jet engines was conducted both on ground test benches and on a Ju 88 converted into a flying testbed. There were plans for submitting the EF 126 to NII VVS for State acceptance trials but they were not put into effect. In October 1947 a ban was imposed for security reasons on the presence of foreign specialists at highly secret test centres, such as LII, and the testing of German aircraft there was halted. In May 1948 two EF 126s were transferred to an airfield at

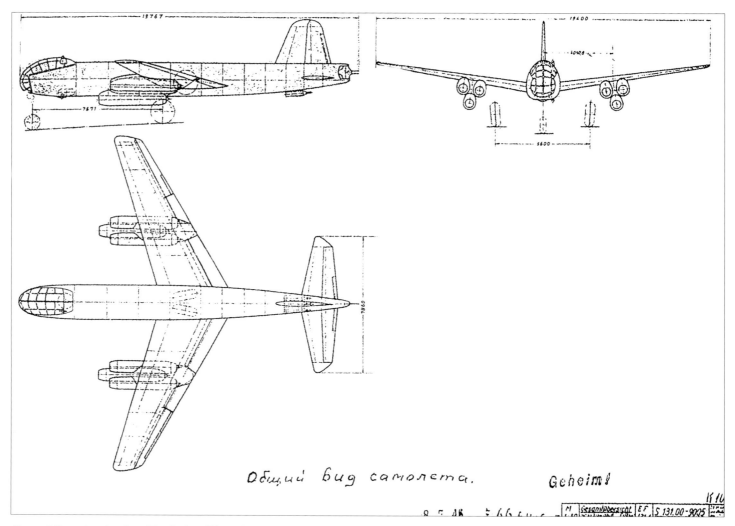

Above: A three-view drawing of the Junkers EF 131 (Ju 287) six-turbojet bomber. The drawing was endorsed on 8th July 1946 and bears the handwritten comment 'General arrangement of the aircraft' in Russian and the rubber stamp *Geheim!* (Classified) in German. Note the JATO boosters under the rear fuselage.

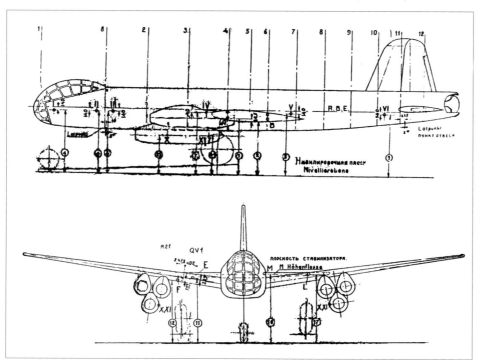

A drawing of the EF 131 from captured German documents, with additional remarks in Russian. The fuselage frames are enumerated in the side view. The cockpit design is typical of late Junkers bombers.

Tyoplyy Stan south of Moscow, but no flight testing was undertaken there. (The area is now part of the city and the airfield is long since closed down and redeveloped.) On 21st June 1948 the Minister of Aircraft Industry issued an order calling for the termination of all work on the EF 126 (as well as on the EF 131 described below).

EF 131 (Ju 287) bomber prototype

One of the turbojet-powered bomber projects developed in the Third Reich during the closing stages of the war was the Ju 287 bomber. This aircraft was the brainchild of Hans Wocke who utilised unconventional forward-swept wings in order to avoid the tip stall problem characteristic of ordinary swept-back wings. On the other hand, forward-swept wings could create aeroelasticity problems; yet Wocke believed these problems could be tackled by optimising the design. Among other things, the engines were to be mounted ahead of the wings' torsional stiffness axis.

The first prototype (Ju 287 V1) which featured two engines under the wings and two

Specifications of the EF 131 aircraft

Powerplant	6 x Jumo 004B
Thrust, kgp (lbst)	6 x 900 (6 x 1,984)
Length overall	20.47 m (67 ft 2 in)
Height on ground	5.7 m (18 ft 8½ in)
Wing span	19.4 m (63 ft 7¾ in)
Maximum speed, km/h (mph)	860 (534) *
Landing speed, km/h (mph)	190 (118) *
Range, km (miles)	1,710 (1,063) *
Service ceiling, m (ft)	12,500 (41,000) *
Fuel load, kg (lb)	7,150 (15,765)
Armament	2 x 13 mm (.51 cal)
Bomb load, kg (lb)	2,000 (4,410)
Take-off weight, kg (lb)	22,955 (50,620)
Crew	3

* estimated

Above: A model of the EF 131 built in the Soviet Union in the course of the development work. The projection above the cockpit is the faired periscope used for aiming the tail cannons. Note that the tail barbette itself is missing.

Above: Another view of the same model, showing clearly the triple engine clusters. In this case the tail barbette is where it should be.

more on the forward fuselage sides, had undergone flight testing in 1944 before it was damaged during a bombing raid against Junkers' Dessau facility. However, the company had begun construction of the second prototype (Ju 287 V2) powered by six BMW 003A-1 turbojets mounted in clusters of three under the wings; the aircraft was to have an all-up weight of 21,200 kg (46,740 lb), a top speed of 800 km/h (496 mph) and a 4,000-kg (8,820-lb) bomb load. It was the incomplete Ju 287 V2 that served as a basis for a new experimental bomber developed by former Junkers specialists in Dessau under Soviet supervision in 1945-46. The project was redesignated EF 131.

On 17th April 1946, In accordance with the Soviet Council of Ministers' directive No. 864-266, Chief Designer of the Dessau-based OKB-1, Brunolf W. Baade, was tasked

The EF 131 V1 (Ju 287 V2) sits beside a pair of Lisunov Li-2 transports during flight tests. Note the bomber's nose-up attitude on the ground.

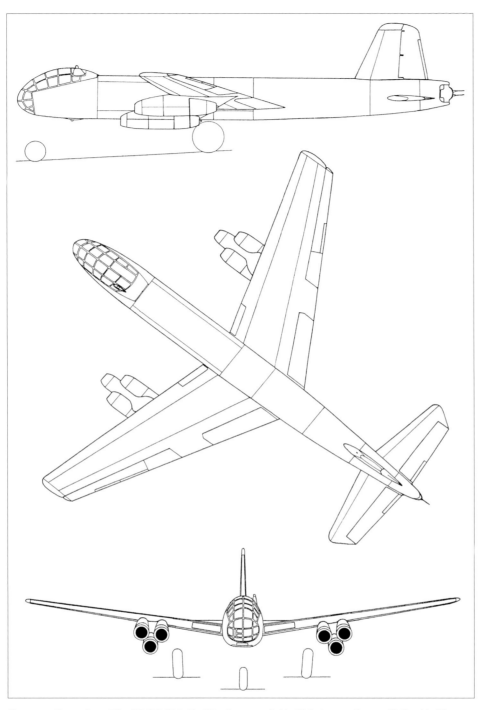

One more three-view of the EF 131. Note that the flaps are divided into two sections, with fixed trailing edge portions in line with the engine exhausts.

with completing development of the EF 131 bomber and submitting it for tests.

Designated EF 131 V1, the first prototype manufactured in Germany underwent a brief flight test programme there before being dismantled and transferred to the Soviet Union. The aircraft was transferred to the State Experimental Plant No. 1 (GOZ – *Gosoodarstvennyy opytnyy zavod*) in Doobna near Moscow. After some delays due to sorting out organisational matters, design and development work was resumed in the spring of 1947. Fritz Freytag was

appointed Baade's deputy, while Hans Wolf became the project engineer. On 15th April 1947 MAP issued an order requiring GOZ No.1 to conduct the flight testing of the bomber before the end of July. It was envisaged that the EF 131 would take part in the annual Aviation Day flypast at Moscow-Tushino along with other new Soviet jet aircraft. A testimony to this is the following MAP directive addressed to Vice-Minister Lukin, GOZ No. 1 Director Abramov and Chief Designer Baade: *'Prepare two prototype EF 131 bombers powered by six RD-10 gas*

turbine engines [...] for participation [...] in the flypast; flight testing of these aircraft shall be completed by 30th July'.

The beginning of the EF 131 bomber prototype's flight tests was postponed because static tests conducted by TsAGI revealed insufficient structural strength of the fuselage. The TsAGI report stated: *'The fuselage meets only 52% of strength standards and possesses sufficient strength only if the speed is limited to 600 km/h'* (373mph).

Nearly two months were spent on reinforcing the airframe of the first flyable EF 131, which was transferred to LII in the autumn of 1946. Concurrently, Plant No. 1 was engaged in the assembly of the second flying prototype, which was completed by the end of the year.

The first flight of the modified EF 131 took place on 23rd May 1947. The aircraft took off at a speed of 250 km/h (155 mph) at an all-up weight of 17 tonnes (37,485 lb). The maximum speed prescribed by the programme for the first flight was 350 km/h, the landing speed was 220 km/h (137 mph), and level flight took place at an altitude of 1,400 m (4,590 ft).

After the touchdown, during the landing run, a small incident took place. A bolt in the attachment of the port main gear fulcrum failed, the aircraft tilted to port and scraped the ground with the port lower engine (in the cluster of three engines).

The damage caused by the incident was relatively minor and was promptly rectified. However, it proved impossible to complete the flight testing of the bomber by the stipulated date. The testing revealed such deficiencies as nosewheel shimmy and vibration of the tail surfaces; curing them took much time. By October 1947 the EF 131 had made only seven flights, logging 4.5 flying hours. The protracted testing and development prevented the German aircraft from taking part in the Aviation Day flypast on 18th August. This caused understandable irritation on the part of the nation's leaders. In September 1947 Mikhail V. Khrunichev, the Minister of Aircraft Industry, sent a strongly worded letter to acting director of Plant No. 1 S. L. Rebenko and to Baade, requiring them to complete the flight testing of the first prototype EF 131 aircraft in October of that year.

Still, this programme was not fulfilled either. In October 1947, in connection with the ban imposed on the presence of foreign specialists at facilities engaged in classified research and development work, an order was issued calling a halt to the testing of the German aircraft at LII; the aircraft and the specialists were sent back to the plant. For several months the EF 131 prototype sat on the airfield, covered with snow. In consequence, as revealed by a subsequent inspection, many rubber parts and wiring components deteriorated and had to be replaced. The overhaul and repairs took several months.

In June 1948 the tests of the EF 131 were about to resume at the LII airfield. Yet, they never did; on 21st June all work on the aircraft was discontinued pursuant to MAP order No.440.

In all, the EF 131 bomber performed 15 flights, logging a total of 11 flight hours. These flights made it possible to study the techniques of piloting a high-speed heavy aircraft, methods of its combat use and operational characteristics of an aircraft featuring an unusual layout and design.

The Council of Ministers directive No. 3206-1301 terminating the work on the bomber was issued somewhat later, on 23rd August. A decision was taken to start the development of a modified version of the EF 131 aircraft which was designated '140'. The decision to halt the testing of German jet aircraft was due to the emergence of a new generation of Soviet turbojet engines which were superior in performance to German engines. These were the AM-TKRD-01 designed by Aleksandr A. Mikulin and the TR-1 designed by Arkhip M. Lyul'ka. The EF 131 powered by clusters of low-powered Jumo engines was already an obsolescent machine.

EF 132 (Ju132-6AMTKRD-01) long-range bomber (project)

Work on the EF 132 bomber was also initiated in 1945 in Germany. The official commencement of the design work must also be dated 17th April 1946 when, in accordance with the aforementioned CofM directive No. 874-266, Chief Designer Baade was tasked with building a high-speed jet bomber powered by six Junkers Jumo 012 engines and submitting it for tests.

In August 1946 the advanced development project (ADP) was completed in Germany and detail design was initiated. The aircraft's design performance included a maximum speed of 950 km/h (590 mph), a bomb load of 4,000 kg (8,820 lb) and a range of 2,250 km (1,398 miles).

After the transfer of the work to GOZ No.1, MAP issued order No. 207 dated 15th April 1947 which tasked the plant's OKB with re-working the ADP to accept Soviet engines – six Mikulin AM-TKRD-01 axial-flow turbojets rated at 3,300 kgp (7,276 lbst) at sea level. Two prototypes of the EF 132 long-range bomber were to be built and submitted for testing by September 1948.

The ADP of the bomber with the new powerplant was endorsed on 10th October 1947; in some documents it was referred to

Design performance of the EF 132

Powerplant	6 x Jumo 012	6 x AM-TKRD-01
Thrust, kgp (lbst)	6 x 3,000 (6 x 6,615)	6 x 3,300 (6 x 7,280)
Length overall	39.4 m (129 ft 3¼ in)	38.475 m (126 ft 2¾ in)
Height on ground	8.0 m (26 ft 3 in)	8.65 m (28 ft 4½ in)
Wing span	34.4 m (112 ft 10⅜ in)	36.40 m (119 ft 5 in)
Tailplane span, m (ft)	n.a.	13.2 (43 ft 3⅜ in)
Wing area, m² (sq. ft)	n.a.	240.0 (2,583)
Maximum speed, km/h (mph)	950 (590)	980 (609)
Landing speed, km/h (mph)	170 (106)	n.a.
Range, km (miles)	3,900 (2,423)	4,000 (2,486)
Service ceiling, m (ft)	11,400 (37,390)	13,300 (43,620)
Fuel load, kg (lb)	40,900 (90,180)	39,200 (86,440)
Empty weight, kg (lb)	n.a.	46,050 (101,540)
Take-off weight, kg (lb)	87,500 (192,940)	90,150 (198,780)
Bomb load, kg (lb):		
normal	4,000 (8,820)	4,000 (8,820)
maximum	n.a.	18,000 (39,690)
Armament	4 x 15 mm (.59 cal)	6 x 20 mm (.78 cal)
Crew	5-7	5-7

as the Ju132-6AM-TKRD-01, Ju being spelled in Cyrillic (Ю-132 6АМ-ТКРД-01). With six AM-TKRD-01 engines the aircraft had a design empty weight of 46,050 kg (101,540 lb) and a normal AUW of 90,150 kg (198,780 lb), including a fuel load of 39,200 kg (86,436 lb). Installation of JATO rockets increased the AUW to 93,750 kg (206,718 lb). The design wing loading was 376 kg/m² (77 lb/sq ft), thrust loading at sea level was 4.62 kg/kgp (lb/lbst). At an AUW of 68,000 kg (149,940 lb) the design maximum speed of 980 km/h (609 mph) was attained at sea level; at 3,500 m (11,480 ft) it decreased to 960 km/h (597 mph) and at 10,000 m (32,800 ft) to 893 km/h (555 mph). The estimated service ceiling at the mentioned AUW was 13,300 m (43,620 ft). Estimated range with a normal fuel load of 39,200 kg (86,440 lb) and a bomb load of 4,000 kg (8,820 lb)

was 4,000 km (2,486 miles); with a medium-sized bomb load it was 3,300 km (2,050 miles), decreasing to 2,300 km (1,429 miles) with the maximum bomb load.

The aircraft featured a more potent defensive armament, too. The dorsal, ventral and tail turrets were to be equipped with twin 20-mm (.78 calibre) cannons, with an ammunition supply of 500 rounds for each pair. The armour plating of the forward cockpit and the tail gunner's station weighed 500 kg (1,102 lb) and 60 kg (132 lb) respectively. The project envisaged installation of the EAP-476 electric autopilot, the RSB-8B and 12RSU-10 radios (transmitter and receiver respectively), the SPU-14 intercom (*samolyotnoye peregovornoye oostroystvo*). Provision was made for the installation of the identification friend-or-foe (IFF) system comprising the **Bariy** (Barium) and **Magniy** (Mag-

The Mikulin AM-TKRD-1 turbojet engine chosen for the Junkers EF 132 and EF 140 bombers. Note that the air intake leading edge assembly is part of the engine itself, not the engine nacelle.

Top and above: A model of the '140' (EF 140), showing the cylindrical engine nacelles and the twin-cannon dorsal barbette. The extreme nose was more pointed on the actual aircraft.

nesium) transponders and the *Materik* (Continent) instrument landing system that were standard for Soviet combat aircraft of the late 1940s. Two aerial cameras could be installed in case of need. Electric power was to be supplied by two 5-kW generators, supplemented by two storage batteries with a capacity of 54 A·h each.

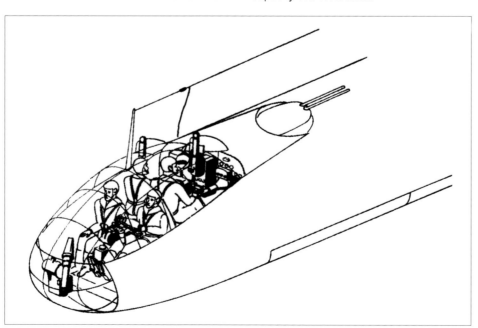

A drawing of the EF 140's flightdeck. The navigator/bomb-aimer sits on the right beside the pilot, while the dorsal gunner and the radio operator/gunner (working the ventral barbette) sit higher, facing aft.

In 1947 the full-size mock-up was under construction and detail design got under way. Some systems and sub-assemblies, such as the landing gear and the cannon turrets, were ordered from other factories. The aerodynamic laboratory of GOZ No. 1 conducted wind tunnel tests. But on the whole the programme was falling behind schedule. It became obvious that it would be impossible to start the testing of the machine at the prescribed time. In December studies were made for fitting the bomber with Lyul'ka-designed engines. But the work did not progress any further: on 12th June 1948, the Council of Ministers issued directive No. 2058-805, pulling the plug on the EF 132 programme.

'140' (EF 140) bomber prototype

As related above, pursuant to the Council of Ministers' directive No. 3206-1301 dated 23rd August 1948, all work on the EF 131 aircraft with forward-swept wings was halted and a decision was taken to develop and build its twin-engined version, which was allocated the designation '140'.

It is worth noting that the aircraft had its inception as early as 1947 as the EF 140 project developed at the initiative of the OKB-1 headed by Brunolf Baade. German designers persisted in giving new aircraft designations in accordance with their traditional system, but in the Soviet Union this system was 'broken down' at an early stage so as not to draw undue attention to the 'authorship' of the machines.

The '140' aircraft (to confuse hypothetical spies, in some documents it was referred to as 'aircraft 001') was intended to fulfil the mission of a high-altitude, high-speed tactical jet bomber. When fitted with special aerial cameras, it could be used as long-range day and night reconnaissance aircraft. The range could be increased by replacing a part of the bomb load by drop tanks installed in the bomb bay. The '140' was an all-metal monoplane with mid-set forward-swept wings. As distinct from its progenitor, the EF 131 prototype, the '140' bomber was fitted with two Mikulin AM-TKRD-01 engines, one on each wing. The aggregate thrust of the Soviet engines, rated at 3,300 kg (7,276 lb), was considerably superior to that of the six Jumo 004Bs. The cylindrical engine nacelles of the '140' aircraft were caried on blended horizontal pylons, adhering to the wing undersurface. The new powerplant necessitated a substantial redesign of the aircraft's fuel system.

The EF 131 had only one gun turret placed in the tail. There was no armour protection whatsoever; the aircraft's speed allowing it to outrun attacking enemy fighters was its primary means of protection.

Above: Front view of the '140' prototype at the Tyoplyy Stan airfield, showing the egg-shaped cross-section of the forward fuselage and the strong wing dihedral.

With the introduction of jet fighters this became obviously insufficient. Therefore the '140' was fitted with two turrets (dorsal and ventral), each carrying twin 20-mm (.78 cal) cannons (each turret was provided with 250 rpg); the cockpit was protected with armour.

The bomber's crew was increased to four. The pilot sat on the port side, with the navigator/bomb-aimer beside him. Seated back-to-back behind the pilot was the gunner operating the dorsal turret. The radio operator, who also worked the ventral turret, was seated behind the navigator facing aft; the cannons were aimed by means of dorsal and ventral periscopic sights. Armour plates – fixed plates with a thickness of 8 to 20 mm ($0^5/_{16}$ in to $0^{25}/_{32}$ in), hinged plates with a thickness of 15 to 20 mm ($0^{19}/_{32}$ in to $0^{25}/_{32}$ in) and

The ventral cannon barbette aft of the bomb bay is visible in this three-quarters view. Note the side-mounted torque link on the nose gear unit, which turns through 90° during retraction.

Three aspects of the '140', showing the shape of the engine nacelles and the blended engine pylons. All landing gear struts were inclined forward. Oddly, the Soviet star insignia were applied to the wing undersurface only. Note the faired rear view periscopes and the bulges in the canopy above the gunners' heads.

Front, rear and three-quarters rear views of the bomber. Unlike the wings, the horizontal tail had zero dihedral. Note the linkage which rotated the mainwheels through 180° with respect to the extended position during retraction (the mainwheels stowed vertically in the fuselage). No armament was fitted.

Above: This rear view shows that the flaps of the '140' were divided into two sections, with fixed trailing edge portions in line with the engine nacelles.

one movable plate – protected the crew from gunfire from the rear (in the cone with an angle of 15° and its apex at the aircraft's axis) and from below. Bombs with a total weight of up to 4,500 kg (9,920 lb) were accommodated in the centre fuselage. The following variants of the bomb load were envisaged:

Bomb load options of the '140'

Number of bombs	Calibre, kg (lb)	Bomb load, kg (lb)
1	1,500 (3,307)	1,500 (3,307)
3	500 (1,102)	1,500 (3,307)
5	250 (551)	1,250 (2,756)
1	3,000 (6,615)	3,000 (6,615)
2	1,500 (3,307)	3,000 (6,615)
6	500 (1,102)	3,000 (6,615)
10	250 (551)	2,500 (5,512)
9	500 (1,102)	4,500 (9,922)
15	250 (551)	3,750 (8,437)

The equipment envisaged for use on the aircraft included the radio transmitter and receiver (RSB-5Ch and 12RSU-10 respectively) and the SPU-14 intercom. Provision was made for the installation of Bariy and *Litiy* (Lithium) IFF transponders and the RUSP-45 ILS (*rahdio'ustroystvo slepoy posahdki* – blind-landing radio device) that were standard for the second half of the 1940s. Radio navigation equipment included the ARK-5 automatic direction finder and the RV-2 radio altimeter. One or two AFA-33/50 aerial cameras could be

installed in case of need. Electric power was to be provided by two 9-kW GS-9000 generators.

The ADP and mock-up construction were completed by 20th March 1948, and detail drawings by 31st March. The programme included a comprehensive range of tests and experiments; wind tunnel tests were conducted in the T-106 wind tunnel at TsAGI.

After the mock-up review the results of the work accomplished so far were endorsed by the Government in the above-mentioned CofM directive No. 3206-1301. Construction of the prototype was considerably speeded up by using the second flying prototype of the EF 131 as a basis.

The aircraft was completed on 22nd July of the same year. Between 7th and 10th August it was disassembled and transported

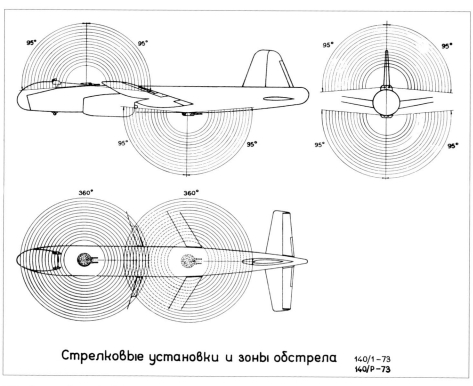

Стрелковые установки и зоны обстрела   140/1–73
140/P–73

This diagram shows the field of fire of the '140' bomber's defensive weapons. The two barbettes provided 360° coverage in both horizontal and vertical planes.

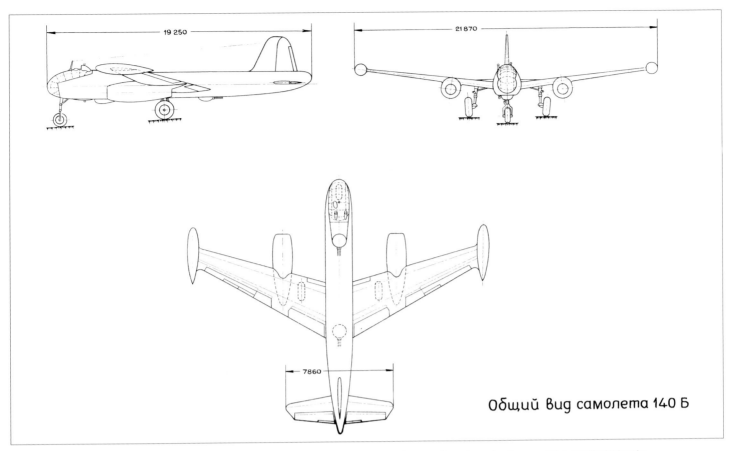

Общий вид самолета 140 Б

Above: This three-view shows the revised '140-B' bomber featuring a bomb-aiming radar in a teardrop-shaped radome and the wingtip fuel tanks.

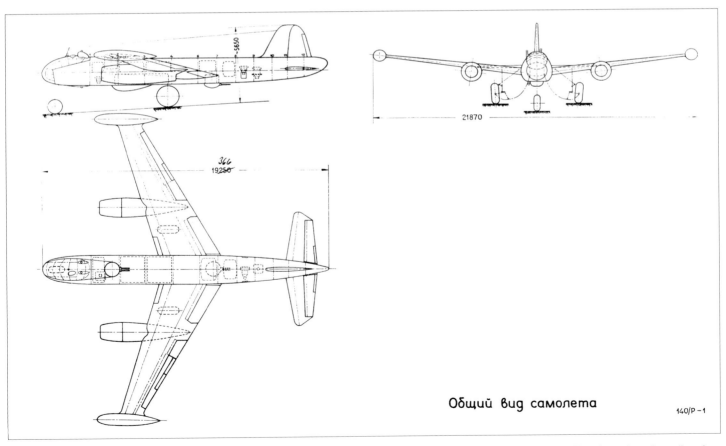

Общий вид самолета

140/P – 1

A three-view of the '140-R' reconnaissance version, showing how the vertical and oblique cameras were housed in the fuselage. Note the reshaped nacelles of the VK-1 engines located closer to the wing undersurface. The drawing shows how the mainwheels rotated around the oleos during retraction.

253

Dimensions and performance of the '140' aircraft

	As per ADP documents	Manufacturer's flight test results
Powerplant	2 x AM-TKRD-01	2 x AM-TKRD-01
Thrust (nominal/take-off), kgp (lbst)	2 x 3,000/3,300 (2 x 6,615/7,276)	2 x 3,000/3,300 (2 x 6,615/7,276)
Length overall	19.6 m (64 ft 3²¹⁄₃₂ in)	19.7 m (64 ft 7 ¹⁹⁄₃₂ in)
Height on ground	5.7 m (18 ft 8¹³⁄₃₂ in)	5.7 m (18 ft 8¹³⁄₃₂ in)
Wing span	19.4 m (63 ft 7²⁵⁄₃₂ in)	19.4 m (63 ft 7²⁵⁄₃₂ in)
Wing area, m² (sq ft)	58.4 (628.67)	58.4 (628.67)
Wing aspect ratio	6.45	6.45
Aileron area, m² (sq. ft)	3.25 (34.94)	n.a.
Tailplane span	7.86 m (25 ft 9½ in)	7.96 m (26 ft 1²⁵⁄₆₄ in)
Stabiliser area, m² (sq ft)	8.0 (86.12)	n.a.
Elevator area, m² (sq ft)	3.9 (41.98)	n.a.
Tailplane area, m² (sq ft)	11.9 (128.1)	11.91 (128.21)
Fin area, m² (sq ft)	3.5 (37.68)	n.a.
Rudder area, m² (sq ft)	2.8 (30.14)	n.a.
Vertical tail area, m² (sq ft)	6.3 (67.82) (5.95/64.05) [1]	6.0 (64.59)
Cockpit volume, m³ (cu ft)	5.3 (57.05)	n.a.
Empty weight, kg (lb)	14,240 (31,400)	14,676 (32,360)
All-up weight, kg (lb):		
normal	n.a.	20,796 (45,846) [2]
maximum	24,500 (54,020) (25,825/56,944) [3]	25,220 3 (55,610)
absolute limit	27,000 (54,535)	n.a.
Landing weight, kg (lb)	16,500 (36,382)	n.a.
Fuel load, kg (lb):		
normal	n.a	5,820 (12,830)
maximum	7,500 (16,540) (9,470/20,880) [5]	8,170 (18,010) [4]
Wing loading, kg/m² (lb/sq ft)	443 (90.7)	356 (72.9)
Thrust loading, kg/kgp (lb/lbst)	3.91 5	3.14
Maximum speed , km/h (mph):		
at sea level	860 (534)	n.a.
at 3,000m (9,840 ft)	n.a.	904 (562)
at 3,500 m (11,480 ft)	885 (550)	n.a.
at 5,000 m (16,400 ft)	n.a.	902 (560)
at 9,000 m (29,530 ft)	n.a.	860 (534)
at 10,000 (32,810 ft)	818 (508)	n.a.
Time to 5,000 m (16,400 ft), min	6.8	n.a.
Rate of climb, m/sec (ft/min):		
at sea level	15.8 (3,110)	n.a.
at 6,000 m (19,685 ft)	9.2 (1,810)	n.a.
at 10,000 m (32,800 ft)	2.2 (430)	n.a.
Service ceiling, m (ft)	11,700 (38,380) [6]	11,000 (36,080) [7]
Tale-off run, m (ft)	880 (2,886) [8]	1,450 (4,756) [9]
Landing run with brake parachute, m (ft):	750 (2,460)	950-1,000 (3,115-3,280) [10]

1. According to the results of weighing and measuring the aircraft after completion of manufacture
2. Without bombs
3. With a 1,500-kg (3,307-lb) bomb load and maximum fuel
4. With two auxiliary fuel tanks in two forward sections of the bomb bay
5. Estimated
6. At an AUW of 19,600 kg (43,220 lb)
7. Altitude actually attained
8. With four JATO rockets
9. At a landing weight of 20,000 kg (44,100 lb)
10. At a landing weight of 16,500 kg (36,380 lb)

to the Tyoplyy Stan airfield where it was reassembled on 3rd September. Thus, it proved possible to proceed from the advanced development project drawings to prototype flight testing within a matter of half a year which on the whole bears testimony to the tempo of work in the Soviet aircraft industry after the war.

The real flying prototype was virtually identical to the configuration envisaged by the ADP. The VDB-6 electrically actuated twin-cannon barbette (**verkh**nyaya distan-tsion*no* [*oopravlyayemaya*] **bahsh**nya – dorsal remote-controlled turret) was used to protect the upper hemisphere, while the NDB-1M barbette (**nizh**nyaya distantsion*no* [*oopravlyayemaya*] **bahsh**nya – ventral remote-controlled turret) covered the lower hemisphere. The size of the mainwheels was enlarged from the intended 1,425 x 520 mm (56.1 x 20.47 in) to 1,450 x 520 mm (57 x 20.47 in). The nosewheel measuring 900 x 350 mm (35.43 x 13.78 in) was left as per the project.

Flight tests of the '140' were conducted at Tyoplyy Stan. The first flight took place on 30th September and lasted about 20 minutes. As stated in the report on this flight, 'the take-off, horizontal flight and landing proceeded normally'. During the second flight which took place on 5th October some faults were revealed in the running of the engines. Unsatisfactory functioning of the so-called 'automatic fuel feed control' installed on the AM-TKRD-01 made a manual control of the engine trust extremely difficult; the engine spontaneously changed rpm, which was accompanied by jolts and swinging of the aircraft in flight. After the seventh flight the tests had to be suspended. Thus, by late 1948 only seven flights were performed, logging in all 4 hours and 20 minutes.

In the first half of 1949 the work on the development of the aircraft went on. After the replacement of engines the testing was continued, and ten more flights were performed. The manufacturer's tests conducted by test pilot Ivan Ye. Fyodorov were completed on 24th May 1949. Their results were as follows: the maximum speed was 904 km/h (562 mph) at an altitude of 3,000 m (9,840 ft) and 824 km/h (512 mph) at 11,000 m (36,090 ft); the range was 2,000 km (1,243 miles).

'140-R' tactical reconnaissance aircraft prototype

On 14th May 1949 the Council of Ministers issued directive No. 1886-696, under the terms of which work on the '140' aircraft was to be continued with a view to turning the bomber into a reconnaissance aircraft. The aircraft was allocated a new designation, '140-R' (that is, [samo**lyot**-] raz**ved**chik – reconnaissance aircraft).

This long-range tactical reconnaissance aircraft was to be fitted with two Klimov VK-1 centrifugal-flow turbojets engines (a derivative of the Rolls-Royce Nene I uprated to 2,700 kgp (5,953 lbst) for take-off) and possess a range in excess of 3,600 km (2,237 miles). The project was developed by OKB-1's preliminary design (PD) projects section under the guidance of Hans Wocke. The complexity of the task stemmed from the very tight development schedule: the aircraft was to be submitted for State acceptance trials in September 1949. Nevertheless, the design team working on the project of the '140-R' reconnaissance aircraft succeeded in curing most of the deficiencies noted by the mock-up review commission which had inspected the mock-up of the '140' in March 1948, and in fulfilling almost all requirements associated with the aircraft's new mission (notably the requirements concerning radio equipment).

The photo reconnaissance aircraft was expected to have a maximum range of 3,600 km (2,237 miles) at an indicated airspeed of 635 km/h (395 mph) during flights at altitudes between 9,300 and 12,800 m (30,500-41,980 ft) at an AUW of 25,543 kg (56,322 lb). The design empty weight was 14,333 kg (31,604 lb); with four additional JATO rockets the maximum weight was to reach 26,503 kg (58,439 lb). The aircraft was expected to take a fuel load of 10,600 kg (23,733 lb). With the mentioned weight characteristics, the design wing loading was 417 kg/m2 (85.41 lb/sq. ft). Maximum speed, at an AUW of 20,000 kg (44,100 lb), was to be 785 km/h (488 mph) at sea level and 837

Estimated range of the '140' aircraft (as per ADP)

Range, km (miles)	All-up weight, kg (lb)	Bomb load, kg (lb)	Fuel load, kg (lb	Flight altitude, m (ft)	Speed, km/h (mph)
2200 (1,367)	25,825 (56,994)	1,500 (3,307)	9,470 (20,880)	10,000-13,000 (32,800-42,640)	760-800 (472-528)
1,870 (1,162)	26,100 (57,550)	3,000 (6,615)	8,210 (18,103)	10,000-13,000 (32,800-42,640)	760-800 (472-528)
1,520 (945)	26,000 (57,330)	4,000 (8,820)	6,650 (14,663)	10,000-13,000 (32,800-42,640)	760-800 (472-528)
1,300 (808)	25,550 (56,337)	4,500 (9,992)	6,110 (13,472)	10,000-13,000 (32,800-42,640)	760-800 (472-528)

km/h (520 mph) at 7,500 m (24,600 ft). At a reduced AUW of 17,000 kg (37,485 lb) the speed at the same altitude was expected to reach 850 km/h (528 mph). Time to 5,000 m (16,400 ft) was to be 8.6 minutes; the service ceiling was to be 14,100 m (46,250 ft). With four JATO rockets the take-off run should not

exceed 980 m (3,214 ft), and the landing run with a brake parachute deployed was to be within 830 m (2,720 ft).

The photo reconnaissance aircraft was to be fitted with the following equipment items: two 9-kW GSR-9000 DC generators, an AP-5 autopilot, an RSIU-3 receiver and an

Top: The '140' streams its brake parachute when landing at Tyoplyy Stan. Above: One more view of the bomber at the same location.

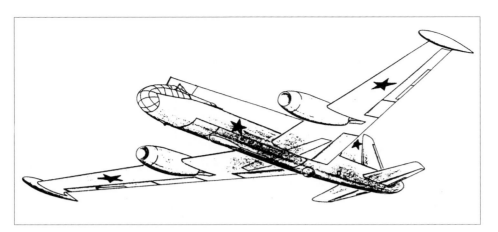

Above: An artist's impression of the '140-R' reconnaissance aircraft from the project documents.

RSB-5 transmitter, an SPU-5 intercom, RV-2 and RV-10 radio altimeters, a Bariy-F IFF transponder and a Materik ILS, a PSBN bomb-aiming radar (*pribor slepovo bombometaniya i navigatsii* – 'blind bombing and navigation device') and four KP-14 oxygen regulators (*kislorodnyy pribor*) with eight 2-litre (0.44 Imp gal) oxygen bottles each. The mission equipment consisted of AFA-33/20, AFA-33/50 and AFA-33/100 day cameras or NAFA-3S/50 night cameras.

The advanced development project of the '140-R' was endorsed on 19th July 1949. In order to modify the '140' bomber prototype into a photo reconnaissance aircraft, the machine was disassembled (a process which took rather a long time) and then transported from the Tyoplyy Stan airfield to Plant No. 1, where it was to undergo modification. The equipment intended for daylight and night reconnaissance (aerial cameras, flare bombs and the like) was to be housed in the forward part of the internal stores bay and in the rear fuselage. Among other things, the aircraft was fitted with:

• new powerplant assemblies, including the VK-1 engines and new engine nacelles adhering to the wings without pylons;

• a new engine control system;

• an extra fuel tank in the fuselage;

• teardrop-shaped wingtip fuel tanks which increased the wing span from 19.4 m (63 ft 7¾ in) to 21.87 m (71 ft 9 in);

• additional equipment for the carriage of eight SAB-100/75 or SAB-100/55 flare bombs or twelve FotAB-50/35 photo flash bombs, and mounts for the installation of aerial cameras;

• additional electric equipment;

• new armament.

The aircraft was fitted with two remote-controlled powered barbettes – a DT-V1 dorsal turret (*distantsionno [oopravlyayemaya] toorel', verkhnyaya*) and a DT-N1 ventral turret (*distantsionno [oopravlyayemaya] toorel', nizhnyaya*), each mounting twin 23-mm cannons with 150 rpg. The cannons were aimed with the help of periscopic gunsights; the turrets were electrically actuated. Should the gunner of the dorsal turret be killed or wounded, his turret could be switched over to the sight and control system of the ventral turret.

In 1949 a test airfield was equipped not far from GOZ No. 1 in the village of Borki because the military were against admitting the Germans to the airfield in Tyoplyy Stan. It was in Borki that the manufacturer's tests of the '140-R' started from September onwards. As had been the case with the original '140', they were conducted by project test pilot Ivan Ye. Fyodorov.

The maiden flight took place on 12th October but had to be curtailed due to strong vibration of the wings. The scenario was repeated on 20th October during the aircraft's second flight. The '140-R' was sent back to the plant for modifications.

During the first half of 1950 the machine underwent development work. Two more flights were performed, the last of them taking place on 24th March 1950. Vibrations of the wings persisted, and after the second flight the testing was suspended. TsAGI specialists joined in studying the problem. It was surmised that the flutter might have been caused by the wing-tip fuel tanks.

The former '140' bomber prototype after conversion as the '140-R'. The new nacelles housing Klimov VK-1 turbojets, the tip tanks and the ventral radome are clearly visible.

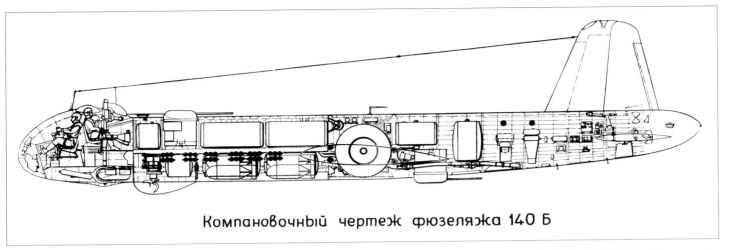

Компановочный чертеж фюзеляжа 140 Б

Above: A cutaway drawing of the '140-B' bomber's fuselage, showing the fuel tanks above the bomb bay and aft of the mainwheel wells. Note the strike cameras further aft.

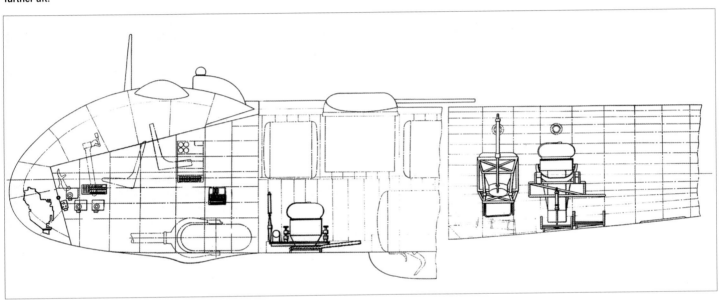

Above: The daylight reconnaissance configuration of the '140-R' with an AFA-33/20 camera ahead of the radome plus AFA-33/75 (oblique) and AFA-33-100 (vertical) cameras in the rear fuselage.

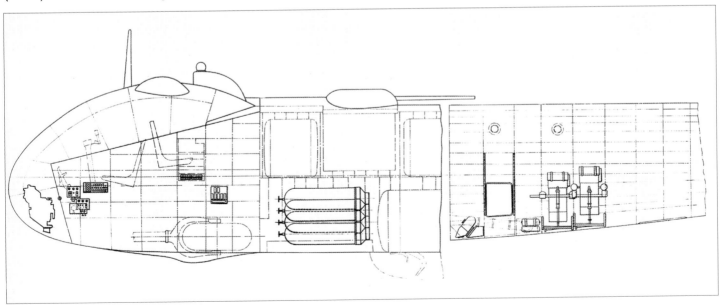

The same aircraft in night reconnaissance configuration. The forward bay is occupied by eight SAB-100/55 or SAB-100/75 flare bombs or twelve FotAB-50/35 photo flash bombs. The rear fuselage houses a so-called 'selenium sight' (light detector) and two NAFA-3S/50 cameras designed for night operations.

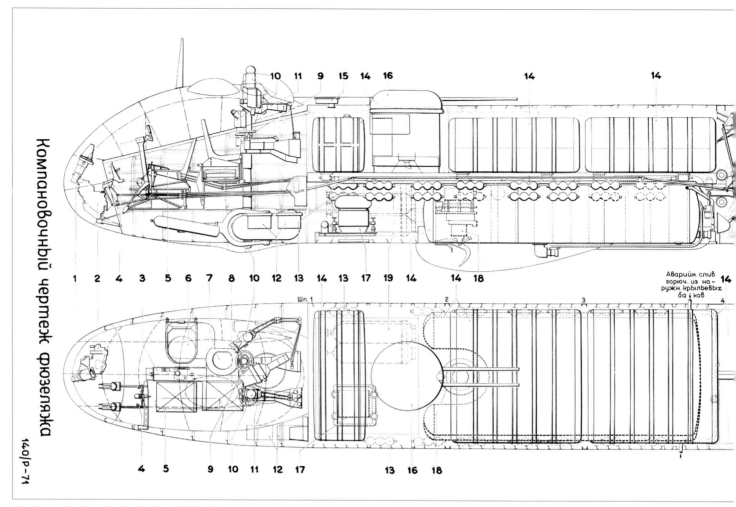

Компановочный чертеж фюзеляжа

140/р-71

A cutaway drawing showing the '140-B/R' dual-purpose aircraft in reconnaissance configuration. Note how the lower forward fuel tank is forked to fit around the radar antenna drive and how the four JATO boosters are fitted under the rear fuselage in tandem pairs.

Аварийн. слив
горюч. из на-
ружн. крыльевых
ба (ков

As a result of this situation, on 18th June (18th July, according to other information) 1950 the Council of Ministers adopted a new resolution No. 2474-974, pursuant to which all work on the '140-R' aircraft was terminated and all the costs associated with this programme were to be written off by MAP.

'140-B/R' tactical bomber/reconnaissance aircraft

The work on a new version of the aircraft designated '140-B/R' started in 1949 in keeping with Council of Ministers' directive No. 3568-1477 issued on 20th August. In Nazi Germany the '/R' suffix to an aircraft designation (for instance, Messerschmitt Bf 110D-1/R-2) stood for *Rüstsatz*, meaning that the aircraft had been upgraded with an additional equipment package. Here, however, the B/R stood for *bombardirovshchik-razvedchik* (bomber/reconnaissance aircraft). The ADP was completed by 12th October; the following day it was submitted to MAP and to GK NII VVS for review and approval.

Retaining the same layout and the same engines as the '140-R' dedicated reconnais-

sance aircraft, the '140-B/R' differed from it primarily in mission equipment. Owing to the improvement of the weapons control system the crew was reduced to three, but the design AUW was nevertheless increased to 26,112 kg (57,577 lb); this figure did not include the weight of JATO rockets. The empty weight, compared to the reconnaissance version, was increased by more than 300 kg (661 lb) to 14,692 kg (32,395 lb) primarily because of additional items of equipment. The design range of the '140-B/R' with a bomb load of 1,500 kg (3,310 lb) and a fuel load of 9,400 kg (20,730 lb) at altitudes between 8,900 and 12,700 m (29,190 and 41,650 ft) was 3,000 km (1,863 miles), the endurance being 4.7 hours. With a bomb load of 4,500 kg (9,920 lb) and a fuel load of 6,530 kg (14,400 lb) the range was 2,000 km (1,243 miles), with an endurance of 3 hours. Maximum speed at 5,000 m (16,400 ft) was expected to reach 866 km/h (538 mph), while at sea level the bomber's top speed could not exceed 828 km/h because of limitations imposed with regard to dynamic pressure and structural strength up to the altitude of 1,700 m (5,570 ft).

The service ceiling was 12,200 m (40,010 ft) at an all-up weight of 18,500 kg (40,790 lb); time to 5,000 m (16,400 ft) was expected to be 8.7 minutes. At the maximum AUW (26,112 kg/57,577 lb plus four JATO rockets) the take-off run was estimated at 1,030 m (3,380 ft), the landing run at a landing weight of 16,500 kg (36,380 lb) should not exceed 1,350 m (4,430 ft) without a brake parachute and 830 m (2,270 ft) with the parachute deployed.

The mock-up of the cockpit section was completed by 5th October, but on 8th October GK NII VVS issued a requirement for a full-scale mock-up of the aircraft. Construction of the latter took just over two weeks, being completed on 25th October. The mock-up was inspected by the State mock-up review commission which finished its work on 5th November. Detail drawings of the aircraft were almost completed by 1st November of that year.

During the first quarter of 1950 the last 100 sheets of manufacturing drawings were handed over to production engineers; the technical documentation for the aircraft had been compiled, comprising the technical

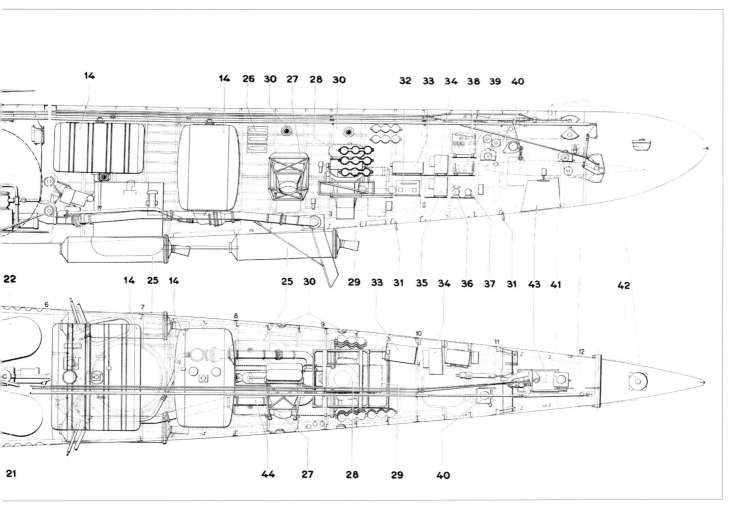

description, flight manual, programmes and instructions for static tests and factory ground tests. Static tests of the aircraft's main assemblies and systems were conducted in April. However, there was no sequel: on 18th June 1950 all work on the '140-B/R' aircraft was also terminated pursuant to the already mentioned CofM directive No. 2474-974.

By the time of issue of the directive closing down the programme the aircraft had been completed and had partially passed ground tests. After the unsuccessful testing of the '140-R' reconnaissance aircraft TsAGI specialists came to the conclusion that the use of forward-swept wings in aircraft construction was undesirable.

RB-2 short-range bomber project

In the late spring of 1948 OKB-1 completed the PD project of a short-range bomber designated RB-2 (*reaktivnyy bombardirovshchik* – jet bomber). The German designers bestowed the nickname *Riese* (giant) upon this aircraft because of its large size (by the day's standards). The specification for the new bomber was drawn up by the Long-Range Bomber Aviation top command and sent to S. N. Zhitkin, Director of MAP's

Comparative characteristics of the '140' aircraft versions

	'140'	'140-R' design data	'140-B/R' design data
Type	bomber	reconnaissance aircraft	bomber/reconnaissance aircraft
Crew	4	4	3
Engines	2 x AM-TKRD-01	2 x VK-1	2 x VK-1
Thrust, kgp (lbst)	2 x 3,300 (2 x 7,275)	2 x 2,700 (2 x 5,950)	2 x 2,700 (2 x 5,950)
Length	19.5 m (63 ft 11¾ in)	19.25 m (63 ft 2 in)	19.36 m (63 ft 6¼ in)
Height on ground	5.7 m (18 ft 8⅜ in)	5.65 m (18 ft 6½ in)	5.65 m (18 ft 6½ in)
Wing span	19.4 m (63 ft 7¾ in)	21.87 m (71 ft 9 in)	21.0 m (68 ft 10¾ in) *
Wing area, m² (sq. ft)	58 (624.36)	61 (656.66)	61 (656.66)
Wing sweep	–19°50'	– 19°50'	– 19°50'
Maximum speed, km/h (mph):			
at sea level	n.a.	785 (488)	828 (515)
at altitude, m (ft)	904/3,000 (563/9,840)	837/7,500 (520/24,600)	866/5,000 (538/16,400)
Landing speed, km/h (mph)	n.a.	205 (127)	205 (127)
Range, km (miles)	2,000 (1,243)	3,600 (2,237)	3,000 (1,865)
Service ceiling, m (ft)	11,700 (38,380)	14,100 (46,250)	12,200 (40,020)
Normal fuel load, kg (lb)	5,820 (12,830)	10,600 (23,370)	9,400 (20,730)
Normal bomb load, kg (lb)	1,500 (3,307)	–	1,500 (3,307)
Take-off weight, kg (lb)	23,000 (50,715)	25,543 (56,330)	26,100 (57,550)
Armament	4 x 20 mm	4 x 23 mm	4 x 23 mm

* between the axes of the wingtip fuel tanks

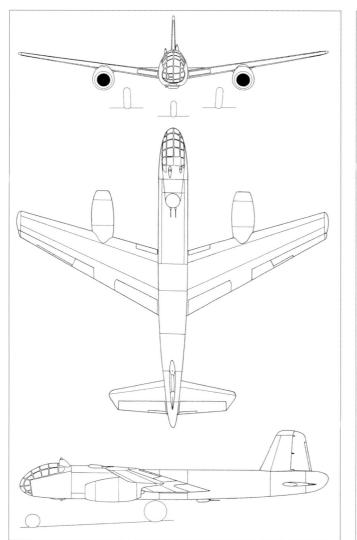
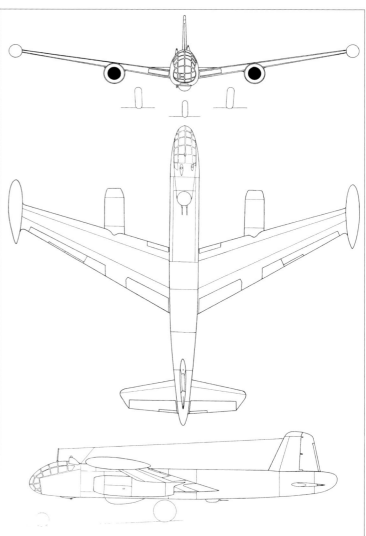

Above: These 'before and after' three-views of the '140' and the '140-R' illustrate well the latter version's increased wing span (not just because of the tip tanks) and redesigned engine nacelles.

A desktop model of the projected RB-2 bomber. Note the dorsal cannon barbette immediately aft of the 'greenhouse' canopy enclosing the pilot and the radio operator/dorsal gunner.

7th Main Directorate (some sources quote his last name as Shishkin), on 22nd May.

By then Semyon M. Alekseyev had been appointed head (or rather chief warden) of the OKB of the State Experimental Plant No. 1. This well-known aircraft designer, the former aide of Semyon A. Lavochkin, was transferred to GOZ No. 1 from the design bureau of the Gor'kiy aircraft factory No. 21 (OKB-21), of which he had been Chief Designer. In this capacity he had developed a number of twin-jet fighters (two of them, the I-211 and I-215, had been built and tested) and the I-218 ground attack aircraft utilising an unconventional twin-boom lay-out with a piston engine driving contra-rotating pusher propellers and a tailwheel landing gear. Formally, however, Brunolf W. Baade remained Chief Designer of OKB-1, with Fritz Freytag and P. N. Obroobov as his deputies; Hans Wocke was chief of the PD section. Earlier Obroobov had been the aid of another well-known Soviet aircraft designer, Viktor N. Belyayev, who had created the highly unorthodox DB-LK bomber utilising the 'flying wing' layout. Lt. (sg) Vlasov was assigned to GOZ No. 1 as the military quality control representative of the Soviet Air Force's Main Directorate of Experimental and Production Aviation Hardware.

Having been tasked with developing and building what eventually emerged as the '150' medium bomber (see below), OKB-1 headed by S. M. Alekseyev worked in close co-operation with TsAGI. The institute's chief specialists in aerodynamics and structural strength matters – Sergey A. Khristianovich, Gheorgiy P. Svishchev, A. I. Makarevskiy, V. N. Belyayev and others – gave OKB-1 recommendations on various aspects of the bomber design. Numerous enterprises and research establishments in the MAP system and within the frameworks of other ministries were involved in the development of the future bomber's systems and equipment.

The ADP was completed in July 1948 and submitted to Minister of Aircraft Industry Mikhail V. Khrunichev and the Director of GK NII VVS on 19th July. On 17th August 1948 the project was submitted for review to Minister of Defence Nikolay A. Bulganin.

According to the ADP the RB-2 short-range bomber was to feature shoulder-mounted wings swept back 38°30' at quarter-chord and swept tail surfaces; the wings utilised a carefully selected range of airfoils with a thickness/chord ratio of 9-11%. The engines – two Mikulin AM-TKRD-02 axial-flow turbojets rated at 4,000 kgp (8,820 lbst) for cruise flight or, alternatively, two Lyul'ka TR-3 axial-flow turbojets with take-off and cruise ratings of 5,000 and 4,000 kgp (11,020 and 8,820 lbst) respectively –were carried under the wings on forward-swept pylons. The normal fuel load was 7,000 kg (15,430 lb), increasing to 18,000 kg (39,680 lb) in overload (maximum take-off weight) configuration. The crew of five was accommodated in two pressurised compartments protected by 15-mm (0$^{19}\!/_{32}$ in) armour plate, plus a bullet-proof glass panel 120 mm (4$^{23}\!/_{32}$ in) thick at the tail gunner's station; the armour offered protection against enemy fighter attacks in the rear hemisphere from within a +15° cone relative to the aircraft's longitudinal axis. All five members were to be provided with ejection seats.

An interesting design feature of the new bomber was the novel bicycle landing gear with outrigger struts under the wingtips. The twin-wheel nose and main units retracting into the fuselage had identical 1,170 x 435 mm (946.0 x 17.12 in) wheels; the outrigger struts had single 600 x 200 mm (23.6 x 7.87 in) wheels. Equally interesting was the designers' idea that in the event of a wheels-up emergency landing the engine nacelles

A provisional three-view of the RB-2 showing the glazed navigator's station and the tail gunner's station.

were to act in the manner of skids, absorbing the load.

The wings and tail unit were to be provided with a hot-air de-icing system. The RB-2 was to have powered controls with mechanical linkages and hydraulic actuators; the control system was to incorporate locking features intended to prevent control surface flutter. The forces on the control column and rudder pedals were to be adjustable.

The RB-2 had a normal bomb load of 1,500 kg (3,310 lb) and a typical bomb load of 3,000 kg (6,610 lb) – a single 3-tonne bomb or a pair of 1.5 tonne bombs; the maximum bomb load was 6,000 kg (13,230 lb), comprising twelve 500-kg (1,102-lb) bombs

or eighteen 250-kg (551-lb) bombs. The defensive armament consisted of five 23-mm (.90 calibre) Nudelman/Suranov NS-23 cannons; the fixed forward-firing cannon had an ammunition supply of 100 rounds, while the paired cannons in the VDB-8 dorsal turret and the KDB-2A tail turret had 200 rpg each. (KDB = *kormovaya distantsionno* [*oopravlyayemaya*] **bahsh**nya – rear remote-controlled barbette.)

The RB-2 was to feature a comprehensive avionics suite comprising RSI-10 and RSB-5 transceivers, an SPU-5 intercom, an ARK-5 ADF, an RV-2 radio altimeter, a Rym-S navigation/attack radar (*rym* is a Russian nautical term meaning 'lifting lug'), Bariy and Magniy IFF transponders and a Materik ILS.

An AV-5 (aka EAP-45) electric autopilot would be used for maintaining course en route to the target. The crew would be provided with KP-14 breathing apparatus and a complement of five or ten 4-litre (0.88 Imp gal) oxygen bottles, depending on the duration of the sortie. Provisions were made for an AFA-33/75 strike camera.

According to calculations the operating empty weight was to be 20,690 kg (45,610 lb); the TR-3 powered version was to have a normal all-up weight of 30,280 kg (66,750 lb) and a maximum AUW of 41,600 kg (91,710 lb). At the normal AUW the wing loading would be 273 kg/m² (55.97 lb/sq ft) and the power loading would be 3.03 kg/kgp (lb/lbst). With TR-3 engines the RB-2 was expected to attain a top speed of 955 km/h (593 mph) at 4,600 m (15,090 ft) and full military power, increasing to 1,000 km/h (621 mph) at 4,700m (15,420ft) with the engines at combat boost (contingency) rating increasing available thrust by 20%. Interestingly, the bomber was to be provided with airbrakes, a feature that would keep the landing speed with a 23,100-kg (50,925-lb) landing weight down to about 179 km/h (111 mph). The RB-2 was expected to climb to 6,000 m (19,685 ft) in 6.3 minutes and to 10,000 m (32,810 ft) in 14.4 minutes. The estimated rate of climb at sea level was 24 m/sec (4,720 ft/min), decreasing to 136 m/sec (2,680 ft/min) at 6,000 m. The service ceiling with an average AUW was estimated as 13,600 m (44,620 ft). The take-off run at full military power was 730 m (2,395ft), with 920 m (3,020 ft) required to reach an altitude of 25 m (80 ft); at combat boost rating the take-off run and take-off distance was 580 and 710 m (1,900 and 2,330 ft) respectively. The landing run was not to exceed 530 m (1,740 ft).

The estimated range figures with a cruising speed of 810 km/h (503 mph) were as follows. With a fuel load of 7 tonnes (15,430 lb) and a 30,280-kg all-up weight (including 1.5 tonnes of bombs), the range at 13,700 m (44,950 ft) and at nominal power would be 2,000 km (1,240 miles), increasing to 2,700 km (1,675 miles) in economic cruise mode. With 18 tonnes (39,680 lb) of fuel and a 41,640-kg (91,800-lb) AUW, including an identical 1.5-ton bomb load, range at 12,300 m (40,350 ft) – the service ceiling was lower in high gross weight configuration, of course – was 4,700 km (2,920 miles) at nominal power and 5,300 km (3,290 miles) in economic cruise mode.

On 24th August 1948 the advanced development project was assessed by an MAP expert panel which gave a number of critical comments. Among other things, the panel noted that the parameters of the bomber's wings and tail should be recommended by TsAGI. Exactly one month later, on 24th September, the ADP was reviewed by GK NII VVS and received a go-ahead, again with a number of critical comments set forth in a special protocol. On 5th October GOZ No. 1 presented the full-scale mock-ups of the forward crew compartment and the tail gunner's station to a GK NII VVS mock-up review commission, which again approved them, except for a few details.

Soon afterwards, however, the RB-2 short-range bomber project underwent a redesign serious enough to regard the resulting aircraft as a separate design described in the next entry.

'150' medium bomber prototype

On 20th December 1948 GOZ No. 1 received a set of recommendations from TsAGI concerning the general arrangement and the internal layout of the projected RB-2 bomber, as well as wing and tail unit design. These were followed on 19th February by more recommendations, this time concerning the structural loads with regard to the bicycle landing gear designed by OKB-1. On 20th February OKB-1 issued the first drawing for the jigs and tooling to be used for prototype construction, followed on 10th March by the first blueprints for the aircraft itself.

The full-scale mock-up of the RB-2 was completed on 20th March 1949; by then the bomber had received the in-house designation 'aircraft 150' (or simply '150'). On 11th

The prototype of the '150' medium bomber (150 V1) at Borki, the airfield of the GOZ-1 experimental plant where OKB-1 was based, a few days after the rollout in December 1951. Note the large 'greenhouse' canopy (an unusual feature for a Soviet aircraft) and the huge parabolic transparency of the navigator's station.

April the mock-up was presented to the State mock-up review commission which endorsed it, accepting the manufacturer's performance estimates but requesting that certain changes be made. Yet, on 20th May OKB-1 was instructed by the ministry to stop all work on the TR-3 powered version and set about redesigning the '150' to take the Mikulin AMRD-04 axial-flow turbojets.

As already mentioned, the bomber's general arrangement and internal layout were developed by the PD team headed by Hans Wocke, with I. L. Makarov as his deputy. The work proceeded in co-operation with the other sections of the OKB-1, notably the aero-dynamics section headed by engineer L. B. Balkind.

The work progressed quickly, in harmony and without any major difficulties. The advanced development project incorporated a number of clever design solutions. The fuselage of the '150' was built in three sections. The entire forward fuselage section was a pressurised compartment accommodating three of the four crew members – the captain, the co-pilot/radar operator (who also performed navigation and bomb-aiming tasks) and the dorsal gunner who aimed the remote-controlled dorsal barbette by means of a revolving periscope sight. The crew compartment was protected from below by armour slabs. The rear fuselage incorporated another pressurised com-

Above: A drawing of the '150' from the project documents. The main gear 'kneeling' feature is illustrated.

partment for the tail gunner. The centre fuselage incorporated the bomb bay, which was large enough to accommodate up to 6,000 kg (13,230 lb) of bombs; it could also house long-range fuel tanks.

The wings swept back 35° at quarter chord were a monobloc (one-piece) structure with skin panels supported by corru-

gated internal stiffeners. The wing centre section accommodated integral fuel tanks. The trailing edge was occupied by two-section flaps (there were no leading-edge devices) and three-section ailerons, while the rudder and elevators were divided likewise into two and three sections respectively. The division of the flaps and control

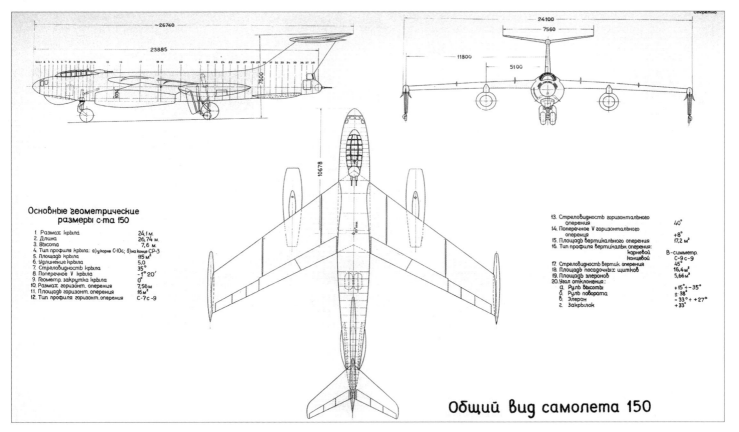

A three-view drawing of the '150' in its definitive form. The fuselage frames are enumerated in the side view; note how the spacing of the frames increases in the area of the bomb bay. Note also the strong dihedral of the tailplanes.

Above: The large diameter and strong taper of the engine nacelles are well visible in this front view. The large chin fairing accommodated the navigation/bomb-aiming radar and the landing lights.

To facilitate bomb loading the aircraft sat fairly high above the ground. The man standing between the twin ventral strakes provides scale, accentuating the bomber's large size. The rod aerial on the centre fuselage is for the IFF transponder.

Above: A fuel bowser based on the ZiS-150 lorry tows the '150' at Lookhovitsy-Tret'yakovo airfield during ground tests. This view accentuates the teardrop shape of the fuselage and engine nacelles; the stabilisers look like the tail flukes of a whale from this angle.

This view shows the angle at which the nosewheels could turn, allowing the '150' to 'turn on a dime'; note how far ahead of the wing leading edge the outrigger strut fulcrums are. It also illustrates the wing fences of unequal height, the wing pitots and the ventral strakes. The '150' carried no insignia.

Left and above left: The '150' makes high-speed taxi runs on the concrete strip at Lookhovitsy.

Top: A still from a cine film showing the '150' in flight.

Above: The bomber takes off on its maiden flight on 5th September 1952.

surfaces into sections was a measure aimed at increasing combat survivability, preventing them from being disabled by a single hit.

Unlike the earlier RB-2 project, the '150' featured a T-tail – a feature subsequently used on many commercial and military aircraft both in the Soviet Union and abroad. Unusually, the horizontal tail had pronounced dihedral.

The unusual design features deserve a more detailed description. The flight control system was particularly noteworthy, since it dispensed with the hydraulic actuators which had become obligatory even for fighters, to say nothing of heavy aircraft, by the early 1950s. The traditional control cables, push-pull rods and bellcranks were replaced by torsional shafts driven by individual electric motors via coarse-pitch screw-and-nut pairs; the electric motors were located in close proximity to the flaps and control surfaces. Give the large size of the '150', the power supply cables for the individual electric actuators were easier to route through the bomber's airframe than traditional mechanical control runs or hydraulic lines.

The proposed electromechanical controls were greeted enthusiastically by some and with deep mistrust by others. The sceptics claimed that the friction in the screw-

and-nut pairs would be insurmountable; they pointed out that manufacturing and assembling the screws and screw sockets would be difficult. Some people questioned the reliability of the electric circuit that was part of the 'pilot to generator to electric motors to control surface' drive train. This time the designers needed not only to convince the sceptics but first and foremost to see for themselves that that their own ideas worked. Since the likes of this control system had not been seen before, the system underwent rigorous testing – both on a ground rig ('iron bird', in Boeing terminology) and on a Junkers Ju 388L bomber, a captured example of which was used by GOZ No.1 as a control system testbed.

A matter of grave concern was that in the event of a dual engine failure all engine-drive generators would become inoperative, putting the flight control system out of action. To preclude this possibility the engineers had to incorporate an emergency generator driven by a ram-air turbine (RAT) with multiple blades; the generator was located in a small streamlined housing and was powerful enough to cater for the needs of both the control system and the cockpit instrumentation in night flying conditions when additional power is required for the lighting equipment.

A small test rig was built to verify the control system mechanics, emulating the controls and featuring the control surface actuators (less electric motors and wiring). The fears about excessive friction in the screw-and-nut pairs were allayed immediately; as the electric engineers set to work adapting the electrical part of the system to the airframe, the technologists opposing the system threw in the sponge and gave the go-ahead. The discussion petered out and the unconventional control system was adopted for the new bomber.

The idea of installing the engines on underwing pylons was floated by the engineers of Arkhip M. Lyul'ka's OKB-165 who had gained some experience with a similar engine installation on the Il'yushin IL-22 bomber prototype of 1947 (the first aircraft to carry this designation). In the latter case (and on the '140' bomber prototype), however, the turbojets were carried on horizontal pylons installed in line with the wing chord, while on the '140-R' the engine nacelles adhered directly to the wing undersurface without any pylons at all. Thus the '150' was the first Soviet aircraft to feature 'real' (that is, swept) pylons setting the engine nacelles apart from the wings. This feature precluded harmful aerodynamic interference between the wings and the engine nacelles, improving the wing aerodynamics. In practice this gave a major increase in wing lift at the expense of only a minor increase in drag as compared to the flush-fitting nacelles; the result was a marked improvement in lift/drag ratio and hence in range. The length of the pylons (and hence the distance between the nacelles and the wings) was limited by the need to ensure an adequate distance between the air intakes and the ground in order to prevent foreign object ingestion. The pylon sweep (79°30') was calculated in such a way as to provide the optimum distance between the engine's centre of gravity and the wing's torsional rigidity axis. Being located ahead of the wing leading edge, the 1,300-kg (2,865-lb) engines acted as anti-flutter weights, effectively damping the wings' self-oscillations caused by bending and torsional loads.

Like its precursor, the '150' was designed with a bicycle gear featuring twin-wheel nose and main units which absorbed 40% and 60% of the aircraft's weight respectively. The nose unit was steerable, steering being effected by the rudder pedals. All units retracted aft. The single-wheel outrigger struts retracted into cigar-shaped wingtip fairings; when extended, the outrigger wheels were in line with those of the main gear unit. The landing gear was hydraulically operated, with a feedback feature; unusually, the hydraulic rams used for gear retraction/extension doubled as the oleo struts (shock absorbers).

It should be noted that part of OKB-1's design staff (which had previously been engaged in developing the flying boats of Igor' V. Chetverikov), as well as the interned German specialists and many MAP employees who were involved in the '150' programme in one way or another, were opposed to the bicycle landing gear, considering it unsuitable for such a heavy aircraft. The unfortunate experience Aleksandr S. Yakovlev's OKB-115 had had with the much smaller Yak-50 experimental fighter (the first aircraft to carry this designation), which was literally blown off the runway by crosswinds, served only to strengthen these misgivings.

The bicycle landing gear had its strengths and weaknesses. The advantages which it offered were easier removal and installation of complete engine nacelles during engine changes; a simpler nacelle structure which did not incorporate a mainwheel well and main gear attachment points; keeping the mainwheel tyres well away from the hot engine jetpipes, the heat from which would otherwise shorten the tyres' service life; the possibility to enlarge the wingtip fairings used for outrigger stowage and utilise

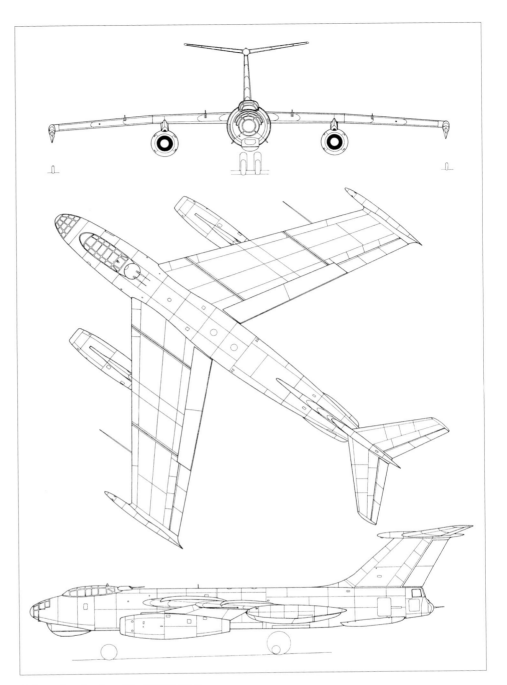

A three-view drawing of the '150' bomber.

them as extra fuel tanks, and the reduction of structural loads at the wing/fuselage joint. The handicaps, on the other hand, were higher drag and increased vibrations as compared to a conventional tricycle undercarriage; the inordinately large dimensions of the landing gear and increased structural weight; a more complicated landing gear control system with long control runs and and/or hydraulic piping (which, again, added to structural weight), operational inconveniences, including more complicated taxiing (especially in the case of large aircraft which required very wide taxiways), and higher manufacturing costs and labour intensity.

The factor which tipped the scales in favour of the bicycle landing gear was undoubtedly the leader of OKB-1, Semyon M. Alekseyev, who successfully tested this landing gear arrangement on his I-215D experimental twinjet fighter. The original arrangement with the outrigger struts under the engine nacelles was abandoned in order to use the wingtip fairings as anti-flutter weights. At Brunolf Baade's suggestion the main gear unit was designed to incorporate a 'kneeling' feature, which increased the angle of attack on take-off by 3°, shortening the take-off run.

In 1949-51 the OKB undertook research and test work under the '150' test programme. Among other things, a hydraulic elevator servo actuator developed for the '150' was tested on the Ju 388L; this testbed was known at GOZ No. 1 as *izdeliye* (product) 145 or 'aircraft 145'. Concurrently the bicycle landing gear was verified on the I-215D, which also had an alternative designation at the plant (*izdeliye* 155). (It should be noted that the first prototype I-215 had a conventional tricycle undercarriage with twin-wheel main units retracting inwards into the fuselage. It was after Alexeyev's transfer to GOZ No.1 that he decided to convert the incomplete second prototype (hence the D for *dooblyor* – lit. 'understudy', which was the Soviet term for 'second prototype' until the mid-1960s) into a bicycle landing gear testbed as part of the effort to create the heavier '150' bomber.

Apart from the tests involving real aircraft, a lot of wind tunnel research was done, using both the plant's own wind tunnel and the TsAGI T-102 wind tunnel. The manufacture of the '150' prototype's airframe and systems components began in 1950 concurrently with the continuing test and research effort.

By 1st June 1949 OKB-1 had issued nearly 1,500 blueprints for the bomber's airframe components and about 500 more for equipment items, and the experimental templates for the wings and fuselage had been manufactured. 30% of the airframe components intended for static testing had been completed and these had undergone 70% of their test cycles.

In early June 1949 the plant received a top-priority assignment requiring it to convert the '140' bomber prototype into the '140-R' photo reconnaissance aircraft in accordance with the aforementioned Council of Ministers' directive No. 1886-696 of 14th May 1949. Hence the work on the '150' prototype had to be suspended, resuming in the second half of July. Before that, on 6th July, MAP went back on its earlier requirements and reverted to the Lyul'ka TR-3A as the powerplant of the '150', eliminating the Mikulin AMRD-04 engines from the programme; hence the parameters had to be calculated anew to match the smaller engines. On 4th July GOZ No.1 received Part 1 of the specific operational requirement (SOR) for the '150' bomber which had

been endorsed by the Soviet Air Force Commander-in-Chief on 14th June; the duly signed protocol of acceptance for the full-scale mock-up of the TR-3 powered '150' followed four days later (on 8th July).

During the second half of July, all of August and the early days of September OKB-1 issued about 1,800 blueprints for various airframe components (wing spars, wing leading-edge fairings, flaps, ailerons, wingtip fairings, reinforced wing ribs, forward and centre fuselage frames, the principal components of the nose and main landing gear units and so on). Within the same time frame Shop 11 of GOZ No.1 completed more than 1,000 parts of the wings' and fuselage's internal structure, while Shop 14 erected the assembly jigs for the flaps, wing leading-edge fairings, wing spars and wingtip fairings. It was a hectic time for F. P. Voznesenskiy, the plant's Chief Engineer.

In early September work on the '150' bomber had to be halted again due to another crash programme calling for the development of the '140-B/R' bomber/reconnaissance aircraft. Some of the OKB-1's design teams were able to resume work on the '150' on 20th October, while the others did not have a chance to do so until November. Since the State mock-up review commission had required numerous changes to be introduced into the design of the '140-B/R' the greater part of the design work on the '150' planned for November 1949 remained unfulfilled.

Scale model tests of the '150' in TsAGI's T-102 wind tunnel were completed in September-October 1949 with encouraging results. High-speed testing of the bomber's wings was conducted in TsAGI's T-106 wind tunnel. In October OKB-1 began a new redesign of the bomber because the powerplant was changed *again*: Aleksandr A. Mikulin's OKB-300 had sent in the specifications of its latest offering, the AMRD-03 axial-flow turbojet with a specific take-off thrust of 8,000 kgp (17,640 lbst). (This engine eventually entered production as the AM-3.)

Meanwhile, the I-215D (*izdeliye* 155) was completed by factory No. 21 and entered flight test in early November 1949 (the exact date is unknown). Like the future bomber, this testbed incorporated a main gear 'kneeling' feature to increase the angle of attack on take-off by 3°. This allowed the I-215D to become airborne without rotation, not requiring the pilot to haul back on the control stick. The aircraft displayed confident ground handling, showing no tendency to tip over on one wing even during sharp turns.

On 21st November Brunolf Baade chaired a meeting at which the specifica-

Performance of the '150' bomber (manufacturer's estimates)

Powerplant	2 x Lyul'ka TR-3A	2 x Mikulin AMRD-04
Empty weight, kg (lb)	24,400 (53,790)	26,300 (57,980)
Normal all-up weight, kg (lb)	35,760 (78,835)	38,120 (84,040)
Maximum all-up weight, kg (lb)	44,760 (98,680)	51,620 (113,800)
Bomb load, kg (lb):		
at normal AUW	1,500-6,000 (3,310-13,230)	1,500-6,000 (3,310-13,230)
at maximum AUW	1,500 (3,310)	1,500 (3,310)
Fuel load, kg (lb):		
at normal AUW	9,000 (19,840)	9,500 (20,940)
at maximum AUW with drop tanks	18,000 (39,680)	23,000 (50,700)
Maximum speed, km/h (mph)	970 (602)	1,050 (652)
at altitude, m (ft)	4,200 (13,780)	5,600 (18,370)
Range with normal AUW, km (miles)	2,400 (1,490)	2,400 (1,490)
at altitude, m (ft)	13,000 (42,650)	14,000 (45,930)
Range with maximum AUW, km (miles)	4,500 (2,795)	5,000 (3,100)
Take-off run, m (ft):		
at normal AUW without JATO boosters	1,100-1,200 (3,610-3,940)	730 (2,400)
at maximum AUW without JATO boosters	1,950 (6,400)	1,450 (4,760)
at maximum AUW with four JATO boosters	1,200 (3,940)	950 (3,120)

Estimated range of the '150' bomber at a cruising speed of 800 km/h (496 mph)

AUW, kg (lb)	Range, km (miles)	Bomb load, kg (lb)	Fuel load, kg (lb)	Service ceiling, m (ft)
38,000 (83,770)	2,400 (1,490)	1,500 (3,310)	9,000 (19,840)	11,000-13,000 (36,090-42,650)
38,000 (83,770)	1,900 (1,180)	3,000 (6,610)	7,500 (16,530)	11,000-13,000 (36,090-42,650)
38,000 (83,770)	1,500 (930)	4,500 (9,920)	6,000 (13,230)	11,000-13,000 (36,090-42,650)
47,000 (103,615)	4,500 (2,795)	1,500 (3,310)	18,000 (39,680)	11,000-13,000 (36,090-42,650)
47,000 (103,615)	4,000 (2,480)	3,000 (6,610)	16,500 (36,375)	11,000-13,000 (36,090-42,650)
47,000 (103,615)	3,500 (2,170)	4,500 (9,920)	15,000 (33,070)	11,000-13,000 (36,090-42,650)
47,000 (103,615)	3,100 (1,925)	6,000 (13,230)	13,500 (29,760)	11,000-13,000 (36,090-42,650)

tions for the powered cannon barbettes (to be manufactured by plant No. 25) were approved. On 30th November he held another meeting in order to finalise the engine type to power the '150' (TR-3A or AMRD-03) in accordance with a query sent by MAP's 7th Main Directorate, which had to make plans for 1950. The preference was given to the TR-3A (by then redesignated AL-5) as more compact and creating less drag; according to some sources, Baade advocated this choice while other sources say it was Alekseyev. The result was felt immediately: calculations (later corroborated by the flight test results) showed that the choice had been a good one.

Another 250 blueprints for the '150' were issued in November 1949. On 6th (or 7th?) December Baade announced the task of modifying the bomber to take AL-5 engines in order to meet more stringent requirements concerning the top speed and field performance posed by the customer. On 23rd December test pilots made the third and final preliminary test flight in the '145' control system testbed (the modified Ju 388L). In all three flights the elevators had been manually controlled; the hydraulic servo actuator was deactivated, pending permission to switch it on. All in all, by the end of the year OKB-1 had released 3,375 blueprints for the '150' (that is, for about 25% of the structure); yet, whereas the first metal had been cut, not a single airframe component had been assembled at the end of 1949.

On 2nd January 1950 the top executives and design team chiefs of OKB-1 had a meeting to discuss the revised blueprint issue schedules for the '150'. The deadline for the final completion of all drawings for the airframe structure was set at 30th March. On 4th February another meeting took place at the factory director's office; the prototype construction schedule was the subject this time and the completion date was slated for October 1950. Hydraulic tests of the Nos. 1 and 2 fuel tanks began that same day.

The following dates from the prototype construction process are given to illustrate the breakneck pace at which the work proceeded.

On 14th February 1950 Baade came back from Moscow, bringing new specifications for the landing gear (first and foremost, the wheel sizes were changed).

On 18th March the director of GOZ No.1 issued the first document dealing in earnest with the construction of the '150' prototype and preparations for series production (order No. 81). On 26th April the first forward fuselage (crew cabin) section was taken out of the assembly jig for further completion work.

On 5th May a sample fuel tank utilising the experimental honeycomb structure developed for the '150' was subjected to the first combat survivability test under a programme held by GK NII VVS – that is, fired upon for the first time. On 23rd May the plant completed the changes to the full-scale mock-up's forward crew compartment and tail gunner's station as required by the mock-up commission. Meanwhile, assembly of the No.2 forward fuselage section began a week earlier, on 16th May; it was completed by 3rd June.

On 24th March 1951 the Council of Ministers issued directive No. 949-469 ordering the development of the '150' bomber and specifying the date of its submission for State acceptance trials, followed shortly thereafter by an MAP order to the same effect. Thus the aircraft finally received official status.

The State acceptance trials (that is, combat survivability tests) of the honeycomb construction fuel tank were completed on 18th April 1951; the tank proved capable of sustaining six hits without catastrophic damage. Ten days later the Air Force endorsed a revised SOR for the bomber and the factory took delivery of the first TR-3A engine. In June and July the plant manufactured the engine nacelles, the wingtip fairings, all four landing gear struts (less wheels) and the tail surfaces.

On 18th July the principal airframe components were moved to the assembly hangar where the fuselage was mated with the wings and tail unit by 1st August; test firing of all three ejection seats took place in the same hangar.

The second airframe (static test article) was being manufactured concurrently; the German specialists at OKB-1 referred to it as the '150 V2' in keeping with the German tradition of designating prototypes. The wings and fuselage of the static test airframe had also been mated (though not yet finally joined together) by 1st August and some airframe components had already been tested. Twenty days later the tail unit was fitted and another two days later, on 23rd August, the static tests began in earnest.

On 16th September 1951 the completed flying prototype was freed from all assembly jigs and work platforms and photographed inside the hangar. Ground system checks began immediately afterwards. These were not trouble-free: one of the integral fuel tanks, which were coated with special RA-6 varnish on the inside, developed a leak when filled with kerosene for the first time.

Around 20th September a crew from LII was assigned to the '150' prototype for holding manufacturer's flight tests. On 15th October two of Arkhip M. Lyul'ka's aides were summoned to the plant to deal with the defects of the AL-5 engines. The following day, when the four drop tanks envisaged by the project were fitted for the first time, the starboard inboard tank suddenly dropped spontaneously because the lock had not engaged properly.

Vibration tests were performed on 25th-28th October. The first weigh-in of the complete aircraft took place on 31st October, followed by the second one on 31st October/2nd November. The result was disheartening: the machine turned out to be 2,000 kg (4,410 lb) overweight.

On 10th November the main landing gear unit's mounting truss failed at 100% of the design load during static tests. It turned out that the diameter of the tubes of which

Close-up of the rear fuselage, showing the DB-25 tail turret, the bulletproof rear glazing of the tail gunner's station, the portside entry hatch and the ejection hatch between the ventral strakes.

A cutaway drawing of the '150' bomber.

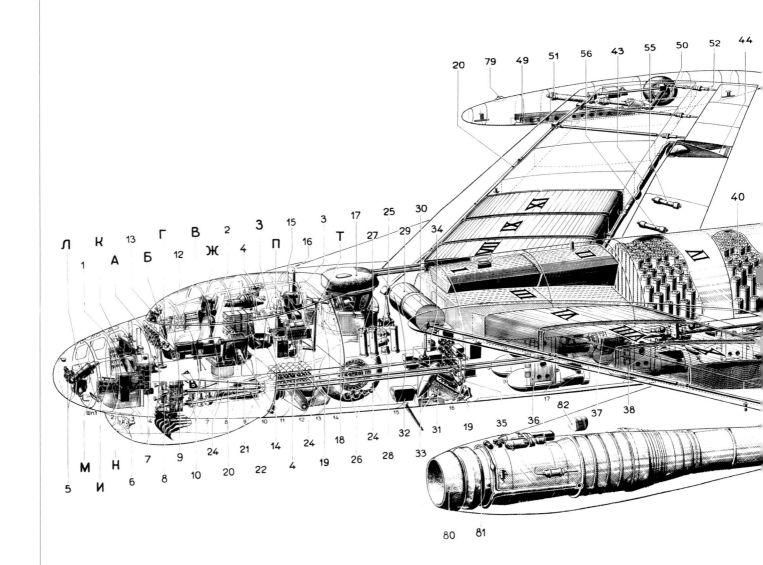

Компановочный че

the truss had been made was too small. That same day the mock-ups of the '150' and the '151', another bomber developed by OKB-1, were moved to another area of the plant and partially dismantled on the orders of the plant's director.

On 22nd November 1951 the Minister of Aircraft Industry signed an order requiring the flight tests of the '150' to take place at

Tret'yakovo airfield in the town of Lookhovitsy near Moscow – that is, more than 200 km (124 miles) from Plant No.1. The reason for this was that Tret'yakovo had an adequately long runway, whereas the runway at Borki (the factory airfield of Plant No. 1) was too short for testing heavy aircraft. (It should be borne in mind that, with an all-up weight of around 38 tonnes (83,770

lb), the '150' was 50% heavier than the '140'.) The aircraft was to be formally delivered to the plant's flight test facility on 31st December; however, the plant obstinately refused to include some crucial test and development programmes (the tests of the 'iron bird', the twin-chamber landing gear shock absorbers, certain hydraulic actuators etc.) into the bomber's completion work

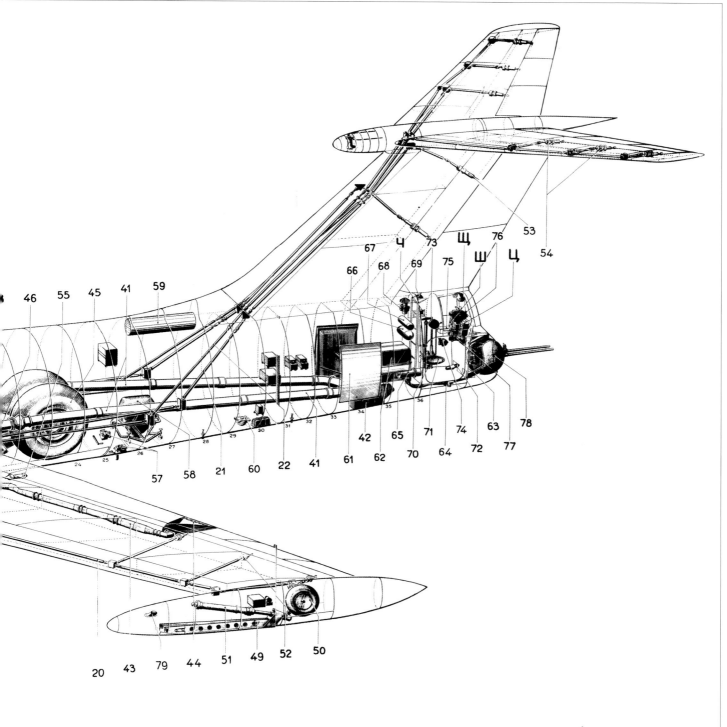

ж самолета   150-7/1

plan; as a result, the complete aircraft could not be accepted because the delay with these programmes was holding up the works. On 8th December Brunolf Baade issued an order forbidding any modifications to the prototype without his personal authorisation.

The following illustrates the difficulties which the engineers of OKB-1 had to tackle when defining and refining the bomber's design. On 11th December the main gear mounting truss failed again during renewed static tests, cracking at 95% of the design load. On 26th December the prototype was finally rolled out, the first engine run taking place the following day; the start-up was not accompanied by anything untoward but the throttles (or rather the control runs from the throttles to the engines) proved to be somewhat resilient, not allowing engine rpm to be adjusted precisely. Fuel usage from several groups of tanks was checked on 26th-30th December; the aggregate engine thrust was also measured on the latter date, constituting 7,500 kgp (16,530 lbst) plus another 750 kgp (1,650 lbst) lost to landing gear friction against the tarmac. With all due corrections made the engines gave 8,500 kgp (18,740 lbst) of total thrust instead of the advertised 10,000 kgp (22,040 lbst). On 30th December the aircraft was hangared again for modifications and additional ground tests. Static tests of the nose gear unit were held on 2nd January 1952; this time there were no surprises, but on 6th January there was trouble with the main gear unit again – the hydraulic downlock failed when the 'kneeling' feature was being checked.

On 8th January the extended flaps refused to retract; it took several attempts to get them up. On 12th January vibration of several actuator screws located in the fin leading edge was detected during checks of the hydromechanical control system; also, the anti-vibration brake of the starboard centre elevator segment failed. On 28th January fuel was somehow forced into the hydraulic system under pressure during a routine engine run; as a result, hydraulic pressure rose by 2.5 kg/cm² (35 psi) and a hydraulic reservoir cracked. This incident also turned up another design flaw in the hydraulic system.

On 30th January the emergency fuel jettison valve of the fuselage fuel tanks was tested; the following day the navigator's ejection seat was successfully test-fired from the aircraft. However, more spills came soon enough. When the landing gear was retracted with the engines running and the nose unit turned through 20° (for the sake of experiment – of course take-off would have been impossible with the nosewheel at such an angle!), it transpired that the nosewheel could not assume the neutral position quickly enough as the gear retracted. As a result, one of the nose gear components was damaged.

On 4th February Brunolf Baade chaired a meeting, stating that he had been ordered by the director of Plant No. 1 to start dismantling the aircraft for transportation to Lookhovitsy by rail. Before the trip could be made, however, more than 50 defects had to be eliminated. The ground test programme, including engine runs, was completed on 19th March. Baade stated that errors had been made in calculating the parameters of the cabin pressurisation system and ordered new calculations to be made.

Disassembly of the '150' prototype began on 29th March. The following day Vice-Minister of Aircraft Industry S. N. Zhitkin came to the plant to examine the aircraft. By 2nd April the technical documentation for the aircraft was still incomplete; therefore Baade held another meeting, ordering that a complete set of documentation be prepared not later than mid-May. The following day a meeting fixed the relocation schedule: the aircraft was to be transported to Lookhovitsy on 15th-20th April and reassembled there on

10th-15th May in order to commence taxiing tests before 1st June, which was tentatively set as the first flight date.

On 17th April 1952 the railway train carrying the crated aircraft and the supporting personnel finally left Bol'shaya Volga station, arriving in Lookhovitsy three days later; the flight test facility of OKB-1 also moved to the new location. On 5th May the plant sent a modified vertical tail for the bomber to Lookhovitsy; manufacturer's tests of the hydromechanical flight control system on the 'iron bird' began two weeks later, on 19th May. On 30th May the pilot's and the gunner/radio operator's ejection seats were sent to LII for manufacturer's tests; the seats were equipped with suitably adapted ejection guns originally developed by the Il'yushin OKB for other aircraft.

On 16th June Baade came back from Lookhovitsy and observed that the ground next to the runway was a grass field with a low bearing strength; a shower of rain was enough to turn it into a bog that was completely unsuitable for landing. On 24th June TsAGI submitted their report on the '150' bomber's structural strength, whereupon it was decided to complete the ground systems checks by 12th July and hand the aircraft over to the flight test facility on 18 July; taxi tests were scheduled for 22nd-25th July.

Thus the relocation to Lookhovitsy caused the flight tests to be postponed until August 1952. Yakov I. Vernikov, a holder of the Hero of the Soviet Union title and a one-time combat pilot who became a Test Pilot 1st Class at LII after the war, was appointed project test pilot. On 8th-11th August he made 19 taxi runs at speeds up to 180 km/h (111 mph) on the paved main runway and up to 120 km/h (75 mph) on the auxiliary grass runway. In the latter case the aircraft was seen to rock dangerously because of the uneven runway surface and the insufficient energy absorption of the landing gear oleos. Hence the oleo struts were removed and reinstalled after modifications had been made. The aircraft was declared ready for flight testing after a few defects had been rectified and a further high-speed run had been made. A high-speed taxi run was performed on 2nd September, the aircraft attaining a speed of 200-220 km/h (124-138 mph) on the concrete runway. The test was marred by failures in the nose gear unit's steering system.

On 3rd September 1952 the '150' was finally ready to fly, but the flight had to be delayed because the airfield had become soggy after a rainfall. Finally, at 13:00 Moscow time on 5th September the bomber became airborne for the first time with Vernikov at the controls and flight engineer Ye. N. Zharkov in the co-pilot/radar opera-

tor's seat; the crew also included a navigator and a radio operator.

The defensive armament was not yet installed for the initial flight tests. After the cannons had been installed, GK NII VVS test pilots took over. S. N. Rybakov was OKB-1's engineer in charge of the flight tests, with I. N. Kvitko being assigned the same responsibilities at LII. OKB-1s Deputy Chief Designer P. N. Obroobov often attended the test flights. The second test flight took place on 9th September, the third flight following on 11th September, the fourth on 24th September and the fifth on 27th September. The flight scheduled for 29th September was cancelled when the communications radio failed.

After the first five flights the following report on the initial flight test was drawn up. Curiously, it was not endorsed until 1953 (it was fairly common practice in the Soviet Union to sign such paperwork with a considerable delay: procrastination on the part of bosses at various levels was the order of the day). The report is quoted in full, as the fact in itself that a heavy jet bomber for the Soviet Air Force was developed from scratch by German engineers is of considerable interest.

'1. Introduction.

The '150' aircraft – a prototype of a jet bomber designed by Baade and powered by two AL-5 engines designed by Lyul'ka – has been built by the Experimental Plant No. 1 of the Ministry of Aircraft Industry pursuant to the resolution of the Council of Ministers of the USSR No.*****.dated *****.

Manufacturer's tests of the '150' aircraft were conducted at the Tret'yakovo airfield belonging to facility No.3 of the Ministry of Aircraft Industry.

Five flights were performed by the '150' aircraft between 5th September and 27th September 1952. Even in the course of these five flights it proved possible to obtain data characterising the aircraft's aerodynamic properties, controllability and handling at high Mach numbers, as well as to assess the functioning of its mechanisms, the most important of which are the bicycle-type steerable undercarriage and the aircraft's hydromechanical control system.

Among other things, the following results have been obtained:

I. Field performance

The aircraft exhibits normal controllability during taxiing, the take-off run and the landing run. The bicycle undercarriage enables the aircraft to move steadily on a straight-line course, and the system of new high-pressure pneumatic shock absorbers has demonstrated good shock absorption qualities.

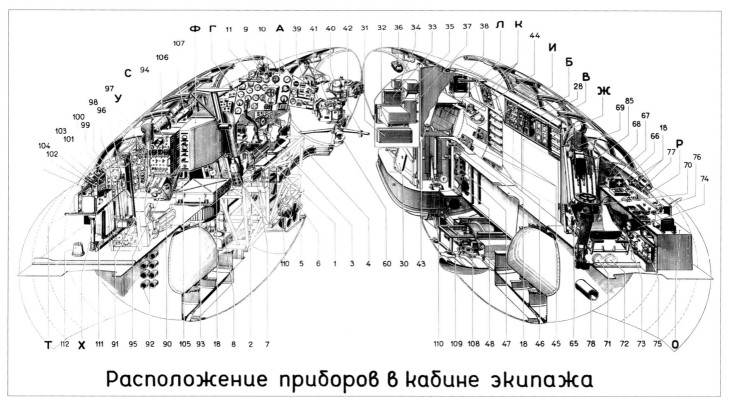

Расположение приборов в кабине экипажа

A drawing from the manufacturing documents showing how the instruments and controls were located in the forward pressure cabin accommodating the pilot, the navigator and the radio operator/dorsal gunner.

The steerable nose gear unit makes it possible to perform precise control of the aircraft up to the unstick speed without making use of brakes or differential engine thrust; at low speeds (during taxiing) it makes it possible to make a turn with a radius virtually equal to the aircraft's wing span.

While performing a take-off run with a normal take-off weight, the aircraft 'kneels' gradually; at the end of this process the take-off angle of attack is reached, followed by a normal lift-off. The obtained take-off run lengths corroborate the estimated characteristics.

All flights were performed with a crosswind speed of 6-12 m/sec [12-24 kts].

The landings were performed at the maximum landing weight; the gliding approach speed was 280 km/h [174 mph].

The braking system designed by Plant No. 279 functioned poorly (the wheels locked); on two occasions this caused the tyres of the nose and rear struts to separate from the wheel rims.

II. Speed

The following figures have been obtained in these flights:
• maximum Mach number 0.9;
• maximum dynamic pressure 3,000 kg/m² [614 lb/sq. ft];
• maximum speed in level flight at 4,600 m [15,090 ft] – 965 km/h [599 mph]; (more exact figures will be given after a calibration flight).

III. Controllability

The aircraft's controllability and handling at speeds from the take-off speed to those quoted above were normal: no reverse roll reaction to rudder inputs was noted, nor was there any aileron reversal. At maximum speeds the aircraft has a positive pitching moment of a value which coincides with the calculated value.

In the pilot's opinion, the functioning of the hydromechanical controls of the '150' aircraft in flight does not differ in any way from that of the usual controls.

IV. Stability

Longitudinal stability with regard to control forces, with the CG at 24%-27% MAC, is normal.

V. Functioning of the aircraft's airframe, units and systems

a) No structural defects worthy of note were discovered.

b) The aircraft's hydromechanical controls functioned normally in all flight modes. No defects were discovered.

c) Despite landings in crosswinds and high-speed taxiing on an uneven surface, the steerable bicycle-type undercarriage proved to be reliable and demonstrated normal shock-absorbing qualities.

d) When tested at altitudes up to 8,700 m [28,540 ft], the pressurised cabin and the high-altitude equipment showed characteristics tying in well with the design figures; the temperature in the cabin was normal (between +16°C and +23°C [+61-73°F]) at an ambient temperature of –43°C [–45°F].

e) The Lyul'ka-designed AL-5 turbojet engines fitted with Tarasov-designed Model 417 hydraulic pumps ran faultlessly in all flight modes.

f) The aircraft's fuel system making use of integral tanks in the hermetically sealed sections of the fuselage and fitted with a new (honeycomb) protection system functions faultlessly.

VI. Defects

1. As a result of imperfect functioning of the braking system, the tyres had to be changed twice on the rear wheels and once on the nose wheels. The defect has been eliminated temporarily. It will be finally cured by Chief Designer Bashta.

2. There are faults in the functioning of the extension mechanism of the tactical air brakes. The faults will be eliminated by removing the hydraulic locks.

3. The captured German fuel quantity indicators are imprecise. They will be replaced by indicators of Soviet manufacture as soon as these are available.

4. Several units of the fuel system and hydraulic system were replaced due to poor-quality rubber parts.

5. The artificial horizon and the mast of the flux-gate compass failed to function and had to be replaced twice; the RV-2 radio altimeter is imprecise.

6. Changes and improvements were introduced into the [flight test] recording equipment.

VII. Particularly notable difficulties encountered during the flight testing

Construction work is still in progress at Lookhovitsy airfield; it comprises not only completion of the construction of the hangar and its amenities and heating, but the work on the runway and taxiways as well, which seriously impedes the fulfilment of the flight test programme, because the work on the runway does not stop even during the flights.

The most essential catering for the needs of the flight test preparations is non-existent: there is no weather service, telephone and radio communication, no marker radio beacon, no kerosene refuelling bowser, no running water, no sewage, no heating, no workshops, no measurement and instrument laboratories, no canteen etc.

All these deficiencies affect very much the tempo of work on the flight-testing of the aircraft.

Conclusions.

1. The maximum speed of 987 km/h [613 mph] attained by the '150' aircraft at an altitude of 4,500 m [14,760 ft] considerably exceeds the maximum speed of 970 km/h [603 mph] stipulated by the specific operational requirement.

2. The maximum Mach number attained by the '150' aircraft during a shallow descent at an altitude of 7,400 m [24,270 ft] is 0.89. The aircraft's behaviour, as well as its stability and controllability, were normal on this occasion.

3. The aircraft's minimum static stability margin is equal to 6% MAC, which meets the general technical requirements.

4. Efficiency of control surfaces, including the ailerons, of the '150' aircraft is quite sufficient in all flight modes, including a sudden failure of one engine.

5. The '150' aircraft is dynamically stable. The degree of oscillation damping that was determined in flight exceeds the calculated value.

6. The values of fuel burn per hour measured on the '150' aircraft's port engine are somewhat lower than the fuel burn values specified by the engine manufacturer and used for calculating the range. Since the speeds attained at these stages match the calculated speeds, there is good reason to surmise that the design range will be attained.

7. The climb rates attained by the '150' aircraft at the engines' nominal thrust rating are 1-2 m/sec [197-394 ft/min] lower than the design value. However, these characteristics are not precise enough because the data required for determining the climb rate were obtained in only two flights; besides, the temperature of the engines' exhaust gases in these flights at nominal rpm was below the normal value. Increasing the turbine temperature to the normal value will, naturally, be accompanied by an increased rate of climb. Further flights within this programme are necessary to obtain more precise results.

8. Field performance: during the take-off run, take-off, landing and landing run the '150' aircraft demonstrates stable and normal behaviour. The take-off run proved to be marginally longer than anticipated because the fuselage angle of attack after the 'kneeling' of the undercarriage was reduced from the 6° envisaged in calculations to 5°. It is possible to reduce the length of take-of run obtained so far by some 150 m [490 ft] by deflecting the flaps simultaneously with the 'kneeling' of the undercarriage.

9. The hydromechanical controls of the '150' aircraft functioned faultlessly and in full accordance with technical requirements. The functioning of the load feel unit must be studied further.

10. The elevator control column travel should preferably be increased in all flight modes except take-off and landing; this can be done by switching off one of the lines of control shafts in flight.

11. The bicycle undercarriage of the '150' aircraft, the nose gear steering mechanism, the main unit 'kneeling' mechanisms and the auxiliary underwing struts' retraction mechanisms functioned faultlessly and in full accordance with technical requirements during the flight tests; they fully ensured the normal execution of take-offs and landings in crosswinds of up to 10-12 m/sec [20-24 kts].

The undercarriage ensured the aircraft's movement in a straight line during the landing run even after the tyres of all four mainwheels were 'shorn off' as a result of the landing with the wheels locked.

12. The wheel braking system incorporating anti-skid unit was repeatedly modified in the course of the tests in accordance with instructions from comrade Bashta, Chief Designer of this system. After modification the system basically met the specifications. However, the tests revealed that performing the braking of an aircraft fitted with this braking system requires the pilot to be very attentive and have some experience, and does not ensure in practice the shortest possible landing run; in some landing situations (such as braking after a touch-down and subsequent ballooning which passed unnoticed by the pilot) one cannot rule out serious damage.

To make this system more reliable and efficient, its design should be supplemented by the following main features:

a) to rule out feeding the full pressure into the brakes before the wheels have accelerated to full rpm during the landing run;

b) to cancel the pressure in the wheel brakes immediately should the wheels stop rotating;

c) to incorporate into the braking system a pressure modulator that will minimise the number of pressure fluctuations during the operation of the anti-skid device.

The abovementioned additions will rule out the locking of the wheels during braking; they will reduce the fatigue stresses on the structural elements of the undercarriage and will ensure the minimum length of the landing run after touch-down.

13. The airbrake, when opened fully at indicated airspeeds of 400-500 km/h [250-310 mph], causes undamped oscillations of the aircraft around the vertical axis. To eliminate this deficiency, it is necessary to change the design of the panels of the air brake by replacing the solid inner panel with a perforated one. Such changes have been developed by now at OKB-1.

In the course of flight testing the aircraft systems, namely:

• the hydraulic system for general controls,

• the hydraulic system for hydromechanical controls,

• the fuel system,

• the navigation system,

• the high-altitude equipment system,

• the powerplant,

functioned faultlessly and fully met the technical requirements.

15. The electric system, after some defects in the warning devices (revealed at the beginning of the tests) had been rectified, functioned faultlessly and fully met the technical requirements.

Compiled by:
(signed) Chief of the flight mechanics team Schumann
(signed) Deputy chief of the team Potashnikov
(signed) Test engineer Lehmann

On 2nd October Chief Designer Baade reported the state of affairs concerning the '150' aircraft to the Minister of Aircraft Industry. The Minister gave orders stipulating the completion of manufacturer's tests and of all the work on the machine by 15th December

1952. On 20th October Deputy Chief Designer P. N. Obroobov issued instructions to start preparing the documentation on the aircraft with a view to submitting it for State acceptance trials and (!) putting it into series production.

In the process of manufacturer's flight tests the wingtip fairings for the outrigger wheel struts were modified and turned into wingtip endplates. This was suggested by aerodynamicist L. V. Balkind as a measure intended to reduce the spillover of the airflow around the wingtip, when the need arose to eliminate the self-induced lateral swinging which developed into swinging around all axes. During a landing approach at altitudes ranging from 300 m to 150 m (from 980 to 490 ft) the machine started wobbling around its CG like a spinning top. When the height of the wingtip fairings was increased and their lower edges were made wedge-shaped, the wobbling disappeared. At the same time the wings' induced drag diminished and ailerons became more efficient.

On 23rd October the state of affairs concerning technical drawings was summed up. A total of 18,023 drawings and 5,943 parts lists for the aircraft had been issued. A schedule providing for the completion of manufacturer's flight tests by 15th December was not endorsed by MAP as obviously unrealistic.

No flights were made until 14th November because of bad weather, but on that day the sixth flight took place, followed by the seventh flight on the following day; after that a leak was discovered in the No. 3 fuel tank of the wing centre section. On 19th November the '150' performed its eighth flight.

On 1st December specialists who came to Plant No. 1 from Lookhovitsy said that the aircraft's lack of speed was due to incorrect calculations when interpreting the flight recorder data. The static pressure had been measured from the bomb bay. Concurrently it came to light that the performance of the AL-5 engines stated by OKB-165 (and purporting to be true) differed from the actual characteristics. Therefore the speeds attained by the '150' aircraft at different altitudes were somewhat altered.

On 22nd December during a conference held by Baade a decision was taken to install spring-loaded rods in the elevator and rudder control linkage; this took some time because of minor alterations that had to be made in the crew section. A month later, on 21st January 1953, when the aircraft was performing one of its regular high-speed runs, the machine went into an uncontrollable turn on the icy runway, brushing one of the fir trees on the edges of the runway; as a result, branches were ingested by one of the engines. Following instructions from Plant No. 165, the engine was removed from the aircraft. On 30th January the factory tests of a photo reconnaissance package with the AFA-33/75 camera (designed for installation in the bomb bay) were completed and the replacement engine was test-run on the aircraft. On 4th February a taxi run was made on the runway covered with hard-packed snow. The next flight was scheduled for the following day, but was cancelled because the pilot did not turn up. On the same day the factory personnel discovered a defect in the nose gear unit's retraction mechanism, whereupon a telegram was sent from the factory to Lookhovitsy calling a temporary suspension of flights.

On 16th February 1953 MAP issued Order No. 216 appointing D. V. Zyuzin as back-up project test pilot due to the departure of test pilot Yakov I. Vernikov on a prolonged mission elsewhere. Until 20th February Zyuzin made several taxi runs; on 23rd February he studied the aircraft's controls on a simulator. On 20th February the Minister of Aircraft Industry signed Order No. 220 on measures intended to speed up the factory tests of the '150' aircraft.

On 13th March Vernikov performed a check-up flight, the ninth in the series, and on the following day he made one more flight as a test sortie. Again a minor leak was discovered in the No. 4 fuselage tank. The first members of the State commission for the testing of the hydromechanical controls arrived at the Plant; they acknowledged that everything was ready for the tests. On 16th March Vernikov performed the 11th flight (in official documents it is listed as the tenth flight, because there are discrepancies in some documents as to the total number of flights performed, the figures differing by just one flight). On the following day the machine made the 12th (11th) flight, again with Vernikov at the controls.

On 19th March information on the progress of the tests was sent to the Ministry of Aircraft Industry; subsequently it was formalised into a special report. All the basic novel design features of the '150', the result of arduous work performed by the creators of the aircraft, functioned without any serious faults. However, certain deficiencies and even peculiarities in the machine's behaviour came to light. For example, longitudinal instability associated with speed and CG changes was revealed; at altitudes between 9,000 and 10,000 m (29,520 and 32,800 ft) during flights at maximum speeds the aircraft had a propensity for small gradual longitudinal oscillations with the control column in the fixed position. Lateral swinging during descent, developing into oscillations around all axes, was eliminated by modifications to the airframe.

The performance target was generally attained and in some cases even exceeded. At an empty weight of 26,860 kg (59,226 lb), the normal take-off weight was 38 tonnes (83,790 lb), the maximum TOW being 47 tonnes (103,635 lb); the maximum landing weight was 32 tonnes (70,560 lb). The normal fuel load was 9,000 kg (19,845 lb), the maximum fuel load with three auxiliary fuel tanks in the bomb bay was 18,800 kg (41,454 lb). Maximum speed was 790 km/h (491 mph) at sea level, 970 km/h (603 mph) at 5,000 m (16,400 ft) and 930 km/h (578 mph) at 10,000 m (32,800 ft); the landing speed was 210-215 km/h (130-134 mph). The bomber climbed to 5,000 m (16,400 ft) in 5 minutes and to 10,000 m (32,000 ft) in 18 minutes. The take-off run on turbojet power alone was 1,200 m (3,936 ft); with the use of four Type 129-1 solid-fuel JATO boosters designed by I. I. Kartukov (each delivering a thrust of 2,000 kgp/4,410 lbst for 17 seconds) the take-off run was reduced to 700 m (2.300 ft). The landing run was 700 m (2,300 ft). The range, depending on the combination of fuel and bomb load, could be anywhere between 1,500 and 4,500 km (930-2,800 miles), and the maximum endurance was 5.6 hours.

On 21st March test pilot D. V. Zyuzin took the machine up for yet another flight. The 13th flight took place a week later. Vernikov was unable to fulfil the flight mission because during climb a window panel of the cockpit canopy incorporating a clear-vision window cracked at an altitude of 9,500 m (31,160 ft). A new window panel was sent to Lookhovitsy on 4th April.

On 31st March a State commission arrived at the factory to watch the testing of the control system. This time the test rig was deemed not ready, and the commission did not commence work until 16th April. The following day Vernikov performed the 16th flight under the programme (listed as the 14th in official documents). The mission again remained unfulfilled because the automatic feel load device in the control system failed (at high altitudes the control forces on all controls 'disappeared'). On landing the wheel brakes were applied prematurely; as a result, the nosewheel and mainwheel tyres were ripped off and the nosewheel rims were deformed. At a conference Baade made a point of the fact that a few days earlier a similar incident had happened with an aircraft designed by Chief Designer Vladimir M. Myasishchev (the aircraft in question was the first prototype of the M-4 strategic bomber – Auth.).

On 9th May, Victory Day in the USSR, Yakov. I. Vernikov finally succeeded in fulfilling the flight mission while performing the 17th (officially the 15th) flight. However, on that day he made one more flight – which proved to be the aircraft's last. When making a landing approach straight into the sun, Vernikov made an error in calculating the glideslope and flared out prematurely. The aircraft ballooned, lost speed and 'fell through', hitting the runway from a height of 5-10 m (16-33 ft) and bouncing violently. The nose gear unit was ripped off, the upper attachment point of the main gear unit was severely damaged, and the machine continued slithering along the runway resting on the engine nacelles and the outrigger wheels; fortuitously, none of the crew were hurt.

A damage assessment was made; the aircraft was deemed repairable but the repairs would cost something between 100 and 300 thousand roubles (within 8% of the aircraft's price). On 18th May Baade declared that the repairs could be done only at the facilities of Plant No. 1. However, this plant was so overburdened with producing missiles that this appeared unrealistic.

Baade quoted the following figures:
- the cost of the flying prototype of the '150' aircraft was 1.9 million roubles;
- the cost of the static test airframe was 1.1 million roubles;
- the cost of the manufacturing jigs and tooling was 800,000 roubles;
- the cost of the test facilities was 500,000 roubles.

All this added up to 4.3 million roubles. Nevertheless, a decision was taken at the conference to start repairing the aircraft immediately.

Although the flight testing had an unhappy end, the flights performed by test pilots had demonstrated that on the whole the '150' bomber met the requirements of the official specification and even exceeded some of them. For example, the maximum speed at sea level was 60 km/h (37 mph) higher than stipulated.

On 2nd June 1953 State trials of the cannon installations were completed at the factory, and 10th June saw the completion of testing of the hydromechanical control system. The preliminary appraisal was positive.

On 3rd June Minister of Defence Marshal Dmitriy F. Ustinov signed Order No. 136 demoting LII test pilot Yakov. I. Vernikov to Test Pilot 2nd Class. The order also contained a phrase about 'deficiencies' of the '150' aircraft and called for curing them.

In May-June the production Plant No. 1 accomplished no work on the systems of the bomber, except for the testing of the photo reconnaissance pack with the AFA-33/100 aerial camera which was conducted between 23rd and 26th June. On 24th June

a Government commission arrived at Lookhovitsy to assess the progress of preparations for the repairs of the aircraft; however, on 2nd July the German specialists resigned in connection with their departure. The results of the work of every design team were summed up in official documents.

On 29th August Baade sent a letter to Pyotr. V. Dement'yev, the then first deputy Minister of Aircraft Industry, in which he contested the contents of the previously issued Order No. 136 dealing with the incident with the '150' aircraft. On 14th September Plant No. 1 received instructions from MAP's 7th Chief Directorate requiring the Plant to disassemble the '150' bomber and stow it away 'until further notice'; from then on, it was a downhill road for the '150'. On 6th October the mock-up of the aircraft was broken up and taken away 'for firewood'. On 19th October, having made a visit to the Ministry of Aircraft Industry, Deputy Chief Designer of OKB-1 P. N. Obroobov broke the news according to which the Government had opted to pull the plug on the '150' aircraft, stipulating that the machine, together with test rigs and design materials, be turned over to higher education institutions.

Between 29th October and 3rd November Plant No. 1 received instructions, according to which the '150' programme was ripped to shreds. The hydromechanical control test rig was to be transferred to Pavel O. Sukhoi's OKB-51, the materials on the aircraft and some units went to Andrey N. Tupolev's OKB-156, and all materials, drawings and reports on the FUGOG-1 system were appropriated by Kartukov's OKB-2.

In December 1953 the '150' aircraft, complete with all documents and equipment, was transferred to the Moscow Aviation Institute (to Chair No. 101) as a teaching aid. Sets of drawings were turned over to the design bureaux led by Gheorghiy M. Beriyev (OKB-86) and Oleg K. Antonov (OKB-153). In February 1954, following instructions from the Ministry of Aircraft Industry, many materials on the '150' aircraft and its drawings were also sent to Plant No. 491 to which the Germans were transferred from the now defunct OKB of Plant No. 1.

Thus, though it fully met the performance target, the '150' bomber failed to proceed any further in its development. It was considered that the successful service introduction of the mass-produced IL-28 tactical bomber and the successful progress of the Tupolev Tu-16 medium-range bomber's State acceptance trials obviated the need for an intermediate-class machine. In addition, in the situation when the Cold War was getting steadily colder, so to say, the introduction of a new heavy aircraft type was considered superfluous.

It should be noted that, despite all this, the work on the development of a jet bomber featuring swept-back wings and the unusual bicycle undercarriage was not wasted. It was used as a basis for the '152' four-engined turbojet-powered passenger aircraft which was built and tested in Eastern Germany shortly thereafter.

'150-R' tactical photo reconnaissance aircraft (project)

In the first quarter of 1951 design work was conducted for the purpose of developing the '150-R' photo reconnaissance aircraft as a derivative of the '150' bomber. Drawings for the full-scale mock-up of the '150-R' were issued and the mock-up itself was built in March, whereupon all work on this aircraft was discontinued.

'152' jet airliner

By the end of 1953 most of the interned German specialists engaged in aircraft and aero engine design bureaux had already 'done their time' and returned to Germany. However, a small group of leading specialists remained in the Soviet Union. In December 1953 they were transferred to aircraft plant No. 431 at Savyolovo, not far from Podberez'ye. The group was tasked with the projecting of the '152' jet airliner. This work was undertaken at the request of the government of the German Democratic Republic (East Germany) which had taken the decision to set up its own aircraft industry and had ambitious plans to manufacture modern jet airliners following the licence manufacture of the piston-engined Il'yushin IL-14P airliner at the Dresden aircraft factory (FWD – Flugzeugwerke Dresden).

Bearing the designation '15.2', the initial project of the airliner was broadly based on the design of the '150' bomber, with appropriate changes dictated by the new role. It was to be powered by four East German Pirna 014 axial-flow turbojets (also known simply as '014') – or two AL-5 engines, like the '150' – and was intended to carry 24 passengers. Later versions of the project, developed from 1955 in the GDR by German specialists that had returned from the Soviet Union, were designated '152', and the number of passengers was increased in each successive study, first to 40 and then to 60, eventually reaching a maximum of 72 tourist-class passengers on medium-haul routes.

The airliner inherited the basic aerodynamic layout and some basic structural design features from the '150' bomber, but it could not be regarded as a mere 'variant' of the latter. For all intents and purposes, this was an entirely new aircraft that had no structural commonality with the bomber.

One of the obvious differences was the new tail unit with a low-set tailplane instead of the T-tail of the '150'. To provide accommodation for passengers, the fuselage diameter was increased from 2.6 to 3.3 m (from 8 ft 6²³⁄₆₄ in to 10 ft 9⁵⁹⁄₆₄ in); the higher all-up weight necessitated an increase in wing area and the size of the tail surfaces. The four Pirna 014 turbojets rated at 3,150 kgp (6,950 lbst) were housed in paired nacelles suspended under the wings on forward-swept pylons. A feature inherited from the bomber was the bicycle undercarriage with twin-wheel nose and main units retracting forward and aft respectively.

Further projecting and the construction of prototypes took place in East Germany at the enterprise VEB Flugzeugwerke Dresden to which the team of German designers led by Brunolf W. Baade had been transferred. Since then various sources spelled the aircraft's designation as '152', VEB 152, EW 152, BB-152 or Baade 152, although only the first of these is regarded as 'official'. It was decided to build three prototypes. The first 'of these, known as the 152 V1 or 152/I V1 (or '152' V-01) and registered DM-ZYA, had a bicycle undercarriage (the main unit of the actual aircraft had two pairs of smaller wheels side by side) and a navigator's station in the glazed nose. It was built by FWD and rolled out at Dresden-Klotzsche airport on 30th April 1958, but the beginning of the flight tests was delayed somewhat, pending the results of the static testing undertaken on the 152/I V2 airframe. DM-ZYA performed its maiden flight on 4th December 1958. This was the first flight of the first German turbojet-powered airliner. Since the Pirna 014 turbojets, initially designed in the USSR and then developed in East Germany, were not yet flight-cleared, the aircraft was fitted temporarily with four Soviet-built Mikulin RD-9B axial-flow turbojets (less afterburners).

Sadly, the flying career of the first prototype tragically ended on only its second flight. On 4th March 1959, when DM-ZYA was on final approach to Dresden-Klotzsche after a 55-minute flight, all four engines quit and the machine crashed, killing the crew of four captained by Willi Lehmann. The cause of the crash was traced to faulty venting of the fuel tanks which caused the bag-type tanks to fold as the fuel was consumed, the vacuum in the tanks cutting off the fuel feed. The crew succeeded in restarting the engines but too late – the aircraft had run out of altitude.

The second prototype, DM-ZYB, known as 152 V4 or 152/II V4 (or even '152A'), made its first flight on 26th August 1960. Representing the production configuration, it differed from the first prototype in several respects. The bicycle undercarriage was

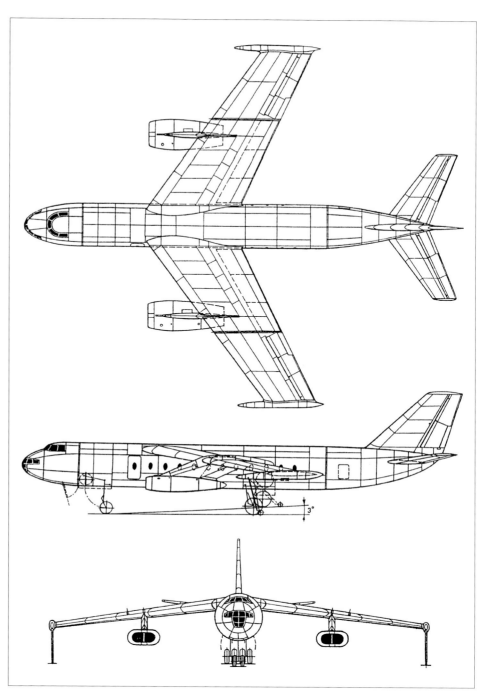

A three-view drawing of the first prototype '152' airliner (152 V1), showing the bicycle landing gear with a 'kneeling' main strut increasing the ground angle by 7°. Note the crew section access hatch.

replaced by a tricycle landing gear; the main units with four-wheel bogies retracted aft into fairings located between the splayed nozzles of each pair of engines, the bogies somersaulting aft through 180° in the process. This arrangement ensured a very wide wheel track of 13.1 m (43 ft). The glazed navigator's station was replaced by a 'solid' nose, the navigator now sitting aft of the pilots. The reshaped engine nacelles now housed the intended Pirna 014 engines. The cabin with a normal seating arrangement for 57 passengers offered enhanced comfort. Wind tunnel tests of a

scale model of this version had been conducted in the USSR at TsAGI. The airliner was capable of transporting 48 passengers and 1,570 kg of cargo over a distance of 2,540 km (1,579 miles) at a cruising speed of 800 to 850 km/h (497 to 528 mph). With 72 passengers and 1,280 kg of cargo the range was reduced to 2,060 km (1,280 miles).

The '152' seemed to have good prospects, yet it proved to be ill-fated. DM-ZYB made its second flight on 4th September 1960, and that was all. The completed 152/II V5 (DM-ZYC) never flew, and a dozen production airframes were never

Above: The rollout of the 152/I V1 (DM-ZYA) on 30th April 1958, with the final assembly shop of Flugzeugwerke Dresden (Building 222) in the background. The navigator's station glazing and the bicycle landing gear with two pairs of wheels on the main unit are well visible. The logo on the nose is that of FWD.

completed. The whole project was terminated as a result of the decision of the East German authorities to close down the aircraft industry in the GDR. Made public on 5th April 1961, this decision reflected the changes in the distribution of economic priorities and specialisation between the member countries of the Council for Mutual Economic Assistance (COMECON) adopted within that organisation (under Soviet pressure, some historians add). The construction of large passenger aircraft was

DM-ZYA at Dresden-Klotzsche on the day of the rollout. Note the upward-hinged entry door and the tail wing fences. Long leather coats were the height of fashion in East Germany in those days, especially among agents of the infamous StaSi secret service.

Above: The 152/I V1 accelerates down the runway at Dresden-Klotzsche, taking off on its maiden flight on 4th December 1958.

Left: Another view of DM-ZYA on its first flight. The flaps and the landing gear are down.

Right: The airliner takes off on its second (and last) flight on 4th March 1959.

Below: This view shows the large slotted flaps, the oval air intakes with vertical splitters and the 'kneeling' position of the main gear unit.

Above: The rollout of the second prototype, the 152/II V4 (DM-ZYB). The second prototype representing the planned production version differed significantly from the first aircraft, featuring a tricycle landing gear, a 'solid' nose, Pirna 014 engines in redesigned nacelles and other detail changes.
Below: A retouched photo of DM-ZYB undergoing taxi tests at Dresden-Klotzsche. The new engine nacelles integrated with the main gear fairings are well visible; the main gear bogies somersault through 180° during retraction. The former outrigger strut fairings at the wingtips are retained, acting as anti-flutter booms.

Opposite page, top left and top right: The second prototype during its second and final flight on 4th September 1961.
Right and below right: The third prototype, 152/II V5 (DM-ZYC), is rolled out from Building 222, towed by a ground support vehicle based on the Tatra 111 lorry. The machine was identical to 152/II V4; it was scrapped without ever being flown. The engine nacelle/main gear fairing design is welll visible here.

Above: This B-25J was used by LII for testing the crew escape system of the DFS 346 research aircraft whose cockpit section is suspended in the bomb bay.
Below: This sequence shows the DFS 346 cockpit being dropped by the B-25, whereupon the pilot's berth is extracted from the cockpit and his parachute opens.

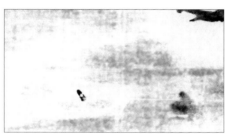
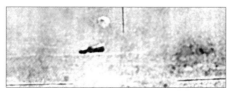
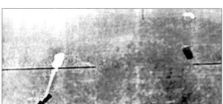

to be concentrated in the Soviet Union, as the national economy of East Germany was deemed lacking the necessary prerequisites for fulfilling that task. Besides, competition from the Tu-104 and Western jet airliners, such as the Sud-Est SE210 Caravelle, made the export prospects for the '152' rather dubious.

The 152/II prototypes were eventually scrapped. By the time the liquidation of the East German aircraft industry was announced, DM-SCA (W.Nr. 008), the first production 152/II for the East German air carrier Deutsche Lufthansa (not to be confused with its West German namesake!), was basically completed, while subassemblies and units had already been manufactured for the machines up to c/n 028. All of these were scrapped, with the exception of WNr 011, the fuselage of which was used as a workmen's hut; in 2001 it was salvaged and was being restored as a museum piece in Dresden.

'346' (DFS 346, Siebel Si 346, EF 346) experimental rocket-propelled aircraft

In 1944 the German Research Institute for Gliding Flight (DFS – *Deutsches Forschungsinstitut für Segelflug*) prepared a project of the DFS 346 experimental aircraft, which was a follow-on to the DFS 228 subsonic high-altitude reconnaissance aircraft intended to be powered by the Walter HWK 109-509 liquid-fuel rocket motor. The DFS 228 was built in 1943 and was tested without the engine, as a glider. As distinct from the DFS 228, the DFS 346 was to have swept-back wings and was expected to reach a maximum speed around 2,000 km/h (1,243 mph). To this end the aircraft was to be powered by two HWK 109-509A rocket motors (sometimes called simply HWK 509A) – the same model as used on the Me 163B Komet

interceptor. According to the project, the DFS 346 was to be lifted to an altitude of some 10,000 m (32,800 ft) by a carrier aircraft (the Junkers Ju 388 bomber or the Heinkel He 219 night fighter being envisaged for this role), and then be released, continuing the flight on its own.

Construction of the experimental superfast aircraft began several months prior to the end of the war and was halted during the closing stage of the war when the fighting moved onto German soil.

It is well known that during the post-war period the Soviet authorities set up several research and development organisations for the purpose of making use of German scientific and technical potential. Several design bureaux were set up in the field of aviation; they were located in Dessau, Berlin, Halle and in other places. One of them, the aforementioned OKB-3 in Halle, was organised in late 1945 on the basis of the Siebel aircraft construction company. It was engaged in the design of not only air-

Wolfgang Ziese, the project test pilot of the '346'. The picture was taken in the early 1950s.

craft but of aircraft engines as well. Since the Siebel company was a relatively small enterprise, OKB-3 had a much smaller design staff as compared to OKB-1 in Dessau (the former Junkers company) and OKB-2 in Stassfurt. In December 1945 the staff of OKB-3 comprised only 41 persons, including 12 designers, four engineers for calculation tasks and two specialists in aerodynamics. Soon, attracted by the food rations offered by the Soviet authorities (no small benefit in war-ravaged Germany), more former employees of the Siebel company joined OKB-3, which also recruited some specialists from the Heinkel and BMW companies. Thanks to all this, the strength of the OKB's personnel grew considerably and in March 1946 as many as 742 persons worked there. General management of the design bureau was effected by Vlasov, a representative of the Soviet Ministry of Aircraft Industry, and by Dr. Seitz, one of the former directors of the Siebel company. Dipl.-Ing. Hans Rössing, a German engineer, was appointed Chief Designer of OKB-3.

Organisationally OKB-3 was divided into two sections dealing respectively with aircraft and aero engines. It was this body that was tasked with resuming work on the projected DFS 346 experimental aircraft. On 17th April 1946 the Soviet Council of Ministers issued directive No. 874-366ss, which tasked the design bureau led by Rössing with developing the Siebel Si 346 experimental supersonic aircraft capable of attaining a speed of 2,500 km/h (1,554 mph) at an altitude of 20,000 m (65,600 ft).

In early 1946 OKB-3 started manufacturing a full-scale mock-up, producing the jigs and tooling and preparing detail drawings of the aircraft. N. A. Heifitz was appointed project engineer for the Si 346 from the Soviet side; on the German side, work on the aircraft was directed by Chief Designer Rössing, engineer Heinsohn (who was chief of the aircraft section's design team) and others. Substantiating the expediency of work on the aircraft, N. A. Heifitz wrote:

'The Siebel-346 aircraft is a flying laboratory intended for studying the problems related to flight at supersonic speeds. (Note: The Russian term letayushchaya laboratoriya (lit. 'flying laboratory') means any kind of flying testbed or research/survey aircraft – Auth.)

Penetration into the field of high speeds and exploration of the conditions of these flight modes has long been a matter of interest for science. In this case not only the methods of studying the problems associated with these flights are new; so is the flight itself: an aircraft's behaviour at supersonic flight modes, flight dynamics, stability, con-

Top and above: A German-built Kranich sailplane – also designed by DFS – was modified to verify the prone position of the pilot chosen for the DFS 346.

trollability, the variation of the drag curve and so on.

Studies conducted on models in supersonic wind tunnels do not give reliable results at present. Wind tunnels having a huge power consumption and dealing with small models do not produce reliable results because of difficulties in assessing the scale effect.

Testing and exploration of these phenomena in flight has always been one of the most enticing and at the same time the most

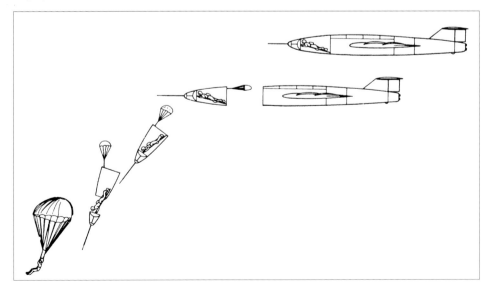

This drawing shows how the crew escape system of the '346' works. The cockpit section is jettisoned and stabilised by a parachute, whereupon the pilot's berth is extracted and the pilot parachutes to safety.

Top and top right: The first prototype of the DFS 346 in TsAGI's T-101 wind tunnel on 12th November 1948. Note the wool tufts on the wings, fuselage and horizontal tail for airflow visualisation.
Above: Another view of the DFS 346 V1 in the wind tunnel, showing the control surface above the stabilisers (the so-called *Paddel*) and the extended landing skid with its bay doors.

difficult tasks. The Siebel-346 aircraft is intended to fulfil this task.'

Here is another quotation from a report prepared by MAP specialists on aviation research conducted in Germany in 1945-46:

'Despite insufficient argumentation to support the project, the aircraft is of great interest as an attempt to undertake the quickest intrusion at random into the field of supersonic speeds, all the more so since factory test pilot Motsch has expressed his wish to conduct tests of this purely experimental aircraft'.

In late July 1946 the Siebel-346 aircraft project was discussed at OKB-3 in the pres-

ence of Deputy Minister of Aircraft Industry M. M. Lukin who had arrived from the USSR. In accordance with the decisions taken at the meeting, some changes were introduced into the aircraft's design; among other things, pressurisation of the fuselage was improved and landing skids were added at the wingtips to protect them during landing.

On 29th September 1946 the recently completed first prototype of the aircraft was rolled out at the aircraft factory in Halle. The second flying prototype was only 40% complete by then, but the static test example was

fully completed. Preliminary ground testing of the first flyable example, designated DFS 346 V1 in keeping with German practice, began in early October.

Here mention must be made of the problems associated with the German liquid-fuel rocket motors. The engine section of OKB-3 was expected to deal with the manufacture of the Walter 109-509 rocket motor for the DFS 346 aircraft and to engage in the study of alternative types of liquid-fuel rocket motors. It was headed by the Soviet engineer Berglezov; German collaborators included K. Schell from BMW, W. Küntzell from the Walter company and G. Reck from the German Aviation Experimental Establishment (DVL – *Deutsche Versuchsanstalt für Luftfahrt*). Yet, there was a shortage of highly qualified specialists on liquid-fuel rocket motors. Chief of OKB-3 Vlasov wrote in his report in May 1946:

'There are no designers, technologists and engineers qualified in engine design and construction. Lists and addresses of the required specialists are available and have been submitted by us to the appropriate organisations [...] Up to now the specialists have been collected by the officers of the Special Technical Bureau, but, since a number of specialists live in the occupation zones of our Allies, we need immediate assistance from appropriate organisations.

During the recent time many valuable specialists on liquid-fuel rocket motors have been taken over by the Allies. [...] In the present situation the Special Technical Bureau is forced to use specialists from other fields of technology and to instruct them in modalities of work on the liquid-fuel rocket motors.'

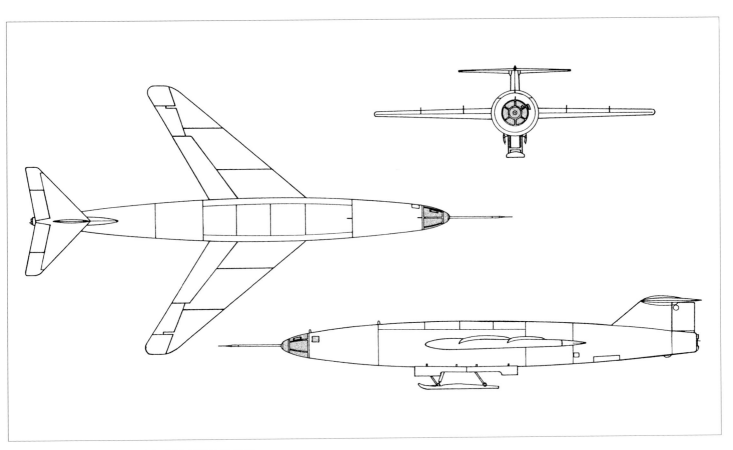

Above: A three-view drawing of the DFS 346 V1 ('346-1').

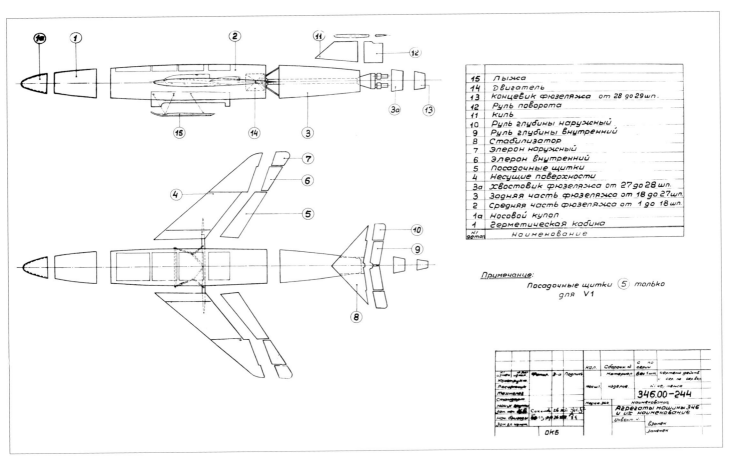

15	Лыжа
14	Двигатель
13	концевик фюзеляжа от 28 до 29шп.
12	Руль поворота
11	Киль
10	Руль глубины наружный
9	Руль глубины внутренний
8	Стабилизатор
7	Элерон наружный
6	Элерон внутренний
5	Посадочные щитки
4	Несущие поверхности
3а	Хвостовик фюзеляжа от 27 до 28 шп.
3	Задняя часть фюзеляжа от 18 до 27шп.
2	Средняя часть фюзеляжа от 1 до 18шп.
1а	Носовой купол
1	Герметическая кабина
№ детал	Наименование

Примечание:

Посадочные щитки ⑤ только
для V1

346.00-244

Агрегаты машины 346
и их наименование

ОКБ

An exploded view of the '346-1'. All inscriptions on the drawing are in Russian, revealing it was completed in the Soviet Union.

Left and above: The first prototype in engineless form known as '346P'. The aircraft has been modified: the *Paddel* is gone, and boundary layer fences have been added to the wings. Note the small outrigger skids under the wings and the absence of the main skid bay doors.
Below left and bottom left: The '346-P' suspended under B-29-5-BN '256 Black' before its first flight on 30th September 1949. The engine nozzles are closed by wooden blanks.

It should be noted that the German rocket motor was built in series, and it proved possible to find many parts for it at different facilities in Germany. The same report noted that it was possible to assemble up to 14 engines from the available stockpile of parts (provided that these parts underwent major overhaul and some missing parts were manufactured anew).

By the autumn of 1946 the engineers of OKB-3 had completed the assembly of seven engines with a thrust rating of more than 1,700 kgp (3,750 lbst) and of two modified models (Walter 109-510) yielding a thrust of up to 2,000 kgp (4,410 lbst). In addition, test benches were manufactured for testing these engines. However, the testing of the liquid-fuel rocket motors was never started. The reason was the absence of the special rocket fuel. A thorough search of the Soviet occupation zone turned up some 55 tonnes (121,250 lb) of fuel components for the liquid-fuel rocket motors developed by the Walter and BMW companies, but their chemical composition made them unsuitable for use. This was the main reason making it impossible to start the testing of the DFS 346 V1.

In October 1946 the staff of OKB-3, together with the other teams of interned German specialists, was relocated to the Soviet Union for further work. All the captured hardware, including the experimental DFS 346 V1, was dismantled and also sent to the USSR for examination, wind tunnel

Above: B-29-5-BN '256 Black' at Tyoplyy Stan airfield near Moscow with the '346P' attached. The propellers are uncomfortably close to the machine's cockpit.

tests and flight testing. By 7th November all aviation specialists that had come from Germany had been distributed and assigned to various MAP enterprises. Specialists in aircraft construction were grouped at the GOZ No. 1 (formerly a plant producing hydroplanes) in the aforementioned settlement of Podberez'ye, while turbojet engine specialists were sent to the experimental plant No. 2 situated not far from Kuibyshev. As mentioned earlier, two new design bureaux were organised at plant No. 1 – OKB-1 under Chief Designer Brunolf Baade and OKB-2 led by Chief Designer Hans Rössing. It was the latter design team that was tasked with continuing the work on the DFS 346 aircraft. Interestingly, the post of Rössing's deputy was occupied by Aleksandr Ya. Bereznyak (the chief designer of the BI – the first Soviet rocket-propelled interceptor), who had a lot of experience in developing aircraft of that kind.

The Soviet staff of OKB-2 and of the production facility consisted of former employees of plant No. 458 and young specialists who had just graduated from institutes and were assigned their jobs; therefore the end of 1946 and the beginning of 1947 were used mainly for preparations for the work. The work on furnishing the necessary equipment to plant No. 1 continued until the end of 1947. In addition to the existing production facilities, the plant was provided with a mechanical laboratory, a static test laboratory and a chemical laboratory; a wind tunnel affording speeds up to Mach 1 was built on the premises, as well as test benches for liquid-fuel rocket motors.

In the USSR the German DFS 346 experimental aircraft was referred to simply as the '346'; in addition, at OKB-2 it was unofficially

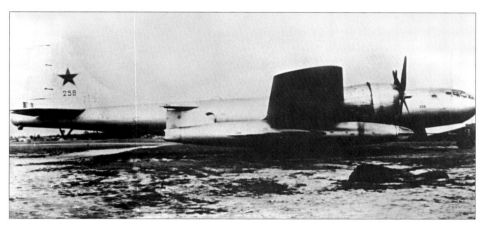

Two more photos of the B-29 'mother ship' with the '346P' attached. The bomber's armament has been removed and the turrets' locations faired over.

dubbed 'Victoria'. The work on it lasted quite some time, the designers delayed the final choice of the layout; the progress of the work was also affected by the interned German specialists' general living conditions.

In the meantime, the DFS 346 V1 delivered from Germany was sent to TsAGI for aerodynamic research. The experiments were conducted in the big T-101 wind tunnel

which permitted full-size aircraft to be tested. The tests showed that, owing to the wing sweepback, severe stalling took place at the wingtips when the wings were set at high angles of attack; the stall quickly spread over the entire wing surface, causing loss of stability. This was not unexpected, since airfoils of the same type were used along the entire span, which is undesirable for swept

Above: The '346-P' lying on its belly after a less-than-perfect landing on 30th September 1949. The damage caused by the collapse of the skid is evident.

Top and above: The '346-1' under the starboard wing of B-29 '256 Black'. Note the special rack on which the machine was carried.

wings. To eliminate this deficiency, it was recommended that four boundary layer fences (two on each wing) be installed on the upper wing surface to limit spanwise air-flow. After the wind tunnel tests the aircraft was also subjected to a structural strength check. Later a model of the '346' was tested in the T-106 – the Soviet Union's first super-sonic wind tunnel. Due to the loss of control authority at transonic speeds the aircraft's maximum Mach number was limited to 0.8.

To minimise drag the cockpit of the DFS 346 was designed so that the pilot was to fly the aircraft in a prone position; there-fore preliminary experiments were con-ducted in LII to study the peculiarities of piloting an aircraft so configured. The Ger-man Kranich (Crane, the bird) sailplane was used for this purpose, with its cockpit refitted for a prone pilot. The glider had gull-type wings with a high aspect ratio. It was towed to an altitude of 5,000 m (16,400 ft) by a Petlyakov Pe-2 dive bomber and then released for independent flights. In 1948 this glider was flown by German pilot-engineer Wolfgang Ziese, who had a 20-year record of flying experience. He had graduated from a flying school attached to the Hannover Avi-ation Institute. Large-scale research was also conducted with regard to the take-off and landing device – the metal skid.

Test pilot Mark L. Gallai, who had flown this machine, later recalled that the prone position of the pilot proved to be very incon-venient for piloting, as might well be expected. Nevertheless, it was decided not to return to the conventional sitting position of the pilot; the idea of fitting the '346' aircraft with a protruding cockpit canopy was dropped because this would have necessi-tated an almost complete revision of its gen-eral layout which, in turn, would inevitably entail an increase of drag. LII specialists also conducted the testing of the detachable cockpit and the ejection device. For this pur-pose the cockpit of the '346' aircraft was sus-pended under the fuselage of a North

American B-25J Mitchell bomber and was dropped in flight. The tests went successfully.

In its final configuration the aircraft was a monoplane of metal construction (with the exception of the cockpit, which had a wooden framework) with wings swept back 45°. As already noted, the pilot lay prone in the forward fuselage. In addition to reducing the fuselage cross-section and hence drag, this arrangement enabled the pilot to sustain greater G-loads than in the traditional seated position. The transparent cockpit canopy with Perspex glazing slid forward to provide access to the cockpit. The latter had provisions for a conventional seat (to be used for testing the airframe) and a berth for the prone pilot. The aircraft was provided with an unconventional rescue system for the pilot. The pressurised cabin (which had been tested in a thermal vacuum chamber at LII and modified upon testing) was attached to the fuselage by explosive bolts and could be jettisoned in an emergency. Attached to the rear wall of the cabin was a parachute which was intended to stabilise its descent after separation. At an altitude of 3,000 m (9,840 ft) a system ejecting the pilot was actuated automatically, the canopy separated and the pilot together with his berth was ejected from the cabin, whereupon his parachute deployed at an altitude of 1,500 m (4,920 ft). The rescue system ensured that the pilot would 'abandon ship' even if he had lost consciousness. In this situation the separation of the pressurised cockpit was effected automatically – the electric fuse of the explosive bolts was brought into action. The landing gear consisted of a skid retracting into the fuselage. The absence of a normal wheeled undercarriage was due to the

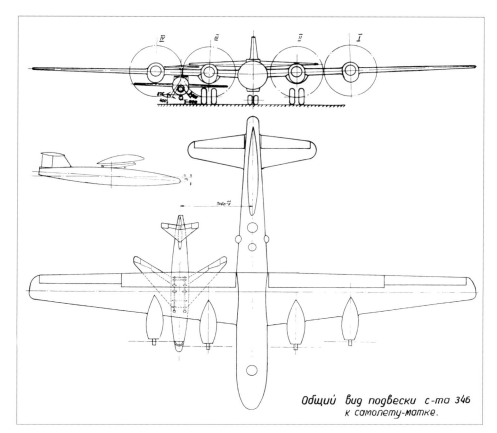

Обший вид подвески с-та 346
к самолету-матке.

Above: A drawing showing how the '346' was attached to the B-29 (Tu-4). The clearance between the '346' and the No. 4 propeller was just 275 mm (10¹³⁄₁₆ in); the ground clearance was 400 mm (15¾ in).

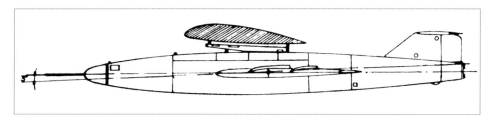

Above: The '346' was carried beneath the wing of the 'mother ship' in a 3° nose-down attitude to assist safe separation after release.

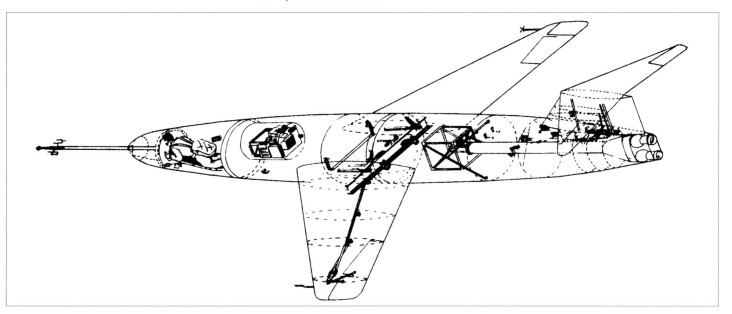

A cutaway drawing showing the DFS 346's detachable cockpit with its parachute system, the location of the rocket motor and control system components.

Above: The other carrier aircraft used in the '346' programme was a Tu-4 (c/n 230503).
Left: Tu-4 c/n 230503 engine running with the '346-3' attached under the starboard wing.
Below left and bottom left: The Tu-4 'mother ship' taxies out and takes off, carrying the '346-3'.
Bottom: A poor-quality but rare shot showing the '346-3' as it glides to a landing; the deployed skid is visible.

fact that the '346' was to be taken aloft by a carrier aircraft (a 'mother ship'). The power-plant consisted of two Walter HWK 109-509A liquid-fuel rocket motors attached to a common engine mount. The fuel tanks held 552 litres (121 Imp gal) of fuel and 1,100 litres (242 Imp gal) of oxidiser. Due to the rocket motors' high fuel consumption this amount was sufficient for a flight of just a few minutes' duration. There was no provision for armament.

To record the progress of the flight, the employees of the plant's OKB-2 developed an onboard data recording unit intended to capture 36 parameters concurrently. Test benches for the rocket motor were also built at the plant, but it was not before the end of 1947 that it proved possible to obtain fuel for the rocket motor. Testing and development of the power-plant went on throughout the year of 1948.

Preliminary experimental research in TsAGI and LII took some time; therefore the construction of the glider version of the '346' aircraft, known at OKB-2 as the '346-P'

(*plahner* – glider), was not completed before the second half of 1948. It had a simplified design: there was no pressure cabin, engine and fuel tanks, and the use of ballast made it possible to change the weight of the machine. In the course of the flight test programme the '346-P' was used for developing the techniques of disengagement from the carrier aircraft; a check-up was made of the machine's stability and handling at different CG positions, experience was accumulated as regards piloting in a prone position and especially landings with the use of a skid. The flight testing of the experimental aircraft in the glider version was conducted by Wolfgang Ziese.

For the purpose of flight-testing the real aircraft it was decided to use a US-built Boeing B-29 Superfortress bomber as the 'mother ship'. The bomber in question, a B-29-5-BW serialled 42-6256, was one of the three Superfortresses that had fallen into Soviet hands not long before the end of the Second World War when they force-landed in the Soviet Far East after suffering battle damage during raids on Japan. A carrier aircraft of Soviet design capable of lifting a suspended load to an altitude of some 10,000 m (32,800 ft) simply did not exist at that time. The bomber was fitted with a special rack under the starboard wing between the engine nacelles for carrying the experimental aircraft. At high altitude the '346' was released and the test pilot performed a gliding descent followed by a landing. On the whole, the testing proceeded successfully.

Despite all efforts to speed up the work of the German designers, it took quite some time to complete the first flyable example of the aircraft incorporating all project modifications. On 5th May 1949 the experimental plant No. 1 submitted for flight testing the '346' aircraft on which a rocket motor had been installed, albeit in dummy form (that is, in non-operational condition). In documents it was referred to as the '346-1'.

The whole summer period and September were used for preparing the '346-1' ('346 V1') for testing at the aforementioned airfield in Tyoplyy Stan. The first flight took place on 30th September 1949, with W. Ziese as the pilot. The aircraft weighing 3,145 kg (6,935 lb) was suspended under the wing of the B-29, which was piloted by A. A. Yefimov and N. A. Zamyatin. The release took place at 9,700 m (31,820 ft). It came to light that the aircraft had some handling deficiencies; these had also been manifest on the '346-P' glider, but the pilot did not consider them to be dangerous at that time. On the '346-1' the situation proved to be different – in certain flight modes it was impossible to make the aircraft change its attitude. Despite the diffi-

Above: Test-firing the upper chamber of the 346 V3's rocket motor in 1950; several access panels appear to be removed. Note the revised tail unit with increased stabiliser sweep and a tapered rudder.

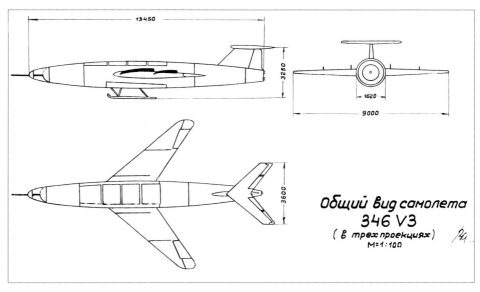

A three-view of the '346' V3, showing the revised tail unit with a tapered rudder and swept stabilisers.

culties, the pilot succeeded in keeping the aircraft under control. However, he misjudged the landing approach and the aircraft approached the airfield at a higher speed than anticipated (some 310 km/h, or 193 mph). After the first touchdown it bounced to a height of 3-4 m (10-13 ft) and flew a further 700-800 m (2,300-2,625 ft). During the second touchdown the skid retracted on impact, and the aircraft slid along the runway on its belly until it came to a standstill. The pilot's berth and harness proved unreliable, too. During the abrupt deceleration after the landing Ziese was thrown forward, hitting his face against the forward transverse beam in the cabin, and was knocked unconscious. Fortunately, the injury sustained by the pilot proved to be minor, and

after some treatment in a hospital he returned to his duties.

A commission headed by test pilot Nikolay S. Rybko was set up for investigating the causes of the accident. The commission came to the conclusion that the accident had been caused by incomplete extension of the skid. The investigation report stated: *'The incomplete extension of the skid during the flight was due to only one possible cause: the incorrect actions of pilot Ziese who had failed to push the button connected to the skid extension lever firmly enough. As a result, the lever of the winch failed to engage, and the skid failed to lock in the extended position'*. One might add to this conclusion that, due to the unexpected difficulties in controlling the aircraft the pilot must have concentrated all his attention on piloting, which is exactly why he had failed to push the said button firmly enough.

The damaged aircraft was repaired; at the same time it underwent some modifications, including changes to the control system, whereupon it was transferred to LII. While Ziese was receiving medical attention, pilot P. I. Kaz'min continued the testing of the '346-1'. In his flights the main attention was given to the aircraft's handling qualities. The rocket motor was not ignited. On his very first flight in the '346' the skid failed to lock down again, but this time the machine landed on a snow-covered field, and everything ended without trouble, the '346-1' suffering virtually no damage. Some time later Kaz'min made his second flight in which the '346-1' was towed by a Tu-2 to an altitude of 2,000 m (6,560 ft) and then cast off to make a free flight. Again the landing was unsuccessful because the pilot undershot, damaging the aircraft. More repairs ensued.

Nevertheless, on the whole the testing proceeded successfully, with the exception of one occasion when Ziese forgot to check the position of the ailerons before the aircraft parted company with the 'mother ship'. As a result, the '346-1' flipped inverted, and the pilot barely managed to bring the aircraft into a level attitude.

The results of the first flights provided the basis for the 'Report on the flight tests of the '346' aircraft'; some excerpts from this report will be of interest for the reader.

(This calls for some explanation, lest the reader should be confused by the designations applied to the German rocket-propelled aircraft in Soviet documents which the reader will encounter further on. In the said Report, which was endorsed on 28th October 1949, one can see such designations as '346A', '346B' and '346D'. In the author's opinion, the designation '346A' refers to the glider version of the aircraft (which was previously mentioned as the '346-P'); the designation '346B' denotes the '346-1' version and the designation '346D' refers to the modified '346-1' with operational rocket motors.)

Report on the flight tests of the '346' aircraft

(Stage 1 of the programme)
Endorsed on 28.X.49
Tests performed by:
test pilot Yefimov;
test pilot Ziese;
project engineer Molochayev.

A summary of the test programme

Tests have been conducted of the '346A' glider, dimensionally identical to the '346B'

airframe and tests of the '346D' without igniting the [rocket] motor. In the course of the testing, techniques were developed for the carriage of the '346D' aircraft by the 'mother ship', as were the release of the '346D' and its landing. A qualitative evaluation of the '346D' aircraft's piloting qualities in a glider version has been obtained.

Purpose of the tests.

The flight tests of the '346' aircraft pursued the following purposes:

1) developing techniques of carrying the '346' aircraft underneath the 'mother ship' No.256;

2) developing techniques of the release of the '346' aircraft by the 'mother ship';

3) checking the stability of the '346' aircraft in free flight with various CG positions;

4) checking the aircraft's handling with retracted skid and without underwing skids;

5) developing techniques of landing on the skid without using underwing skids.

Test results

In the course of the testing, four taxi runs and five flights were made. When the taxi runs showed that the '346' aircraft behaved normally when suspended, the first flight was made. The first three flights involving the carriage and release of the '346' aircraft were performed for the purpose of developing the release procedure. The aircraft's weight in the first three flights was 2,180 kg [4,810 lb], the CG position being at 29.3% MAC. In two flights the release of the '346' aircraft was effected in a gliding mode at a gliding speed of 300 km/h [186 mph] and a sink rate of 4 m/sec [787 ft/min]. In one of the flights the aircraft was released at a speed of 350 km/h [218 mph] with a sink rate of 6 m/sec [1,180 ft/min]. After that it was established that the release was best performed at 300 km/h and a sink rate of 4 m/sec. In the fourth flight the weight of the '346' aircraft was 1,880 kg [4,154 lb], the CG position being at 27% MAC. In one of these flights the pilot failed to check the position of the ailerons before disengagement with the 'mother ship'; as a result, immediately after the release the aircraft flipped over, losing nearly 2,000 m [6,560 ft] of altitude before it could be brought into gliding flight. In the fifth flight the '346' aircraft was carried with the rocket motors installed, but these were not ignited. The flight weight was 3,145 kg [6,930 lb], the CG being at 27% MAC. The aircraft was released at an altitude of 9,700 m [31,825 ft]. In this flight it was established that the elevators of the '346' aircraft had no aerodynamic balance, while the ailerons were overbalanced. For these reasons it was impossible to make any changes of the aircraft's attitude at speeds in excess of 300 km/h. When the

landing skid was extended, it failed to lock down. At the moment of touchdown at an excessively high speed of 300 km/h the skid retracted, the aircraft suffering minor damage.

The 'mother ship' was piloted by A. A. Yefimov and N. A. Zamyatin, the '346' was piloted by Ziese.

Conclusions

1) Techniques have been developed for the carriage and release of aircraft '346' by aircraft No. 256;

2) Qualitative assessment has been obtained of the '346' aircraft's stability and handling at CG positions of 29% and 27% MAC.

3) The functioning of the onboard data recording unit has been verified.

Project engineer of LII V. Ya. Molochayev 25.10.49

Conclusion:

1) It is recommended that after the inspection of the '346' aircraft the flying personnel of LII should take training.

2) Testing of the aircraft (after repairs) should continue in the powered version in accordance with the approved programme.

Deputy chief of facility No.1 Kvitko

(Note: The 'aircraft No. 256' mentioned here is the aforementioned B-29-5-BW (c/n 3390) whose original USAAC serial 42-6256 had been amended to '256 Black' when Soviet insignia were applied. Stating the proper designation of this aircraft in Soviet documents was out of the question because the fact of its existence in the USSR was top secret. Moreover, in some copies (such documents were usually typed out in six copies) of the abovementioned report the number '256' was altogether blacked out by ink or scrubbed out, which testifies to the top-secret status of the American 'booty'.)

A total of 29 flights were performed in Tyoplyy Stan in the '346-P' ('346A') and '346-1' aircraft in 1948-49; these included 24 flights of the '346-P' ('346A') on tow behind a B-25, four flights of the '346-P' ('346A') in a suspended position under the B-29 and one flight of the '346-1' ('346D') with rocket motors installed, but not running. The test pilots and engineers came to the conclusion that the experimental aircraft's piloting properties were generally satisfactory and that it was possible to commence the main part of the test programme involving powered flights. For this purpose the second prototype was prepared, with the rocket motor already installed; it received the designation '346-3'. Its assembly was completed in May

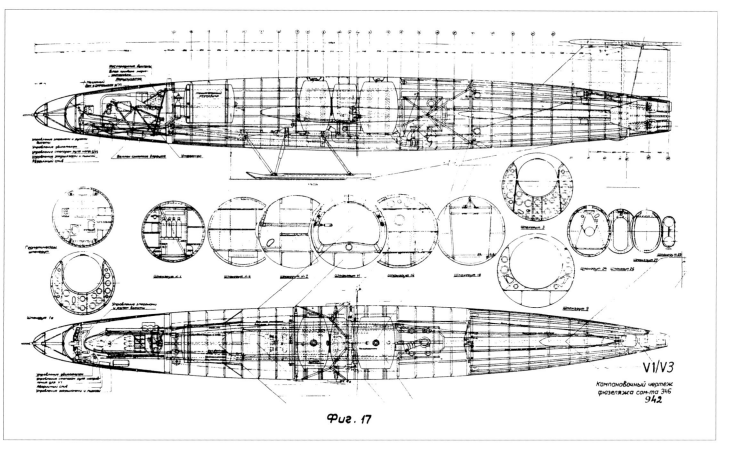

Фиг. 17

Above: A cutaway drawing from the aircraft's Soviet manual enumerating the fuselage frames and naming some of the equipment items. This was based on a German drawing of the first prototype with amendments made in the Soviet Union to show the changes made on the second prototype.

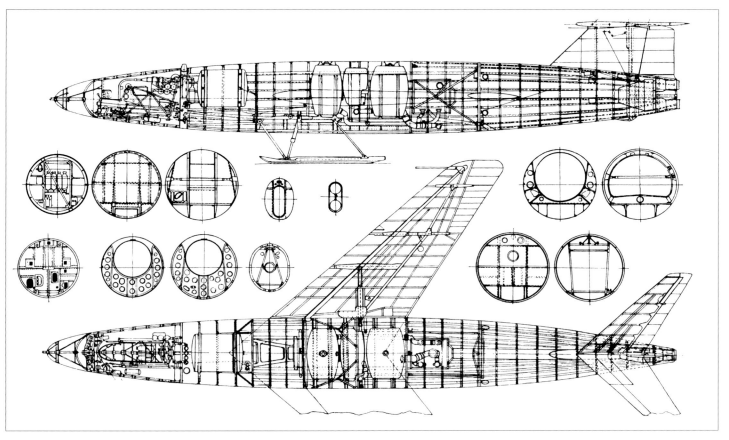

A similar drawing of the '346' V3. Note the lightening holes in some of the bulkheads.

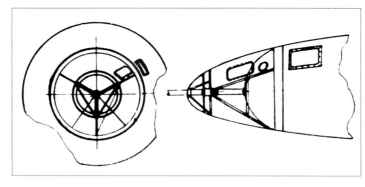

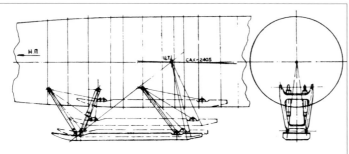

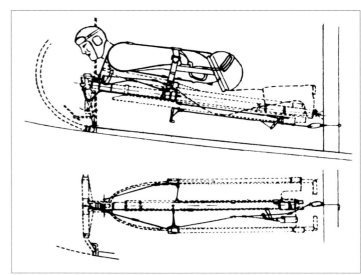

Above: The pilot's berth, control stick and rudder pedals.
Above left: The sliding parabolic canopy featuring the transparent pressure dome and the strut-braced pitot boom.
Left: The main landing skid in no-load, ground static and retracted positions.
Below: The horizontal tail of the '346-3' (top) and the '346-1'.

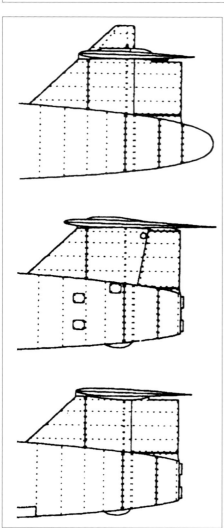

Top to bottom: the rear fuselage and tail unit of the '346' wind tunnel model; the rear fuselage and tail unit of the '346-3'; and the rear fuselage and tail unit of the '346-1'.

1950. The '346-3' differed from the '346-1' in having a horizontal tail with a thinner airfoil (9% instead of 12%) and greater sweepback, and in having no landing flaps. The vertical tail was also made thinner (likewise with a thickness/chord ratio of 9%) and the rudder was tapered, not rectangular. Nevertheless, an attempt to enhance the ailerons' effectiveness under the conditions of a shock stall proved unsuccessful, and TsAGI imposed stringent limits on the flight speed: the Mach number should not exceed 0.8 for the '346-1' and 0.9 for the '346-3'.

Construction of a new factory airfield specifically for the purpose of testing the '346-3' was undertaken at a location some 100 km (62 miles) south-east of Moscow, near the town of Lookhovitsy (the airfield was called Tret'yakovo). Construction work, manufacture of test equipment and transportation of the hardware to the new site took several months. In the meantime, ground runs of the powerplant were conducted on the '346-3'. The fuel used was a mixture of hydrazine hydrate with methyl alcohol and water, 82% hydrogen peroxide being used as the oxidiser.

In early 1951 Wolfgang Ziese, who had recovered from his injuries, started training flights in the '346-P' ('346A') glider, and on 6th April he made the first flight in the '346-3' without igniting the rocket motor. Interestingly, it was only at the initial stage of the tests at Lookhovitsy-Tret'yakovo that the US-built B-29 '256 Black' was used as the 'mother ship'; further on it was replaced by its Soviet analogue – a Tupolev Tu-4 bomber manufactured by the aircraft plant No. 23 in Fili near Moscow (c/n 230503; the aircraft had no serial).

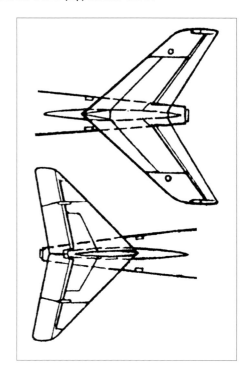

On 10th May 1951 Ziese made a flight in the '346-1', and on 16th June he performed the first flight in the '346-3'. In both flights, which ended well, the rocket motor was not ignited. Bearing in mind the strict speed limits imposed, it was decided to use only one combustion chamber during powered flights, gradually increasing the amount of fuel.

On 15th August Ziese made the first powered flight. Due to maximum speed limitations only one chamber of the rocket motor was used, the maximum thrust of the engine reaching 1,570 kgp (3,530 lbst) on that occasion. The powerplant was ignited at an altitude of 7,000 m (22,960 ft) 100 seconds after separation from the carrier aircraft. The rocket motor ran for 90 seconds, followed by a gliding flight and landing.

The flight turned out to be a sore trial for the pilot. During powered flight strong lateral instability was experienced, and Ziese constantly had to roll the aircraft level by applying ailerons. To make matters worse, due to the poor functioning of the heating regulator the cockpit temperature rose to +40°C (+104°F), and flying the aircraft in these conditions was extremely difficult. Ziese said later that he was on the point of fainting.

In all, Ziese made three flights in the '346-3' with the rocket motor running. After the installation of ventilation valves in the cabin the following flight took place on 2nd September and passed quite uneventfully, but the third powered flight, performed on 14th September, ended in an accident. In that flight the fuel load was 60% of the maximum amount. The '346-3' was released from the carrier aircraft at an altitude of 9,300 m (30,510 ft). The rocket motor was fired at an altitude of 8,500 m (27,880 ft) and the aircraft started climbing rapidly. At first the pilot maintained a constant speed by increasing the climb angle, but then the speed started growing. At an altitude slightly in excess of 12,000 m (39,360 ft) the speed exceeded 950 km/h (590 mph) and the aircraft lost lateral controllability, performing, as the pilot reported, a spontaneous flip. The '346-3' started rolling uncontrollably. Some time later the pilot regained control of the aircraft and managed to put it into a dive. When recovering from the dive at an altitude of some 7 km (22,960 ft), the machine started rolling again. Ziese came to the conclusion that he would not be able to cope with the aircraft before he ran out of altitude. He decided to bail out and detached the pressurised cockpit by detonating the attachment bolts. In all, the free flight of the '346-3' had lasted just over 3.5 minutes.

For about ten seconds the cockpit section fell, tumbling crazily; then the stabilising parachute deployed automatically and the cockpit section began a smooth descent in a nose-down attitude, rotating at a speed of one revolution per second. At an altitude of about 3,000 m (9,840 ft) the pilot was ejected together with his berth and the nose fairing of the cockpit. During the descent the nose fairing went upwards and Ziese easily detached himself from the berth, parachuting to safety.

Since all the data recording equipment was destroyed together with the aircraft, the cause of the crash was never established with certainty. According to one suggestion voiced by the 'tin kickers' investigating the crash, the '346-3' started rolling uncontrollably when it exceeded the speed limit

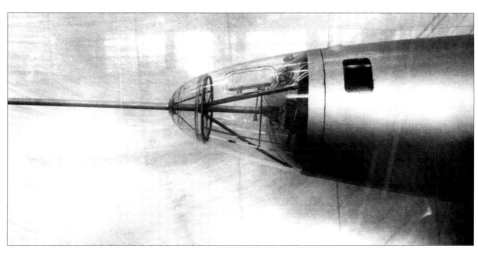

Above: The closed canopy of the '346', showing the pitot boom with its supporting structure and the hinged maintenance access panel.

Above: Here the canopy is slid fully forward together with the pilot's berth, giving access to the cockpit. Note the pressure dome integrated into the canopy.

Wolfgang Ziese is strapped into the berth of the '346-P' as it hangs beneath the wing of the B-29.

Above: The cockpit section of the '346', seen from the rear. Note the four explosive bolts and the stabilising parachute. This example was dropped from the B-25J during tests of the rescue system.

The extended main landing skid. Note the cutouts in the doors suggesting that the latter were to close, once the skid had been extended.

imposed by TsAGI and the ailerons lost their effectiveness. During the dive the aircraft went supersonic, the shock stall was left behind and the '346-3' regained controllability. After the shutdown of the rocket motor and the ensuing recovery from the dive the speed began to decrease, the aircraft re-entered the transonic speed area and lost lateral control again; it began to tumble, hit the ground and was destroyed by the ensuing fire.

After this accident, work on the '346' aircraft was terminated. Yet another 'Report on the flight tests of the '346' aircraft' contained the following conclusion:

'Despite the accident involving the '346' aircraft, it must be considered that the purpose of the testing, with due regard to speed limits, has been achieved and the tests that have been conducted have shown:

1) Good, reliable operation of the liquid-fuel rocket motor, both during ground tests and in flight on the '346' aircraft; reliable ignition of the motor, using hypergolic propellants, at high altitude.

2) Impeccable functioning of the rescue system which was ensured on the '346' aircraft by separating the pilot's pressurised cockpit from the fuselage, with the subsequent ejection of the pilot at low speeds, which had been tried out both during the accident and during preliminary tests.

3) The possibility of piloting an aircraft in a prone position which permits the pilot to sustain considerably higher loads on his system in comparison with the conventional position.

4) The feasibility of landing an aircraft fitted with a skid landing gear on an unpre-pared natural ground airfield at speeds of up to 330 km/h (205 mph).

5) High rate of climb at all altitudes and the ability of rocket-propelled aircraft to accelerate rapidly.

6) Satisfactory operation of all the hardware.

Despite the positive results obtained, further testing of the remaining flyable example of the '346-1' aircraft is inexpedient for the following reasons:

1) Further flights of the '346' aircraft cannot yield substantial results.

2) The remaining first flyable example of the '346' aircraft has a lower speed limit (Mach 0.8) as compared with the example that was lost in the accident (Mach 0.9).

3) Aerodynamic refinement of the remaining example for the purpose of lifting the speed restrictions is inexpedient due to the ageing of the airframe which has been in open storage for a long time and cannot guarantee the safety of eventual further flight testing.'

Since the aircraft attained a speed in excess of 900 km/h (559 mph) when using less then half the maximum available thrust, one can surmise that with both chambers ignited it would have been able to exceed the speed of sound. However, taking into account the insufficiently perfected aerodynamic layout, the designers refrained from the risk of undertaking such a test.

Thus, between 12th October 1950 and 14th September 1951 a total of 19 flights was performed at Lookhovitsy. These included 12 flights of the '346-P' glider on tow behind a Junkers Ju 388 bomber acting as a tow-plane, two flights of the '346-P' glider suspended beneath a B-29 bomber, one flight of the first prototype, the '346-1' ('346D') with rocket motor inoperative, one flight of the second prototype, the '346-3', with motor inoperative and three powered flights of the '346-3'.

In the course of the tests the following performance of the '346' aircraft was obtained: a maximum altitude of 12,000-13,000 m (39,370-42,650 ft), a maximum speed of 950 km/h (590 mph), a maximum Mach number of 0.9-0.95 in horizontal flight, a maximum climb rate of 100 m/sec (19,680 ft/min). The diving speed in the last flight with the rocket motor running was presumed to be supersonic.

The development of the '346' experimental aircraft became the most costly programme of the experimental plant No. 1. As can be seen from documents, 55 million roubles were spent on this programme between April 1946 and September 1951, which was an exorbitant sum for that period, even by the standards of the Soviet aircraft industry which was receiving heavy investments.

Interestingly, some time after the completion of the test programme Chair 101 of the Moscow Aviation Institute (MAI) received an example of the '346' aircraft with a modified tail unit for use as an instructional airframe. Since we know that the second prototype featuring such a tail unit had crashed, one may surmise that the institute received the '346-P' glider variant which, judging by the 1949 test report, was dimensionally identical to the '346B' machine (that is, the higher-speed version of the aircraft).

The '346' aircraft in detail

Type: Single-seat high-speed research aircraft. The airframe was almost entirely of riveted duralumin construction.

Fuselage: The aircraft's fuselage was cigar-shaped and featured a high fineness ratio of 8.3; the cross-section changed to oval at the rear. The maximum diameter was 1.62 m (5 ft 1 in), the length was 13.45 m (44 ft 1½ in). The fuselage consisted of three main parts joined by bolts. The metal framework of the fuselage consisted of duralumin frames and stringers; these were riveted to stressed skin panels, also made of duralumin.

The *forward (nose) section* was an axisymmetrical body with a contour formed by the NACA 00121-0,66-50 airfoil. It was followed by a cylindrical section and by the aft section whose cross-section smoothly changed from circular to elliptical with the larger axis vertical. The nose section had a glazed front fairing with a strut-braced pitot boom mounted at its foremost point. The nose dome had double Perspex glazing. The forward fuselage accommodated a pressurised cockpit, which had a wooden framework. The pilot lay prone on a special berth. The cockpit section was attached to the fuselage by explosive bolts; in an emergency it could be detached from the rest of the airframe by detonating the bolts. The cockpit section was separated from the rest of the fuselage by a pressure bulkhead. The canopy slid forward together with the berth, giving access to the cockpit. Attached to the pressure bulkhead from behind was a drag parachute used to stabilise the cockpit section in an emergency after the latter's separation from the fuselage. The pilot's berth was provided with an ejection device which fired him from the jettisoned cockpit after it had detached itself from the fuselage in an emergency.

The *centre fuselage* (also an axisymmetrical body) was occupied entirely by fuel and oxidiser tanks. A small recess was provided for the landing skid using a parallelogram retraction mechanism and another for a beam carrying the attachment points for the port and starboard panels of the wing. The centre fuselage also housed strain gauges for monitoring the wing stresses and the onboard data recording unit with test equipment.

The *aft fuselage* housed a small amount of fuel, as well as turbopump units for the fuel feed and chambers of the liquid-fuel rocket motors suspended of a common engine mount.

Wings: Cantilever mid-wing monoplane wings of swept-back planform with rounded tips; sweepback at quarter-chord 45°. The wings were of all-metal two-spar construction and featured a NACA-0,012-0,55-1,25 airfoil along the entire span, with a thickness/chord ratio of 12%. The wing area was 19.87 m² (213.9 sq ft). Two boundary layer fences were installed on the upper surface of each wing panel. The wings were fitted with hinged landing flaps (346 V1 only), plus inboard and outboard ailerons with recerse taper (the chord increased towards the tips). The inboard and outboard ailerons were mechanically interlinked; the gearing ratio could be changed by the pilot. At low

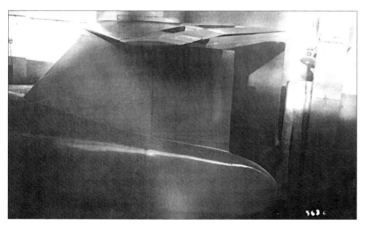
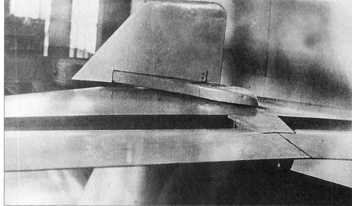
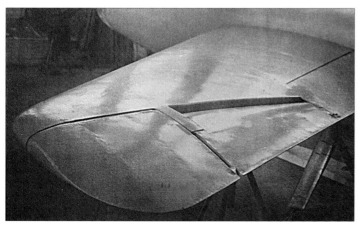

Above left and right: A model of the DFS 346 V1 tested in TsAGI's T-106 supersonic wind tunnel. Note the Paddel and the fairing replacing the rocket motor nozzles. Left and right: The '346' had two-section reverse-tapered ailerons with aerodynamically balanced inner sections.

Above: The front end of the pilot's berth and the horizontal banks of instruments, which the pilot had to literally look down on. The instruments are German ones. The ejection button is on the transverse bar ahead of the pilot.

Below, left and right: More instruments and equipment items were located on the cockpit walls.

speeds both sections of the ailerons deflected to the same angle, while only the outboard sections were to move at high speeds (during the testing the gear ratio from the control wheel to the outboard ailerons was made twice higher than the gear ratio to the inboard ailerons.

Tail unit: Cantilever all-metal T-tail. On the '346P' the rudder was rectangular. The horizontal tail was swept-back and incorporated adjustable stabilisers, the incidence being −2°40' to +2°, and two-section elevators of similar design to the ailerons. The two sections of each elevator deflected to different angles in a fashion similar to the ailerons. Placed above the stabiliser was a small movable surface – the so-called *Paddel* ('paddle' in German). At small inputs from the rudder pedals the deflection of the rudder was produced by the lateral aerodynamic force arising on the *Paddel* during the latter's deflection. At big inputs from the rudder pedals the action of these was to be switched directly to the rudder. In the course of further work the *Paddel* was removed.

The first prototype ('346-1') had a rectangular rudder and a horizontal tail with 40° sweep at quarter-chord. On the second prototype ('346-3') the tail unit was modified: the fin's area was increased, the rudder became longer and received a noticeable taper, the stabiliser sweepback at quarter-chord was increased to 45°. At the same time the elevator area was reduced, as was the taper of the horizontal tail.

Dimensions of the '346' aircraft

Length overall, including pitot:	
'346-1'	15.81 m (51 ft 10½ in)/15.987 m (52 ft 5½ in) *
'346-3'	16.55 m (54 ft 3½ in)/16.387 m (53 ft 9 in) *
'346-P'	16.355 m (53 ft 8 in) *
Length less pitot	13.45 m (44 ft 1 in)/13.642 m (44 ft 9 in) for the '346-1'
Fuselage length	13.25 m (43 ft 5½ in)
Height on ground	3.25 m (10 ft 8 in)/3.030 m (9 ft 11 in.) *
Fuselage cross-section area, m² (sq ft)	2.06 (22.18)
Wing span	9.005 m (29 ft 6½ in)
Gross wing area , m² (sq ft)	19.87 (213.9)
Net wing area, m² (sq ft)	14.87 (160.07)
Wing centre section area (inside fuselage), m² (sq ft)	5.00 (53.82)/5.07 (54.58) *
Horizontal tail span	3.6 m (11 ft 9⁴⁄₅4 in)
Horizontal tail area, m² (sq ft):	
'346-1'	3.8 (40.9)
'346-3'	4.02 (43.28)
Vertical tail area, m² (sq ft)	3.85 (41.44)
Fin area (without rudder), m² (sq ft)	2.158 (23.23)
Rudder area, m2 (sq ft):	
'346-1'	0.8 (8.61)
'346-3'	0.65 (7.0)
Flap area (total), m² (sq ft)	2.45 (26.37)
Area of each aileron, m² (sq ft):	
inboard	0.5 (5.38)
outboard	0.4 (4.3)
Elevator area, m² (sq ft):	
inboard	0.44 (4.74)
outboard	0.36 (3,88)

* Different documents give different figures

Weights and take-off performance of the '346' aircraft

	'346-1' ('346D')	'346-3'	Notes
Empty weight, kg (lb)	2,300 (5,070)	n.a.	
Thrust/weight ratio, kgp/kg (lbp/lb)	0.7	n.a.	
All-up weight, kg (lb):			
in the glider version (without motors)	1,880-2,180 (4,145-4,807)	n.a.	
with motors, but without fuel	3,125-3,145 (6,890-6,935)	n.a.	
maximum (with motors and fuel)	5,260 (11,598)	5,230 (11,532)	
Landing weight (minimum), kg (lb)	3,260 (7,188)	3,320 (7,320)	
Wing loading, kg/m² (lb/sq ft)	265 (54.28)	263 (53.87)	
Motor thrust (single chamber), kgp (lbst)	n.a.	1,570 (3,462)	
Fuel/oxidiser ratio	n.a.	1:2.13	
Maximum Mach number	0.8	0.9	According to limits imposed by TsAGI
Altitude for release, m (ft)	10,000 (32,800)	10,000 (32,800)	Design figure
Speed at the moment of release, km/h (mph)	520 (323)	520 (323)	
Altitude attained, m (ft)	n.a.	12,000 (39,360)	
Rate of climb attained, m/sec (ft/min)	n.a.	100 (19,690)	
Landing speed, km/h (mph)	200 (124)*	200 (124)**	
Motor operation time, sec	–	165	In the last flight

* In accordance with TsAGI-imposed limit with flaps set at 14°

** In accordance with TsAGI-imposed limit with flaps set at 15°

Above: A model of the projected '468' rocket-powered interceptor. The large size of the vertical tail is noteworthy.

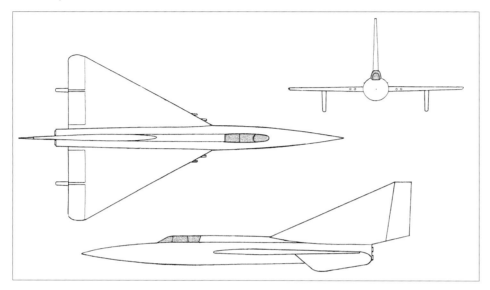

Above: A provisional three-view drawing of the '468' or the very similar '470'. Note the twin ventral fins housing the main landing skids.

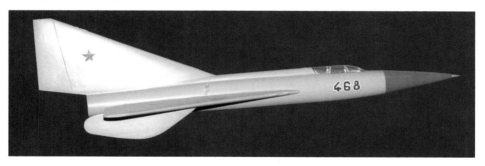

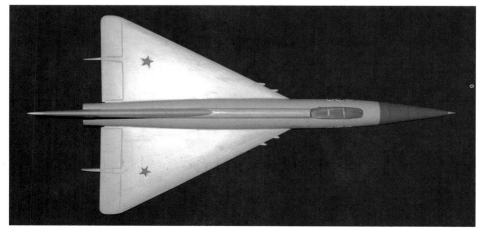

Top and above: A desktop model of the '468', showing the four cannons buried in the wing roots.

Landing gear: Since there was no need for independent take-off from an airfield, the undercarriage was limited to a skid which retracted into the fuselage.

Powerplant: The rear fuselage housed a Walter HWK 109-509A twin-chamber liquid-fuel rocket motor delivering a total thrust of 3,740 kgp (8,250 lbst) at sea level and 4,000 kgp (8,820 lbst) at altitude. The overall amount of fuel (kerosene), oxidiser (nitric acid) and catalyst (hydrogen peroxide) was 1,900 kg (4,190 lb). It was sufficient for two minutes' running of the rocket motor at full thrust. To save fuel, only one combustion chamber was ignited.

Supersonic interceptors with multi-chamber liquid-fuel rocket motors ('466', '468' and '470' projects)

In the late 1940s and early 1950s several project versions of a supersonic interceptor featuring a tailless layout with low-aspect-ratio delta wings were developed in OKB-2 under the direction of Siegfried Günther, a former designer of the Heinkel company, and Aleksandr Ya. Bereznyak, deputy Chief Designer of OKB-2. A more powerful multi-chamber liquid-fuel rocket motor was envisaged as a powerplant for the fighter. The take-off was to be performed with the help of a take-off dolly, the fighter subsequently landing on a skid. The projects had the factory designations 'izdeliye 466', 'izdeliye 468' and 'izdeliye 470'.

Models of the '466' and '468' were produced for wind tunnel tests; as for the '470' version of the project, its development was conducted with due regard to the results of these tests.

The '470' aircraft was an interceptor of tailless-delta layout with a multi-chamber liquid-fuel rocket motor. The vertical tail surfaces comprised a main fin/rudder and two underwing strakes at mid-span. The wing trailing edge was occupied by ailerons and elevators (inboard and outboard of the strakes). The landing gear comprised a front skid and two main skids accommodated in the abovesaid strakes. The aircraft was to take off from a special dolly or sled fitted with solid-fuel boosters, or with the help of a jettisonable undercarriage without boosters, using the skids for landing.

The interceptor was to be powered by a four-chamber liquid-fuel rocket motor, which was also under development at OKB-2 of plant No. 1. According to calculations, the overall thrust of the motor was to be 8,376 kgp (18,469 lbst) at sea level, rising to 9,830 kgp (21,670 lbst) when the fighter climbed to 20,000 m (65,600 ft).

To ensure the pilot's survival in an emergency, the fighter was to be equipped with an ejection seat; in addition, the use of a high-altitude pressure suit was envisaged. The cockpit was hermetically sealed and provided with an atmosphere revitalisation unit. According to the project, the aircraft was to be provided with a Korshun (Kite, the bird) radar, a **Kremn**iy (Silicone) IFF interrogator/transponder and an OSP-48 ILS (*oboroo*dovaniye sle**poy** po**sahd**ki – blind landing equipment).

Three armament options were envisaged. One included four 23-mm (.90 calibre) Shpital'nyy Sh-3 cannons with 90 rpg; another was armed with two ORO-132 automatic three-tube rocket launchers holding six 132-mm (5.19-in) TRS-132 rocket projectiles, while the third option was a strike version with four FAB-50M9 high-explosive bombs and a bombsight ensuring accurate delivery. Of these, the cannon-armed version received the most detailed treatment in the advanced development project.

The aircraft's armour plating provided protection for the pilot in the forward hemisphere from the front and from below. It comprised a 110-mm (4²¹⁄₆₄ in) bulletproof windscreen, a front armour plate of 16 mm (0⅝ in) thickness and a lower armour plate 8 mm (0⁵⁄₁₆ in) thick.

The 'Conclusion on the advanced development project of an interceptor powered by a liquid-fuel rocket motor (manufacturer's designation '470')', signed by Lieutenant-General of Engineering and Technical Service Volkov (acting chief of the Air Force's Aircraft Materiel Committee) and endorsed by Major-General of Engineering and Technical Service Shishkin (deputy Commander of the Air Force for prototype aircraft construction) contained the following remarks from the military. These may be of interest for the reader wishing to get a clearer idea of this project, which was quite a departure from the usual Soviet aircraft construction practices, as well as the reaction of the military to this project:

'1. The aerodynamic layout and structural design of an aircraft with low-aspect-ratio delta wings ensures flight at speeds up to Mach 1.8 and raises no objections. Delta wings without a horizontal tail have a lifting capacity inferior to wings fitted with high-lift devices and combined with a normal horizontal tail. However, delta wings without a horizontal tail can have greater area and a relatively lower weight than swept-back wings.

2. The project materials contain a sufficiently detailed study of the optimum airfoil for this aircraft. More that 70% of the total amount of fuel is used for climbing to an altitude of 22,000 m [72,160 ft]. The endurance and range of level flight at a given altitude is determined by the amount of fuel remaining

Design performance of the '470' interceptor as per ADP documents

Maximum speed at altitudes in excess of 11,500 m (37,720 ft), km/h (mph)	1,910 (1,187)
Landing speed, km/h (mph)	182 (113)
Time to altitude, minutes:	
to 20,000 m (65,600 ft)	2.24
to 22,000 m (72,160 ft)	2.33
Horizontal flight range with the rocket motor ignited, km (miles):	
at an altitude of 22,000 m (72,160 ft) and a speed of Mach 1.5	213.6 (133)
at an altitude of 13,000 m (42,640 ft) and a speed of Mach 0.8	264 (164)
Range at an altitude of 22,000 m, taking into account the distance covered during climb and gliding descent, km (miles)	502 (312)
Endurance in horizontal flight with the rocket motor ignited, minutes:	
at 15,000 m (49,200 ft) and Mach 0.8	18.25
at 22,000 m (72,160 ft) and Mach 1.5	8.09
Endurance with the rocket motor ignited, minutes:	
at Mach 1.5, at 22,000 m, taking into account the time for take-off, acceleration and climb	10.42
at 22,000 m, taking into account the time for take-off, acceleration, climb and gliding descent after the shutdown of the motor	35.56
Take-off run, m (ft)	
from a dolly (sled) with rocket boosters	171 (560)
with a jettisonable undercarriage	680 (2,230)
Landing run with airbrakes deployed, m (ft)	610 (2,000)

after a climb to this altitude. Therefore it is necessary to make additional calculations for level flight at altitude, analysing possible deviations in the motor operating modes and in the take-off mode, for the purpose of determining the influence of these deviations on the range.

3. One of the project's strengths is that that much attention has been paid to the aircraft's stability and handling. However, the static stability and controllability characteristics need to be explored and checked by testing aircraft models in a wind tunnel. It is also necessary to determine by calculation the dynamic characteristics and to study in relation to high altitudes the character of minor longitudinal and lateral oscillations, their frequency and damping, and the character of the aileron input when banking the aircraft and levelling it out again.

4. The aircraft's range and endurance are determined on the assumption that the fuel is consumed fully in level flight. The fuel reserves necessary for performing an instrument landing making use of the OSP-48 equipment have not been taken into account in the calculations.

5. The wing span chosen when defining the configuration of the aircraft is undersized. With the landing weight of some 4,500 kg (9,920 lb) the specific loading for the square of the wing span (sic) is as high as 90 kg/m² [18 lb/sq ft], whereas for modern fighters it is just about 40 kg/m² [8 lb/sq ft]. This makes the landing more difficult.

6. The sink rate during the landing approach has been calculated for the con-

figuration with the landing gear retracted, and will be, according to the project, 10 m/sec [1,970 ft/min]. With the landing gear extended the sink rate can be expected to be about 18 m/sec [3,540 ft/min]. Bearing in mind that, the lower the lift/drag ratio, the greater should the relative speed reserve be during the gliding descent, the sink rate during a gear-down landing should be calculated at a speed ensuring a flat flare-out.

7. The ADP envisages the possibility of using the ailerons as trim tabs. If the ailerons, when used as trim tabs, are slightly raised, this will worsen the effective wing aspect ratio; this should be taken into account when calculating the aircraft's landing performance.

8. Worthy of note is the statement made by designer Comrade BEREZNYAK [...] that it is possible to increase the range of powered flight to 600 km [373 miles] and the endurance in powered flight to 1 hour without major modifications of the aircraft while retaining the other performance characteristics listed in the ADP. This may provide a solution to the question of returning to base and ensure acceptable landing performance.

9. Two alternative take-off techniques have been studied in the project: a take-off by means of a take-off dolly (or sled) with solid-fuel rocket boosters, and a take-off with a jettisonable undercarriage without making use of boosters. The jettisonable undercarriage reduces the optimum range of the aircraft by some 5%, but is simpler in operation and also ensures acceptable take-off performance.

10. The airbrakes envisaged on the aircraft reduce the maximum speed of level flight at 15,000 m [49,200 ft] by 40% in the course of 33 seconds and enable the aircraft to dive vertically from an altitude of 24,000m [78,720 ft]. However, their effectiveness has been determined only by calculations and requires checking by means of wind tunnel tests.

11. The landing speed of 182 km/h [113 mph] specified in the project can be obtained only in the case of landings performed with an angle of attack up to 24°.

12. The multi-chamber rocket motor envisaged by the ADP has quite realistic design performance and meets modern requirements. This motor has in part been developed, built and tested by OKB-2 of MAP plant No. 1.

13. The use in the motor of the Kenaf (Ambary) concentrate which is added to kerosene before injection of the latter into the combustion chamber calls for additional experimental work connected with determining the properties of this admixture. The final development of techniques of using Kenaf may require a more exact definition of the general layout of all powerplants.

[…]

15. It is necessary to preclude the possibility of a fire in the event of the tanks holding the Kenaf concentrate being hit by a cannon shell.

16. The project makes no provision for a device which ensures normal fuel feed in a flight with negative g forces during the aircraft's gliding descent.

17. The project envisages the use of solid-fuel boosters for take-off. These boosters are very costly because the nitroglycerin powder used in them is in short supply and because they are not reusable. In addition, the thrust and burn time of these boosters depend to a considerable extent on the ambient temperature. Therefore it is more expedient to foresee the use of liquid-propellant rocket boosters for this purpose. Liquid-propellant rocket boosters are also superior to solid-fuel booster as regards the specific weight.

[…]

23. The dimensions of the cockpit have not been specified in the project and cannot be assessed.

[…]

25. The ADP contains calculations determining the limitations for safe ejection of the pilot. The results of these calculations […] show that at altitudes below 17,000 m [55,760 ft] the ejection seat does not guarantee the pilot's survival the whole range of speeds afforded by the aircraft's aerodynamics and airframe strength. In this case ejection may be possible only after shutting down the motor and decelerating the aircraft. However, the limits of safe ejection cited in the project are too high. Tests show that the trajectory of an ejection seat with a man in it passes much lower above the fin as compared to the trajectory of a seat with a dummy. Also, the limits of safe ejection determined by the impact of the slipstream on the pilot have been used in calculations at too high values.

26. The project specifies the KP-15, KP-18 and KP-20 oxygen apparatus which cannot be used for the high-altitude rescue pressure suit.

27. For the purpose of airframe strength calculations the design all-up weight is presumed to be 6,500 kg [14,330 lb] which is equal to the aircraft's all-up weight after take-off and climb to 8,000 m [26,240 ft].

The design dynamic pressure limit has been chosen as 5,000 kg/m2 [1,024 lb/sq ft], which permits the aircraft to fly at a maximum speed corresponding to Mach 1.8 only at altitudes in excess of 11,400 m [37,400 ft]; this can be considered admissible for this type of aircraft. At an altitude of 8,000 m [26,240 ft] the admissible flight speed must not exceed Mach 1.4.

28. The control surfaces installed on the wings are subdivided into elevators and ailerons. This distinction in the functions and the provision for eventually using the ailerons as trim tabs is expedient, because this allows the aircraft to be controlled manually in the event the powered control system fails.

29. The control rods to the aircraft's control surfaces are grouped together and accommodated in a fairing in the upper side of the fuselage; this is not expedient from the point of view of the aircraft's survivability because in this case a single shell can disable all controls of the aircraft.

30. In the event one of the hydraulic accumulators or one of the oil tanks or one of the control boosters fails, the entire powered control system is disabled, which is inadmissible from the point of view of survivability.

31. The ADP envisages a sideways-hinged cockpit canopy, which is inexpedient from the point of view of flight safety in the event of the canopy opening spontaneously in flight.

32. In accordance with the advanced development project the interceptor's armament has been projected in three versions:
- four 23-mm Sh-3 cannons with an ammunition complement of 90 rpg;
- two automatic three-tube launchers with six TRS-132 rocket projectiles;
- four FAB-50M9 bombs for precision bombing.

On the first prototype of the fighter it is expedient to install cannon armament comprising:
- two 30-mm [1.18 calibre] cannons with an ammunition complement of 50 rpg;
- two 23-mm cannons using VYa ammunition (that is, suitable for the Volkov/Yartsev VYa cannon – Auth.), with 70 rpg.

According to a statement made by designer Bereznyak, it is possible to install this armament on the aircraft.

[…]

34. Simultaneously with the installation of cannon armament on the aircraft the following armament options should be studied on the drawing board:
- six TRS-190 spin-stabilised rocket projectiles;
- two 100-kg [220-lb] anti-aircraft bombs or two OFAB-100M bombs.

[…]

42. […] It is expedient to install the RSIU-3M radio with two receivers.'

The same document contained the following conclusions:

'1. The ADP of an interceptor with a multi-chamber liquid-fuel rocket motor developed by designer A. Ya. Bereznyak (manufacturer's designation '470') contains sufficiently comprehensive calculations substantiating the design performance.

The design performance specified in the project basically meets the Air Force requirement posed for this type of interceptors.

2. The aerodynamic calculations have been made proceeding from the results of the '466' and '468' models' wind tunnel rests and from theoretical studies; wide use has been made of technical literature published abroad. Therefore it is necessary to adjust the calculations proceeding from the results of wind tunnel testing of the '470' aircraft model, conducted at TsAGI. Characteristics of the static stability and controllability shall be refined by wind tunnel tests of the aircraft's model. It is also necessary to determine by means of calculations the aircraft's dynamic characteristics and pay special attention to ensuring acceptable characteristics of the gliding descent prior to a landing and of the landing itself.

3. The design characteristics of the multi-chamber liquid-fuel rocket motor intended for the aircraft meet modern requirements posed for engines of this type. It is expedient to continue the development of this motor, which is conducted in OKB-2 of MAP plant No. 1.

4. In accordance with the aircraft's mission it is expedient to fit it with cannon armament comprising two 30-mm cannons and two 23-mm cannons using VYa ammunition. At the same time drawings should be prepared of two armament options: the installation of six TRS-190 spin-stabilised rocket

projectiles and the installation of antiaircraft bombs.

5. During the final improvement of the aircraft's ADP the designers shall take into account the remarks on deficiencies made in the conclusion on the ADP.'

Next came the Conclusion itself.

'1. The advanced development project of an interceptor with a multi-chamber liquid-fuel rocket motor developed by designer A. Ya. Bereznyak has been prepared in sufficient detail. Owing to its design characteristics this aircraft is of interest for the Air Force.

2. It is considered expedient to task designer Bereznyak with developing a rocket-powered interceptor with due account of the remarks stated in the conclusion on the aircraft's ADP.'

However, as early as the middle of 1951 it became obvious that the use of liquid-fuel rocket motors on combat aircraft was inexpedient because of the all-too-short endurance. In June 1951 MAP stopped funding new projects of OKB-2. Shortly thereafter the design bureau was closed down and its personnel was transferred to other departments of the Plant.

Lastly, the author would like to draw the reader's attention to an interesting fact. In the 'Advanced development project of the '470' interceptor' and in the 'Conclusion on the Advanced development project of the '470' interceptor' A. Ya. Bereznyak is named as the aircraft's designer. There is no mention at all of German designers.

Sänger 'superbomber' (long-range hypersonic bomber project)

In 1946 Soviet authorities undertook an attempt to establish a special technical bureau for the purpose of further work on a long-range hypersonic bomber based on a project of the Austrian scientist Dr. Eugen Sänger. During the war Sänger was working in Germany on a project of a bomber capable of delivering a bomb strike against the USA. In August 1944 he published in Germany a report 'On a rocket motor for a long-range bomber'. The report contained a description of a vehicle, propelled by a powerful rocket motor, which was expected to make a horizontal take-off from a monorail structure and zoom obliquely to an altitude of between 40 and 250 km (25 and 155 miles) in the course of 4 to 8 minutes of powered flight. Having used up all the fuel, the aircraft would continue its flight in a hypersonic glide along an oscillatory-type (multiple-pass) trajectory. Upon reaching the predetermined target the aircraft would drop its bombs and then return to base or to another landing site, making a large-radius

turn. The estimated maximum speed was 20,000 km/h (12,420 mph), with a landing speed of 170-180 km/h (105-111 mph). The engine thrust was 100 tonnes (220,500 lb), the all-up weight reached 100 tonnes (220,450 lb), with fuel accounting for 85-90% of this figure. The bomb load was between 1,000 and 6,000 kg (2,205-13,230 lb), depending on the range. According to Sänger's concept, such a bomber would be capable of making a strike against targets at a distance of up to 20,000 km (12,420 miles); simultaneous use of a big number of such bombers would ensure the destruction of large area targets – including capitals of hostile states – anywhere in the world.

The military leaders of the Third Reich did not undertake any practical steps for the implementation of this concept, realising it was clearly beyond the capabilities of the German industry, which was overburdened by other tasks.

After the war two copies of Sänger's report were found by Soviet specialists in Germany. One of them came to the knowledge of General Kutsevalov, chief of the Air Force section of the Soviet Military Administration in Germany. He was so impressed by Sänger's concept that he wrote to his superior, Soviet Air Force Commander-in-Chief Air Marshal K. A. Vershinin, suggesting that a special scientific and technical bureau be set up in Germany for the purpose of developing a hypersonic bomber. The proposed bureau was to be staffed by German specialists, including Sänger himself and his colleagues; they should join forces with Soviet specialists. Vershinin gave his support to this proposal; so did the leaders of NII-1 (a research institute dealing with rocket propulsion, subordinated to MAP) who described the development of an ultra-long-range bomber for the Soviet armed forces as an imperative and urgent task.

Professor Sänger's participation was considered essential for the success of the undertaking, and much emphasis was placed on getting hold of him, as well as of his associates. However, the efforts to establish contact with Sänger proved fruitless, because from July 1946 he resided in France, where he took part in experiments with rocket-powered aircraft. Apparently, this was one of the reasons why work on this project was not conducted on any substantial scale.

However, in 1946-47 NII-1 did undertake some studies based on Sänger's project. The institute's specialists called into question the possibility of developing a liquid-fuel rocket motor with the thrust yield required by the original project. In consequence, they opted for a bomber with a mixed powerplant comprising liquid-fuel rocket motors and

ramjet engines. The latter were to be mounted at the wingtips. Estimated performance of the bomber included a maximum speed of 25,200 km/h (15,650 mph), a service ceiling of 250-260 km (155-161 miles) and a range of up to 40,000 km (24,840 miles). The studies conducted by NII-1 were concentrated on the powerplant for the hypersonic bomber, while the detail design of the aircraft itself would have to be undertaken by some other organisation – but that part of the project was apparently never dealt with.

It may be added that Sänger's project had actually captured the imagination of Soviet leaders and high-ranking military officials. It was given special attention at two meetings held in the Kremlin in 1947 where some projects of German engineers (Wernher von Braun, Wagner, Hosse, Sänger) were discussed. On those occasions Grigoriy Tokayev (the aerodynamics expert mentioned above) expressed an utterly sceptical attitude to this project, thus entering a conflict with the prevailing opinion among the top brass.

Aero engines developed by German specialists in the Soviet Union

Described below are engines developed by German engineers under Soviet supervision after the war. They are arranged in the following order:

1) piston engines: Jumo 224;

2) turbojet engines: BMW 003C and Jumo 004F; BMW 018; TRD-7B, Jumo 012; 014 (Pirna 014).

3) turboprop engines: TVRD; '028'; '022' (TV-2) and its derivatives; TV-2F and its derivatives, including 2TV-2F; TV-12 (NK-12).

Piston engines

Jumo 224 (M-224) diesel engine

Among the projects handled by the aero engine section of OKB-1 at Dessau was an attempt was to resurrect the Jumo 224 diesel engine, development of which had begun in Germany in 1943 and then had been suspended in favour of speeding up the development of turbojet engines. By the time Dessau was temporarily occupied by the Allies, some 80% of detail drawings of the engine were ready and manufacture of some parts was started. However, the original technical drawings were burned in April 1945.

The Jumo 224 was a 24-cylinder in-line liquid-cooled engine incorporating four Jumo 207 six-cylinder diesels joined together in an X-type configuration. Its design power rating was 4,800 hph. Every cylinder of the Jumo 207 had two pistons;

thus, the Jumo 224 had 48 pistons, which made the engine unique in its layout. The Jumo 224 captivated the imagination of several Soviet engine specialists, notably the chief designer of Plant No. 500, F. Ya. Tulupov, who advocated the resumption of work on this engine. In his opinion, the promise of exceptionally high power output, coupled with the higher fuel efficiency of diesel engines, made the Jumo 224 a suitable powerplant for long-range heavy bombers. The engine also had its opponents – for example, V. M. Yakovlev, chief of the diesel engine design bureau at TsIAM who stuck to the opinion that the complexity of the Jumo 224 precluded its development to production status.

Nevertheless, work on the Jumo 224 received a go-ahead in April 1946, and a special team for diesel engines was set up within OKB-1; Manfred Gerlach (a former Junkers engineer) was appointed project engineer for the Jumo 224. His team set about producing anew the technical drawings of the engine; eventually, construction of the prototype engine began, but its progress was slow because of the lack of the necessary machine tools (much of the equipment of German enterprises in the Soviet occupation zone had been shipped off to the USSR). In the meantime came the month of October and with it, the relocation of OKB-1 (as well as all other similar design bureaux) to the Soviet Union.

The team headed by Gerlach was relocated to Plant No. 500 at Tushino near Moscow (now part of the city) which was engaged in the design of diesel engines. The team resumed its work on the Jumo 224, also called M-224 in the USSR (M for *motor* – engine) to conceal its German origins. According to the requirement issued by MAP on 10th April 1947, the M-224 was to be completed and submitted for bench testing in the first half of 1948.

By 1st August 1947 the German specialists had finished adapting their project to Soviet production standards; the feasibility of attaining the design parameters of the Jumo 224 was checked by preliminary tests involving the use of the Jumo 205 and Jumo 207 six-cylinder engines brought from Germany. The scene was set for starting the manufacture of the Jumo 224 (M-224) prototype. However, at this juncture unforeseen obstacles arose. The most serious of them was the negative attitude to the M-224 on the part of V. M. Yakovlev who, as Chief Designer of OKB-1 at Plant No. 500, supervised the work of the German specialists. He flatly refused to give any assistance in the development of the Jumo 224 to which he had voiced his opposition earlier, as mentioned above. His attitude may well have had some-

thing to do with the fact that he was himself responsible for the projecting of the indigenous M-501 diesel aero engine with a design power output of 6,000 hp. Yakovlev succeeded in obtaining an MAP decision halting the work on the M-224 and then made his next move: he insisted that the German specialists should leave Plant No. 501 because of security concerns, given the secret nature of other projects handled by the plant.

Manfred Gerlach contested the decision to suspend the work on the M-224 in his letters to Minister of Aircraft Industry Mikhail V. Khrunichev and Minister of the Interior S. N. Kruglov. The official reaction to his pleas is unknown; his group remained at Plant No. 500 in 1949. Yet, the M-224 engine was not mentioned in the plan for prototype engine construction for 1948-49. In 1950 Gerlach, together with the members of his team, was transferred to Experimental Plant No. 2 where he headed a group engaged in projecting combustion chambers for turboprop engines.

It might be added that the rapid advance in turbojet propulsion technology made the use of diesel engines (or any other piston engines) for long-range bombers decidedly pointless.

Turbojets

Jumo 004 and BMW 003 turbojets – boosted versions
The use of the captured Jumo 004B and BMW 003A turbojets and their Soviet copies (the RD-10 and RD-20 respectively) in early Soviet jet aircraft has been described in the previous chapter, as have been the modifications of these engines developed by Soviet design bureaux. In parallel with that, it was decided to task the former Junkers and BMW designers and engineers working under Soviet supervision (respectively at OKB-1 and OKB-2) to develop boosted versions of these engines which are described below.

Jumo 004C (Jumo 004F)
The engine section of the Dessau-based OKB-1 headed by A. Scheibe was tasked with developing an uprated version of the Jumo 004B. German sources credit it with the designation Jumo 004C), while Russian sources (notably D. A. Sobolev) refer to it as Jumo 004F (F in Cyrillic – ЮМО-004Ф), denoting *forseerovannyy*, boosted or uprated – or afterburning (though not in this case). Plans were in hand to test five examples of the Jumo 004F in 1946. This was a modified version of the standard Jumo 004B with a thrust rating of 1,200 kgp (2,650 lbst) – exceeding that of the Jumo 004B by 300 kgp (660 lbst). The measures designed to

ensure this thrust augmentation included increasing the injector (spray nozzle) diameter, reinforcing the turbine guide vanes, forced cooling of the inside surface of the jet-pipe cone (centrebody). Additional augmentation of thrust at take-off was to be achieved by water injection.

The first example of the Jumo 004F was completed in May 1946. During bench testing it proved impossible to attain the design thrust rating of 1,200 kgp due to combustion chambers' burnout, warping and disintegration of turbine blades and other complications. It was decided to restrict the boosting temporarily to a thrust value of 1,050-1,100 kgp (2,315-2,425 lbst) in the hope that detail modifications would make the design thrust rating attainable at a later stage. In the course of testing at Dessau the Jumo 004F succeeded in passing 25-hour tests, but the thrust did not exceed 1,050 kgp, which was not a significant increase over the standard Jumo 004B.

After the transfer of the team led by A. Scheibe to Experimental Plant No. 2 in the USSR the activities of that team, known as OKB-1 of the mentioned plant, were concentrated on the development of more powerful engines, while further work on the uprated versions of the Jumo 004 was assigned to the aero engine plant No. 26 responsible for the series manufacture of the RD-10 – the Soviet copy of the Jumo 004B.

BMW 003C
The Stassfurt-based OKB-2 headed by Karl Prestel was tasked with developing an uprated version of the BMW 003A engine. By the end of 1945 this design team developed a project of the BMW 003C version with a static thrust of 1,050 kgp (2,315 lbst) at sea level, as against the 800 kgp (1,764 lbst) delivered by the BMW 300A. The thrust augmentation was achieved by increasing the engine speed from 9,500 to 10,000 rpm, and by raising the temperature in the combustion chamber from 780°C to 850°C. To ensure a reliable operation of the boosted engine, it was necessary to introduce changes into the design of the combustion chamber, the jet-pipe and the turbine. Despite the difficult conditions of work at Stassfurt, the first prototype of the BMW 003C (or simply '003C') was submitted for bench testing on 14th June 1946; by October seven engines of this version were manufactured. Initial testing revealed the same sort of problems as with the Jumo 004F: the high turbine temperatures caused the turbine blades to warp and crack. Eventually these problems were solved; in August the engine scored an uninterrupted bench run of nearly 35 hours, including 1 hour and 340 minutes at maximum thrust rating (1,050 kgp).

The development of the BMW 003C was resumed after the transfer of the team headed by Karl Prestel to the Soviet Union where the group was reinstated as OKB-2 at Experimental plant No. 2. A Government directive dated 11th March 1947 required OKB-2 to complete the development of the BMW 003C and submit it for flight testing by August 1947. However, the work ran into some difficulties, primarily associated with the absence of the heat-resistant alloys that had been used in Germany for turbine blades. The use of the Soviet El-403 steel alloy instead of the German *Tinidur* entailed a reduction of the engine's capacity for running at maximum thrust, which did not exceed 25 hours due to turbine blade failures, albeit in the normal (unboosted) mode the engine had passed a test run of 100 hours. Soon it was deemed expedient to relieve OKB-2 of this work, which was entrusted to Plant No. 26 in Kazan' (this enterprise was producing the BMW 003A as the RD-20). The Kazan' plant succeeded in raising the TBO of the BMW 003C to 50 hours, introducing some improvements into the design of the combustion chamber, the turbine and the jet pipe. This engine was manufactured there as RD-21 and was installed in some versions of the MiG-9 fighter (see previous chapter).

TRD-7B turbojet (project)

In an effort to use the German intellectual potential for the needs of the Soviet defence industry to the full, the Soviet authorities resorted to seeking out appropriate specialists among the prisoners of war that were held in camps on Soviet territory. Close to 1,600 skilled specialists were selected in this way; among these, there were several dozens of aviation engineers, including the former technical director of the Argus aero engine company, Manfred Christian. The German specialists were assigned to the specially set up design bureau (OKB-36-2)

at aero engine plant No. 36 in Rybinsk. Its staff also included some Soviet specialists who had been persecuted and worked as detainees. This OKB was tasked with designing and building the TRD-7B turbojet (**toor**bor**eaktiv**nyy **dvig**atel' – turbojet engine) which should represent a further development of the Jumo 004 and BMW 003 engines. The engineering project of the engine was to be completed by early 1947. No information is available on the progress of this work which must have been abandoned after the Soviet Union came into possession of the Rolls-Royce Nene and Rolls-Royce Derwent turbojet engines.

'032' (P 130) turbojet engine with a piston-engine-driven compressor (project)

On 11th March 1947 the Soviet Council of Ministers issued a directive on prototype aero engine construction which, among other things, tasked OKB-1 (Chief Designer A. Scheibe) at Experimental Plant No.2 with designing and building the '032' turbojet engine with a piston-engine-driven compressor, yielding a thrust of 2,000 kgp (4,410 lbst). This project had been proposed by the Dessau-based team led by A. Scheibe before its transfer to the Soviet Union. The work on the '032' had actually been started in Dessau where it bore the designation *Luftstrahlgerät* P 130. In this project, the seven-stage compressor of a turbojet engine was to be driven by a built-in two-row 10-cylinder radial engine instead of using the energy of a turbine; this was believed to ensure greater fuel efficiency for an equal thrust rating.

In the opinion of Ye. V. Urmin, a well-known Soviet aero engine designer who made a report on German engine projects for MAP in October 1946, the '032' project did not tally with the mainstream lines of aero engine design at that time, but it 'did represent a certain interest'. This rather

sceptical comment proved justified. The '032' engine was to be submitted for manufacturer's bench testing in the third quarter of 1948. However, work on this project was discontinued in September 1947 because studies and calculations had shown that at high speeds and altitudes this type of engine would have no advantages over the pure turbojet.

Jumo 012 ('012A', '012B') turbojet

The Jumo 012 axial-flow turbojet with a design thrust of 3,000 kgp (9,840 lbst) was the most powerful turbojet designed during the Second World War. Its projecting was initiated at the Junkers aero engine factory in 1944. In the spring of 1945 the prototype engine was ready for final assembly, but before this could begin, the Dessau factory was overrun by US troops. When Dessau was taken over by the Soviet occupation administration, Soviet specialists did not find anything substantial on the Jumo 012: much of the documentation had been destroyed, and some subassemblies, such as the turbine and the compressor of the Jumo 012, were captured by US specialists and taken to the USA for study. Thus, the work on the Jumo 012 had to start from scratch.

A full set of technical drawings was completed at OKB-1 in Dessau in May 1946, and the prototype of the engine was ready on 23rd June. Five more examples of the engine were being manufactured at that time. The bench testing of the prototype proceeded uneventfully until 9th August when an incident accompanied by engine damage happened. During bench running the engine, after having reached 4,300 rpm, started accelerating spontaneously and did not respond to attempts to shut it down. Finally, when the speed of rotation exceeded 6,000 rpm by a substantial margin, the engine stopped abruptly and caught fire. The prototype engine was damaged beyond repair. The cause was traced to a failure of

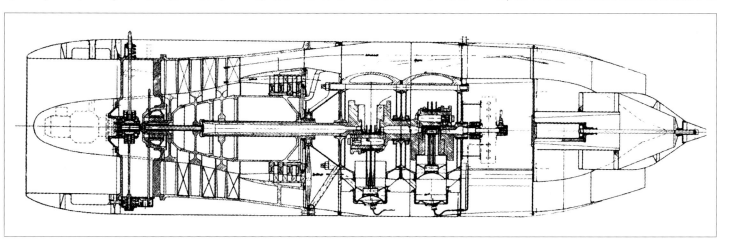

A cutaway drawing of the project's '032' (P 130) jet engine, showing the piston engine driving the compressor and the translating nozzle centrebody.

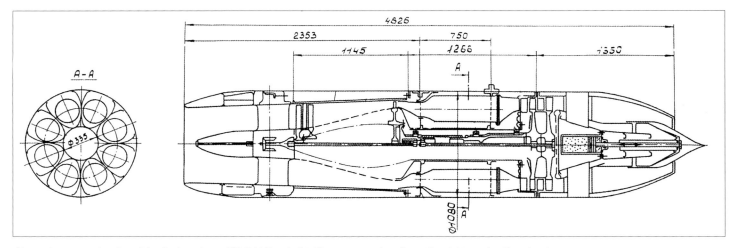

Above: A cutaway drawing of the Junkers Jumo 012 (012A) turbojet. The cross-section shows the eight combustion chambers.

Above: A prototype of the '012B' turbojet undergoing bench testing in 1948.

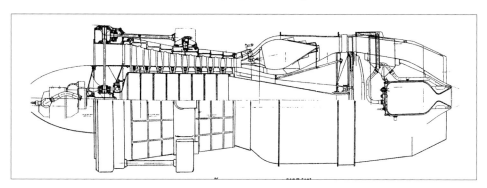

The designation '012' was used for several rather different engines. This is the projected '012D'.

the engine control linkage which automatically put the fuel feed at its maximum. The testing was continued on the second and third examples of the engine. (Some Russian sources refer to the resurrected Jumo 012 as '012A'). The work was still at its early stage when on 23rd October 1946 all the German-staffed design bureaux, including the Dessau-based OKB-1, were moved to the Soviet Union.

Development of the Jumo 012 was resumed at the Junkers-staffed OKB-1 set up at the Experimental Plant No. 2 near Kuibyshev. An important new element was the change in the customer's requirements: instead of being developed as a powerful turbojet, the Jumo 012 was to form the basis for a future turboprop engine (this line of development resulted in the '022' turboprop, see below). However, work on the pure turbojet version of the engine continued. The engines manufactured at Dessau and brought to the Soviet Union (two examples, according to some sources; four, according to others) were modified with a view to increasing their service life. Changes introduced into the design included, among other things, a new combustion chamber which constituted a combination of the annular chamber characteristic of BMW engines and individual combustion chambers featured by Jumo turbojets.

In late 1947 construction of the modified engine dubbed '012B' started. Testing began in the summer of 1948, upon completion of five prototypes (somewhat different dates are quoted in some sources). The testing was plagued by incidents and mishaps, such as the failure of a compressor bearing and the appearance of cracks in the turbine blades and compressor guide vanes. This necessitated a new series of modifications. In October 1948 the '012B' was finally submitted for the 100-hour State acceptance testing, which was

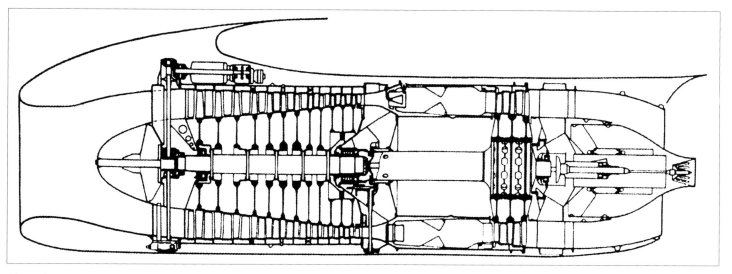

Above: A cutaway drawing of the BMW 018 turbojet installed in a conformal underwing nacelle.

conducted on engines Nos. 11, 12 and 14. Everything seemed to proceed well, yet on the 94th hour one of the turbine blades suffered a failure. Eventually the work on the '012B' was discontinued. This decision was due to the fact that in 1948 production was started in the Soviet Union of the RD-45 turbojet which was a Soviet copy of the Rolls-Royce Nene. The RD-45 had the same thrust rating as the '012B', but it had much smaller dimensions, and, importantly, it weighed some 25% less than the German engine.

In October 1948 a project was developed of one more version of the basic engine; it was designated '012D'. The design philosophy of the version boiled down to reducing the weight as much as possible, increasing the service life and simplifying the design. The '012D' featured an eight-stage axial compressor, which was expected to ensure an efficiency of 85% on the basis of 'extensive use of British research materials'. The annular combustion chamber was designed on the basis of experimental work conducted by the BMW company at Berlin-Spandau. Provision was made for short-time thrust augmentation by means of using an auxiliary liquid-fuel rocket motor which was to be accommodated in the jet nozzle cone. Design thrust rating of this combination for take off was 3,000 kgp (6,615 lbst) + 1,940 kgp (4,278 lbst).

BMW 018 turbojet

When the BMW aero engine factory in Stassfurt resumed its activities under Soviet supervision as OTB-2 (later OKB-2), the German staff there was tasked, among other things, with resurrecting the BMW 018 turbojet, the prototype of which was nearing completion before Germany's defeat. This was an engine of considerably greater thrust (3,400 kgp/7,495 lbst) as compared to 1,050

kgp (2,315 lbst) of the BMW 003C; while sharing the latter's general layout, the BMW 018 was appreciably more complex. It featured an 18-stage compressor and a three-stage turbine (as compared to the seven-stage compressor and single-stage turbine on the BMW 003C). With a length of 5,000 mm and diameter of 1,270 mm (16 ft 5 in and 4 ft 2 in respectively) it was also rather bigger. The staff of OKB-2 faced the difficult task of making anew the calculations and technical drawings, since neither hardware, nor documentation on this turbojet had survived. The situation was further compounded by the lack of some essential items of equipment and the need to move the production facilities from underground mines, where they had been located by the Germans, to normal premises on the ground.

The first prototype of the BMW 018 was completed by 18th October 1946 and put on the test bench, but the testing had to be suspended at its initial phase because on 23 October the former BMW engineers were transported to the Soviet Union and sent to Experimental Plant No. 2 at Upravlencheskiy Gorodok (lit. 'Executive township') near Kuibyshev. This team, headed by Karl Prestel and known, again, as OKB-2, was originally supposed to continue the work on the BMW 018 turbojet, the sole example of which was delivered from Germany in 1947. (A German source states, obviously in error, that three examples of this engine had reached the Soviet Union).

However, in late 1946 the Soviet 'customers' changed their priorities somewhat. A new task came to the fore, namely the

An incomplete BMW 018 engine (the parabolic fixed spinner is missing). The eight radial struts of the air intake assembly are visible.

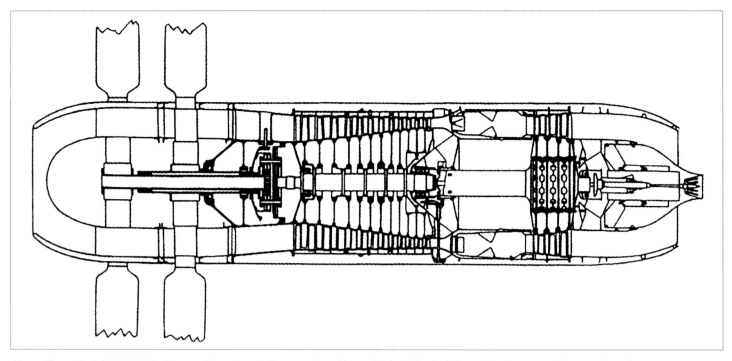

Above: The projected BMW 028 turboprop with contra-rotating propellers. Unusually, the air intake is located in the centre of the propeller spinner.

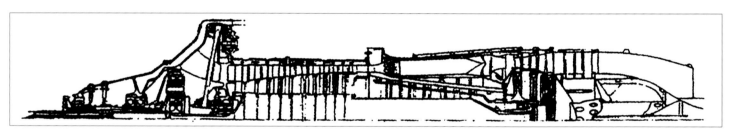

A partial cutaway drawing of the '028' turboprop's core.

development of turboprop engines. An idea came up of tasking OKB-2 with creating a turboprop engine based on the BMW 018. After consultations with the German specialists the task was formulated in more precise terms. It envisaged the projecting and prototype construction of the '028' turboprop engine delivering 6,800 ehp, possibly related in some way to the BMW 018. (For further details see below under the '028' heading.) As for the BMW 018 turbojet as such, it was not mentioned in the new task for the team and, apparently, must have been deleted from the prototype construction plan. The sole BMW 018 was used at Experimental Plant No. 2 as a teaching aid for young Soviet specialists.

'014' (Pirna 014) turbojet
As related above, a group of German specialists was assembled at Savyolovo in December 1953 and tasked with designing the '152' jet airliner for the nascent aircraft industry of the German Democratic Republic. This group included engine specialists who made initial project studies for the 014 turbojet intended to be used in the power-

plant of the new airliner. These project studies formed the basis for the subsequent engineering project of this engine which was developed by German specialist after their return to the GDR. The engine was eventually built there as Pirna 014 and used in a prototype of the '152' airliner.

Turboprop engines

TRDV turboprop engine (project)
As mentioned above, a team of German specialists selected in the camps of German prisoners of war was assigned to OKB-36-2 at aero engine plant No 36 in Rybinsk. In 1947 the leader of this team, Manfred Christian, together with his colleagues prepared a project of a turboprop engine which in Soviet documents was referred to as TRDV (*toorboreaktivnyy dvigatel' s vintom* – turbojet engine with a propeller). Its design performance included output of 5,060 shp or 5,600 ehp. This power was to be transmitted to two co-axial propellers measuring 3.2 m (10 ft 6 in) in diameter via a planetary gearbox. The engine incorporated a 12-stage axial compressor with a pressure ratio of 7.

The project was submitted to NII VVS where it received a favourable assessment and was recommended for prototype construction. A special section was set up within OKB-36-2 for the implementation of this project; the number of specialists and workers involved (both German and Soviet) was as high as 1,000 persons. However, in the summer of 1948 OKB-36-2 was disbanded owing to a decision to curtail the plan of experimental work and prototype construction in the aircraft industry. The work on the TRDV was to be continued within the framework of Kolosov's OKB at Plant No. 16 in Kazan'; for this purpose a group of eight German specialists headed by Christian was transferred to that plant.

The final version of the project was to be completed in March 1949. However, M. Christian did not get a chance to bring his project to fruition. In early 1950 he was sent to Experimental Plant No. 2 at Upravlencheskiy Gorodok where the work on the '022' (TV-2) turboprop engine was showing good progress. Christian was expected to take part in the development of that engine. Enraged at being sent further eastwards instead of being sent back home to Germany, as he had hoped, Christian declared a boycott and refused to turn up at his workplace. The sad consequence of this was his renewed arrest and exile to Magadan in the Soviet Far East. Relating this episode, the Russian historian Dmitriy Sobolev does not mention the ultimate fate of the TRDV project, which was presumably abandoned.

'028' turboprop (project)

As far back as 1940 the BMW company had projected a powerful turboprop engine designated BMW-109-028. The engine would feature a 12-stage axial compressor, a four-stage turbine and coaxial contra-rotating propellers; its output in cruise was to reach 7, 940 ehp. This project served as a starting point for the development of the '028' turboprop engine, which was pursued after the war by a team of former BMW employees under the direction of Karl Prestel working in Stassfurt under Soviet supervision.

When this team was moved to the Soviet Union in October 1946, it was assigned to Experimental Plant No. 2 at Upravlencheskiy Gorodok and organised as OKB-2 with K. Prestel as chief designer. A directive issued by the Soviet Council of Ministers on 11th March 1947 tasked OKB-2, among other things, with designing and building the '028' turboprop delivering 6,800 ehp. The work on this engine proceeded in parallel with the work on the '022' (Jumo 022) turboprop which was conducted by OKB-1 (Chief Designer A. Scheibe) at the same plant. By the end of 1947 both teams had completed their theoretical calculations and started issuing detail drawings and tooling up for the construction of prototypes. Three versions of the '028' were under development. One of them, featuring a 10-stage compressor, a three-stage turbine, an annular combustion chamber and contra-rotating coaxial

propellers driven via reduction gear, was to have an output of 6,570 ehp. However, the work was hampered by the shortage of test benches and other equipment. In consequence, in 1948 a decision was taken to merge the two OKBs into a single design bureau and to concentrate all efforts on the projecting of only one turboprop – the '022' (see below). That meant the cancellation of the '028', the project work on which was stopped in 1949.

'022' (Jumo 022, TV-022) turboprop engine and its TV-2 derivatives

As stated above, in 1948 the two German design bureaux set up at Experimental Plant No.2 (led by A. Scheibe and K. Prestel respectively) were merged into a single joint OKB with A. Scheibe as Chief Designer. A decision was taken to concentrate its efforts on the development of the '022' turboprop engine (sometimes referred to as TV-022). It was projected on the basis of the Jumo 012 turbojet; the concept of the 022 (Jumo 022) dated back to 1944, but it failed to materialise at the time. In 1948 the German designers were in a better position: the Jumo 012 turbojet, providing the starting point, had already been tested and sufficiently developed. However, this basic design had to be revised to a very large extent to turn the turbojet into as turboprop. The '022' differed from the Jumo 012 in having a three-stage turbine, apart from the addition of propeller, reduction gear and rpm governor.

Preparation of detail drawings was completed in mid-1948, followed by the manufacture of three prototype engines. In 1949, when the development work on the engine was in full swing, Experimental Plant No. 2 received a new chief – it was Nikolay D. Kuznetsov, the future famous aero engine Chief Designer. Thus, the 022 and its successors came to be developed under his

overall supervision. Manufacturer's tests of the '022' were started in June 1949.

In 1951 the '022' turboprop was renamed TV-2 (TV = *toorbovintovoy* [*dvigatel'*], turboprop engine). Actually, this was a modified version which differed from the original TV-022 in having a new oil system with oil pumps of greater output, a new turbine starter and new AV-41B propellers instead of the original AV-41s. Having successfully passed 100-hour State acceptance tests, it was put into series production. The engine yielded an output of more than 5,000 ehp (4,663 shp plus 469 kgp/1,034 lb of residual thrust).

In 1951 two TV-2 engines were flight-tested in a Tu-4 bomber converted into a flying testbed. They were installed instead of the Nos. 1 and 4 Shvetsov ASh-73TK radial engines. The aircraft logged 70 hours in 27 flights with the turboprops installed.

The subsequent career of the TV-2 is connected in part with the OKB-19 aero engine design bureau led by Pavel A. Solov'yov. This OKB modernised the TV-2 raising its power output to 7,650 ehp in the TV-2M version. The TV-2M driving three-bladed contra-rotating propellers was used on the prototype Tu-91 attack aircraft. The TV-2M engines derated to 7,000 ehp were planned for Tupolev's '101' military transport and '111' passenger aircraft which remained paper projects.

The TV-2M served as a basis for the first Soviet turboshaft engine intended for helicopters – the TV-2VM which was used on the Mi-6 prototypes.

TV-2F turboprop engine and its derivative, the paired 2TV-2F engine

German specialists who had taken part in the development of the '022' (TV-2) engine were rewarded with money bonuses; furthermore, after the successful testing of the engine a group of German specialists and

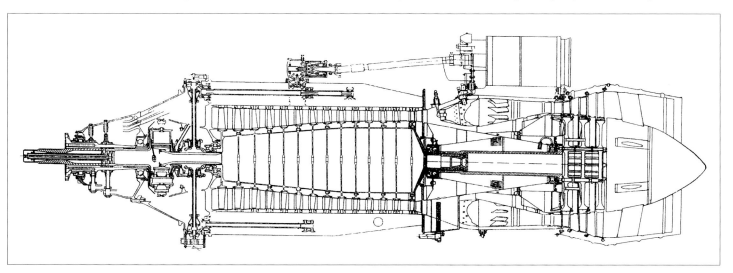

The '022' (Junkers Jumo 022) turboprop. Note the long accessory drive shafts and the aft position of the accessories.

Above: The Kuznetsov TV-2 turboprop derived from the Jumo 022.

their families received permission to leave the USSR, as they had been promised. In 1950, 241 German specialists (with family members, 610 persons) went back to Germany from Upravlencheskiy Gorodok. However, several hundred engineers and workers from Germany were left at the plant. Their services were needed for a new task – the development of the TV-12 turboprop engine of an enormously high power output – 12,000 ehp. Engines of this performance were needed for the new Tu-95 strategic bomber, then under development in the Tupolev OKB.

In the meantime, an interim solution was sought in utilising the TV-2 engine in a paired configuration, coupling the two engines to a common gearbox. But, before doing that, it was necessary to uprate the existing TV-2. This was achieved by raising the temperature of combustion and by increasing the volume of airflow through the engine. The resulting TV-2F (*forseerovannyy*, uprated) produced an output of 6,250 ehp during bench testing in 1951. In the same year two prototypes of a paired installation of these engines were completed; designated 2TV-2F, they incorporated two engines

arranged side-by-side, one of the engines being slightly moved back. They transmitted their torque to four-bladed contra-rotating propellers measuring 5.8 m (19 ft 0¹¹⁄₃₂ in) in diameter. After some development work an example of the 2TV2-F passed manufacturer's 100-hour bench tests. Without waiting for the results of the State acceptance tests, which were scheduled for December 1952, four coupled engine packages were installed in the first prototype of the Tu-95 bomber ('95-1') which made its first flight with these engines on 12th November 1952. In the meantime, two examples of the 2TV-2F were consecutively subjected to State acceptance tests in January and April 1953; in both cases the reduction gear failed due to insufficient fatigue strength. Inexplicably, flight testing of the Tu-95 prototype went on. On 11th May 1953 this aircraft crashed after an engine fire, traced to the disintegration of a gear wheel in the reduction gear. Subsequently steps were taken to improve the fatigue strength of the reduction gear of the 2TV-2F engine, but it never came to power any aircraft: on the Tu-95 it gave place, as originally planned, to the TV-12 (NK-12) engine producing the same power output in a single unit.

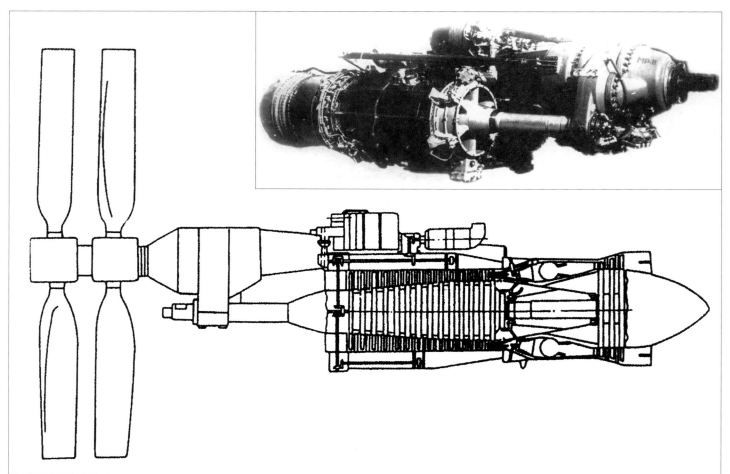

This drawing and the inset photo depict the 2TV-2F turboprop consisting of two TV-2Fs driving a pair of contraprops via extension shafts and common reduction gear.

As for the TV-2F (the single unit), in 1953 ten examples of this engine together with its technical documentation were transferred from OKB-276, led by Nikolay D. Kuznetsov, to the OKB-478 aero engine design bureau led by Aleksandr G. Ivchenko in order to provide the latter with know-how in the field of gas turbine design. Ivchenko's OKB took up further development of the engine and eventually produced its own version, designated TV-2T. It power rating was raised to 6,250 ehp as compared to the 6,000 ehp of the TV-2F (these figures do not quite tally with the 6,250 ehp rating of the TV-2F quoted in a different source). The TV-2T was intended for the prototype of the Antonov An-8 transport; seven engines were built.

The TV-2T served as a basis for the projecting of the TV-20, later renamed AI-20. This turboprop delivering 4,250 ehp was built in large numbers; its numerous versions powered the An-10 and Il'yushin IL-18 airliners, the An-8 and An-12 transports and several other types of aircraft.

In 1955 Ivchenko's OKB also produced on the basis of the TV-2F a version intended for the first prototype of Kamov's Ka-22 compound helicopter. Designated TV-2VK, this engine had a maximum rating of 5,495 ehp. The engine displayed insufficient gas-dynamic stability and had to be replaced by Solov'yov D-25VK engines on subsequent Ka-22 prototypes.

NK-12 (TV-12) turboprop engine

The NK-12 turboprop engine occupies a special place in the range of engines developed in the USSR with the participation of German engineers. The projecting of this engine began in 1951 under the designation TV-12. Intended as a powerplant for the Tu-95 strategic bomber, it was to deliver 12,000 ehp for take-off. The projecting of the engine was conducted at Experimental Plant No. 2 at Upravlencheskiy Gorodok near Kuibyshev under the overall direction of Nikolay D. Kuznetsov; Soviet engineers took part in this work from the outset together with the German team of designers led by engineer Ferdinand Brandner, the former technical director of the Junkers aero engine plant at Dessau. He was responsible for detail design in the joint OKB which was eventually formed at Plant No.2 by merging OKB-1 and OKB-2 initially set up there.

To attain the very high design power rating, the number of turbine stages was increased to five. The use of the new nimonic heat-resistant alloy made it possible to raise the engine pressure ratio and to increase the turbine temperature. New features incorporated in the design included the use of special inserts intended to minimise the turbine blade tip clearance, and

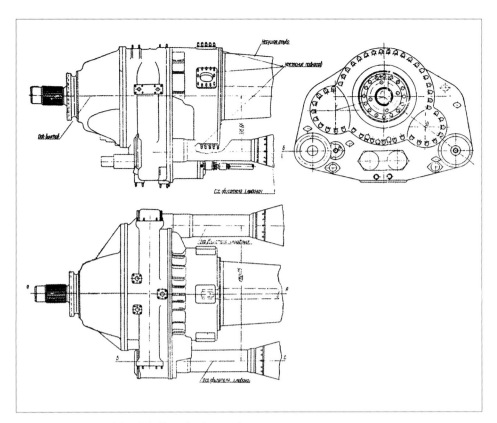

Above: Three views of the 2TV2-F's reduction gearbox.

the introduction of hollow cooled turbine blades. The power generated by the engine was to be transmitted via reduction gear to a pair of large-diameter contra-rotating propellers; both the reduction gear and the propellers were developed by Soviet specialists with assistance from their German colleagues. Numerous experiments and tests of engine systems and subassemblies were conducted during the projecting and prototype construction stage. As a result, the new engine attained the stipulated power output and proved reliable and fuel-efficient. Its specific fuel burn was much lower than that of its predecessor, the TV-2.

The first example of the TV-12 was completed in early 1953. The successful bench tests of the engine corroborated the design

power rating of 12,000 ehp, which was unrivalled at that time. Its operational characteristics were also good, including, in particular, the sufficiently long time between overhauls (TBO) which initially was 100 hours. In 1954 the engine passed 100-hour tests; later the TBO was raised to 150 hours.

In late 1953 German specialists engaged in the work on the TV-12 (renamed NK-12 after the initials of Nikolay Kuznetsov, the plant's chief) left the plant at Upravlencheskiy Gorodok and returned to Germany. The final testing and subsequent development of the engine was handled by the design staff of OKB-276 led by Kuznetsov. The NK-12 was put into production and used on the Tu-95 bomber/Tu-142 anti-submarine warfare aircraft family, the

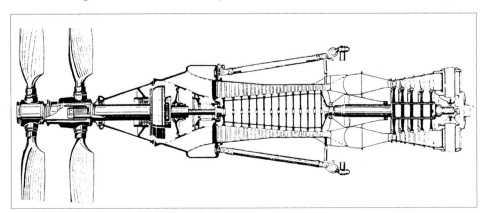

The Kuznetsov NK-12 turboprop. The reduction gear is housed in the intake centrebody.

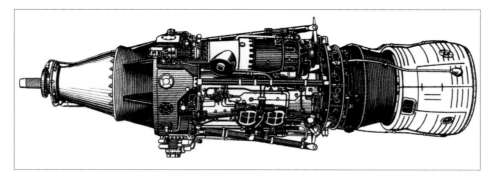
Above: The NK-12 minus propellers. Note the radial struts linking the reduction gear housing with the engine casing.

Tu-114 long-haul airliner and Tu-126 AWACS aircraft. In 1955 a new, more powerful version was produced; designated NK-12M, it had a TBO of 300 hours. A production run of the NK-12/12M totalled 848 engines. These were followed by the NK-12MA and NK-12MV versions (for the An-22 heavy transport and the Tu-95/Tu-142 family respectively) with the same power rating; the service life was eventually raised to 6,500 hours. The most powerful version on the NK-12 was the NK-12MP tested in 1978 and launched into production in 1979; with its output of 15,000 ehp it remains to this day unsurpassed in power output among production turboprops of the world.

Summing up
Assessing the final results of the activities of German-staffed design bureaux in the USSR, we have to return to Aleksandr S. Yakovlev's memoirs quoted at the beginning of this chapter. Yakovlev regretfully states that the German specialists did arrive in the Soviet Union, *'but the attempt to make use of their services failed to bring positive results, despite the huge expenses involved'*. This assessment may well be too categorical,

albeit it is true to some extent. It is echoed by some later Russian researchers (for example, D. A. Sobolev) who point out that the work of German specialists in the USSR did not give any tangible results in the development of Soviet aviation. Indeed, none of the aircraft designed by German-staffed OKBs in the Soviet Union and built in prototype form were put into series production; at best, some of the technical features developed by German engineers and incorporated in these aircraft proved of interest for Soviet aircraft designers and were used in their projects. One of the reasons explaining the poor yield may be found in the fallacious choice of some basic design features by German designers. Experience showed, for example, that swept-forward wings failed to gain acceptance and wide use in aviation; the same is true for liquid-fuel rocket motors or pulse-jets, or the bicycle undercarriage that was only rarely used on production aircraft. (It was probably the Soviet Union with its Myasishchev M-4 bomber and its derivative, the 3M, as well as the Yakovlev Yak-25/-26/-27/-28 series of twinjet tactical aircraft, that made the most out of this undercarriage layout.)

However, this was not the main factor. The meagre results of the German design bureaux in the USSR in the post-war years were due primarily to the wrong way of organising their activities. This is where one can recall Yakovlev's words that had been quoted at the beginning of the chapter. Indeed, the German specialists working in isolation from the rest of the world and from their Soviet professional colleagues could not acquire new knowledge so necessary for generating new ideas. They had no contacts with TsAGI, TsIAM, LII and other scientific centres, nor could they freely communicate with specialists from other design bureaux. Thus, they could only share their previous experience which reflected the level of technology attained by the end of the war.

Yet, it would be a mistake to underestimate the influence exerted by the work of the German engineers on the development of Soviet aviation technology.

The most noticeable contribution made by German engineers to the development of aircraft technology in the Soviet Union was the development of the mighty TV-12 (NK-12) turboprop engine which proved to be a very valuable asset, indeed. These engines formed the powerplant of the Tu-95 strategic bomber which became the mainstay of the Soviet long-range aviation and, like its US counterpart (the Boeing B-52), soldiers on to this day in its Tu-95MS and Tu-142MZ versions.

Even more profound was the general influence of the German know-how and experience on the development of jet aviation in the Soviet Union. The first Soviet jet aircraft could not have made their appearance as early as 1946 without the German turbojets placed into series production in the USSR. Moreover, despite their low thrust, the German jet engines, such as the Jumo 004 and the BMW 003, provided much useful experience in the designing of axial-flow turbojets that came to dominate the jet aero engine field supplanting the centrifugal-flow turbojets. In the long run, this experience proved to be more fruitful than the experience gained with copying the British Nene and Derwent engines. The results of German research in the field of high-speed aerodynamics, including the studies on swept wings, proved of much value in shaping the approach of Soviet designers to the projecting of jet aircraft in the late 1940s and early 1950s. The Soviet aircraft industry, aeronautical science and technology made a leap into the domain of jet propulsion and then quickly achieved a stage of self-sufficiency permitting them to wage successful competition with other major air powers.

The German design staff of OKB-2 in 1954.

Chapter 6

GERMAN AIRCRAFT IN THE USSR/RUSSIA AFTER THE MID-1950S

Cooperation between the Soviet Union and Germany in the field of aviation between the early 1950s and 1991 (the year when the Soviet Union collapsed) can be broadly described as a 'reversal of the flow' (that is, the flow of technology and know-how). To make the point clear, one should bear in mind the radically altered political scene that served as a background for the developments in the domain of aviation. The period in question was dominated by the Cold War; in Europe, it was characterised by the splitting of Germany. The two German states, the Federal Republic of Germany and the German Democratic Republic, happened to be on the opposite sides of the divide between the East and the West. The Soviet Union maintained very close ties with the GDR, while its relations with the Federal Republic were initially very strained but gradually improved in the course of time, reflecting all the ups and downs on the world arena.

For ideological and political reasons, imports of aviation technology to the Soviet Union from the West after 1947 virtually came to a halt. The West was opposed to selling anything that was deemed 'sensitive' from a military/security standpoint to the Soviet Union. The latter had to rely on its own resources and, through a concentrated effort, attained self-sufficiency in the aeronautical sphere. These circumstances alone precluded any imports of aircraft from West Germany (quite apart from the fact that the aircraft industry was non-existent in the Federal Republic of Germany during the first decade after the war – its resurrection began in the mid-1950s).

In consequence, for quite some time the Soviet Union's links with Germany in the aeronautical sphere were limited to East Germany (the GDR). But, as distinct from the pre-war period, this time it was not the Soviet Union but (East) Germany that became the recipient of aviation hardware and technology (hence the 'reversal of the flow'). However, this aspect of the interaction between Russia/the Soviet Union and Germany is beyond the scope of this book and must be treated as a separate subject.

One may surmise that, as the aircraft industry in West Germany was revived, giving birth to interesting projects of both civil and military aircraft, Soviet designers must have followed these developments with keen interest. For example, the experiments conducted in West Germany with VTOL aircraft making use of thrust vectoring and lift engines must have been particularly interesting to Soviet aviation specialists. It may be presumed that all available information on the West German projects of such aircraft was carefully studied by Soviet specialists. To be more specific, one can mention the Dornier Do 231 vertical/short take-off and landing (V/STOL) civil transport project and the VFW-Fokker VAK 191B experimental V/STOL strike/reconnaissance fighter. However, it is difficult to speak of any direct influence in this case.

* * *

The first signs of a thaw in aeronautical contacts between the Federal Republic of Germany and the USSR began to appear in the late 1980s and early 1990s, after the onset of Mikhail Gorbachov's *perestroika* which touched off far-reaching changes in the Soviet Union's internal development and its relations with the outside world.

Claudius Dornier Seastar – plans for licence production in the USSR

In early 1990 reports appeared about the intention of the West German Claudius Dornier SEASTAR GmbH & Co KG company to establish co-operation with a Soviet enterprise. The British magazine *Flight International* wrote in its 17th-23rd January 1990 issue: *'A team from the financially troubled Claudius Dornier Seastar is to visit Moscow next week for talks on co-operation in amphibious aircraft – a move which could lead to licence production of the Seastar amphibian in the Soviet Union'*. According to the British magazine, the German company was insolvent, and financial problems had halted the development of the Seastar amphibian weeks short of certification. *'A successful deal in Moscow would give unprecedented access to the Soviet aviation market and could lead to sales of up to 200 Seastars in the Soviet Union, virtually doubling overall sales prospects for the West German 12-passenger amphibian.'*

A few words about the machine in question. The Seastar CD2 was an all-composite,

unpressurised 12-passenger amphibian. The wings, carried above the fuselage on a set of struts and braced by sloping struts, were a classic Dornier design, unswept and with zero dihedral. The powerplant comprised a pair of Pratt & Whitney Canada PT6A-135A turboprops mounted back-to-back on top of the wing centre section in a push-pull configuration. Lateral stability when afloat was ensured by sponsons, which also housed the fuel tanks and the main units of the tricycle undercarriage. The aircraft had been under development since 1981 and was intended to enter production in 1990, but financial troubles in 1989 caused a slippage in the programme.

According to *Flight International*, the discussions about co-operation were initiated by the Soviet organisation Aeroprogress, which had contacted Seastar officials in January 1990. At that time this was a newly established small private design bureau with modest financial assets and production possibilities, but big ambitions. Somewhat later these found their expression in a number of projects ranging from light utility aircraft to medium-class airliners and amphibian aircraft. One of Aeroprogress' designs, the An-2-class T-101 Grach (Rook) utility aircraft, was actually built in small numbers but failed to gain a foothold in the market. The enterprise changed names and financial sponsors several times and finally became an aviation subdivision of the M. V. Khrunichev State Space Research & Production Centre rocketry concern (GKNPTs Khrunichev).

Nothing was heard ever since about the progress of the intended negotiations; it is to be understood that the idea was dropped as the West German company presumably found a different solution to its financial problems. (Significantly, *Flight International* made no mention of the negotiations with Aeroprogress in its later article about the Seastar amphibian published in May 1990.) However, the whole story left its visible trace in one of the projects developed by Aeroprogress. Designated T-130 *Fregat* (Frigate), this was a light amphibian bearing a strong similarity to the Seastar in its overall layout, albeit this does not imply directly copying the German design. The obvious difference between the two designs includes

This model of the MM-1 commuter airliner/utility transport was displayed at the MAKS-93 airshow.

the T-130's strut-braced wings attached directly to the fuselage, pylon-mounted engine pod and tailwheel undercarriage (although a version with a tricycle undercarriage was under development). The basic T-130 was to be powered by two Czech Walter M-601E turboprops; alternative options included two Lyul'ka AL-34-1 turboprops, or one Glushenkov TVD-20 turboprop, or two Garrett AiResearch TPE 331 turboprops. The T-130 did not reach the hardware stage.

The period after 1991
The dissolution of the Soviet Union and the emergence of the Russian Federation as its successor, along with the appearance of a number of independent states – former Soviet Republics – brought about dramatic changes both within Russia and in Russia's relations with the rest of the world. Russia's transition to market economy and a Western-style political system removed, on the face of it, the ideological barriers and political obstacles for normal economic relations and comprehensive contacts and co-operation between Russia and the West. (In reality, the shaping of new relations proved to be an arduous and controversial process.)

One of the consequences of these changes was the opening of the Russian market for imports of aircraft from the West. The former monopolist in the field of air transport – the state-owned Aeroflot – was split into hundreds of more modestly sized airlines, mostly based on private ownership; these started importing airliners and other types of commercial aircraft of European and US origin. This created new chances for the aeronautical industry of the Federal Republic of Germany, which by then had established itself as a well-developed branch of the national economy. The reunification of Germany made the Federal Republic the sole German partner for Russia.

However, this was accompanied by the creation of supranational European concerns with the participation of German aircraft manufacturing enterprises. For example, in 1992 the Eurocopter concern was founded by Aérospatiale (France) and Daimler-Benz Aerospace (DASA, Germany), the ownership being 70% French and 30% German (as of 1997). Another case in point is Airbus Industrie, now forming part of European Aviation, Defence and Space (EADS).

During recent years Russia has been purchasing or leasing airliners manufactured by Airbus Industrie and helicopters produced by Eurocopter. It is rather difficult to single out the German element in these imports. Moreover, Russia's relations with international aircraft manufacturing corporations are, strictly speaking, outside the scope of this book; for this reason, the authors restrict themselves only to a brief review of some aspects directly related to Germany.

The Airbus airliners imported into Russia in the course of the sixteen years since 1991 or ordered for delivery in the coming years comprise the A310-200 and -300 for Aeroflot Russian International Airlines, Diamond Sakha, Transaero and Sibir' Airlines (now S7 Airlines); the A319-111 for Aeroflot and Rossiya State Transport Co.; A320-200 for Aeroflot, Ural Airlines and Vladivostok Air; the A321-200 for Aeroflot; the A330 ordered by Transaero; the A350XWB ordered by Aeroflot. The German content in these airliners may vary, depending on the type.

In addition to imports, Airbus Industrie and its parent concern, EADS, have established co-operation with the Russian aircraft industry enlisting its services in the production of components for some airliners of the Airbus family.

Speaking about helicopters, the two Eurocopter types of 'German descent' that have been imported into Russia are the Eurocopter (née MBB) Bö 105 and the BK117. The first two Bö 105CBS-5SF-SAR machines were delivered to Russia in late 1994. Purchased by the Ministry for Emergency Situations (EMERCOM, the Russian

civil aid and protection agency), they were assigned to the Moscow-based Central Airmobile Unit used in the search-and-rescue and ambulance roles. By mid-1997 four examples had been delivered. Unfortunately, the first of these machines, coded '390 Black' (c/n S 900), was lost in a fatal crash during a rescue operation on Mt. Fisht near Sochi on 30th June 1996; the other three – '903 Black', '910 Black' and '912 Black' (now RF-32762) – continue their service to this day.

As for the BK117, a single example of this type was purchased by EMERCOM in 1998. This was BK117C-1 c/n 7523 (test registration D-HMBG); its Russian registration (not applied visibly) was RA-73607. The machine was displayed at the MAKS-99 airshow in August 1999. It is now coded '914 Black'. Another BK117C-1 registered RA-01881 and named *Miracle 7* (c/n unknown) was seen at the MAKS-2007 airshow; it is operated by Moscow Air Services, a division of the Moscow Government.

The MM-1 (M-112) joint venture commuter airliner (project)
The year of 1993 saw the emergence of an interesting project of Russian-German co-operation in the field of aircraft construction. The idea arose of establishing a joint venture enterprise with the participation of German and Russian companies for the purpose of designing and building a small turboprop airliner intended for local services. The initiative came from Jürgen Krause, a businessman from Bavaria. He wished to enlist the support of Russian aircraft constructors in resurrecting a project of a small turboprop aircraft developed in the Federal Republic of Germany in the late 1970s and early 1980s. The development work had reached the full-scale mock-up stage, but the project had to be shelved for lack of financing. In the early 1990s some analysts came to the conclusion that a niche existed in the air transport market for aircraft of that class and that the project could become viable.

This initiative found a positive response from the Russian side; in March 1993 two contracts forming the basis of this co-operation were signed in Munich by Krause with Russian organisations. The main Russian partner was the Myasishchev Experimental Machine-building Plant (EMZ), the successor of the Myasishchev Design Bureau which had produced the well-known M-4 and 3M four-turbojet strategic bombers (*Bison* in NATO parlance). It was joined by the King company – a small enterprise headed by Aleksandr Kudryavtsev, a young Moscow businessman. On the German side, the development work was to be performed by the German division of TEC Avia Inc. The project was sponsored by Deutsches Ostforum.

The airliner that was to be designed and manufactured as a result of this partnership received the designation MM-1 (MM stood for 'Moscow – Munich'). According to the original optimistic plans, the prototype was to be flown in 1995, with series manufacture starting in 1996. The Myasishchev EMZ 'adopted' the project and embarked on its further development; allocating to it the in-house designation M-112. It was a multi-purpose aircraft with a payload of up to 3,000 kg (6,610 lb). Its cargo hold could be easily converted into a passenger cabin of any class. The M-112 was a high-wing monoplane featuring an upswept tail with a rear cargo hatch and a loading ramp. It was to be powered by two Pratt & Whitney turboprops driving six-blade propellers; alternatively, the Soviet Glushenkov TVD-20M or RKBM TVD-1500 turboprops could be installed. Basic specifications included a maximum all-up weight of 9,200 kg (20,280 lb), a normal payload of 2,400 kg (5,290 lb), a range of 830 km (515 miles) and a cruising speed of 450 km/h (279 mph). With a crew of two the M-112 would carry 28 passengers.

Work on the project continued for several years (it was still advertised at the MAKS-97 air show in 1997), but the promised financing from the German side failed to materialise and the project was eventually shelved.

British/German BR710 engines for Russian aircraft

During the period after 1991 Russian aircraft manufacturers, guided by the wish to enhance the export prospects for their products, have resorted to making use of Western powerplants on Russian aircraft. In most cases the engines in question came from the US, Canada or Great Britain. In at least two cases attempts were made to make deals which envisaged using jet engines of German manufacture. In both cases the engine concerned was the BR715 turbofan. This engine was manufactured in Dahlewitz by Rolls-Royce Deutschland, the German branch of the famous British company.

This engine was proposed for the Tu-334 medium-haul twin-engined airliner. During the ILA-2002 airshow an agreement was signed between the RSK MiG corporation (responsible for the series manufacture of the Tu-334 at that time), the Tupolev PLC and Rolls-Royce providing for the installation of the BR715 in the Tu-334. The participants of the agreement intended to undertake a feasibility study with a view to working out the more practical aspects of this co-operation later. To date, nothing has been heard of practical results of this venture which may have stumbled on the erratic development of the whole Tu-334 project over the years (its series production was due to begin in 2007, after a long delay, but has been called into question again). Nevertheless, the list of prospective versions of the Tu-334 includes the Tu-334-120D and Tu-334-220 version powered by BR715-55 (56) engines and the Tu-336 – a Tu-334 version with the BR710H2 engines using alternative types of fuel. The latter version features a dorsal liquefied natural gas (LNG) tank.

The other candidate for receiving the BR715 engine is the Beriyev Be-200 amphibian, which is produced by the Irkut Corporation in Irkutsk. A project of the 'westernised' version powered by these engines and tentatively designated Be-200RR was studied by the Russian side in co-operation with the marketing specialists of the EADS concern. It was assumed that re-engining the Be-200 with BR715s would help solve some of the operational problems and enhance the aircraft's prospects on the Western market. In 2005 EADS and Irkut reached an agreement on establishing a joint enterprise known as EADS Irkut Seaplane S.A.S. (based in France). There were plans for producing the Be-200RR version prototype in 2006-2007, but the project has apparently stalled. According to some reports, no customers have yet been found for this version of the amphibian.

Dornier-728 medium-haul airliner – a joint venture that failed to take place

Around the turn of the century the joint US-German enterprise Fairchild Dornier ran into financial difficulties which, by the year 2002, had brought it to the brink of bankruptcy. In an effort to save the enterprise, negotiations were started with a Russian company based in Siberia about the possibilities of co-operation in the production of the Dornier Do 728 twin-turbofan short/medium-haul airliner. The 13th August 2002 issue of the German newspaper *Handelsblatt* carried a report to the effect that the Basic Element holding concern controlled by prominent Russian industrialist Oleg Deripaska was studying the feasibility of this project. The Russian side was interested in joint manufacture of the Do 728, which would provide employment for the Aviacor aircraft plant in Samara with its sorely under-utilised production facilities. Had the deal gone through, the Russian share of joint production would have amounted to some 40%, according to Thomas Brandt, Commercial Director of Fairchild Dornier. Apparently the negotiations brought no positive result, and the Do 728 programme was eventually abandoned. The completed first prototype was destined never to fly, becoming a ground test vehicle at the DLR research agency in Germany.

Cryoplane: A Russian-German co-operative venture on cryogenic fuels

In 1990-1992, German and Russian firms co-operated closely in investigating prospective cryogenic fuels for aircraft: liquid hydrogen (LH_2) and LNG. The study was sponsored in part by the German Federal Ministry of Economics. The goal of the study was to determine if the use of cryogenic fuels, that is, very low-temperature, liquefied gases, was technically feasible and environmentally and technically practical for aviation applications. It was possible to answer these questions in the positive, with the reservation, however, that the fuels in question were not at that time commercially competitive with kerosene. Russia was particularly interested in using its rich supplies of natural gas in such applications, but Russia's partners did not view this as a permanent or universally applicable solution to the problem. Consequently, the work was concentrated on liquid hydrogen. Due regard was taken to the fact that this study could benefit from the considerable experience gained by the Russian partner with the Tu-155 research aircraft, which tested the use of both LNG and LH_2.

The partners in the German-Russian feasibility study comprised two Russian enterprises and 13 German firms. The Russian ones were the Tupolev Company and the Samara-based 'Trud' Production Association (formerly the Kuznetsov Engine Design Bureau). Among the German partners mention must be made of DASA/Airbus acting as project coordinator, of the Daimler Benz, MTU and Dornier companies and such firms as MAN-Technologie, Max-Planck-Institut, Garrett GmbH, Messer-Griesheim, UHDE, Deutsche Lufthansa and others.

The partners intended to continue their co-operation on Cryoplane (as the eventual cryogenic-fuel airliner was named). A tentative study was made of a possible adaptation of an existing airliner to the LH_2 fuel; an A310 derivative was visualised as carrying this fuel in cylindrical tanks of considerable size placed atop the fuselage inside a full-length fairing. It was estimated that the high calorific value of hydrogen would enable such an aircraft to carry more payload than a comparable kerosene-fuelled aircraft of identical take-off weight and range. The study concluded that, assuming favourable conditions, a series-produced hydrogen aircraft could enter service around 2010 (apparently a forecast that proved too optimistic). The co-operative study went on, and in 1995 there were press reports about the intended conversion of a Dornier Do 328

Top and centre: An uncoded Eurocopter Bö 105CBS-5SF-SAR operated by EMERCOM of Russia lowers a rescue worker by means of its electric hoist as it hovers over the scene of a simulated accident during an airshow.

Above: Here, an 'accident victim' is hoisted aboard Bö 105CBS-5SF-SAR RF-32762 (ex '912 Black', c/n S 912). One of EMERCOM's Bö 105s ('910 Black', c/n S 910) lacked the hoist, being used as an air ambulance.

Above right: This Bö 105CBS-5SF-SAR makes use of a rescue cage during an EMERCOM exercise involving a simulated fire at an offshore oil rig.

Right: RF-32762 was demonstrated at the ILA-2006 airshow at Berlin-Schönefeld with a gyrostabilised optoelectronic observation system 'ball'.

'914 Black' (RA-73607), the sole Eurocopter BK117C-1 operated by EMERCOM of Russia, takes part in an exercise involving a simulated fire at an oil rig.

regional airliner into a flying testbed for a powerplant using LH_2. The Tupolev PLC, too, continued studying various projects based on the use of cryogenic fuels.

As a direct follow-up to this co-operation, the Tupolev PLC came up with a proposal for an aircraft intended to be a technology demonstrator. This aircraft featured a fairly unusual layout with two wing centre sections located in tandem; the rear wing centre section carried the outer wing panels, while the forward wings were flanked by the engine nacelles. The rear ends of the latter were extended aft to join the main wing and served as fuel tanks. The project, initially referred to as the Tu-XXX ('Demonstrator') was eventually transformed into the Tu-136.

However, there has been no tangible evidence of real progress in these matters; some sources ascribe this to the reorganisation of the Dornier and Deutsche Airbus companies.

Imports of German light aircraft.
During recent years quite a few light aircraft and helicopters were imported from the West by Russian private companies and individuals; some of these machines (though not many) are of German origin. The known cases are listed below.

FK9 Mark III light aircraft.
This is a two-seat light aircraft developed in Germany by FK Planes and manufactured jointly by Germany, Poland and France (the French division is B&F Technik situated in Toulouse). It is a high-wing strut-braced monoplane with a fixed tricycle undercarriage, powered by an 80-hp Rotax-912 engine. One such aircraft (identity unknown) was purchased in France by the Russian oil company Udmurtneft' based in Izhevsk, Udmurtia, and was operated by it in 2002. Another example registered ФЛА РФ 01975 (that is, FLA RF 01975) was demonstrated at the 'Civil Aviation-2002' airshow held at Moscow-Domodedovo airport in August 2002. It belonged to the Aist-M air club based in the vicinity of Moscow.

Stemme S10VT
This is a two-seat powered glider developed by the Stemme company (Germany). At least one example of this type was acquired by the Irkut Corporation based at Irkutsk and was converted into an 'optionally piloted' UAV designated Irkut-850 which was among the exhibits of the MAKS-2005 and MAKS-2007 airshows in Zhukovskiy. It was coded '242 Black' and named Viktor Chanchikov.

The Irkut-850 can be operated in both manned and remote-controlled mode; this makes it possible to avoid restrictions that can be imposed on UAV flights due to the absence of the necessary legal regulations. The converted air vehicle has an AUW of 860 kg (1,900 lb), a 200-km (124-mile) radius of action and an endurance of 12 hours. Its mission equipment includes an IR/TV camera on a gyro-stabilised platform, sensors for chemical, radiation or weather monitoring etc., a high-resolution digital photo camera, a first-aid package (for delivery to those in distress), and a three-dimensional laser mapping system (LIDAR). The equipment associated with the UAV role is installed in the cockpit instead of the right-hand seat. Part of the mission equipment is carried in streamlined pods suspended under the wings.

The Irkut-850 ('242 Black') makes a demo flight in piloted mode at the MAKS-2007 airshow. The nosecone is slid forward, allowing the propeller to spin. The underwing equipment pods are well visible.